FINDING A GOOD FIT

FINDING A GOOD FIT

The Life & Work of Architect Rand Iredale

by Kathryn Iredale
with Sheila Martineau

BLUE*im*PRINT

Co-Publishers:

BLUE*i*MPRINT
501 – 5525 West Boulevard
Vancouver BC   V6M 3W6
Canada

and

Kathryn Iredale
1537 Wesbrook Crescent
Vancouver BC   V6T 1V9
Canada
iredale@shaw.ca

Finding a Good Fit:
The Life & Work of Architect Rand Iredale

Editor, Designer, Researcher:
Sheila Martineau PhD (UBC 1999)
(sheila@shaw.ca / sheilamartineau.com)

Copy-Editor: Neall Calvert
Indexer: Renee Fossett

© 2008 Kathryn Iredale
All Rights Reserved
Printed and bound in China

No part of this book may be reproduced by any means whatsoever without the prior written permission of the author, with the exception of brief passages cited in book reviews and relevant research materials.

Every effort has been made to contact copyright holders of material used in this book. Please notify the author of any oversights, which will be corrected in future editions.

Remarks by Premier Gordon Campbell: Copyright © Province of British Columbia. All rights reserved. Reprinted with permission of the Province of British Columbia. www.ipp.gov.bc.ca.

Unless otherwise indicated, most of the photographs are from Rand Iredale's project archives and Kathryn Iredale's private collection. Vertical graphic images on or adjacent to Section and Chapter title pages were reproduced from the Rhone & Iredale brochure (circa 1970), with Bill Rhone's permission. Uncredited images in published reprints were uncited in the original articles and/or either taken or commissioned by, and subsequently submitted by, Rand Iredale.

We gratefully acknowledge the support of the Canada Council for the Arts and the BC Arts Council for our publishing program.

Contributors:

Bogue Babicki, D.Sc., P.Eng., RCA

Peter Busby, C.M., AIA, FRAIC, MAIBC, MAAA, MOAA, BCID, LEED AP,
Managing Director, Busby Perkins + Will

Rainer J. Fassler, MAIBC, Senior Associate,
Architecture & Interior Design, Stantec

Jennifer Iredale, Senior Curator, Heritage Branch,
BC Ministry of Small Business, Tourism & Culture

Richard Iredale, MAIBC, MRAIC, P.Eng., LEED AP,
Partner, Iredale Group Architecture

Talbot Iredale, P.Eng., Software Development Manager,
Diebold Election Systems Inc.

Charlotte Murray, M.Arch., MAIBC (retired)

William Rhone, BA(Arch) Hons., MA, MAIBC, PP, FRAIC

Liz Scremin, Architectural Designer & Technician

Library and Archives Canada Cataloguing in Publication

Iredale, Kathryn, 1930-
Finding a good fit : the life & work of architect Rand Iredale / Kathryn Iredale, Sheila Martineau.

ISBN 978-1-894965-90-3

1. Iredale, Rand.   2. Architects—British Columbia—Biography.
I. Martineau, Sheila, 1945-   II. Title.

NA749.I73I73 2008   720'.92   C2007-904924-9

*This book is dedicated
to all of those people who so loyally worked
with Rand Iredale.
They enriched his life
and helped him to fulfil his dreams.*

*It is also dedicated to our children
— Jennifer, Talbot, and Richard —
who were such an important part of Rand's life;
and to their children
— Lauren, Marlies, Julie, Adam, Meg,
Benjamin, Rylan, and Brodan —
in the hope that they may know their grandfather as
Pioneer, Architect, and Mentor.*

Acknowledgements

Many people assisted me in creating this book.

I want to thank Trevor Boddy for his *Tribute* to Rand, written shortly after Rand's death in 2000. It was much appreciated by all of my family.

We are especially grateful to Bill Rhone, Rand's professional partner in the Rhone & Iredale practice for 20 years (1960–1980), for so kindly sharing his generous and thoughtful memories of Rand.

Charlotte Murray, Rand's professional partner in The Iredale Partnership for 20 years (1980–2000), also graciously agreed to be interviewed and to write an essay about her many experiences as his long-time friend and colleague.

Many thanks to Bogue Babicki, Peter Busby, Rainer Fassler, and Liz Scremin, who each were interviewed, and who recalled their colourful memories of Rand from the Rhone & Iredale days and The Iredale Partnership days.

Much appreciated, too, is Professor Abraham Rogatnick for helping me to recollect our family's Venice experience. He was most generous in sharing his memories of UBC's Studies Abroad Program in Venice, Italy and allowing me to include a few excerpts from his booklet, *UBC in Venice, 1969–70*.

I want to thank my children—Jennifer Iredale, Talbot Iredale, and Richard Iredale—for contributing to this book by writing essays on memories of their relationships with their father, each one quite different.

The book also contains excerpts from a letter written by Rand's mother, Betty Iredale, and published in her book, *Stories of the Sod Shack, and Other Reminiscences* (1991). Her letter recounts the aura of Rand's childhood—of growing up during the Great Depression of the 1930s, which had a considerable impact on his values and personality.

My thanks to Gordon Price, Director of the City Program of Continuing Studies, Simon Fraser University at Harbour Centre, for his enthusiasm that I complete this book and, in so doing, add to the documentation of Rand's era in the development of downtown Vancouver. The interest and support of Colin Wong, Director of Communications at the Architectural Institute of British Columbia, has also been most heartening.

This encouragement by Gordon Price and Colin Wong, together with the rich memories of those who contributed to the book and the decision to include some of Rand's own writings, caused the book to take on a life of its own. What began as a reminiscence intended for Rand's family, friends, and close colleagues has become a book worthy of wider distribution in the architectural community and beyond.

Additional thanks go to Granville Island Publishing for pre-press assistance, to Neall Calvert for his copy-editing skills, and to Renee Fossett for her thorough indexing of the book's subject matter. They helped enormously in finalizing the book for print. And many, many thanks to Dimiter Savoff of BLUE*IM*PRINT for expediting its publication and distribution.

I particularly want to thank Sheila Martineau for her persistence, encouragement, and enthusiasm, and also for her designing, interviewing, writing, and editing skills. Whereas I had been able to draw on personal memories and project materials from Rand's files, Sheila's contributions provided a broader view of *Rand Iredale the man* and the times in which he lived. Without her help I could not have brought this book to fruition. ∎

Kathryn Iredale
Vancouver 2007

Contents

Acknowledgements — vi
Editor's Note — xiv
Tribute: In Memoriam — xviii
Preface: Remembering Rand — xxi

PERSONAL PLACES

1 Pioneer, Architect, Mentor — 3
    Rand's Résumé — 3
    Starting Out — 8
    The Business of Just Surviving — 14

2 'The First Step in Any Journey' — 17
    The Great Outdoors — 17
    Careers for Canadians — 20
    I Guess We Just Clicked — 22
    BC Hydro: A Bit of History — 27
    Developing a Mission Statement — 28
    Rand's Partners — 29
    Project: Channel 8 Television Studios — 30
    Project: Grouse Mountain Chalet — 34
    Elemental Estimating — 36

3 Island of Dreams — 39
    Mayne Island — 39
    Rand's Vision — 40

The Early Years	42
School of Architecture Workshops	45
Building the Dome	48
Building the Log House	54
The Bell Bay Bare Land Strata	56
The Gingerbread House	58
Moving to the Log House	60
Horse-Logging, Sheep-Farming, & Barn-Building	61
Family Settlement	63
The Future	67

PUBLIC PLACES

4 Beyond Functional Necessity — 71

Architecture at the Peace	73
Project: Portage Mountain Lookout Building	75
Lunch at '21' with Dr. Shrum	77
Project: Hudson's Hope Housing	79
Project: George W. Pearkes Elementary School	80
Perspective of the Power Scheme	82
The Intake Structure	83
Project: The Central Control Building	85
A Great Friend & Collaborator	88
Project: The Powerhouse	90
Project: Tourist Development Master Plan	92
The Emotional Function	97

5 The Earth on Which We Build — 99

Design for a University	99
Simon Fraser University Competition	101
Statement by Chancellor Shrum	101
Architectural Competition	102
Second Prize Winner	106
A Contest of Ideas	108
Project: The Science Complex	110
A 'School' for Architects	114
A New Structural System	115
SFU Archives	116
SFU Building Chronology	117
Site Analysis	118

6 Generosity of Spirit — 123

Project: The Westcoast Transmission Building — 124
The Most Significant Building in Canada Today — 127
The Landmark Westcoast Transmission Office Building — 127
An Interactive Design Process — 129
Can We Build This? — 130
Structural Efficiency — 131
Open to the Ideas of Others — 131
A Powerful & Innovative Idea — 132
Skyhook Tower — 134
Design Excellence — 141
Project: The Sedgewick Undergraduate Library — 142
A Great Deal of Weeping & Wailing — 146
A Whole Lot of Gyrating Around — 146
Space Planning — 150
Site Zoning — 151
1969: An Ingenious Plan — 152
1973: A Very Human Library — 153
A Popular Place — 154
Underground Library Has Many Advantages — 156
Finding a Good Fit — 159

7 Imagining a Different Reality — 161

The Venice Venture — 165
Creating a Culture of Design — 166
Rhone + Iredale Brochure — 172
A Historic Hike Up the Chilkoot Trail — 174
Project: Chilkoot Trail — 176
He Let You Shine — 179
Project: Seymour Medical Building — 180
Project: Burrard Medical Building — 182
Project: Manning Park Housing Study — 184
Architecture is a Team Sport — 185
A Lifelong Friendship — 186
The Way We Worked — 189
Project: BCIT Master Plan — 190
Project: BCIT Campus Building — 191
The Nature of Creativity — 192

8 The Heart of the Design Process — 195

The Strength of a Good Idea — 196
Vancouver Board of Trade Leadership Summit — 196

Project: Vancouver Centenary Study	198
A Major Contribution	206
Bennett Wants $50-Million Promise from Clark	207
Project: Downtown Stadium Proposal	211
A Multidisciplinary Practice	212
Project: False Creek Housing (The Lagoons)	215
Project: Fairview Townhouses I & II	216
Project: Steamboat Heritage House	218
An Iterative Design Process	220
The Schematic Design Phase	221
Changing Times	222

PEOPLE PLACES

9 'God is in the Details' — 227

One Door Closes …	227
… And Another Door Opens	230
Project: Bell Bay Strata Plan	231
Project: Vancouver City Block 15	232
The Heritage Partner	236
Project: Hodson Manor	239
Project: Gingerbread House	240
Memories of Dad	244
Project: Steamboat Heritage House	250
Key Details	253
Vancouver's Park Site 19	254
Project: Barclay Heritage Square	255
Heritage Park Plan	256
A Heritage Community	257
Vancouver's Model Park	258
Conservation Through Adaptive Reuse	263

10 Each Step of Our Exploration — 265

About the RAIC Award Competition	266
Governor General's Medals for Architecture	267
The Jurors (1986)	268
Church Buildings	270
Project: St. Helen's Anglican Church	271
This Beautiful Timber Structure	272
Project: Burnaby Village Museum	274
Project: Still Creek Park	275

Project: UBC Heritage Building Study	278
Pushing the Boundary of Technology	284
Applying New Techniques	289
Project: Greenwood Village Townhouses	290
Project: Bennett Road Townhouses	291
Project: Ladysmith Heritage Harbour	292
Project: Kamloops Indian Centre	293
Letting Everybody Speak	294
Deep-Freezing & Brain-Storming	294
Project: The Old Territorial Administration Building	295
Quality Control	301

11 We Build a Shared Vision — 303

The Peg Board of the Past	304
The Future of the Firm	305
Grand Gestures & Simple Sketches	306
Project: Norquay Elementary School	310
1995 City of Vancouver Heritage Award Nomination	311
City Honours School With Heritage Award	314
Check & Double-Check	315
Norquay Elementary School: The Three R's	316
In My Father's Footsteps	318
Project: Squamish Railway Museum	322
Project: Minnekhada Heritage Park	328
He was a Magician with a Spreadsheet	333
Shared Values	334
A Shared Vision	335

12 Place of Song and Dance — 337

Travelling Together	337
Retiring Together	341
Creating a Cohesive Design	342
History in the Making / Bâtir un passé	344
Project: Maillardville Heritage Square	346
An Urban Design / Heritage Preservation Submission	347
Brutally Tight Budgets	351
An Environment of Collaboration	355
Context Analysis	356
A Natural Curiosity for Life	358
Place of Song and Dance	361

Index — *369*

Editor's Note

The professional career of a prominent architect is inevitably built with a bold mixture of success and dissent—luck and talent, conflict and creativity, innovation and innuendo: all pave the pioneer's path of promise and purpose, and Rand Iredale's journey was no exception. It is not the intention of this book to emphasize or exaggerate accomplishment, nor to deny or diminish controversy; rather, it is to recognize a man's life and his work through the dual lenses of record and reminiscence.

༄

Finding a Good Fit, which incorporates documented data alongside recollected anecdote, takes its direction and inspiration from Rand Iredale's enthusiastic approach to his life and his work, and from Kathryn Iredale's desire to acknowledge her husband's contributions and achievements. In a close collaboration, Kathryn and I agreed from the outset to avoid creating an idealized story in favour of capturing the realized story.

This book is not, by any means, a critical social analysis of the times, events, and projects that circumscribe the making of a successful career or that document the development of a world-class city. Nor is it a seamless construction; rather, it reflects the spirited messiness of a life well lived, as it both reveals and replicates the collage of collaboration that resided at the core of Rand's character.

Content

The book's contents are arranged along two intersecting paths, one *thematic* and one *chronologic*, as Rand's life and work can be neither rendered in, nor reduced to, straight lines. Multiple perspectives necessarily overlap and interplay, alongside the revisionist tendencies of remembering. While not representing the definitive record, the contents register the scope and significance of Rand's life through his personal activities, interests, and relationships, and through his key projects, partnerships, and collaborations.

In addition to Kathryn Iredale's narratives and the reprints of published articles on Rand's projects, the pages of *Finding a Good Fit* are seasoned with insights provided through essays by, and interviews with, some of the people who knew Rand best:

- daughter Jennifer Iredale, who shares her love of historic buildings and places and her "memories of Dad" as mentor and maverick;

- son Talbot Iredale, who describes his and Rand's joint fascination with "pushing the boundary of technology" and developing organizational methodologies;

- son Richard Iredale, who expresses his recollections of Rand as a father, mentor, and collaborator, as well as a man of great curiosity, optimism, and enthusiasm;

- Rand's partners Bill Rhone (Rhone & Iredale, 1960–1980) and Charlotte Murray (The Iredale Partnership, 1980–2000), who each reminisce about their heartfelt experiences of working with him;

- structural engineer Bogue Babicki, who recalls his abiding personal and professional relationship with Rand, which began in the 1960s;

- architect Rainer Fassler, who worked for Rand in the late 1960s and early 1970s, and who recounts his admiration for Rand as an exceptional mentor and collaborator;

- architect Peter Busby, who worked for Rand in the late 1970s, and who provides a colourful characterization of the man he knew and admired;

- long-time employee Liz Scremin, who worked for Rand in the 1990s, and who recalls him as a master of both the simple design and the grand gesture.

These essays and interviews have been edited for clarity and consistency, while the authentic voice of each contributing speaker and writer has been retained to the greatest extent possible. Individually, the contributors' comments convey some of the same events and vignettes from different standpoints. Collectively, they portray the qualities of Rand's multi-faceted career and character, thus providing texture to the telling and retelling of his story.

Rand recorded his developing philosophies and methodologies in his *Project Manager's Manual*, which evolved to document the smooth operation of a professional practice. First conceived in 1968, the Manual appeared in four subsequent editions over the next 29 years. Edited excerpts from the 1997 Edition are included throughout this book to illuminate specific projects and exemplify Rand's poetical and practical approach to the profession he loved (the titles of these excerpts are italicized in the Table of Contents).

The book begins with architecture critic Trevor Boddy's eloquent Tribute, written and published shortly after Rand's funeral in 2000. Kathryn's Preface follows, in which she shares a little about herself and her life with Rand and why she wanted to undertake this project. The book concludes with the Miner's Bay Band Stand, donated by the Iredale family in Rand's memory and built on Mayne Island in 2006. In between are selected projects and anecdotes depicting the places and people that influenced, and were influenced by, Rand Iredale.

Chapters

Section One: Personal Places

Section One provides a brief overview of Rand's life and work and an introduction to his education, marriage, and career in the 1950s.

Chapter 1 summarizes Rand's personal and professional life and includes an excerpt from his mother's autobiography. Chapter 2 introduces Rand's great love of the outdoors, his early years as an architect, and the beginnings of his 20-year partnership with Bill Rhone. It also covers two early projects, the Channel 8 Television Studio and the Grouse Mountain Chalet. Chapter 3 illustrates the Iredale family's lifelong love affair with Mayne Island, and their changing roles over the years from rural pioneers, to land developers, to family homesteaders.

Section Two: Public Places

Section Two covers the heady years of the 1960s and the 1970s, highlighting Rand's collaboration on major projects for major clients, and his emergence as an urban planner with a compelling vision for the City of Vancouver.

Chapter 4 covers the Portage Mountain Hydro Electric project for BC Hydro. Chapter 5 covers the competition to design Simon Fraser University on Burnaby Mountain and the resulting commission to design its new Science Complex. Chapter 6 covers both the landmark development of the Westcoast Transmission Building in downtown Vancouver and the innovative design of the undergraduate Sedgewick Library for the University of British Columbia. Chapters 7 and 8 span the transforming decade of the 1970s. Amidst the stimulating environs of diverse cities and cultures, these chapters illuminate the Iredale family's evocative journey to Venice, Italy and Rand's emerging and increasingly influential involvement in urban planning and downtown development.

Section Three: People Places

Section Three contrasts Rand's abiding interest in computer technology with his pioneering promotion of heritage conservation, seemingly strange bedfellows that accompanied his ever-evolving approach to project management during the 1980s and 1990s.

Chapter 9 introduces the shared interests of Rand and his new professional partner, Charlotte Murray, in developing heritage projects and establishing heritage policies and practices in Vancouver. Chapters 10 and 11 emphasize Rand's work on schools, churches, museums, and townhouses, alongside his fascination with new computer technologies. Chapter 12 covers the winding down of Rand's practice while affirming his expertise as a master planner; in this context, it also conveys the sometimes controversial mix of partnership and collaboration, as evidenced in the episodic completion of Place des Arts at Maillardville Heritage Square in the City of Coquitlam.

Context

Chapter titles are drawn from Rand's life and work: the first and final Chapters are named after the family's memorial plaque and the band stand built for Rand on Mayne Island; Chapter 3 is named for his dream of developing the land on Mayne Island; all other chapter titles are lifted directly from the excerpts of his *Project Manager's Manual*. Taken together, they aptly depict Rand's lifelong journey of exploration and discovery.

Finding a Good Fit is a compilation of diverse materials. Though best read from front to back, the book's format is not unlike that of a magazine: chapters and segments are self-contained, and one can begin reading at almost any point. To assist the reader, different texts are identifiable through the use of different fonts and page formats, as follows:

- Kathryn Iredale's writings – plain white pages
- contributors' essays and interviews – bordered text boxes
- partial or whole reprints of published materials – headers and shaded pages
- excerpts from Rand Iredale's *Project Manager's Manual* – 'dog-eared' text boxes
- excerpts from some of Rand's Studies and Reports – headers and white pages

Kathryn's texts derive both from her writings and from my interviews with her. The end of each individual entry—whether text, essay, interview, or reprint—is marked by a small black square [■]. Rand's writings conclude with his name. Citations for excerpted reprints and other references are contained in footnotes; all known authors are named.

A note to readers: the four seasons are capitalized throughout the text, acknowledging Dr. David Suzuki's commitment to honouring the Earth, and recognizing Rand's interest in protecting the environment.

※

It has been a great pleasure to work for, and with, Kathryn Iredale on a project so close to her heart. Her careful collecting and cataloguing of archival materials rendered the editing process remarkably manageable. Through the making of this book I have come to know and admire Kathryn and, through the memories of many, to also know and admire Rand, whom I never had the pleasure of meeting.

The book's title, Finding a Good Fit, *captures Rand's approach to life and work. Just as he consistently searched for a good fit in architecture, so he always sought a good fit in his personal and professional relationships. By all accounts, Rand loved his life and his work. By all accounts, he found a good fit.* ■

Sheila Martineau PhD

Vancouver 2007

Tribute: In Memoriam

This tribute to Rand Iredale, written by architecture critic Trevor Boddy, M.Arch. following Rand's death, was published in The Canadian Architect *and is reprinted here in full.*

☙

Over the course of the 20th century, there was a shift in the cultural identity of the architectural profession—from architect-as-master-builder to architect-as-artist. This is why we know so much about Frank Gehry hanging out with the artists and sculpting maquettes for the laser scanner, but almost nothing about Randy Jefferson, the Canadian whose wide-ranging skills are essential to getting Gehry's projects built. We venerate Louis Sullivan—delineator, writer and designer—but tend to forget the contributions of partner Dankmar Adler—inventor, manager and designer.

These thoughts dominated when I joined a huge sample of the Vancouver architectural community for the funeral of Randle Iredale in August [in St. Anselm's Anglican Church on University Boulevard]. Arthur Erickson is Iredale's only rival as the architect who most shaped the Vancouver architectural scene over the past few decades. Because Iredale's greatest skills were as architectural manager, leader, researcher and in-house critic rather than designer, his legacy may not be so easily named, but it is real.

Consider the key architects who had their first responsibilities under Iredale's tutelage at his firm Rhone and Iredale and who then went on to make their own important contributions as designers or specialists: Richard Henriquez, Peter Busby, Peter Cardew, Rainer Fassler, Terry Williams, Andrew Gruft, Robert Lemon, Charlotte Murray, C.Y. Loh (frequent structural engineer to most of these and subject of a recent UBC exhibition), and one of Seattle's top design firms first founded as a Rhone and Iredale satellite, Miller and Hull.

In terms of current leadership of the West Coast design community, these alumni of Iredale's much smaller firm now cast a shadow at least as long as alumni of Erickson's. Indeed, history might have been different had Rhone and Iredale won the 1963 competition for Simon Fraser University, rather than placing second to Erickson and Massey.

Randle Iredale was born in Calgary in 1929 and moved to Vancouver before completing high school. He graduated in one of UBC's first architecture classes in 1954, and soon founded a firm with colleague Bill Rhone. An early success, and one of the most underrated achievements of Modern Architecture in Canada, are Rhone and Iredale's installations for the Bennett Dam on the Peace River.

Iredale's intellect shone at the Friday afternoon design panels that were a fixture of his firm, and alumni architects describe his skill at pre-design studies and process thinking, delineating site and program issues to set a design direction continued by others. According to current partner at the successor firm The Iredale Partnership, Charlotte Murray, "He had to *know* everything, [and then] was very trusting of the people he employed." Richard Henriquez has a similar view: "Rand was an extremely argumentative person; he thought that a good building is the result of conflict."

Rather than a gifted artist in the mode of Erickson, Iredale was a master builder and a major figure in the Vancouver architectural community. We owe him—and other under-recognized talents like his—a continuing debt.[1] ■

---

1 Trevor Boddy, "In Memoriam: Randle Iredale Dies at 71," *The Canadian Architect* (October 2000): 7.

Preface: Remembering Rand

My husband, Rand Iredale, died suddenly and unexpectedly on August 20th, 2000 from an aorta aneurism. He died 'with his boots on,' having spent the previous week hiking and camping in Manning Park with two of his grandchildren, Rylan and Meg. Rand shared his great love of the outdoors with all of our grandchildren, teaching them how to set up camp and cook their meals. Manning Park was one of their favourite places.

A Partnership of Equals

Rand and I met on a blind date at a high school dance at University Hill High School in 1946. We went on to attend the University of British Columbia together in 1947. I studied Math and English, took a year out to earn tuition, and received my BA in 1952.

After my graduation, while Rand continued his studies in the School of Architecture, I did a bit of travelling, taking the train to Toronto via Everett and Chicago with a friend, and staying on in Toronto. I had a wonderful time living in Yorkville with my girlfriends, and working for Dr. Eugene Faludi at Town Planning Consultants Ltd.

In the Spring of 1953 Rand came to Toronto, and we were married at Hart House at the University of Toronto on May 6th. I was 23 and Rand was 24. In a remarkable coincidence, we were married by the same Minister, Cecil Swanson, who had confirmed Rand in Calgary and confirmed me in Vancouver when we were children.

Following our honeymoon at the summer home of my aunt and uncle just north of Toronto, we relocated to Ottawa. We spent the Summer there and lived at Kirk's Ferry while Rand worked as a Second Lieutenant with the Canadian Officers' Training Corp (COTC), Reserve Army. He still had another year of university to complete and so we headed back to Vancouver in the Fall.

Driving west through the northern United States in a '47 Chevy, we stayed at roadside motels along the way. After one such overnight stop, we each thought the other had put our luggage in the trunk of the car, but about 200 miles down the highway we discovered we had no luggage. We had to drive all the way back to pick it up. After that we were a little more careful!

We hadn't yet figured out who was going to do what in the marriage, though we eventually worked it all out. I managed our home and Rand managed his office. We raised three children together—Jennifer, Talbot, and Richard—and later we worked and travelled together. We were high school sweethearts who became great companions throughout our life together.

I didn't have a profession like young women do today, and Rand didn't make his own breakfast and iron his own shirts! Due to family circumstances, I was brought up by my maternal grandparents, George and Margaret Swaisland, and so my sense of what I was supposed to do in the world was more traditional.

Grampa was a bank manager and Grannie had trained as a nurse at Johns Hopkins University in Baltimore, Maryland. They were married in 1905 and Grannie ran the household; she made a lot of the decisions, but they worked as a team and they were my role models. They were equals, each carrying different responsibilities, and that's the way Rand and I were, too. We complemented each other, we were mutually supportive, and we had an equal partnership.

A Labour of Love

Rand contributed so much to others, both personally and professionally, that I felt a book deserved to be done in recollection of his life and in recognition of his work. I wanted to make a memory of him, for both present and future generations of our family and friends, and also for the public record.

I hope that this book will find its way into the libraries of family and friends, colleagues and collaborators, and architectural schools and professional associations. I also hope it will serve as a resource for related works that may be undertaken by others concerning the social and political history of Rand's era in the City of Vancouver and the Province of British Columbia.

Bringing this project to fruition has been a labour of love for me and my family. We adored and admired Rand and we miss him terribly.

Kathryn Iredale

Vancouver 2007

Adjacent:
Our Wedding Day
Hart House, Toronto
May 6th, 1953

Photo: Bill Carter, Toronto

Opposite:
William Randle Iredale
1929–2000

Photo: Schiffer, Vancouver (1975)

PERSONAL PLACES

1 Pioneer, Architect, Mentor

Rand Iredale was a Member of the Architectural Institute of British Columbia and a Fellow of the Royal Architectural Institute of Canada. As an architect and an urban planner, he practised his profession in British Columbia for over 40 years, from the time of his registration in 1958 until his retirement in 1999. What follows is a chronology of his résumé.

Rand's Résumé

Upon graduation from the UBC School of Architecture in 1955, Rand apprenticed first with McCarter, Nairne and Partners for two years and then, in 1957, with McKee and Gray, Architects and Engineers, where he briefly joined the firm as a junior partner.

Rand became a member of the Architectural Institute of British Columbia (AIBC) in 1958 and started a small professional practice as Randle Iredale Architect, which he operated for two years. He was a Founding Partner of Rhone & Iredale Architects for 20 years (from 1960) and Managing Partner of The Iredale Partnership for another 20 years (from 1980).

During his career Rand set up subsidiary companies to accommodate his interests in planning and design. In 1963 he founded Tecton Structures Ltd. to develop prefabricated modular building systems, and in 1968 he established Canadian Environmental Sciences (CES), an interdisciplinary environmental planning and engineering group. One of the partners in CES, Art Cowie, eventually left the firm and started EIKOS, which was the first Vancouver firm to emphasize interdisciplinary planning as a major component of landscape design.

Tecton, which won the Canadian Industrial Design Award in 1967, merged with Fabco Ltd. in 1968 to form Fabtec Structures Ltd. Fabtec became the largest manufacturer of school, hospital, and industrial camp buildings in British Columbia. Rand was Chairman of the Board and Director of Research until the company was sold in 1971.

THIS IS TO CERTIFY THAT

W. Randle Iredale

is a

MEMBER

of the

ROYAL ARCHITECTURAL INSTITUTE
OF CANADA

Founded in the year of our Lord, One thousand nine hundred and seven, and afterwards constituted under Royal Charters granted by King Edward the Seventh, King George the Fifth, and Queen Elizabeth the Second, a body politic and corporate, to establish and maintain a bond between The Royal Institute and component or allied societies, to promote architectural appreciation and the interchange of knowledge pertaining to the practice of architecture, and to encourage and recognize worthy aspirants to the profession.

IN WITNESS whereof Officers of the Royal Institute have hereto set their hands, and the Common Seal of the Institute has been hereto affixed under authority of the Council dated the 21st *day of* **September, 1962.**

President

Honorary Secretary

Rand at the time of his appointment as a junior partner with McKee & Gray, Architects and Engineers (Associates of The Rankin Co. Ltd. in Montreal, Brown and Blauvelt in New York, and Hooper, Belfrage and Gray in London UK).

Photo:
Williams Bros., Vancouver (circa 1957)

Early in his career, Rand was involved in award-winning designs for the Portage Mountain Hydro-Electric Development at the W.A.C. Bennett Dam, the Science Complex at the new Simon Fraser University, the Westcoast Transmission Building in downtown Vancouver, and Sedgewick Library at the University of British Columbia. He went on to design a range of building types for public and private clients throughout British Columbia.

In addition, Rand was in charge of many urban planning projects that included campus planning, inner-city planning, and master planning for cultural and municipal centres. His input was pivotal, for example, in determining the downtown developments of BC Place, False Creek, and Expo '86, and he was lauded as "an architect responsible for much of Vancouver's urban landscape" at the time of his death.[1]

Rand was also a pioneer in promoting heritage preservation policies and practices and in developing computerized project management systems. His work has been recognized with 18 international, national, and local awards and has been published in Canadian, American, British, German, and Japanese professional journals.

Rand loved learning and experimenting, and early on he embraced the new computer technologies. In 1968 he studied Computer Sciences at the University of Washington and in 1976 he studied the Management of Planning & Design through Harvard University's Graduate School of Design (Continuing Education). He took courses in computer languages and developed innovative and award-winning project management systems in his professional practice.

In the 1970s Rand developed the Ri-Rite program, which ran on a large IBM machine in downtown Vancouver, to track billable time and tasks on projects. In the 1980s, at the beginning of the computer revolution, he became an enthusiastic beta tester for AutoCAD systems.

---

1 "Died: Randle Iredale," *The Report Newsmagazine* (October 2000). Source: Internet (author unknown).

THIS IS TO CERTIFY THAT

W. Randle Iredale

was elected on the 2nd day of February 1977

FELLOW
of the
ROYAL ARCHITECTURAL INSTITUTE OF CANADA

Founded in the year of our Lord, One thousand nine hundred and seven, and afterwards constituted under Royal Charters granted by King Edward the Seventh, King George the Fifth, and Queen Elizabeth the Second, a body politic and corporate, to establish and maintain a bond between The Royal Institute and component or allied societies, to promote architectural appreciation and the interchange of knowledge pertaining to the practice of architecture, and to encourage and recognize worthy aspirants to the profession.

IN WITNESS whereof the Officers of the College of Fellows have hereto set their hands, and the Common Seal of the Institute has been hereto affixed under authority of the Council dated the 28th day of June 1977

Charles H. Cullum
President of the Royal Institute

Chancellor
Dean
Registrar

Registered Serial No. 457

The technology revolution fascinated Rand, such that The Iredale Partnership was one of the first architectural practices to embrace computers, with all of their possibilities and frustrations.

Rand's systems were recognized in industry publications and in invitations to speak at the American Institute of Architects seminars in Seattle, Sun Valley, and Chicago. Rand also took courses in *synectics*, a brainstorming tool for creative problem-solving that would influence his thinking throughout his architectural practice.[1]

Rand was an esteemed mentor and teacher to students of architecture working in his practice. He believed the design and implementation of a project to be a team effort, and he gave recognition to all who worked on his projects. During the course of his career, he was a Visiting Lecturer at Pennsylvania State University and Wisconsin University and an Adjunct Professor at the University of British Columbia.

In 1984 Rand was appointed Professional Advisor to the Royal Architectural Institute of Canada (RAIC) Governor General's Medals for Architecture Awards Program. Mandated to review the program, he produced the Iredale Report; its recommendations were accepted by the RAIC Council in 1985. The new awards program was held in Vancouver in 1986 with jurors John Andrews, Fumihiko Maki, Kurt Forster, and Moshe Safdie. Rand worked closely with the jury and the jurying process and edited the 120-page quadrennial catalogue of the winning projects.[2]

As a committed citizen of Vancouver, Rand volunteered his time, energy, and expertise to work with numerous associations and committees. His volunteer activities included positions as Chairman of the Architects, Engineers & Building Inspectors for the Certified Professional Program Task Force; Chairman of the Vancouver Board of Trade Civic Affairs Committee; and Chairman of the Downtown Vancouver Association Planning Committee.

Rand also volunteered with the Vancouver Chapter of the AIBC (as Vice-President and later as Chairman), served on the Vancouver Heritage Advisory Committee, and acted as a Professional Advisor for local design competitions.

☙

This summary of Rand's résumé just traces the contours of his career. His many personal and professional accomplishments, associations, and adventures are expanded upon in this and later chapters.

---

1   *Synectics* (William Gordon, 1961) is a comprehensive approach to creative thinking. Taken from the Greek word *synectikos*, which means "bringing different things into unified connection," it employs analogy and metaphor for developing creative problem-solving, internalizing abstract concepts, and disrupting traditional methodologies. Source: Internet (2006).

2   *Royal Architectural Institute of Canada: 1986 Awards Program* (Downsview ON: Douglas & McIntyre, 1986).

Starting Out

Just as Rand's professional life was defined by partnership and mentorship, and by innovation and collaboration, so his personal life was defined by family and friends, and by activity and adventure. He was as excited about exploring new ski hills and hiking trails as he was about experimenting with new technologies, such as computers and camcorders. Rand was an exceptional husband and father who very much enjoyed spending time with his family. His personal and professional lives were well integrated: he was as likely to discuss new design ideas with his family at the dinner table as he was to bring his family with him to both work and play at the office.

Rand was born in Calgary on June 1st, 1929, the only son of William E. Iredale and Isabel (Betty) M. Iredale. His early years were spent in Calgary, where he attended the Strathcona School for Boys (now Strathcona / Tweedsmuir) and developed his great love of the outdoors. One of his fondest memories was a camping trip with his parents, the three of them driving through the Canadian Rockies in the old Ford and camping for several days near the Hot Springs at Radium.

Rand, third from the left, setting out with school friends on a bike trip from Calgary to Banff in 1944

At age 15, along with three friends, Rand embarked on a gruelling 80-mile bicycle trip from Calgary to Banff. The boys struggled uphill against a strong westerly wind and camped overnight next to the road, their bicycles providing the only shelter. On another of many such adventures, Rand and his friends travelled to Vancouver Island to explore uncharted caves.

Though Rand enjoyed an active and adventurous childhood, memories of his family's struggles during the Great Depression left an indelible imprint, such that throughout his life he hated to waste anything and often found imaginative, economic solutions to otherwise costly problems.

Rand Iredale
High School Graduation
University Hill Secondary
1947

Photo: Artona Studio, Vancouver

In 1945, when Rand was 16, his family sold their house in Calgary and moved to Vancouver, eventually purchasing a home in the University Endowment Lands at 1729 Acadia Road. He attended University Hill Secondary School, graduated in 1947, and went on to attend UBC, where he was an active member in the Players' Club (drama club).

After two years of undergraduate studies, Rand enrolled in the new five-year B.Arch. program. At that time the Department of Architecture, headed by Frederick Lasserre, was housed in old army huts that had been brought to UBC by Dr. Gordon Shrum to accommodate all of the World War II veterans returning to their university studies.[1]

As money was scarce after the Depression and the War, Rand sold World Book Encyclopedias during the winter months while he was attending university. One summer he worked on the CPR boats to Alaska, and then he joined the Canadian Officers' Training Program (COTC) and attained standing as a Second Lieutenant. After joining the COTC, Rand spent his school summers in their training programs at Chilliwack, Jericho (in Vancouver), and Ottawa.

Rand graduated from UBC's renamed School of Architecture in 1955 (he would have graduated in 1954 but he needed one more course to complete his studies). He had written his senior thesis on designing a new television station and, following our marriage in Toronto in 1953, and in the interests of his research, we visited every television station we possibly could on the return motor trip from east to west!

After returning to Vancouver we stayed with Rand's mom and dad for about a month. Rand returned to university, I found a job, and we rented a suite in the upstairs of a house on West 2nd Avenue, near Alma Street. It was quite a dreary house, heated by a sawdust furnace that filled the house with smoke in the middle of the night! For $50 a month we had a kitchen, a bed-sitting room, and a shared bathroom.

I went to work for Bill Watts with Watts Marketing & Research, but there was nobody else in the office and I was bored to tears. I finally found an interesting job with Forest Industrial Relations, working for Don Lanskail, who later became the Mayor of West Vancouver.

---

1   The Vancouver Board of Trade passed a resolution in 1945 urging UBC to establish an architecture department. Concurrently, students in second and third year Applied Science formed a Pre-Architecture Club to lobby for the implementation of an architectural program. The Department of Architecture was subsequently established in 1946 within the Faculty of Applied Science, under the direction of Frederick Lasserre. In 1950, the Department was reorganized as the School of Architecture. Lasserre, who became Director of the School, continued in this capacity until his death in 1961. Originally housed in several old army huts, in 1962 the School moved, together with the Department of Fine Arts, into the Frederick Lasserre Building. The School originally offered a five-year undergraduate programme leading to a B.Arch. degree. Source: www.library.ubc.ca/archives/u_arch/scharc.html (2006).

Our children were born during those early years while Rand was establishing his architectural practice: Jennifer in 1956, Talbot in 1957, and Richard in 1959. We purchased a cottage at 4273 West 12th Avenue for $6,500. It was a real cottage, with floors going every which way! It had no furnace—it was heated by an oil stove—but had a large lot and a garden. It was home.

It was about the same time that Rand was introduced to Bill Rhone, who had completed his education in California, but was living here and looking to start a practice. Memory is fallible, but I recall that Rand and Bill Rhone met through Harry Pickstone, at that time a planner at City Hall. It is Bill's recollection, however, that they met through my sister, Daphne, who trained as a nurse with Bill's wife, Louise, at Vancouver General Hospital. Perhaps both events occurred!

The Rhone & Iredale Years: 1960–1980

Rand and Bill got together and formed a partnership—Rhone & Iredale—and, as they had no money, their first office was set up in the attic of Rand's parents' home at 1729 Acadia Road. They worked there for about a year and then, in 1961, they purchased a ramshackle house at 1095 West 7th Avenue on the Fairview Slopes, which they renovated for their offices. The whole area was rundown at that time; it was red-lined and you couldn't get a mortgage. It was considered a 'slum,' but it was also in transition.

By 1967 Rand and Bill had outgrown the house and sold it to Charles Flavelle of Purdy's Chocolates; Charles used it for his office and purchased the adjacent building for his chocolate factory. When he eventually sold the property and moved his operation out to Kingsway, the Chocolate Factory was redeveloped by Mary and Harold Spence-Sales as their home, and Charles Flavelle's Choklit Park was gentrified.

Rand and Bill bought the much larger house across the street at 1100 West 7th Avenue, which had previously been a house of ill repute! Their office was a non-conforming use—the area was still zoned industrial—but the City turned a blind eye, as their office use was significantly better than the previous owners! The firm grew to some 30 people and they stayed in these premises until 1980, when the partnership of Rhone & Iredale was dissolved.

Rhone & Iredale
1095 West 7th Avenue
Vancouver

The Iredale Partnership Years: 1980–2000

In 1980 Rand formed The Iredale Partnership and, as the Managing Partner, invited architect Charlotte Murray to join him. They remained at 1100 West 7th Avenue until 1985, when the property was sold for a townhouse development. The Iredale Partnership then moved to the Steamboat Heritage House at 1151 West 8th Avenue, which Rand had preserved as an adaptive reuse Professional Office Building in the late 1970s. Rand and Charlotte both had a keen and consuming interest in heritage preservation.

Charlotte became the Heritage Studio Partner, though Rand still participated in this area with notable heritage projects throughout British Columbia. In 1990 our son, Richard Iredale, with degrees in architecture and civil engineering, also joined the firm and soon became a Studio Partner. Richard's training permitted the firm to participate in seismic upgrading projects, which included several schools; consequently, in the 1990s educational facilities became a large part of the practice.

Kendall Jessiman joined the firm as a Studio Partner in 1996, and James Emery joined the firm in 1997, becoming a Studio Partner in 2000. During this time of transition, Rand stepped down as Managing Partner in 1999 and turned the role over to Richard. Charlotte Murray postponed her retirement plans in order to complete her crowning work, the heritage restoration of the interior of Christ Church Cathedral in downtown Vancouver, and finally retired in 2004 to embark on her long-awaited journey around the world.

The firm continued to operate as Iredale Group Architecture—with partners Richard Iredale, Kendall Jessiman, and James Emery—and to occupy the Steamboat House, with its views of False Creek, downtown Vancouver, and the North Shore mountains. The house was sold in 2006, and Iredale Group relocated to One Alexander Street in Vancouver's historic Gastown.

Below, left:
Rhone & Iredale
1100 West 7th Avenue
Vancouver

Below, right:
The Iredale Partnership
1151 West 8th Avenue
Vancouver

Our Family Home

Once Rand and Bill Rhone had established their practice in the early 1960s, we moved the family from our little cottage on West 12th to a house at 4514 Langara Avenue, where we lived for five years. This house was eventually too small for our growing family; we liked living there, but it was tight quarters and not worth renovating. Rand's mother, Betty, sold real estate in the University Endowment Lands, and we told her we were looking for a four-bedroom house because I wanted a bedroom for each of the kids.

With Betty's help, we found our family home at 1537 Wesbrook Crescent in 1967 and had no need to move again. Our children could go to University Hill High School, where Rand had graduated, and his mother, Betty, lived just three blocks away. She was now living on her own, as Rand's father had died a few years earlier. Though she was highly independent, it was nice to be close at hand. One time she called us on Christmas Day; there was a torrential rain, her basement was flooded, and she needed help, which was easy for us to provide. Also, the kids could drop in and visit her after school. Rand was an only child and they were her only grandchildren. So it was a very good arrangement.

The kids grew up and left home, and Rand and I continued to live here. When we retired we set up our offices at home. I still live here with Rand's golden retriever, Bing, whom he named after Bing Crosby. I sometimes think of moving, but I like it here and I enjoy the garden. It's home.

Our Family Life

Our life together was never dull. We were always doing something, and Rand was ever-ready with his camera to record our activities. If we weren't working, we were skiing, camping, hiking, fishing, or travelling.

Rand, Jennifer, & Kathryn
Fishing at Wells BC
Summer 1977

During the 1970s our winter weekends were spent skiing at Whistler with the family. Often, on a sunny winter day, Rand would take his skis to the office, work in the morning, and leave about 1:00 in the afternoon for a few hours of skiing on the local mountains, returning to the office around 5:00. When our sons were teenagers, Rand took them helicopter skiing on virgin snow in the Rocky Mountains.

One time we all went camping in Washington State; I remember this trip because we had our first golden retriever, Corby (named after Le Corbusier), with us. It was teeming rain, but Rand was determined to camp! We had to hike up a long hill in the rain with all of our gear and equipment. As we were soaked to the skin, and in an effort to keep our tent and sleeping bags dry, I insisted that everyone strip off their wet clothes before climbing into the tent. The next morning we awoke to a glorious sunny day.

Rand and Kathryn enjoying their shared hammock on Mayne Island

Summers were spent on Mayne Island, with the whole family building projects and camping out. We fished, hiked, and water-skied, and in the evenings we sang around the campfire. Rand had a wonderful baritone voice and could often be heard singing enthusiastically. His favourite song was *Clementine*. He was the guiding light of our annual summer lamb bake, when friends, family, and colleagues would gather for feast and fellowship. It's a tradition that continues to this day.

There are so many memories of Rand: his daring outdoor adventures, our travels all over the world, and the years we spent working together at the Steamboat House. These and other reminiscences are sprinkled throughout the pages of this book.

Early on a summer morning, Rand would rise about 4:00, make himself a thermos of hot coffee, and take off in the boat to go fishing. The early morning when the sun was just rising was one of his favourite times of the day, and he would drag along whoever was willing to go with him. Sometimes I'd go, but I'm not an early riser. He usually came back around 7:00 or 7:30 and wanted breakfast. So of course I'd make him breakfast, and then he'd curl up in the hammock and have a siesta! He enjoyed it so much. He loved Mayne Island. ■

The Business of Just Surviving

by Betty Iredale

The following text, excerpted from the Epilogue of Betty Iredale's autobiography, explains why her son, Billy (Rand), born in 1929 during the Great Depression, was raised as an only child.[1]

The Depression years had been hard on everyone. The business of just surviving, of feeding, housing, and clothing oneself and one's family made it impossible to consider a larger family.

Upon returning from our honeymoon, my husband and I quickly realized that young Billy was on the way, which was a slight shock. We were so beautifully broke. The stock crash was beginning to cast its shadow. Wise men saw the handwriting on the wall, and big business began to tighten its belt. We were out of jobs with a baby on the way and plenty of money on the books against us.

"You've got a little boy," [the nurse] told me. I moved my head on the pillow and closed my eyes. I was content; I'd wanted a little boy. Things got more difficult after the baby came. We had to find cheaper lodgings, and car sales were dropping. The Crash came in November 1929. Bill lost his shirt like everyone else; he lost his job and he was overdrawn. Things looked decidedly bleak.

By the time Billy was three years old business was getting worse. The Depression was underway, and many of our friends were out of work and remained out of work until we wondered how they lived.

---

1 Betty Iredale, "Epilogue" in *Stories of the Sod Shack, and Other Reminiscences* (Vancouver: Iredale Family, 1991), 197–212. Excerpts (197–99, 202, 204–05, 210–12) have been edited for clarity.

Continued

The oil company Bill worked for laid off one or two men, it seemed, every time there was a sales meeting. In our hearts we worried, but I always felt we would somehow manage. We planned all of the things we might do if the worst came to the worst and how we would keep Billy fed and healthy, for there was plenty of evidence that children were suffering from malnutrition.

It was all about poverty and anxiety, and those who gave up and went on relief, and those who pulled their belts tighter and put their chins a little higher and stuck it out on God-only-knows what: hunting, hunting, hunting for work. A day here, a dollar somewhere else, and no money was ever spent more cautiously or with such thought and consideration as were those precious dollars. Every ounce of nutrition was considered in the spending.

We might have had another baby then. But was it fair? No one was having babies—not the thinking ones. We had a job, but common sense told us there was every likelihood that we wouldn't have one from one week to the next. There were appeals in the paper every night to help those in need. Children whose parents had been driven into indescribable hovels by poverty were starving in tumbledown buildings at the edge of the city.

I think 1934 [when Rand was five] was the worst year of the Depression. People's courage was beginning to weaken after the long strain, and the resources of both individuals and industry were nearing their end. There seemed to be no break in the gloom. Poverty, fear and hunger existed all around us.

Then the armament race began. Slowly, slowly, it began to have its effect. Worry for ourselves and for our friends began to lessen. We attacked our pile of debt with new vigour. It was slowly whittled away, and teeth that had been neglected and clothes that were patched beyond further repair were replaced, and after that I began to put a few dollars away again.

That year Billy began school. I took him over on that Monday morning in his little grey suit that I'd made for him, and after I'd met his teacher and she'd shown us to his seat, we both cried a bit and I left him. Now Bill and I talked about his education. A man had to be equipped with the best education the country could provide in this super modern world. Our next job was to buy a home and educate Billy.

There was no thought of a larger family now. The time for that had passed. It had flown by so quickly while we had been taken up with the business of living and outwitting an enemy that pounded at our doors for admittance. We'd held our own against the Depression of the 1930s, and that was all we'd had the courage to attempt. ∎

Betty Iredale

Photo: Schiffer, Vancouver (1975)

2 'The First Step in Any Journey'

> *I touched on Rand's great love of the outdoors in Chapter 1 by recounting a few of his boyhood adventures and family camping trips. But that is only the tip of the iceberg! He loved to sail and ski, camp and hike, and fish in the early morning, and the whole family became involved in one way or another in his many outdoor activities and adventures.*

The Great Outdoors

Sailing

While at university, Rand and his friend Bob Campbell learned to sail in the waters of English Bay. As junior members of the Royal Vancouver Yacht Club, they purchased the sailboat *Orswim*. Rand and Bob had very little money, so maintenance of this wooden-hulled boat and its canvas sails called for a good deal of ingenuity. The sails required drying and mending, and many hours were spent—with girlfriends to help out—caulking, sanding, and painting the hull. Later, Rand purchased a Star sailboat which, with its deeper and heavier hull, was more stable. It was a great thrill to be out on the water on a sunny summer's day. Alas, the Star sank dockside in a bad storm and was not salvageable.

After marriage and the arrival of babies, we had to give up sailing because it was not possible to pursue this activity without babysitters. Also, as the winds would die down in the late afternoon, we could not guarantee our return home by the agreed upon time.

Left:
These snapshots are from one of Rand's early photo albums; the sailboat *Orswim* is in the background

Right:
Kathryn and Rand enjoy an afternoon excursion up Malahat Drive while visiting relatives in Victoria (1950)

Rand was a real adventurer and a risk-taker. The second time he went skiing in the Bugaboos he went with a neighbour of ours, Gordon Harris. I received a very short phone call that evening from Rand: "Kathryn, I can't talk, but we're okay. Phone Doris." There had been an avalanche and several people had been lost. It was a dangerous sport but, all in all, Rand loved it.

Skiing

Also while at university, Rand took up skiing on the local mountains. Again, with the shortage of money, he adapted his old army boots into ski boots. Skis were the long wooden variety with 'bear trap' harnesses. We would ride the new wooden gondola up Grouse Mountain where the new rope-tows and T-bars lifted us to the top of the runs. These were not the groomed runs of today but, rather, were very icy and covered with moguls.

One of these rope-tows was thick and would perform a large vertical sine wave when it was running. On one occasion when Rand rode this particular rope-tow, as the rope performed a sine wave high in the air, he found himself hanging on tightly, dangling about 20 feet above the snow!

Skiing was a lifelong love of Rand's and it became a treasured family activity. When Whistler was developed in 1965 we were one of the first families to ski there. Over that first Christmas we stayed at the Cheakamus Lodge, which had just opened. We rode the train to Whistler and unloaded at Alta Lake into huge snowdrifts. Richard was about six years old and he landed, completely covered in snow, into one of these snowdrifts. We had to lug Richard and our gear to the road with our toboggan and then trudge a couple of miles on to Cheakamus Lodge.

In 1972 we purchased a ski chalet at Highland Village Lodge and, during the ski season, alternate weekends were spent skiing at Whistler with all the family and friends. Fresh snow in the Back Bowl provided many hours of good skiing. Other family ski trips were made to Silver Star near Vernon and to Big White near Kelowna.

When our sons, Talbot and Richard, were in their teens, Rand took them on a challenging ski holiday in the Bugaboos, high up in the Canadian Rockies, where skiers were helicoptered from Bugaboo Lodge to the tops of mountain ridges. The runs back to the lodge on virgin snow were steep and long, and Rand was proud of his ability to keep up with his much younger sons.

Camping & Hiking

Our camping expeditions included trips to the Canadian Rockies and to the Arrow Lakes in the West Kootenays, as well as the trip to Portage Mountain, and travelling up the Parsnip and Finlay Rivers prior to the area being flooded to create the huge lake for the Peace River Dam. If you went camping with Rand in a car, he would go down the most incredible 'roads,' which weren't even roads, to the very end until you thought you were lost! He had to explore. Sometimes I got uneasy and a little scared. I was the cautious one, but he always handled whatever came up.

Rand, grandson Brody, & dog Bing attending 'Camp School' in the backyard May 1999

When the grandchildren were old enough—ages five, six, and seven— Rand taught them about the great outdoors. He ran a kind of 'Camp School' on Mayne Island for a couple of weeks, teaching them how to plan a trip, cook their meals, and collect their water from the streams. He'd have them putting tents up and taking them down, as well as packing dried foods and going on hikes. Weight in your backpack is a problem when you're hiking, and Rand believed that it was essential to know how to pack carefully.

Fishing

When we purchased the Mayne Island property in 1958 (see Chapter 3), we frequently camped in a small clearing. Later, after we built the Sholi, Rand purchased a 10-foot dinghy and fished for salmon and rock cod. Later on, we acquired a 19-foot motorized runabout. Rand would often take off in the boat, heading down Campbell Bay toward the islands off Saturna for several hours of fishing. We enjoyed many good salmon barbecues after these fishing trips. When we went camping, Rand always took his fly-fishing gear along. ∎

Reprinted from *The Post* (Mathers, 1949)

An old newspaper clipping was found tucked away in an envelope at the back of one of Rand's photo albums (dated 1944–59). The article was published in 1949—the same year that Rand entered the School of Architecture at UBC—and is reproduced here in full.[1]

---

1 A.S. Mathers, "Careers for Canadians—VII: Opportunities For Young Architects Are Plentiful But Best Are Found In Our Smaller, Growing Cities," *The Post*, 1949 (Toronto; specific date and page number are unknown).

"ALVAN S. MATHERS, 54, of Mathers and Haldenby, Toronto architects, a past president of the National Construction Council of Canada, started practice in Toronto 30 years ago, entering the partnership in 1921. Among the buildings he's responsible for are the Botany Building, the School of Hygiene and Whitney Hall at the University of Toronto; the Dunlap Observatory, Richmond Hill, Ont.; Vancouver plant of Coca-Cola of Canada Ltd.; [and] St. John's Hospital, Willowdale. He's a Fellow of the Architectural Institute of Canada, [and] chairman of the advisory technical committee, Toronto City Planning Board."

Careers for Canadians

Opportunities For Young Architects Are Plentiful But Best Are Found In Our Smaller, Growing Cities

By A.S. Mathers (Mathers & Haldenby, Architects, Toronto)

Mentally, a successful architect should be alert and imaginative. He should be observant and possess a good memory, particularly of things he has seen. He should possess a pleasing personality and be able to get along well with all sorts of people.

The best training for an architect is a combination of formal academic study and practical experience on construction work, both in an architect's office and in the field. Experience in the administrative end of architectural work is essential.

Summer holiday jobs are extremely helpful. The student should spend at least one vacation period as a laborer on an important construction project. Summer work in an architect's office is, of course, a requirement for graduation from most architectural schools, but in taking work of this kind the student should get into a busy office regardless of the salary offered.

On the question of whether students should strive to head their class each year at the expense of their sport and social activity, or be content with lower marks and more fun, a reasonable balance is desirable. Fun and social activities should, however, not be permitted to interfere with the acquisition of knowledge. The academic years provide the only period when the basic education of an architect can be obtained. Fun can be had later.

Distinction in school and university sport and social activities are definitely an asset for later success, but again distinction academically must be the main consideration. Postgraduate work at another university in Canada, U.S. or abroad is not nearly so important as travel, for the student who intends to practice his profession. I consider postgraduate work of little value except for those who intend to teach.

20 | 'The First Step in any Journey'

Reprinted from *The Post* (Mathers, 1949)

Many Openings

How hard is it to get into this field?

The field is not overcrowded and there are many openings for the young architect who is prepared to establish himself in smaller cities. It is fairly difficult to get established in large cities where competition with recognized architects must be met.

As to probable first-year earnings, the young graduate can expect a salary of between $3,000 and $3,500 as assistant draftsman in an architect's office. As an employee, the salary after five years would be $4,500, after ten years $5,200, and after 15 years might reach $10,000, depending on the man. As a practicing architect, he would earn upward of $10,000 a year.

> Want to be an architect? Be prepared to study long and hard; be prepared for long, irregular hours of work, constant pressure. But you can look for plenty of variety.
>
> That's the advice of A.S. Mathers in this, the seventh in The Post's series designed to help young Canadians—and their parents—decide the all-important question of their future.
>
> The field is expanding, the outlook is good for the future, there are plenty of openings in our smaller, expanding communities, adds Mathers.

The field is expanding and the outlook is good for the future. Architects prosper in any period of national growth and prosperity. But a depression of serious proportions is extremely hard on them for their employment depends entirely on capital expenditure and investment. Bad times don't affect architects at first, but eventually they find the going tough. And they are among the last to benefit by a recovery. The lag is about a year in both cases.

The young architect should not marry too early if he intends to practice on his own. Many brilliant young men have denied themselves the possibility of later success by assuming the financial burden and restrictions on travel imposed by marriage before their earning power was sufficient.

What about setting up on your own? It is better to start as an employee. At least four years of sound office experience and the experience of being in charge of work is essential before it is wise to consider hanging out your shingle.

Considering the matter of starting and staying in a smaller city, or starting there and moving on to a big city later, the young architect would be well advised to start in a smaller city and stay there unless he is well known professionally in a large centre. The exceptions, of course, are many, but it takes outstanding ability to make one's way in a big city.

Being an architect involves long and irregular hours, night work and on week ends; constant study, terrific bouts of work and fairly constant pressure for about 10 months in the year. Usually there is a slight letup in November. In depression years there is little to do but worry.

As far as spending money on social activities and club memberships is concerned, even if such expenditures pinch, these things are of minor importance professionally; too much can be detrimental. Public activity, such as board of trade, art gallery and perhaps a service club, is desirable but not essential. Attention to business is the main thing if clients are to be satisfied.

How To Get In

I would advise a young man seeking his first job in architectural work to follow the old reliable method of writing letters to prospective employers and following this with a personal interview with those interested in his application. At least, that is the way I like applicants for jobs to approach me. As for aptitude tests in selecting new employees, I do not regard them as being of any use at all.

Training and experience in architecture can definitely be used as a stepping stone to success in other fields, certainly on the administrative side. I know of at least three men who left architecture to assume direction of large corporations as managing directors.

What are the things I like about architecture and the things I don't?

I like the interesting problems and the variety. I like to see the dream the architect puts on paper take form in the solid permanent structure. I like to return to work previously built and examine it over again. There is nothing I don't like about it—except the long hours.

There is no single thing in architecture most essential to success, but several. Architects succeed if they can design buildings well and economically, and if they administer the funds placed under their direction with care and thoroughness. Constant and thorough attention to details is essential. Unfortunately, there are no books which tell the whole tale of architecture or its people, but the student would be well advised to read *The Architect in History* by Martin Briggs (Oxford Press, 1927). ■

I Guess We Just Clicked

From an interview with Bill Rhone.

Ticking Along Fairly Nicely

After graduating from the University of California at Berkeley in 1952 with an MA in Architecture, I spent 21 months in the US Army in the Corps of Engineers as a Junior Officer. In those days it was universal draft, so you either signed up with the draft board and were subject to being drafted as a private in the army, or you took what was known as ROTC (Reserve Officers' Training Corps). And then when you graduated you got a commission as a Second Lieutenant and signed up to serve as a Junior Officer.

While in the US Army, I became a specialist in soils and asphalts and was sent to Texas A&M University. I took a special training course developed by the US Air Force and became an 'expert' in soils and asphalts and airfield construction. My MOS (Military Occupation Specialty) was Airport Engineer, a rather pompous sounding title for a First Lieutenant! I was offered a really nice job if I'd stay on, a promotion to Captain, but I said, "Nope, I want to be an architect!"

When I got out of the army I came up to Vancouver because my parents lived here. I was offered a job working for Bill Knoppe, which I took and that's how I got started. Bill was a Belgian and he had some of the most hair-raising World War I war stories I've ever heard. He was a bit of a maverick and a bit controversial, a difficult kind of a guy. But he did interesting work, and I learned a lot from him.

So I graduated in 1952, and then I was in the army. I got out in 1954 and worked in Vancouver for two years. Then my wife, Louise, and I went over to England for a year. After we came back, I worked for Bill Knoppe again and then started my own practice in 1959. We rented a large Tudor house on Point Grey Road that has since been demolished. I had two rooms upstairs, and I got some plywood and nailed it all together and had an office up there and was ticking along fairly nicely. And finally Rand and I got together in 1960.

Opportunity Knocks

While working for Bill Knoppe in the late 1950s I had an opportunity to design a radio station, and the first private television licence was coming up for grabs. It was called VanTel (Channel 8). Prior to then all television was handled by the CBC.

I had met Art Jones a few times, as he was a graduate of McGee High School where I'd gone for a while, so I went to see him. He was quite approachable and we had a couple of meetings. Art had a little studio on Richards Street. He was a photo-journalist and quite adventurous. If there was a plane wreck 300 miles north of Prince George, Art would be there taking photographs, wearing a parka, boiling beans over a campfire, and talking into a microphone!

I met some of the other guys down at the station and thought, well, if this opportunity comes along, I can't handle it alone. So I called Rand because he had experience in managing projects: "Here's an opportunity that I think is coming up and it's a nice size project. Why don't we work together on the proposal?" Rand knew how to interview consultants and set up filing systems and run and manage projects. He was really good at that and that was great. He brought these skills to the table and I brought the initial contact, and it just worked like a charm. It really did. We were both young and had ideas, and I guess we just clicked.

So, that's how the partnership started. We decided we'd jointly go after this project, which we were awarded. I heard later that VanTel had interviewed the larger firms in town, but they went with us.

Continued

At that time, Rand's office was on the second floor of his parents' home on Acadia Road. So we set ourselves up and that's where we did most of the project. It worked out very well because Betty Iredale was an active real estate agent and when she was out we answered the phone and took messages for her and then if we were out at meetings, if she happened to be home, she'd answer the phone for us. This was before cell phones and instant communications with anybody anywhere in the world! It was kind of cramped, but we did most of the VanTel project there.

The Fairview Slopes

We were going to get bigger and we didn't have room to expand. The Fairview Slopes was a forgotten little ghetto in those days, with bumpy streets and potholes. Down below, where the False Creek flats are, it is now very much sought-after real estate, with places to live and walkways and trees and everything! But then it was just broken down industrial buildings and polluted grounds and old generators and wrecked trucks. It was a real eyesore. There were beehive burners still in existence down there. There were sawmills and log booms everywhere, and the smoke rising out of False Creek was amazing.

But the view of the mountains from the Fairview Slopes was great, and we found this old house at 1095 West 7th Avenue and we bought it for next to nothing. We tore it apart by hand, the two of us working until 1:00 in the morning, and we pasted it back together and that was our first architectural office. So now we had room to do things.

It was a small house with a boardroom plus a washroom. At one time we had 14 people in that little building. In 1964 we purchased 1100 West 7th Avenue and moved diagonally across the street. It was a great big house. We had three floors, and we finished the attic and put plywood up there and got some old furniture and that was the coffee room. We had maybe 25 people there, and we still owned and used the house across the street, too. ∎

Bill Rhone at
his drafting table
1095 West 7th Avenue

The 1st architectural office of Rhone & Iredale

1095 West 7th Avenue Vancouver (1960s)

The view looking north from 1095 West 7th; the BC Hydro building dominates the downtown skyline; log booms float in the False Creek flats (early 1960s).

The view north from across the street (that's 1095 in the foreground); the swath of the old chair lift is visible up the side of Grouse Mountain; the Gondola was not built until 1966.

The 2nd architectural office of Rhone & Iredale

1100 West 7th Avenue Vancouver (1970s)

Above & Below: unidentified staff members

Drafting tables had not yet been replaced by desktop computers (circa 1970s)

The Portage Mountain / Peace River Project, spearheaded by Premier W.A.C. Bennett and Dr. Gordon Shrum, the Chairman of BC Hydro, "was one of the largest developments of its kind in the world. It provided thousands of jobs and stimulated industrial growth. The G.M. Shrum Generating Station has an average energy capability of 1,310 gigawatt hours."[1]

The WAC Bennett Dam and Williston Reservoir at dusk

1   Source: www.powerpioneers.com/BC_Hydro_History/1962–1972/ (2006).

Reprinted from the Internet (BC Hydro, 2006)

BC Hydro: A Bit of History

Beginnings

The founding of the Victoria Gas Company in 1860 began the BC Hydro legacy. 23 years later, inventor and entrepreneur Robert McMicking turned on the first commercial electric lights in Canada. Along with a group of local investors, McMicking incorporated the Victoria Electric Illuminating Company and electric lights lit up the streets. The age of electricity had arrived.

Vision

BC Electric was the brainchild of financier Robert Horne-Payne and future Lieutenant-Governor Frank Barnard. With money raised from investors in England, they set out to build the coast's first hydroelectric plant near Victoria in 1898. After several years of prosperity and growth the company was taken under control by the Montreal-based Power Corporation in 1928.

Progress

In 1945, the provincial government created the BC Power Commission. This public sector enterprise began acquiring small utilities, extending electrification in rural or isolated areas, and building or modernizing both generating plants and transmission systems. By 1961, it served over 200 communities all over the province, many with small diesel generating units.

Growth

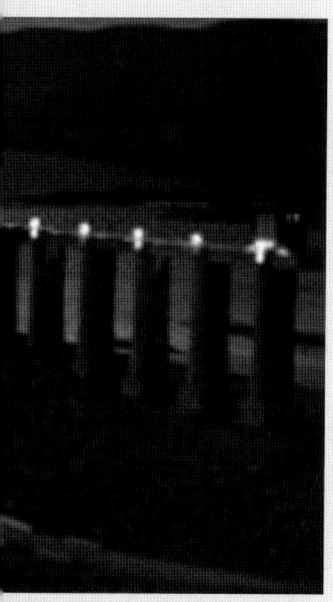

To enable the development of Peace and Columbia River projects, the provincial government stepped in and bought BC Electric in 1961. A year later the government amalgamated BC Electric with the Power Commission to create a new Crown corporation: the British Columbia Hydro and Power Authority, known more familiarly as BC Hydro. The '60s and '70s saw BC Hydro take on some of the most ambitious hydroelectric construction projects in the world.[1] ▪

Why does this history matter? It matters because of life's fortuitous foreshadowing! Not only did the BC Hydro building dominate the Vancouver skyline and the view from 1095 West Seventh Avenue, but one of its "ambitious projects" would also dominate the first decade of Rand's professional career: namely, designing the buildings at Portage Mountain in BC's Peace River Country. In addition to the vast hydro-electric facilities, these buildings would include a school and housing for construction crews and operating staff (see Chapter 4).

---

1   Excerpts of history article. Source: www.bchydro.com/info/history/history1027.html (2006).

> "The first step in any journey is the most important" (Plato).
>
> Begin, not by presenting a solution, but by asking questions.

DEVELOPING A MISSION STATEMENT

"The first step in any journey is the most important" (Plato).

As architects, our first urge when presented with a new project is to create a design. This urge is natural! Your initial thumbnail sketches, while they may reflect genius, however, too often take the first step in the wrong direction. Begin, not by presenting a solution, but by asking questions to gain an understanding of the situation and the needs to be fulfilled. Before you start designing you need to start developing a mission statement.

First we need to establish why the project is being built. If it is a school it is probably to educate children. What age of children? How many? What kind of education?

As everything flows from this mission statement, try to get it right. If you cannot agree with the mission, then resign. A client who wants a very ordinary building will frustrate an architect who is trying to win an award. You need to understand the client's needs and aspirations and either commit to them or quit. The best mission statements are short and simple, such as:

- design a school to suit the latest advances in teaching techniques [Hudson's Hope, Ch. 4]
- celebrate the wonder of the largest hydro-electric project in North America [Portage Mountain, Ch. 4]
- build a head office that reflects the client's leading edge technology [Westcoast Transmission, Ch. 6]

Rand Iredale, Project Manager's Manual (1997)

Rand's Partners

The firm was originally established in 1957 as Randle Iredale Architect. From 1960–1980 the firm operated as Rhone & Iredale Architects (RIA), a partnership between Bill Rhone and Rand Iredale.

RIA was dissolved in 1980 and Rand formed The Iredale Partnership with Charlotte Murray to carry forward the RIA years of practice in award-winning and cost-effective design. Charlotte retired in 2004 after a 24-year career that focused on the preservation, restoration, and adaptive reuse of heritage buildings.

Richard Iredale joined the firm in 1990 and became a partner in 1992. He integrated structural engineering—with particular expertise in seismic design—into the firm's architectural practice. Kendall Jessiman joined the partnership in 1996 with a practice that specializes in building envelope science. James Emery joined the firm in 1997 and became a partner in 2000. He specializes in structural engineering and LEED facilitation.

William Rhone, M.A.Arch., MAIBC, FRAIC

Randle Iredale, MAIBC, FRAIC

Charlotte Murray, MAIBC, M.Arch.

Richard Iredale, MAIBC, MRAIC, P.Eng., LEED AP

Kendall Jessiman, MAIBC, MRAIC

James Emery, IA AIBC, MRAIC, P.Eng., LEED AP

Project: Channel 8 Television Studios

The first collaboration between Bill Rhone and Rand Iredale was designing and building the Channel 8 Television Studios for VanTel Broadcasting in 1960. The opportunity to pursue this project together—based on their combined contacts, interests, and experiences—was the impetus for forming the partnership of Rhone & Iredale Architects.

Rand had done the necessary research to program a television station and had gained experience managing projects of similar size and scope, and Bill had already designed a radio station and had resourceful contacts in radio and television. Thus, VanTel Broadcasting entrusted the newly formed Rhone & Iredale to design and build the first television studio in Vancouver (now BCTV).

Television was still a new media in the 1950s, and Rand had chosen to research and design a television station for his graduating thesis from the UBC School of Architecture. On the return automobile trip from Ottawa to Vancouver in late August 1953, he particularly spent many hours visiting a television station in Chicago to gain an understanding of the layout and space requirements for this new form of communication.

While working on his thesis, Rand had also worked closely with Charles Smith, Chief Engineer, and the staff of CKWX Radio in Vancouver, who were at that time planning to build the first television station in Vancouver: CKWX-TV. His aim had been to gain an understanding of administrative needs, technical installation, and building design. He had discussed with department heads their respective needs, which included production, news, traffic, writing, and accounting. ▪

VanTel Reception Area

Photo: Graphic Industries

Channel 8 Television Studio
1219 Richards Street
Vancouver BC
1960

Photo: ArtRay Ltd. / Art Jones

Channel 8 Television
Studios, Offices, &
Sound Stage

Photo: Graphic Industries, Vancouver

Sketch: William Rhone

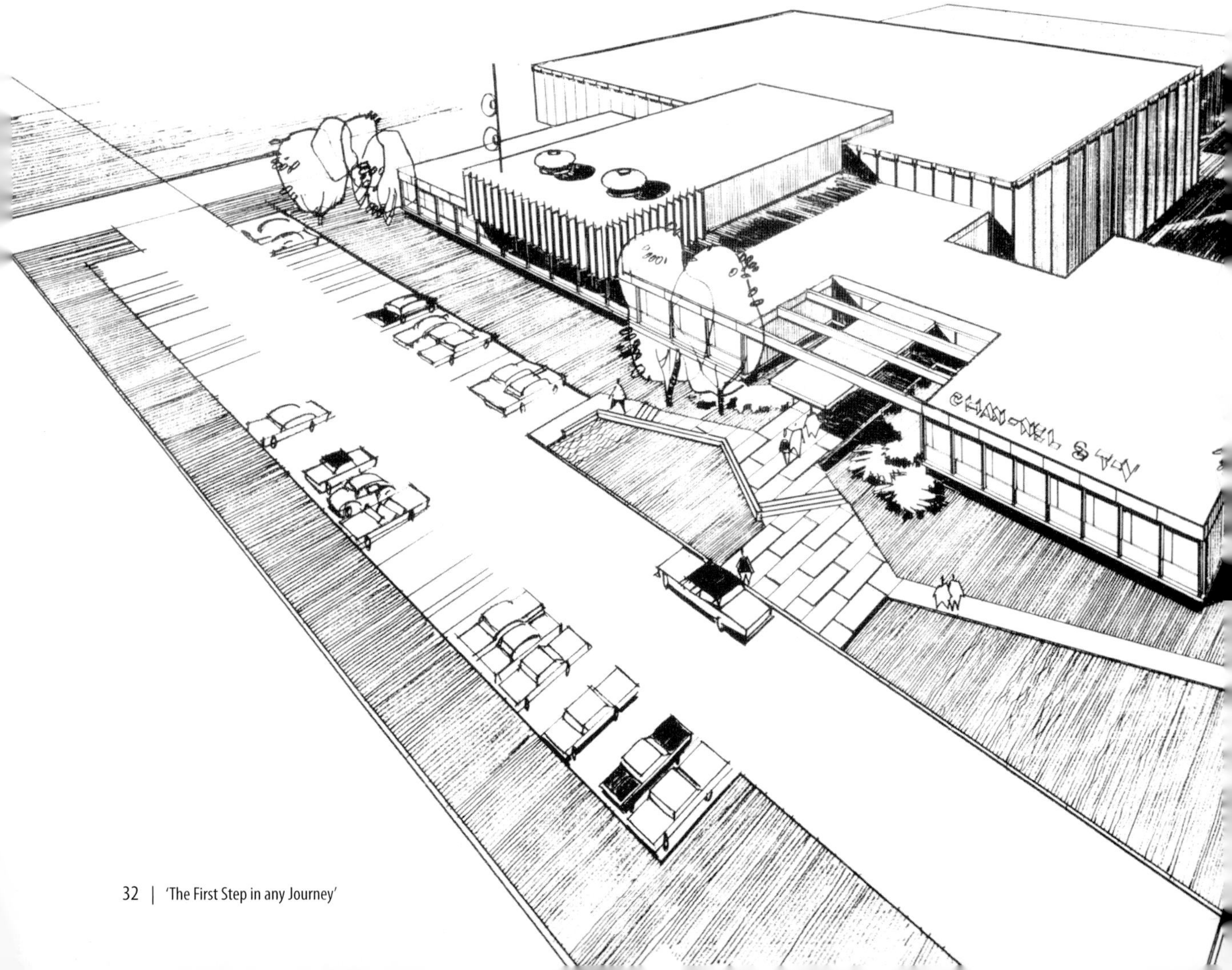

Owner

VanTel Broadcasting Company

Lake City Industrial Estate, Burnaby BC

Project Team

Architects
Rhone & Iredale

Structural Engineer
Read Jones Christoffersen

Mechanical Engineer
D.W. Thomson

Electrical Engineer
Simpson & McGregor

General Contractor
Smith Brothers & Wilson

Rand's projects during the two-year period 1958–1960, while operating his own practice and before joining forces with Bill Rhone, were primarily homes and churches. After the formation of Rhone & Iredale and their completion of the VanTel Studio, Rand added more churches, as well as corporate clients, to his project roster.

Rand also designed and built the first tecton cottage (made of prefabricated modular building systems) in 1962. Completion of the tecton cottage was followed by his commission to design the new Grouse Mountain Chalet for Grouse Mountain Resorts.

Project: Grouse Mountain Chalet

The Grouse Mountain Chalet, a large traditional log-cabin structure and a landmark dear to Pacific Northwest skiers, was destroyed in a spectacular fire in August of 1962 that lit up the peak of Grouse Mountain, which overlooks the City of Vancouver.

In a departure from the traditional log structure, Rand proposed that the entire structure of the new chalet be fir plywood–sheathed timber frame to exploit wood's inherently rustic and warm qualities, as the first chalet had done. Rand drew from his knowledge of A-frame construction, in which plywood played a primary role.

Contemporary in design, the new chalet retained a picturesque 'alpine' quality that blended perfectly with the rugged mountain terrain. During the winter, the chalet would provide skiers with a lunchroom, dining area, toilets, and ski rental shops and in the summer it would provide such tourist facilities as dancing and bar facilities.

Grouse Mountain Chalet
Grouse Mountain Resorts
North Vancouver BC
1964

Photos, adjacent & opposite:
William Dekur, North Vancouver

The chalet was oriented so that prevailing winter winds would keep the entrance free of snow. The maximum recorded single snowfall in the area at that time was 32". With snow loads of up to 300 lbs. per square foot, it was decided to adopt a rigid frame formed by braced equilateral triangles of the floor and roof structures. This frame was developed to withstand both vertical and asymmetrical loading.

The foundations were constructed of wood treated with preservative, as the site was not accessible to concrete trucks. The overhanging south wing is supported on poles cut on site, and the rest of the ground floor is of frame construction with plywood-braced shear and exterior walls.

During reconstruction of the new chalet in 1962, when the structure was framed but still only partially sheathed with plywood, it withstood the blows of Typhoon Freda! ▪

Project Team

Architect
Rhone & Iredale

Engineer
McKenzie & Snowball Co.

General Contractor
Tecton Ltd. /
Minty and McLean Ltd.

Award

Honourable Mention,
Massey Medal Competition

Publications

RAIC Journal
(November 1964), 56

The Canadian Architect
Vol.10 (11)
(November 1965), 50–51

Sylvaply & MBPR Wood Product NEWS
(Winter 1965), 3–4

ELEMENTAL ESTIMATING

How do we establish the square foot costs for space that isn't even designed? We start with Marshall & Swift's square foot costs, which give us average costs for different space types; e.g., office, residential, and institutional. Combined with our experience in similar buildings, this data provides a reasonable estimate of the final project cost, accurate at this stage to plus or minus 25%.

Even at inception of the project, the implications of the square foot prices in terms of building systems can be determined. I discovered this fact in 1961 when designing BCTV, the first television facility in Western Canada. The owner needed to know the cost of the building to arrange financing. Based on our experience and other costs, we were able to tell him our estimated cost for his office space and for the storage portions of the building. But the cost of television studios was unknown.

Elemental Estimating System

We obtained prices from Texas of $10.00 per sq.ft. and from the CBC in Toronto of $100.00 per sq.ft. It was at this point that we discovered the idea of *elemental costing*. We knew the structure had to be concrete to keep the noise of aeroplanes and traffic out of the studio. We asked our structural engineers, Read Jones Christoffersen, what a concrete long span structure would cost per sq.ft. That gave us our structure cost.

We knew the finishes were simple, except that the floor needed to be dead flat for rolling cameras and the walls and ceiling needed to have 2" of fibreglass for sound absorption. This knowledge allowed us to develop our costs for finishes. The fittings for control consoles could also be costed. Then we asked our mechanical and electrical engineers what budget they would need to provide the air-conditioning and theatre lighting required for a television studio.

Presto! This process generated an estimated cost of $910,000 for the building and provided a design budget for all of the participants.

The owner and the contractor didn't trust our 'new-fangled' estimating system, however, so well-recognized quantity surveyors were called in. After asking us every question they could think of with regard to systems and finishes, they came up with a 2"-thick quantity take-off and an estimated cost of $650,000. The building was constructed under a management contract with Smith Bros. & Wilson.

Toward the end of the project the contractor's billings were exceeding the $650,000 budget. Meetings were called to establish what was wrong. The quantity surveyors waved their thick book of quantities, the contractor defended his efficiency and unit prices and the owner screamed that his whole financial structure was in jeopardy. Finally, the contractor's senior estimator said, "Let's stop the bull! The final cost of your building is going to be $910,000!" Our elemental estimating system had arrived at the right answer!

Quantity vs. Quality
It is our policy to bring projects in on time and on budget. You cannot do this if your initial budget is unrealistic! Clients are happiest when budgets come down. They will blame you if they have to raise new money; therefore, this initial budget must be adequate.

Now is the time to bring the bad news if what the client wants cannot be afforded. At this stage stop being the optimist. Be the voice of caution! When the owner feels that your prices are high because he has heard of other buildings that cost less, go item by item through the specifications and determine which items he is willing to reduce or to live without.

There are only three variables to work with in construction budgeting: the amount of space, the quality of the construction, and the budget. For long-term satisfaction it is better to reduce the amount of space than to lower the quality of construction.

An allowance for contingencies is the final key to keeping a project on budget. Failure to have a reasonable contingency sum makes the construction process a constant battle over extras between the owner, the consultants, and the contractor.

Rand Iredale, Project Manager's Manual (1997)

> There are only three variables to work with in construction budgeting: the amount of space, the quality of the construction, and the budget. For long-term satisfaction it is better to reduce the amount of space than to lower the quality of construction.

Japanese-Canadian Families on Mayne Island Pre–WW II

A number of Japanese-Canadian families settled on Mayne Island from 1900 to 1942, eventually comprising one-third of the population and providing more than half of its economy.

The Hardships of Early Pioneers

"They set to work, felling trees, digging out stumps, removing large rocks, and generally experiencing … the hardships of early pioneers everywhere in this new country. Only then could the land be made suitable for farming. They proved to be an enterprising lot, for there is reference to various projects being started such as cattle-breeding, poultry farming, and even a sawmill operation. Some became involved in fishing.

"Greenhouses were built, and proved to be a boon, for fresh produce could be brought to market weeks earlier than before. Tomatoes and cucumbers grew well and showed every promise of becoming profitable commodities much in demand. …

"Then came 1942, and the forced mass evacuation, incarceration, and loss of land and property, which shattered the hopes and dreams of these inhabitants of Mayne Island. Furthermore, once removed, they were declared to be 'enemy aliens,' unwanted back."[1]

Active Pass Growers' Association

Lynn Nagata's family summered on Mayne Island, where her father, John Nagata, had grown up in the 1920s. His weekend chore as a schoolboy "was to polish the reflector in the [Georgina Point] lighthouse." Lynn's paternal grandfather, Kumazo Nagata, "grew hothouse tomatoes (in the Campbell Bay area) and founded the hothouse cooperative called Active Pass Growers' Association, which grew and packed 'Island Brand Tomatoes and Cucumbers.'"

John Nagata was a founding donor of the Japanese Garden at Dinner Bay on Mayne Island, developed to commemorate the Japanese families who settled and developed the land. It was dedicated in 2002 by BC's Lieutenant Governor, Her Honour the Honourable Iona Campagnolo.[2]

---

1 Correspondence from Victor Kadonaga, who believes that the first Japanese immigrant to settle on Mayne Island was Gontarô Kadonaga. His text is taken from the on-line correspondence project that led to the publication of Michael Kluckner's book, *Vanishing British Columbia* (UBC Press, 2005). Source: www.michaelkluckner.com (2007).

2 Notes from Lynn Nagata, *ibid.*

3 Island of Dreams

> *In 1997 our daughter-in-law Lael Whitehead suggested that Rand and I write a history of Iredale Place on Mayne Island so that her generation and future generations would be aware of the early history and evolution of this land that is so precious to our family. The occasion of Rand's approaching 70th birthday in 1999 inspired me to attempt to tell the story—with Rand as my 'historical consultant'—based on our memories and photographs.[1]*

Mayne Island

The first generation of Iredales to arrive on our quarter section of Mayne Island in 1958 found a primitive and isolated land. Rand and I were the pioneers. Prior to this time, a few Japanese people had occupied an open field (near our Log House), where they had grown many of the hothouse tomatoes that supplied the Lower Mainland prior to World War II. We hacked out a place in the heavily forested land and made ourselves a campsite. We camped out and enjoyed our Summers there without benefit of modern conveniences, but always with many good friends and wonderful memories. Over the years the land has gradually become tamed and habitable.

The next generation has added, and will continue to add, the modern conveniences of the civilized world. In 1999 our son Richard undertook to bring BC Hydro power to the settlement. Richard and his wife, Lael, have built their permanent home on the site and our daughter, Jennifer, and her partner, Peter, have built their dream cottage. In the future our son Talbot and his wife, Paddy, will also build their own cottage.

It is our hope that future generations will love and tend this land and find a balance with nature. My thanks to Rand for his comments and memories, and for his patience in helping me scan the photographs into the text, and to Talbot, who helped us recall dates and events.

Rand's primary interest as an architect had been in developing the land. His dream, inspired by the English landscape and a visit to Stourhead (a celebrated landscape garden in Wiltshire), is gradually being realized.

Mayne Island is 21 sq. km. in size and is now home to 900 residents. It is located in Georgia Strait off southwestern BC, and is accessed by ferry from Vancouver, Victoria, and several of the Gulf Islands.

---

1 This chapter is an abridged and edited version of our booklet, "Memories of Iredale Place on Mayne Island."

Rand's Vision

In 1958, five years after we were married and after Jennifer and Talbot were born, Rand found the chance to fulfill his dream of having a family retreat in the Gulf Islands. At that time there was no Deas Island Tunnel, and the only access to the Gulf Islands was via Captain New's private ferry from Steveston to the Gulf Islands, which ran twice a week. In 1960, Premier W.A.C. (Wacky) Bennett established the BC Ferry Corporation to build a new ferry terminal at Tsawwassen that would provide fast, efficient service to the Gulf Islands and Vancouver Island.

An engineer friend whom Rand had gone to university with, Jack Wood, was working with Swan Wooster Engineering and designing the new terminal. With Jack's help, Rand obtained marine charts and aerial photographs of the Gulf Islands. He was looking for a large acreage within easy travel time from the new terminal.

Rand found two possible sites in a 12-mile radius: one was at Whaler's Bay on Galiano Island, and the other at the head of Campbell Bay on Mayne Island.

Whaler's Bay was subdivided, but Campbell Bay had a quarter section at the head of the Bay with the name John Hart on the legal map. Rand researched the 160-acre Campbell Bay site and discovered that it was still owned by the estate of the late John Hart, who had been Premier of British Columbia in 1910.

Rand wrote to the trustees of the estate in Victoria, offered $6,500 to purchase the quarter section, and assumed that it would take several years to settle the estate. Six weeks later Rand received a reply from the trustees: "In response to your offer we have advertised the property and received no better offer. Please send us your money."

The wilderness as we found it 1958

Of course, being young, fresh out of university, and starting a growing family, we had no money! We had paid $6,500 for our first house at 4273 West 12th Avenue in Vancouver. So Rand went to his father, Bill, and asked if he would finance the purchase. Bill and Betty agreed, and the property was purchased and registered in the name of Bill Iredale. Ownership of the property was divided between the three of them: Bill with 37.5%, Betty with 25%, and Rand with 37.5%.

Rand's only knowledge of the property was from marine maps and an aerial photograph that showed forest and a sandy beach at the head of Campbell Bay. Wanting to visit the property to see exactly what they had bought, Rand and Bill took Captain New's ferry to Mayne Island to explore. There was no road into the densely wooded site, and they could only drive as far as the end of the road at Captain Waugh's farm. They bushwhacked by foot from there to the beach at Campbell Bay. Rand and Bill stayed at the Springwater Lodge at Miners Bay, which at that time was owned by the pioneering Mayne Island Bennett family.

The only partially open area was the site that had been occupied by Japanese prior to WW II. They had built extensive greenhouses and a boiler for heat and water on the neighbouring quarter section. The Japanese had been interned off the West Coast and had their property confiscated during the war. Later when we surveyed our property we found that the greenhouses, abandoned and slowly falling down, had inadvertently been partly built on John Hart's property. When we received the title we were pleased to find that the original Crown grant, one of the few issued prior to 1886, included mineral rights and did not require payment for provincial stumpage on logging.

My first of many visits to Mayne Island ensued. We brought our tent and camping gear and that first year our only access was to the end of the road at Captain Waugh's farm, so we camped above the cliffs on Edith Point.

In 1960 Fred Bennett, Sr. of the Highways Department approached Rand for permission to push a road through our property to complete a circle around that part of Mayne. Rand and Bill agreed, as it would give us access, too. It was a rough gravel road, and remained a class 12 road passing through private property until we did the Bell Bay Strata development in 1980.

Early one morning we heard bullets ricocheting through the leaves over our heads. Rand dashed out to the road to inform the deer hunters in no uncertain terms that they were shooting at his family! Unaware that we were camping in the woods, they apologized and slunk off. This and similar incidents resulted, a few years later, in the prohibition of hunting on Mayne Island.

Aerial View of Campbell Bay Site 1960

After the road was put in, we camped in the area where the Sholi now stands. I have memories of camping one May 24th weekend in a heavy rainstorm. We scraped a small area out of the forest for a campsite; Betty and Bill had their tent and Rand and I had ours, and the children slept in the car.

Jennifer recalls waking in the night and becoming aware of a dark figure peering into the car, which she thought was a bear. It was her father checking on her.

The Early Years

Once we had three small children in diapers we did not visit our property very often, as it would have meant taking everything we needed with us (quite a packing job!). Also, it was difficult for toddlers to play in the forest.

In 1964 (six years after purchase), Rand and I decided we needed some sort of shelter from the elements and a storage place to leave things so we didn't have to cart everything back and forth with us. By 1969 the new ferry service with the *MV Island Princess* was in place and we had direct service from Tsawwassen (the Deas Island Tunnel was built in 1960). Rand was deeply involved in Tecton, a company he founded to build prefabricated buildings; he designed a small basic shelter and had the pieces prefabricated at the Tecton factory. We named our shelter the 'Sholi'; it consisted of one 10' x 14' room with sliding doors across the front. There were no windows, as we wished to leave items there and did not want strangers looking in and stealing our precious camping gear.

On a hot and sunny May 24th weekend all of the pieces were loaded onto a large truck, which Frank Brown (then a student at UBC who was living with us) drove to the site. We followed Frank in our Valiant and Betty Iredale followed us in her car. Richard Feilden (Betty's nephew and Rand's cousin) had also been invited along to help put the Sholi together. Rand had arranged for Jack Mummery—who was logging for us so that we could get some stumpage income—to bring the bulldozer Rand had bought for him and to do the logging required to create a level area for the new Sholi.

The pieces of the new building were unloaded at the site and, along with the three children, we spent the weekend assembling the new building. I remember Richard, at age 5, helping to nail the shingles on the roof!

At night in this small building we would lay foamies on the floor for our sleeping bags, which were then rolled up in the morning to provide floor area for living. After much soul searching, we purchased a potbelly stove to provide warmth; it cost $50, which seemed like a fortune to us. We raked and planted grass on the freshly bulldozed soil and, as the site was so clear and open and very warm in the hot weather, one year Rand transplanted a small hemlock tree to provide more shade. Today it is a large tree and the entire area is quite shaded.

Most of our cooking was done outside, picnic style, on either a hibachi or a Coleman stove. We would take five-gallon water jugs in the car to the hand-pumped Community Well at the intersection of Fernhill and Gallagher Bay Roads to obtain water. A well with a hand pump was added in the field about 1975. Rand and the boys laid a line to suction water to the Sholi.

The moon and stars were our only night-time sources of light, though we also had a Coleman lamp. We only spent time there on long weekends in the Spring and Summer, as the facilities were inadequate then for Winter habitation.

Kathryn, Jennifer, Talbot, & Richard on the beach (1960)

Kathryn cooking on the open fire

Our camp was quite primitive and our closest neighbours were Wilbur Deacon and Captain and Mrs. Waugh. I did not like staying there on my own with the children, as our campsite was isolated in the forest.

But many happy Summers were spent on Mayne Island. Much time was spent on the beach, clamming and digging for oysters, and walking in the woods and down to Edith Point (Richard was so small he completely disappeared in the salal!). We purchased an eight-foot Sabot pram and, with only 3" of freeboard, we would take trips out into the bay as far as Three Tree Island. (Islanders who saw us worried that we would swamp.) Around 1967 we invested in a 14' outboard runabout, the *Summer Wind*.

The 14-foot *Summer Wind* on the beach

Water-skiing behind the *Summer Wind*

The Community Well

A good day of fishing

Patrick and Patricia Oswald and their children joined us for a happy weekend in 1969, during which time we were to teach them how to camp. On this weekend Rand and Patrick, having imbibed a little too much alcohol for dinner, caused some Australians camping on the beach to flee in terror.

The Australians had anchored their boat and come ashore to cook dinner over a campfire. Rand and Patrick were not too happy with their fire, which was built on a large log round. After dinner, well fortified with gin and tonic, Rand and Patrick decided to tow the fire out to sea. After making a dramatic circle around the bay with the fire spewing flames in the dark, they decided to return the fire to the Australians; however, the painter from our boat had become ensnared in the Australians' anchor line and proceeded to tow their rather large sailing vessel into the shore.

Rand and Patrick were unaware that this boat was bearing down on them until the Australians suddenly leaped up and into their dinghy and rowed frantically out to their boat. The lines were unsnarled and the Australians were put out to sea, never to return for another encounter with the wild barbarians of Campbell Bay.

Below: After 1970 Charlotte Murray and her husband, Gordon, were frequent visitors to Mayne Island. John and Jania Gaitanakis and their children shared many of our Summers, too.

Adjacent: The view of Campbell Bay, looking out from the Log House, includes the two tall trees that appear at the beginning of Kathryn and Rand's original booklet on Mayne Island.

Charlotte & Gordon's vintage Caravan, beside the Sholi (1974)

The view of Campbell Bay

School of Architecture Workshops

The First Workshop

The first 10-day School of Architecture Workshop was held on our Mayne Island property in 1970. The students were brought over by the chartered yacht *Norsal*, dumped on the beach, and told to explore and find living arrangements. Masses of food were shipped in, along with other necessities of life. Rand had arranged to bulldoze out a couple of platforms to provide cooking and dining areas.

Professor John Gaitanakis was in charge, and Charlotte Murray was the Den Mother in charge of food preparation; teams of students were assigned times and responsibilities to help her.

During this workshop the students built a wood-burning sauna at the mouth of the stream that now runs down to the beach, next to the site where the Dome was later built. They would take a sauna and then dash down the stairs to plunge naked into the cold ocean.

When it came to the final feast of the week, we discovered that no one had thought to buy retsina for the lamb and salmon bake. Rand raced to the local telephone and called the charter air service to tell them the problem: we needed two or three cases of retsina for our Greek lamb bake! They had a float plane just over Nanaimo, and they set up a four-way conversation with the pilot, a Nanaimo taxi driver, themselves, and Rand, who negotiated the purchase and delivery of the wine. To the amazement of the pilot, as he landed in Campbell Bay and taxied up to the beach, he was greeted by a mob of naked figures flying over the cliff from the sauna and down into the ocean!

The students befriended a local elderly Indian named Red and persuaded him to show them how to smoke salmon 'Indian style.' The technique involved building a large wood fire and smoking the salmon over it; unfortunately, however, when the school had obtained permission from the local fire department to cook in the open, it was stipulated that the fire must be charcoal and not wood, as there was a danger to the forest from flying embers. Red went back to the village and,

The first lamb bake at the first workshop (1970)

Rand & students at lunch at the first workshop

Jania & John Gaitanakis, Kathryn & Talbot, at the lamb bake

One of the early lamb bakes, in front of the Sholi (1973)

in a somewhat drunken state, bragged about teaching the students how to cook the salmon.

The local RCMP heard about the event, and the next morning an RCMP officer, accompanied by Hugh MacFarlane, a retired police officer, turned up on the property to lay charges for violating the Fire Act. All of the UBC School of Architecture staff vanished into the woods, and Rand was left to deal with these irate men. As diplomatically as possible, Rand tried to persuade them that Red had had too many drinks and was exaggerating. He offered to show them around, hoping to introduce them to some of the faculty.

No sooner had the tour begun than Rand smelled the sweet odour of marijuana—oops! A federal drug charge loomed! He quickly escorted the authorities to their car and bid them farewell. The young RCMP officer in charge did not want to lay charges and, fortunately, his will prevailed.

The Second Workshop

The second UBC School of Architecture Workshop was held a year or two later, again in the first week of September. And, again, the students were brought by boat and dumped on the beach. This year they erected a large ex-army parachute in the shape of a geodesic dome to provide cover for the kitchen and eating areas.

Bud Wood was in charge and Charlotte Murray was once more the Den Mother, attending to, and doing a superb job of, organizing the food department. Masses of food were provided to feed about 50 students and staff for a full week.

One of the major events during this workshop was the Grand Celebration in Secret Cove, which the students had spent the week devising for the final evening. They built a massive raft and mounted a large throne for Henry Elder, the head of the school. Henry arrived on the final day and was dressed in a toga and garland. At sunset he was placed on the throne and pulled by willing student slaves around to Secret Cove. Many candles decorated the throne, and it was a most impressive and dramatic sight. Two bands provided music—modern and Elizabethan.

During the previous week the students had built an amphitheatre in Secret Cove out of available driftwood, with benches stretching along the shore into the ocean. Candles lit the recesses of the sandstone rocks around the cove and also floated in the water.

A sumptuous dinner had been prepared for all attendees, who were greeted at the bottom of the path-stairway to the cove by a well-endowed lady serving potent drinks. Dinner was served on sawn cedar plates, and the ceremonies began. Then the candlelit ceremonial raft with Henry presiding on his throne arrived in the cove. Dark-haired and tanned architect Bruno Freschi, dressed in a white toga and looking very much a Caesar, stood ankle-deep in the waters of the ocean to greet Henry and give a silver-tongued address to the assembled disciples.

It was a grand and exotic evening. Rand and I walked the site in the wee hours to check and cover sleeping bodies that had fallen wherever they happened to be when the festivities ended.

Students on the path down to Secret Cove

Faculty, students, and a young Talbot building the fire for the Feast

Primitive Shelter / Student Workshop

Wood-burning sauna built by students

Rand, removing the fat from the lamb

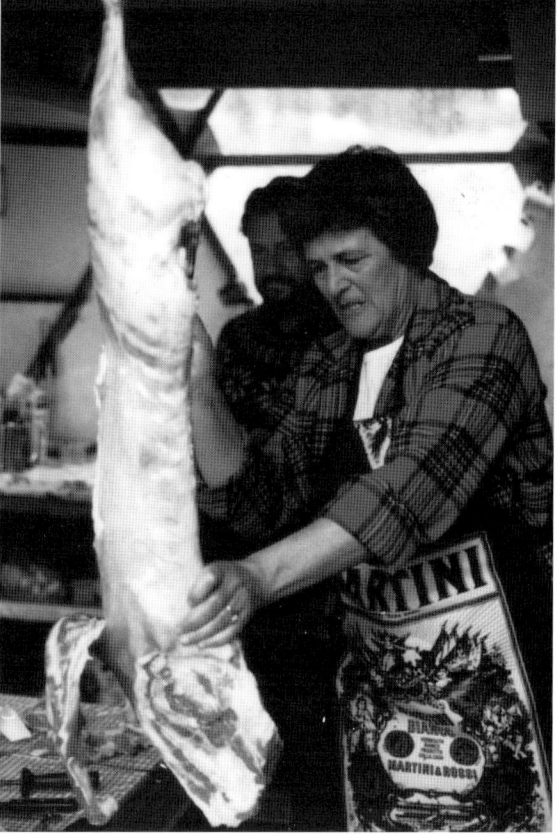
Charlotte, inserting garlic cloves under the skin of the lamb

Building the Dome

After the second School of Architecture Workshop and at the time of the expiration of the copyright on Buckminster Fuller's geodesic dome, there was a great deal of interest in developing buildings using the geodesic form. We needed more space and so Rand, an architect with an inventive spirit, undertook to design a geodesic-domed cottage on a site just west of the Sholi and over the mouth of the gully running through the field down to the ocean.

All of the structural members were pre-cut in the Tecton factory and trucked to the site, where crews of young men assembled them. I was given the dimensions of the glass, which had an unusual shape, and asked to order it from a shop in Vancouver. When I arrived at the shop, the staff couldn't believe I wanted glass of this size and shape; however, as they were being paid in advance, they agreed to my request and cut the glass to these unusual shapes. At $600, it was the most expensive element in the building.

During the course of building our Dome, two young men in their early twenties, Phil Vernon and his pal Donny, emerged out of the woods. They were American conscientious objectors to the war in Vietnam. They had crossed the border into Canada, but were not here legally and did not have work permits. I particularly remember Phil. He was a vegetarian and a Quaker with a great musical talent. We befriended him and he enthusiastically volunteered to help us build the Dome. Until it was habitable, Phil built himself a dome-like plastic shelter in the field previously used by the Japanese. Phil and Donny did a lot of the work, along with Richard, Talbot, Jennifer and, of course, Rand. I mostly did the cooking, picking up, and gophering for them. The project covered two Summers. During the first Winter Phil lived in the Dome, which had a second-hand wood stove to keep him warm.

We had a lot of fun, and there are many wonderful memories of building the Dome and of Phil. Although young, he took pride in his work and became a skilful carpenter. He was also a wonderful musician who played both guitar and piano. Many a Summer's evening, after a day of working on the Dome, he entertained us by playing the guitar and singing Bob Dylan songs. He sang *Mr. Tambourine Man* with such feeling. He was a gentle and generous human being. Later, with Donny, he would build our Log House.

We also met Ron Pither at this time (then a young man), who was keen on growing a garden. Together, Ron, Phil, and Donny undertook to cultivate the area around the future Goat House and to grow a garden there. It was the era of the hippies and the love-not-hate mentality, partly in rebellion against the war in Vietnam. These young people did not live by the law of the government but by their own idealism.

Some of the adjacent photographs are from the *Mayne Dome* book,[1] which documents the plans and building of our domed cottage. After we completed it, a young lady from the *Toronto Star* wanted to write an article. She furnished the Dome with 'hip' furniture, and when the article was published the editor suggested we create a booklet so others could purchase the plans and build their own dome. We produced the Dome booklet and sold copies for $12.00 each. The proceeds funded a wonderful trip to England, which included a charter boat trip down the River Thames.

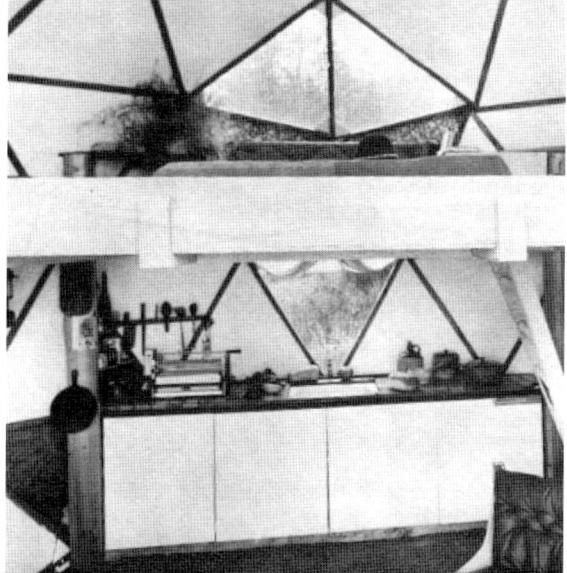

---

1   *Mayne Dome* (Vancouver: Kara Resources, 1973). The interior photos were taken by John Fulker.

Island of Dreams | 49

During many a happy Summer in the Dome, we would awaken to the early morning sun rising over Campbell Bay. Bunks were built in the Sholi to provide additional sleeping spaces for our children and their friends. Most of our cooking and meal preparation still took place outdoors on the hibachi or the Coleman stove or over an open charcoal barbecue pit.

Jennifer, Talbot, and Richard were now into their teenage years. We purchased a 20-foot trihulled boat with an inboard Volvo engine, which we stored during the Winter for a few years at the Lummi Island Marina. On a few occasions we boated from Tsawwassen to Campbell Bay.

Rand became keen on fishing and would boat down to Cabbage Island before sunrise. Warmly dressed and packing a thermos of hot coffee, he and whoever was with him would fish for a few hours, often returning with salmon or rock cod for a wonderful barbecue that evening.

The boat put us more in touch with the ocean. We fished, hunted for oysters, and toured the islands. We visited Salt Spring and the Penders and, on two or three occasions, attended the lamb bake on Saturna Island. One Fall day Jennifer and a boyfriend, along with Rand, were marooned in Active Pass in a dense fog when the motor failed. It was a bit scary until the fog finally lifted.

The ultimate use of this new boat, however, was for water-skiing. Rand, Jennifer, Talbot, and Richard and many of their friends spent Summer days being towed behind the boat. Campbell Bay is a water-skiers' paradise, as it is deep, long, narrow, and protected. Talbot's friend David McIlraith water-skied from Campbell Bay across Georgia Strait to Tsawwassen on a still, clear day. Douglas Bell, who learned to water ski on Lake Mowack in New Jersey, would ski barefoot right from the beach. I did a little skiing but was not that brave, preferring to watch the others from the beach.

Unfortunately, due to lack of maintenance and very much due to lack of time, the Dome eventually deteriorated and became dangerous. A sight to see from out on Campbell Bay, it was torn down in the mid-1990s and is no longer a landmark.

Kathryn and Rand fishing at Campbell Bay (1972)

Reprinted from *Mayne Dome* (Iredale, 1973)

MATERIALS LIST [for one dome]

5 Pressure-treated poles with an 8" butt – see text for length

Edge Beam – 5   2" x 12" Fir 10'6 3/4" with a 72° angle cut at both ends

Main Beam – 2" x 12"   2 cut out of 18' length

Joists – 2" x 10"   3 cut out of 16' length
   4 cut out of 14' length
   2 cut out of 12' length
   2 cut out of 6' length
   joist hangers – 10
   lag bolts, spikes and nails for framing

Deck - 1/2" tongue and groove fir plywood
   7   4' x 8' sheets
   1½" annular grooved nails

Struts – 2" x 2" clear, kiln dried fir, see schedule in text; total 900 linear feet

Connectors
   15 pentagons of 020 gauge aluminum
   70 hexagons of 020 gauge aluminum
   1½" annular grooved nails

Loft Beams 2" x 12" fir
   2 out of 12'0" material
   2 out of 6'0" material
   ¾" plywood deck – 3 sheets 4' x 8'
   4   ¼" x 3" long ring bolts
   4   2" diameter washers
   hangers – ¼" 6 x 19 galvanized hempcore rope
   4   2" x 4" stringers cut out of 8' material
   4   8" long x 1" wide pipe hanging straps
   material for ships ladder
   spikes and 1½" annular grooved nails

Sheathing Material
   4' x 8'   ⅜" sheathing grade exterior plywood
   ¼" thick float glass (safety glass) and plastic;
      see schedule in text
   Lepage's White Carpenter Glue or
      Phenolic Resorcinal Glue
   1½" annular grooved nails
   binder twine
   staples and staple gun
   suction grips
   1 doz. tubes Dow silicone caulking (small joint
      sealant) and gun

Reprinted from Mayne Dome *(Iredale, 1973)*

¼" rubber tap washers, 6 per window
electricians' vinyl tape
1½" galvanized #8 round head screws; 6 per window

Climbing Mast
    8" long ⅜" bolt
    60' climbing rope
    ½" climbing rope carabinier and harness

1 Door with frame and hardware

Entry Stairs or Bridge

3 Vents — 1' x 2' ⅜" plywood hinged vent doors and fly screen

Umbrella Vent
    5 Whitco hinges
    5 2" x 2" struts, 1½" longer than 'A'
    1 Pentagon connector (listed in connectors)
    5 special connectors of 020 gauge aluminum
    5 perimeter struts cut to shape shown
    plywood or plastic sheathing
    25' x 8" wide butyl rubber flashing

Rolled Roofing — area to cover plywood, plus 25% for flaps and waste
    asphalt roofing gun
    roofing nails

Insulation — 1" thick Styrofoam 4' x 8' sheets; order quantity equal to plywood sheathing material used
    waterproof lino cement
    batt insulation material under floor deck

Bench — 2" x 12" out of 10'0" length

Built-In Bench — made of plywood and 2" x 4" framing

Kitchen Cabinets and Sink

Acorn Fireplace and Yukon Chimney

Furnishings

Misc. 2" x 4" for scaffold, centre post, diagonal bracing, pegs, batter board, etc.

Carpentry Tools as required [1]

---

[1] This Materials List was reproduced from *Mayne Dome*, 11–12.

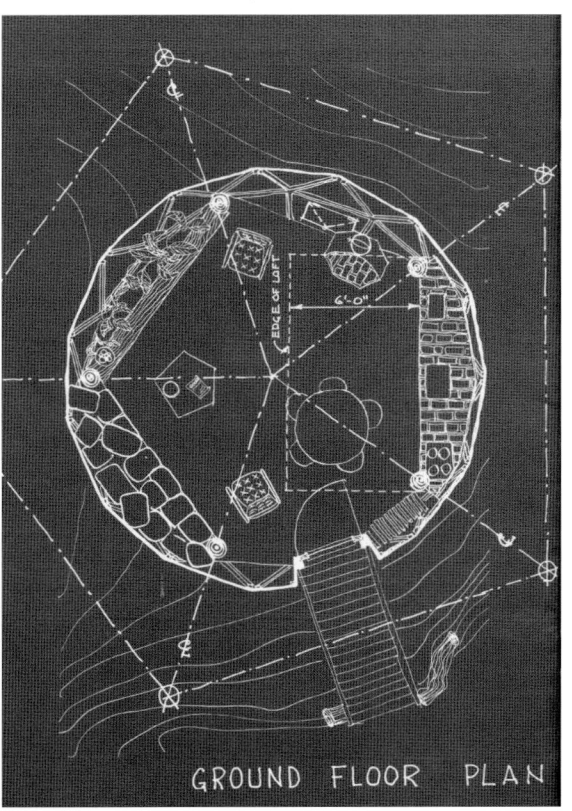

GROUND FLOOR PLAN

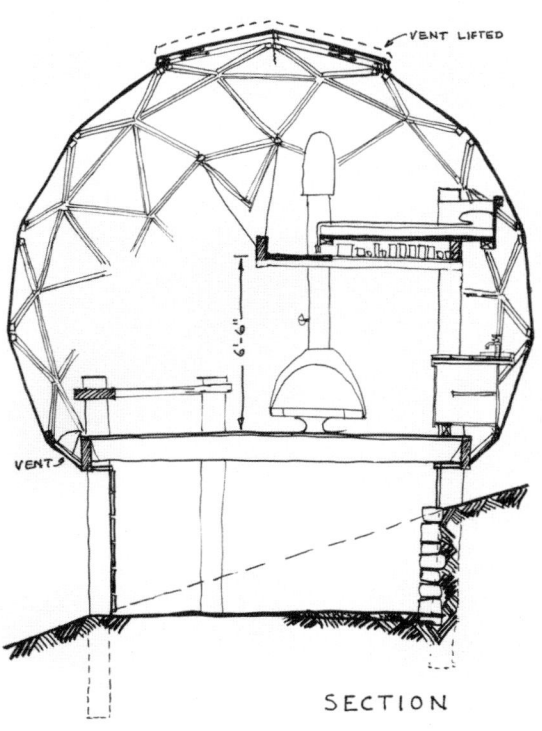

SECTION

Building the Log House

The decade of the 1970s was an anti-establishment time, largely influenced by the hippies and by revulsion to the undeclared and ultimately unsuccessful war in Vietnam. Many young American men fled to Canada to escape the draft. It was a time of questioning our values. One of the responses to this questioning was a desire to return to the land and a simpler way of life.

After the inventiveness of the geodesic dome, there was renewed interest in building log structures. Our two young American friends, Phil and Donny, were still with us and camped on the property. They suggested that they would like to build three log cabins. We agreed that they could build a log house with three bedrooms, which Rand would design. The logs would be cut off the land and peeled, and the house would be erected on the high ground next to the field where the Japanese had grown their tomatoes.

Great excitement followed.

Rand drew the plans and took a course in log building with Talbot, while the young men went to work cutting down trees. Barry Wilkes excavated the site as partial payment for the bulldozer he purchased from us. Local stone provided the foundation, at the cost of a bag of cement and sand hauled from the beach. The first Summer the felled logs lay in the field drying; we spent many a day peeling the bark off and letting them dry. In the Spring the logs were lifted with a skyline rigged between the old arbutus tree and a fir on the hillside.

The close fit between logs was accomplished by placing the next log over the last, which leaves it about six inches high, as no saddle notch has been cut. The new log is then scribed to the profile of the log under it and rolled over. The scribe line is then chain-sawed from both sides to create a v-notch.

We had many long discussions about whether the v-notch should be filled with Fiberglas or caulked with moss in the traditional manner. We finally agreed on Fiberglas (with reservations on the boys' part), as it would not rot or attract insects. Cedar shingles were obtained for the roof.

After the roof was on, Phil and Donny moved from the Dome into the shell of the Log House, with only a wood stove for warmth, no running water, and toilet facilities in an outhouse. Coleman lamps provided light during the long, dark, rainy Winter.

The next year Phil fell in love with Maggie; she joined the group, and commuted to her job in Vancouver. The following Summer brought more work on the Log House. After two or three years, however, Maggie and Phil had a baby and they found living in the Log House without hot water or electricity too difficult. They left to live in the city, which broke up our fledgling commune.

We were left with the Log House, the exterior of which was finished—recycled windows had been put in place—but with no interior partitions. We paid Phil and Donny $8,000 for their work on the Log House, which we hoped they would use to buy their own land.

The Log House, under construction

The Log House, completed

The Bell Bay Bare Land Strata

In 1978 we decided to cut off 24 acres of the property to create the Bell Bay subdivision in the form of a bare land strata. Property taxes had become onerous and we were 'land rich and cash poor.' We hoped that selling off some of the property would generate sufficient cash to help carry the cost of keeping the rest of it.

The Mayne Island Zoning By-Law only allowed subdivision into 10-acre parcels, which would have been difficult to service and would have cut our 110 'land' acres into 10 or 11 equal pieces (50 of our 160 acres are under the water in Campbell Bay). Considerable time was spent drawing up plans and negotiating with governing authorities, including the Islands Trust.

A plan was agreed upon in 1979 and we applied for a development permit. Final approval would not be granted, however, until after we had built the roads and provided services, such as well water, electrical power, and tests for septic fields.

The firm of Crooks and Money built the private road and logged much of the site to open up the land. They also cleared the upper field, where Richard would eventually build his house. The Winter of 1981 saw the burning of a massive pile of stumps and branches.

After the field was created we picked up rocks with Islanders Jeannine and John Dodds so the field could be planted with grass and the Dodds could use it as a cattle field.

Three years elapsed from the time of our initial idea until all of the approvals were in place. In the meantime, the BC real estate market collapsed.

In 1983 nine of the ten lots went on the market but they did not sell. Our hopes of generating extra cash evaporated and it became an anxious time for us (this economic depression was generated by high interest rates of 20% or more, and lasted until Expo '86 put Vancouver on the world map).

Five lots were eventually sold to Americans, whose dollar was much stronger than ours. Our initial prices were based on a 1979 professional assessment of $150,000 per lot, but we ended up selling them for $50,000 each.

When the Dodds gave the field up it grew hay, but it was difficult to maintain our farm property tax status as there was an oversupply of hay on Mayne Island.

We then partnered with Ken Sommerville to raise sheep. For the past several years sheep and their lambs have grazed on the grass and kept the field from returning to nature.

Adjacent:
Artist John Thompson's gift of 'cut-out' cows in the new field

Opposite:
Map of the NE 1/4 Section 11 Mayne Island

Map created by Rand Iredale (1998)

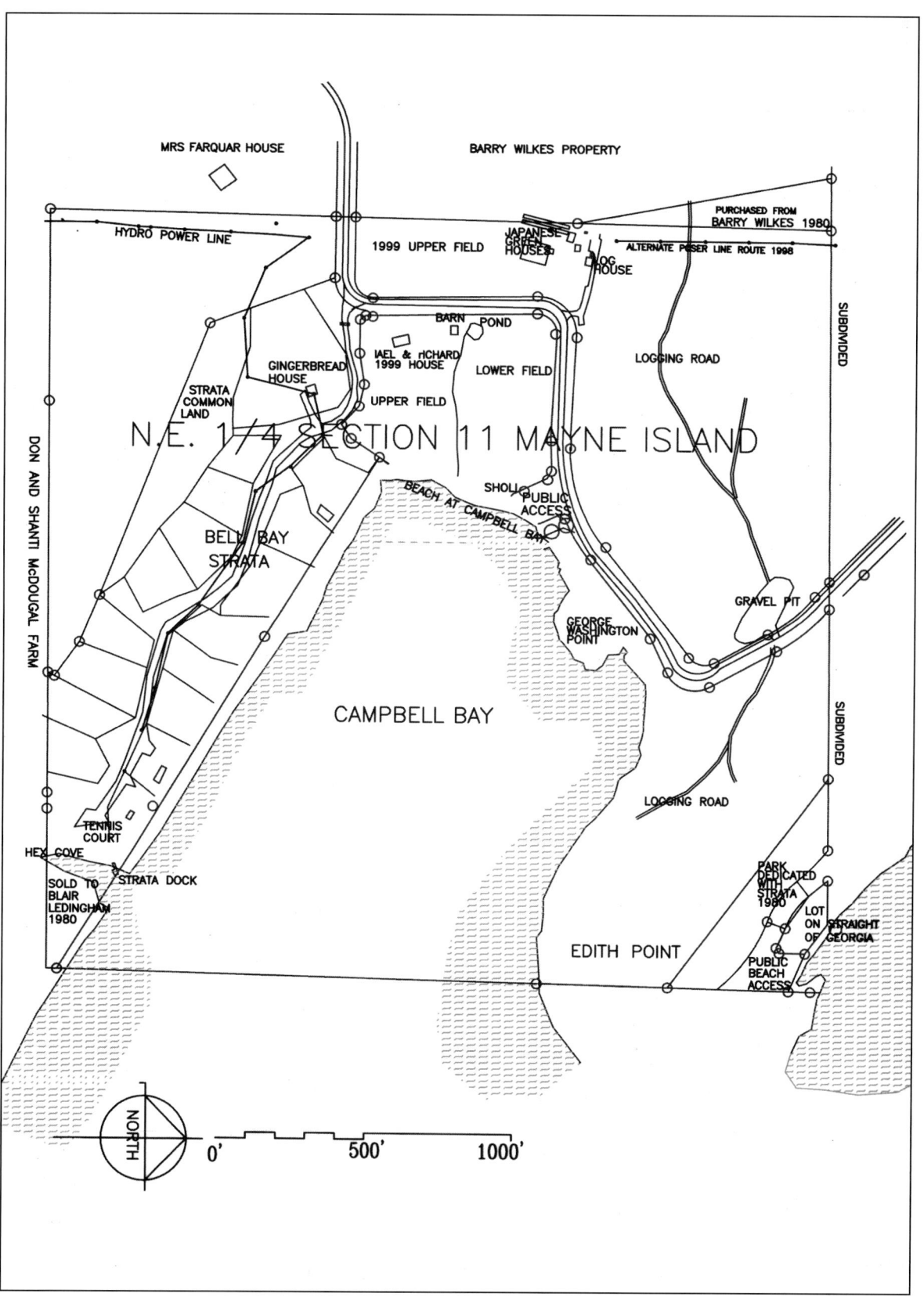

The Gingerbread House

Sometime during the late '70s and early '80s our daughter, Jennifer, took it into her head that the Gingerbread House on West 7th Avenue on the Fairview Slopes must be saved, and she persuaded Rand that it should be moved to Mayne Island. She negotiated with the developer, Piconi, who had bought the property for redevelopment, to purchase the house with all of its gingerbread trim for $1.00. The house had to be moved off the site, as Piconi wished to build townhouses. Nickel Bros. was hired to move the house and ship it by barge to David Cove on Mayne Island and then by bogie wheels to its present site.

The house-moving took place on October 31st, 1980 between midnight and 6:00 am during a torrential rainstorm. Hydro and telephone lines had to be moved and reconnected. Parked cars had to be towed and replaced. All went well until someone noticed that the BC Telephone people had not arrived to remove their wires. A series of 4:00 am telephone calls to every Mr. Smith in Burnaby finally got the response, "Yes, my husband works with the telephone company," and "I thought you said Friday," and the acid reply from the Nickel Bros. foreman, "It is Friday!"

Everything had to be put back in place except for the house, which was now sitting on bogies out on the street. The house kept Alder Street closed that Friday and, as the street is extremely steep, it was blocked in place and guarded by a full-time watchman. The next night the wires and traffic lights were again taken down and the parked cars were moved, and the house was finally towed to Granville Island. It sat on a wharf for several weeks before finally being barged to Mayne Island.

The evening before the Gingerbread House was to be moved off site by Nickel Bros., I received a telephone call at the office from the construction manager for Haebler Construction. He knew that Mr. Haebler had agreed with Jennifer that we could disconnect the power to his construction site; however, Mr. Haebler was in Europe and the manager was pouring concrete at 7:00 am Friday. If we failed to have the power back on their site by 7:00 am, they would hold us liable for a cost of $40,000 per hour. I was flummoxed. A call to Nickel Bros. convinced me not to worry, they would take care of the problem. And they did.

Upon arrival at David Cove, the house was trucked to its present location. The only problem was that the subdivision was not complete, and Rand and Jennifer had to locate the position of the house by peering through the trees.

After Nickel Bros. situated the house on site, a new foundation was built, the house was gutted, and new interior finishing was undertaken, including heating, electrical, and plumbing fixtures. Jennifer oversaw the project and spent considerable time finding authentic Victorian-type finishes and fixtures. Landscaping was also undertaken.

Lamb bake at Gingerbread House (1982)

Gingerbread House (1995)

We owned the Gingerbread House for just a few years, but enjoyed many good times there.

In 1983 our son Richard and Lael Whitehead were married in St. Mary Magdalene Church on Mayne Island. The wonderful wedding ceremony, which expressed their deep attachment to our land, was followed by a sit-down dinner for 150 guests in the field behind the Dome, in a hollow beneath the large maple tree.

Planning and preparing the dinner was quite a challenge, as we had neither electricity nor cooking facilities for such an undertaking; however, we still had the Gingerbread House! Richard and Lael's wedding made use of its facilities.

We enjoyed our lamb bakes there, too. Robin and Freda Pierce, visiting from England in 1984, spent the Summer in the house, and Robin planted a garden.

In 1985 the house was sold to Ken and Karen Sommerville, who did a wonderful job of furnishing it in the Victorian Style and, for several years, of running it as a Bed and Breakfast.

Charlotte and Rand carving the lamb

Rand and Kathryn entertaining guests at the Gingerbread House

The Bride and Groom in the field

Ken and Karen Sommerville's garden

Moving to the Log House

During the course of doing the Bell Bay Subdivision in the early 1980s and moving the Gingerbread House from the Fairview Slopes in Vancouver, Jennifer and her partner, Peter, and some of their friends lived in the Log House.

After selling the Gingerbread House to the Sommervilles, Rand and I moved back to the Log House in 1986 as our centre of operations. Many improvements had been made over the years.

A new Elmira Wood Stove, manufactured by the Mennonites in Ontario, had been purchased. The water well was drilled and the pump-house built. The shed that we built to store the boat—which now got only sporadic use, as our water-skiing children were grown—collapsed in the Blizzard of 1996 and demolished the poor boat.

With the help of contractors, Rand and I finished the interior, laid a tile floor, changed the front door, and added French doors leading to the outdoor patios. In 1998 we had a septic tank installed and added field and indoor plumbing. A Honda generator was purchased to provide electricity for lights on dark winter evenings.

All of these improvements made the Log House more of a year-round abode. We had discovered that the next generation was not willing to put up with the primitive lifestyle that we had been willing to put up with when we were young!

In the mid-90s Rand relocated the driveway from the field side of the Log House to its present location. He enlarged the grassy area and built the first stone wall (with the aid of Kevin Weinstaup's excavator), being careful to leave the old arbutus tree undisturbed; unfortunately, it was killed by the weight of the stone wall at its roots.

The Log House (photo by David Dibble)

'Death of the Fibreform Boat in the Blizzard of 1996'

Farm kitchen of the Log House (photo by David Dibble)

Charlotte standing in the doorway: another lamb bake underway!

Horse-Logging, Sheep-Farming, & Barn-Building

In 1996 we undertook to log the Hall Hill portion (on the north side of Campbell Bay) of our remaining 80 acres. Jennifer researched an ecological form of the "high-grading" we had used, previously called "selection logging." John Bartlett, our forestry consultant, marked all of the trees to be removed. He based his selection on removing scrub trees and opening the canopy to improve growth of the remaining trees.

Kevin Weinstaup undertook the logging contract, which paid us $40,000 in stumpage over two years. These funds built a new fence and the barn, and also paid for tree planting by Brinkman & Associates (Charlotte Murray's son-in-law, Dirk Brinkman). They planted 9,000 seedlings that, with proper care, will be ready to crop in 60 or 70 years.

The upper field was cleared during creation of the Bell Bay Bare Land Strata. Now it became necessary to maintain it as a field and not allow it to return to nature. With John and Jeannine Dodd's help we had picked stones, fertilized, and laid grass seed. For the first few years, John and Jeannine had the use of the field to graze their cattle. Unfortunately, one year the slaughtered beef was hung next to some venison and the meat became tainted. The Dodds lost their customers for the beef and decided to abandon cattle.

For the next few years we grew hay. We were dependent on the local hayers to cut the hay in June. As this was a community affair, we were usually the last on the list. Then the market for hay collapsed and this endeavour also failed.

In a joint partnership with Ken Sommerville, we then undertook to raise and breed sheep. We were to supply the field, and fence it. Ken would look after the sheep and with our help take the lambs to market. One of the advantages was that we would have our own lamb for our lamb bake. Since 1995 we have seen the ewes and their offspring in the fields. In early July some lambs are kept for further stock and the rest are taken to market. In 1996, Ken purchased a Sussex ram, two Sussex ewes, and two Sussex yearlings to improve our stock.

The Blizzard of 1996 and the loss of our shed for fodder storage persuaded us that it was necessary to build a new barn. Rand designed the barn and researched the requirements that would provide storage for sheep hay and a birthing arrangement for new lambs. The present site is close to the pond and was chosen for its accessibility to Ken and to the road in bad weather.

We needed wood to build the barn. The horse-logger, Tonio, and his two magnificent Belgian horses were hired to bring the required trees out of the woods. Bernardo's portable sawmill was set up in the field and the wood was sawn for the new barn. A large fir tree that stood in the way of the new barn was cut down and also sawn up for lumber.

Grant, a contractor who was working on Mayne Island, built the barn during the Fall of 1997.

When our son Richard and his wife, Lael, moved to Mayne Island, Ken Sommerville asked if he could be relieved of his share in the sheep-raising partnership. Ken and Karen's store, the Island Cottage, was requiring more of his time and so we bought out his share. While Richard commuted to Vancouver three days a week to tend to his architectural practice, Lael and their three daughters took over the sheep operation.

The Spring of 1998 saw the addition of horses Halo and Rastas to the farm; they are company for Obedia, the donkey Ken had purchased to deter dogs from attacking the sheep.

Tonio's Belgian horses hauling logs (sheep grazing in background)

Tonio, the horse-logger, with his Belgian horses

Collecting horse manure to sell

Obedia in the Upper Field

Bernardo and the portable saw, cutting wood for the Barn

Building the Barn

Sheep grazing in the Lower Field

Family Settlement

Beginning in 1985 Rand and I witnessed the birth of the third generation. First there was Lauren, quickly followed by Marlies and Julia, to Lael and Richard; then Adam and Meg to Jennifer and Peter; and Benjamin, Rylan, and Brody to Talbot and Paddy. The Log House has been a meeting place each Summer for all of them and has seen birthday parties, Easter egg hunts, Summer lamb bakes, Thanksgiving dinners, and many other happy occasions.

With eight grandchildren, though, the Log House is really too small to accommodate the expanding multitude. Our children and their families have expressed great love for the land and they return frequently to spend time there. There is a great sense of space and peace and tranquility. The children can ride their horses, and the beach and water activities provide many hours of pleasure. More young people are settling on Mayne Island and the commercial facilities are expanding. The annual lamb bake continues to attract cousins and friends and coworkers and is a major event.

With the growing traffic congestion and densification of Vancouver, Richard and Lael decided to sell their home in West Vancouver and move to Iredale Place on Mayne Island in 1997. They selected a site in the upper field and built their permanent home there. Jennifer and Peter also had a long-standing desire to build a cottage as an addition to the Log House, and in 1999 their dream took shape. Tab and Paddy, too, hope to build a cottage and, in the meantime, they share the use of the Log House.

The first step was to provide electricity for their new homes, and it was decided to extend the line to service the Barn and the Log House. Clearing the right of way for BC Hydro proceeded; trees were cut down, massive piles of log debris were collected in the upper field and, with the help of Matt Taylor's bulldozer, the debris was burned in the wet and rainy Winter.

Richard designed the two houses, and Rand assisted on Jennifer's house. Once the designs were agreed upon, Richard contracted out and oversaw the challenging construction.

Richard drilled a new well on his site, which produced an incredible volume of 16 gallons a minute. The Winter rains and winds came, and water and mud were everywhere. Many of the construction crew lived in the Log House; the woodpile shrank and the old pump gave out and was replaced by an electric pump. The hot-water supply was troublesome. The Elmira stove caused problems. Delivery trucks got stuck in the mud. Richard frequently found himself up to his knees in water while trying to lay or fix drainage systems. But Spring came, the earth dried out, and the houses were soon finished.

This isolated property that Rand and his parents purchased in 1958 is becoming a settled community. ∎

Rand and Talbot, carving the lamb (circa 1990)

The Log House

Adjacent:
Kathryn (in her sun hat) with the next generation building sand castles on the beach … (daughter Jennifer is on her left, and daughter-in-law Lael is on her right)

Opposite:
Rand with Bing and Kashi on Mayne Island (1998)

Below:
'The Gang' of all eight grandchildren on Brody's 4th birthday (1998)

The Future

The future belongs to our children and to their children. As grandparents, we will watch and enjoy their contributions to Iredale Place.

We all love this land. The youngest generation has returned, along with their parents, time and time again.

Here, the cousins can play and share their lives. Some will stay and, no doubt, some will wander on.

We wish them joy.

Kathryn & Rand Iredale

May 1999

PUBLIC PLACES

While Rand was building his architectural practice, I was raising our three children, running a busy household, and organizing many of Rand's travels and activities. This photo of me with the children in the TR3 was one of Rand's favourites (1960).

4 Beyond Functional Necessity

Some of the most important and exciting institutional projects for which Rand Iredale was the Partner in Charge were the many buildings at Portage Mountain, near Hudson's Hope, in the Peace River Country of northeastern British Columbia. These facilities were designed and constructed in the 1960s when BC Hydro & Power Authority was building the Bennett Dam.

BC Premier W.A.C. Bennett and BC Hydro Chairman Dr. Gordon Shrum spearheaded the massive hydro-electric project at Portage Mountain. Dr. Shrum believed that this new community should have buildings designed by architects and that even the Powerhouse should have architectural input.

In addition to the W.A.C. Bennett Dam and the Gordon M. Shrum Generating Station, the programs and buildings of the Portage Mountain Hydro-Electric Scheme that Rand was involved in included:

- Portage Mountain Lookout Building
- Hudson's Hope Housing
- George W. Pearkes Elementary School
- Central Control Building
- The Powerhouse
- Tourist Development Master Plan
- Hudson's Hope Hospital (prefabricated by Tecton Industries, the firm that Rand founded in 1963 to develop modular building systems)

This chapter covers Rand's Portage Mountain projects during a significant period in the history of BC Hydro. It includes newspaper clippings and journal articles as well as excerpts from interviews with two of Rand's collaborators, his partner Bill Rhone and his structural engineer Bogue Babicki. It concludes with Rand's insightful approach to developing a Mission Statement for Portage Mountain. ∎

"Spotlight on Art: PORTAGE – The Proof of a Growing Sensitivity to Esthetic Values" by Joan Lowndes, *The Province*, April 7, 1967: 10. Caption: "Portage Mountain Dam … why should it not be romantic?"

"Beauty and Power too" by Bob McMurray, *The Province*, April 4, 1967: 16. Caption: "W.R. Iredale (left) and Dr. Gordon Shrum examine model of 'esthetic' control centre and visitors' centre at Portage Mountain Dam."

"Construction Has Big Impact: Dams Pour $1 Million Daily Into Economy" by Frank Rutter, *The Vancouver Sun*, May 30, 1967, Progress Edition: 6A. Caption: "POWER OF THE PEACE is symbolized in design of the central control building … Here architects Randle Iredale and Alan Scott admire their work—a scale model of the project now under construction—which proves there can be beauty even in the rawest of basic industry …"

Reprinted from Industrial Architecture (1967)

"Preliminary studies were initiated early in 1965. Working drawings were begun in March 1966 and were completed in July of that year; tenders were invited two years later and called in December ... General completion [was] scheduled for August 1968 and first power [was] due to be generated later the same year" (IA, 581).

Architecture at the Peace

Future visitors to the massive Portage Mountain project on the Peace River will find it more meaningful as the result of an early blending of engineering and architectural skills. One of the largest of its kind and the largest in the Western Hemisphere, the project has been designed not only to function efficiently but also to permit people whom it serves to visually appreciate and understand it.

Portage Mountain is located in north-east British Columbia. It derives its name from the early explorers having to portage their canoes at this point due to unnavigable rapids. Peace River originates in north central British Columbia at the confluence of the Findlay and Parsnip rivers. It flows from west to east through British Columbia into Alberta. The closest major town to the project is Fort St. John, some 80 miles to the east ...

The designers of the hydro-electric works are International Power and Engineering Consultants of Vancouver, a subsidiary of the British Columbia Hydro and Power Authority for whom the scheme is being carried out. Rhone and Iredale Architects, also of Vancouver, were appointed as architectural consultants for the total project, but are primarily responsible for ... design of the central control building, generator breaker buildings, finishes to the powerhouse, the portal structure and overall landscaping. *Industrial Architecture* feels sure its readers will agree that ... their professional colleagues in Vancouver have made a notable contribution towards the future design of power projects and we offer them unqualified praise for their inspired achievements.

In the structures now being built ... can be seen the outcome of a policy in which the originators recognized a fundamental need beyond the immediate technical function. That is, the need to let form express the essence; the human need to derive an enduring visual/emotional experience of satisfaction in human accomplishments. As a result of this initial perception a relationship of specialists unique in Canadian construction history was created between engineers and architects.

Working on a team headed by the engineers, the architects participated in the development of general layouts ... [and were] responsible for the visual and emotional impact of the design in the same way that the structural consultants were responsible for their stability. As a result, a group of structures that might otherwise have risen as a technically efficient but diverse complex, is emerging with visual harmony, the form of individual parts suggesting their function and contributing to an overall impression of the project's purpose and magnitude.

This has been the role of the engineers and architects—to integrate through design the power, the purpose and the essential creativity of the total concept.[1] ∎

---

1 "Architecture at the Peace: The Portage Mountain Hydro-Electric Scheme," *Industrial Architecture* (December 1967): 581–86 (581). Contents of the article are hereafter cited in this chapter (in-text) as IA, followed by the applicable page number(s); e.g., (IA, 581).

Inaugural event at the Lookout Building; visitors and dignitaries fill the deck overlooking the Peace River Canyon below.

Photo:
William Dekur, North Vancouver

Project: Portage Mountain Lookout Building

The Portage Mountain Tourist Lookout was one of the first buildings to be constructed. Tourists were eager to see the work in progress and it was thought that a building overlooking the site was needed. It was located at the edge of the 400-foot cliff on the east bank of the Peace River Canyon, immediately downstream from the hydro-electric dam. The building was designed to accommodate a minimum of two bus loads of sightseers and included accommodation for a residential caretaker. It was articulated so that the view could be maintained in three directions and so that this portion of the building could be placed as close to the cliff edge as possible. ∎

Project Team

Randle Iredale
Partner in Charge

William Rhone
Consulting Partner

Glen Cividen
Project Architect

Award

Massey Medals
for Architecture,
Honourable Mention,
1964

Publication

The Canadian Architect
(November 1964): 57

Photo:
Gunnar Johannessen, Vancouver

Portage Mountain
Tourist Lookout Building

Photos: William Dekur,
North Vancouver (1965)

76 | Beyond Functional Necessity

Lunch at '21' with Dr. Shrum

From an interview with Bill Rhone.

After Rand and I started up our partnership, we talked about getting good support people for the firm. We needed a lawyer and an accountant just to run the practice. So Rand suggested Gordon Shrum, who he had gone to school with and who was Dr. Shrum's son. Well, that sounded pretty good because I didn't have any contacts with lawyers and accountants.

Gordon lived with his dad on Chancellor Boulevard and one day he phoned up and said, "Rand, we need some outdoor work, we need a deck off the back of this place." So we went around to this house and Dr. Shrum was there. He was a towering figure in the academic world, a brilliant administrator at UBC, a dean, a department head, and he'd been appointed co-chair of the BC Hydro & Power Authority (with Hugh Keenleyside).

In those days the Bennett government took a giant leap forward and decided to develop the Peace River system and the Columbia River system for the production of massive amounts of hydro-electric power. They weren't into all of the environmental issues like today; we needed power in those days! Dr. Shrum handled the Peace River project and Hugh Keenleyside handled the Columbia River project.

But we didn't know about any of that at first. We just started out, a couple of young architects brought around to look at putting a deck at the back of this house. It turned out to be quite successful; we put planters and handrails in and did a really nice job of the deck. Dr. Shrum came around a couple of times when we were out there looking after the project, and one day he asked, "Rand, why don't you get Bill and come down and have lunch at BC Hydro?" This was quite something!

So we went up the 21st floor of the BC Hydro building and they had a private dining room and we sat and chatted about various things. And out of that contact we did a little project up at the Peace River Dam and then we did some housing and other things, and then ended up designing the Central Control Building, and that one contact from adding a little deck at the back of a house emerged and blossomed into a whole series of projects for the BC Hydro & Power Authority.

At the beginning we worked on the Tourist Lookout Building together. Then there was a very nice little row-house project and then some private houses. And then there was a school, a couple of schools, as a matter of fact. And then some work associated with the dam itself, and then the Central Control Building. I didn't

Continued

spend much time on that building; it was designed principally by Rand and the team. It was a major project.

And in association with that project, we were consulting architects on the power generator project, which was a huge underground building with generators. The perspective goes into infinity and there's nothing but generators. We recommended materials and colours for that one and then there were a number of similar projects; I was on the periphery because I was working on other things at that time.

But there is an interesting anecdote to tell about the row houses. It was two-storey housing; we built it up, and then had a basement because you have to carry the concrete right down below the frost line because the ground up there freezes so hard. So it was quite nice and we developed this very sculptural design and looked at materials that were available.

The 'board and batten' look was really what we wanted, where the battens are about 1" x 2" and separated by about 6". We looked at the best way of getting all that cedar up there and so we invented a certain look: We'll just put plywood sheathing on and flash it at the edges and join it together and put the battens right on the plywood sheathing.

And so we went to the Plywood Association and they said that, with some technical adjustments, our plan would work just fine. So that's the way we did it. The crew put the raw plywood up and then stained it.

In the meantime, Dr. Shrum had flown up to look at the project and he comes along to the housing and he thinks it looks terrible! Just the stained plywood! And we got this angry telephone call, "This building is absolutely unsatisfactory!" Just like that, from the top of Mount Olympus, we had an avalanche come down on top of us! So Rand said, "Well, I'd better get up there and take a look. It sounds pretty serious!"

So Rand flew up there and, in the meantime, the battens had arrived and they were starting to put the battens up. Rand went around to the project and couldn't see anything wrong; it looked good. So he's on the telephone to Dr. Shrum and he says, "I think it looks terrific." Dr. Shrum almost blew his head off again! But Rand said, "Well, it looks good!"

Then Dr. Shrum called one of his chief engineers and asked him to take a look. So the chief engineer for the whole dam came up and he met Rand on the site. The chief engineer then phoned Dr. Shrum and said, "Well, it looks pretty good!" Finally, it got sorted out and the project was very nice. It was published and received several awards. ∎

Project Team

Architects
Randle Iredale
Partner in Charge

Glen Cividin
Project Manager

Structural Engineer
Snowball & MacKenzie

Mechanical Engineer
J.D. Kern & Company

Electrical Engineer
Arnold Nemetz Engineering

Project: Hudson's Hope Housing

This $4 million project was located on a 50-acre site adjacent to the small wilderness community of Hudson's Hope, which was under development to attract top personnel for construction of the Portage Mountain Hydro-Electric project. Different types of housing were grouped to provide residences for construction workers and operating personnel.

All of the units were manufactured buildings, realizing savings through factory construction on the isolated site. Standard frame construction was used on full concrete basements. The board and batten effect of the exterior walls on individual and row houses and on fencing was obtained by applying 1" x 2" battens directly to single-skin exterior prefabricated plywood panels.

Placing houses in groups of six or eight, with the clusters separated from each other by groups of trees, avoided the endless vista common to many suburban tracts. The jury of the American Public Power Association Awards Program for utility design stated: "The Hudson Hope Housing project is a remarkably good solution to the housing needs of this construction site." ■

Hudson's Hope Housing

Photo:
William Dekur, North Vancouver

Awards

American Public Power Association Honourable Mention, 1969

National Design Council's Centennial Award for Residential Design, 1967

Massey Medal Finalist, 1967

Canadian Housing Design Mention, 1966

Canadian Wood Design Award, 1966

Publications

Architecture-Batiment-Construction (April 1967)

Canadian Builder (October 1966)

Project: George W. Pearkes Elementary School

The Hudson's Hope community was developed to serve the Portage Mountain hydro-electric construction project, 700 miles north of Vancouver. Due to concerns of the technical staff for the education of their children in this isolated area, the School Trustees (School District No. 83) requested a school that would provide the latest advances in teaching techniques. Educational specifications to the architects called for the best possible environment to facilitate team-teaching, upgraded classrooms, and progressive curriculum. It was necessary to take into account the problems of a diminishing school population even as construction crews worked to complete the project.

In their initial study, the architects drew heavily on the Ford Foundation educational research facilities. It was determined from this research that primary students received direct instruction from the teacher only about 32% of the time. They received most of their instruction in small groups of 10 to 14, rather than the traditional group size of 30 to 40. Consequently, there was little justification for a classroom to accommodate 35 students, and it was decided that a large space designed to accommodate 175 students and a team of five teachers was the best approach.

Hudson's Hope School
Open Plan

Photo: BC Hydro

The plan is a system of three octagons, geometrically spaced to allow for further octagons if required. The school has two main teaching clusters that accommodate about 175 students plus five portable trailer units to accommodate another 175 students, for a total of 350 students. The trailer units are arranged around the third octagon, which is the activity room. Spaces between clusters were increased in size over a normal corridor and used for general exhibition areas. In the team-teaching method, grading is not used; children move around during the day with their tote trays and can be in contact with all of the teachers. Upon completion of the hydro-electric project, the portable classrooms were removed and sold to other school districts. ∎

Project Team

Randle Iredale
Partner in Charge

Robert Todd
Project Manager

Hanna Skapski
Planning

Publications

Friedemann Wild, "Vorschule and Grundschule in Hudson Hope" in *Entwurf und Planung* (München: Georg Callwey, 1971): 112–13

"Diminishing Schools," *The Canadian Architect* Vol. 13 (September 1968): 52–55

"Project '68': Hudson's Hope Elementary School, BC," *The Canadian Architect Year Book* (1967): 63

Above:
Hudson's Hope School Activity Room

Below:
Hudson's Hope School general view of core

Photos:
William Dekur, North Vancouver

Reprinted from *Industrial Architecture* (1967)

Perspective of the Power Scheme

"The Portage Mountain Project [as] viewed from the east end of the downstream side of the dam. Rising from the reservoir some 300' north of the curving crest of the dam are the 10 intake towers with their gantry crane stationed at the east end of the platform.

"Below the dam, viewed in a southerly order, are: tourist parking facilities—access road—the central control building and maintenance shops—the generator breaker buildings—the transformer pockets and blastwalls—the 300 kv relay building—and the switchyard" (IA, 582). ∎

Perspective drawing of the power scheme

Sketch: Rhone & Iredale Architects

Reprinted from *Industrial Architecture* (1967)

The Intake Structure

"With sleek economy of form, the 10 penstock intakes rise from the waters of Portage Mountain reservoir some 300' north of the dam crest. It is through these intakes that Peace River water will be directed into the penstocks and thus to the 10 turbines in the underground powerhouse.

"The architectural aim here was to find an apt form for the visible portion of the intakes, aiding visitors to comprehend their function.

"Horizontal emphasis of an intake operation deck for the intake gates was overcome by extending the concrete towers above the deck. The resulting vertical lines suggest the downward movement of the energy-producing water. The towers also house stairways providing access to control equipment. Windows placed in the walls of the operating deck indicate, by their size, the relatively large mass of the structure" (IA, 582). ∎

Artist's impression of the intake structure

Sketch: Rhone & Iredale Architects

Adjacent:
Artist's impression showing another view of the Central Control Building. The tall structure on the right houses the lift shaft.

Sketch: Rhone & Iredale Architects

Reprinted from *Industrial Architecture* (1967)

Project: The Central Control Building

What should a central control building look like? The architects' answer to that simple question was that it should symbolize both electric power and the building's basic function—to transform everything that happens at Portage Mountain into directed energy. The result is a design resembling an enormous transformer. The structure's concrete and steel mass [stands] 100' high with broad, powerful lines at the base evolving to a more sophisticated form in the crown.

The building [functions] as an administrative and control centre for the whole project; as maintenance shops for the whole project, including maintenance of the 500,000 volt transformers; and as a tourist centre for guided tours and information on the fundamentals of electricity, a history of the area, and details of the construction.

The structure is of reinforced concrete on spread footings, which are 50% on bedrock and 50% on fill. The upper structure is steel framed with aluminium cladding. External finish is of structural concrete with recessed form ties and score lines at pour joints. The pre-finished aluminium cladding is pop riveted to corrugated aluminium profile sheet, 1½" deep, with 2" rigid insulation and interior aluminium liner sheet.

The metal cladding is designed on the rain screen principle, a method that eliminates the need for external caulking. The outer sheet sheds the rain and air movement is invited between the outer sheets and the profile sheet, maintaining equal pressure. The weather-tight seal is provided on the inner face of the cladding where the caulking acts as an air seal and is never exposed to the weather.

Double glazing is incorporated throughout the Central Control Building. Hermetically sealed units are used for the air-conditioned ... control and tourist floors. Double glazing for the maintenance areas consists of ¼" plate grey-tinted outer sheet and ¼" plate wired inner sheet. Frames are neoprene-glazing gaskets.

A tall concrete tower on the west side of the building repeats the effect of the Intake Towers. Its approximate height above ground level is 120', but it also descends below ground to a depth of 620'. It houses two 4,000-lb. capacity lifts operating at speeds of 500' per minute. It also houses the necessary communications antennas and a microwave dish, which provides a direct telephone link with Vancouver.

Internal finishes include prefinished aluminium framed demountable partitions having plastic laminate panels. The lift shafts are lined with rough cedar boarding to give a textured finish. Floors generally are of lino tiles in the offices and tourist areas. Concrete hardener and quarry tiles have been used in the maintenance shop levels. Ceilings are of acoustic tiling in the offices and sprayed asbestos over the tourist areas (IA, 584–85). ∎

Below:
The climatic conditions that had to be taken into account entailed a temperature range of -50°F to +90°F. The structure is designed for a 60-lb. / sq. ft. snow load over the roof area and a 30-lb. / sq. ft. wind load against the sides of the building.

(The large disk on the lift shaft is most likely a satellite dish for receiving telephone signals.)

Reprinted from *Industrial Architecture* (1967)

Some Statistics

Some statistics for the Central Control Buildings are:

- rock excavation 8,000 cu. yd.
- other excavation 17,000 cu. yd.
- fill 70,000 cu. yd.
- reinforcing steel 1,000 tons
- structural steel 573,000 lb.
- poured concrete 16,440 cu. yd.

Inside the Central Control Building

The team concept for the design of the project served more than the external appearance. The interior of the Central Control Building, for example, is designed to accommodate the spectator—from the tourist lobby on the middle floor of the crown, through the control room on the lower floor … to the power house below ground. The sectional drawing shows each of these areas, together with the adjacent 50' high transformer untanking area and service shops extending outward from the base (IA, 585). ■

Sectional Drawing of the Central Control Building

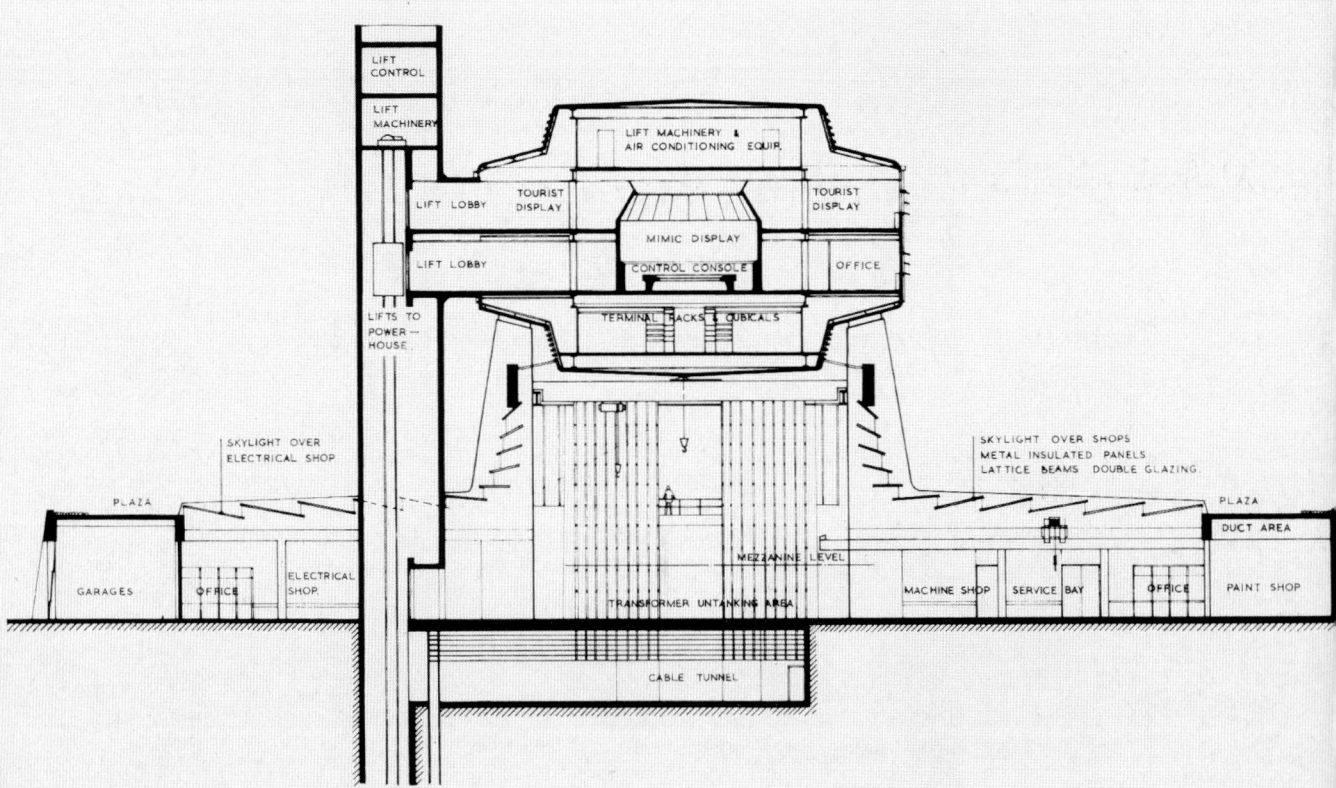

Project Team

Architects
Rhone & Iredale

Structural Consultants
Bogue Babicki & Associates

Heating & Ventilating
Consultants
Dexter, Bush & Associates

Awards

American Iron & Steel
Institute Design in Steel
Citation for Excellence in
Design, Public Works,
1971

American Public Power
Association Award of Merit,
1971

Publications

Industrial Architecture
(Britain, December 1967):
581–86

Murray Perry, "Bird's
Eye View of the Peace,"
Progress (BC Hydro, 1963):
"Nerve centre of Hydro's
Portage Mountain Dam
will be a Central Control
Building shaped like a giant
transformer"

Photo, far right, bottom:
William Dekur, North Vancouver

A Great Friend & Collaborator

From an interview with Bogue Babicki.

Vancouver Was Just a Small Town

I immigrated to Quebec from Poland in the late 1950s with a Masters Degree in Engineering from the Warsaw University of Technology. Because I spoke French, my first job in Canada was as a surveyor on the construction of the Great Lakes St. Lawrence Seaway System in the Port of Montreal. My wife, Maria, later joined me from Poland and, as part of a holiday, we drove across Canada to Vancouver in 1959.

Vancouver was just a small town behind the Rocky Mountains! But it was a very attractive place; we loved it and decided to stay. I completed the requirements of the Association of Professional Engineers of BC by writing my thesis on a fully prefabricated high-rise building I had done in Poland. My first job in Vancouver was with Read Jones Christoffersen, already a well-known firm of consulting engineers, where I worked for three years.

In 1962 I established Bogue Babicki and Associates Inc., Structural Designers and Consulting Engineers (BBA). One of the first architectural firms BBA began collaborating with was Rhone & Iredale. Over the years we worked together on many projects, but four were particularly significant: the Grange Industrial Plant, the Central Control Tower, the SFU Science Complex, and the Westcoast Transmission Building. These award-winning projects were recognized in Canada and abroad for their novel and unique design solutions.

A Rare Adventure on the Peace River

From the beginning Rand and I were very close friends and collaborators, and the 'proof' of it was in the Portage Mountain project. The Central Control Tower was challenging, but together we came up with an interesting and rational design. It also provided us with a rare adventure and unforgettable memories.

Our two families—Maria and myself, Rand and Kathryn, and their three children—decided to travel down the Peace River by canoe before the dam was closed and the river valley was flooded. We were among the last people to see the area in its natural state. It was 1967; Jennifer was the oldest child, about 11 or 12, and Maria was pregnant. We had two longboats, with two Indian guides and a trapper who was famous in the area to help us. We camped on the riverbank, and a week later the dam was closed and the surrounding environment was changed forever.

Continued

The time we spent on the Peace River was fantastic, and very interesting from an ecological perspective. The Indians showed us imprints of prehistoric animals in the stones—made when the stones were not yet stones. I remember it very clearly. It was the middle of the summer, and everything would soon be flooded, and so it was the last moment to see these archeological wonders. We canoed down the river, and slept in tents along the way or in the trapper's cabin.

After that trip, Rand and I often skied and travelled together. We loved the same kinds of things and activities.

Special Memories

Years later Rand's sons Talbot and Richard, both young engineers at the time, worked in my office. Richard worked on the geodesic dome at Expo '86 (now Science World) and was using the computer system in our office, which was connected to the computer centre at UBC. These are special memories, because the whole computer revolution was starting to happen: the new computers, the new way of approaching design. It was a very exciting time. And I was truly honoured when Richard then asked me to make a speech at his wedding.

The friendship between our families continued, with Rand and Kathryn visiting Maria and me in the South of France in the 1990s and helping us with the *vendange* (grape harvest). Rand will forever stay in my memory as a great friend and collaborator.

I Could Always Rely on His Word

Rand was a very honourable person. If he said he would do something, there was no doubt that he would keep his promise. He was always on time and he had a very positive, very wonderful personality. His approach was open and straightforward; there was no manipulation, and so I could always rely on his word.

The greatness of Rand was his willingness to go and learn himself, to convince himself, to spend time really learning enough about the structure that would allow him to accept new ideas. So here was Rand, working together with the 'newcomer,' who was telling him that Canada was a bit behind! And Rand accepted that and was willing to go ahead and do something new.

Because of his open mind and willingness to do something special, Rand also realized that he needed the help and support of somebody else. So there was a real collaboration between us. I was very lucky to meet Rand at that time and to be able to introduce different ideas. ∎

Bogue B. Babicki,
D.Sc., P.Eng., RCA

Reprinted from *Industrial Architecture* (1967)

Project: The Powerhouse

The accompanying perspective portrays very well the dramatic impact of this cathedral-like hall ... excavated in bedrock 500 feet below the dam's left flank. In fact, what is seen here is the main floor of the world's largest underground powerhouse [at the time].

The hall is about 60 ft. high and 900 ft. long. Ten great generators are to be viewed and serviced through access covers at floor level. Riding along tracks under the concrete roof, cranes will have access to each turbine and generator, whose rotors can be seen through plexiglass domes. Tourists will use the gallery shown on the right of the hall for viewing activities in this energy-producing heart of the hydro-electric project.

Once again, the design is straightforward, conveying an impression of size and power. This impression is heightened by steel-panelled walls, concrete supports, and blue steel access plates around each rotor head.

The overall effect is integrated by the colour plan and lighting pattern. Concrete columns and crane beams are left natural, metal in-fill panels are blue, the 250-ton crane is yellow, and the floor around the blue access panels is mainly quarry tiling. In the centre of the light fixtures situated in the roof arch are red cones to reflect the focal point of the turbines. This was felt necessary, to introduce scale, in order to convey to the tourist the size and extensiveness of the powerhouse. The twin star shapes on the end wall represent the BC Hydro and Power Authority's house symbol (IA, 585). ■

Artist's impression of the Powerhouse interior, with viewing gallery on the right and the BC Hydro twin star house symbol on the end wall.

Sketch: Rhone & Iredale Architects

Reprinted from *Industrial Architecture* (1967)

Project: Tourist Development Master Plan

In this sketch the various components of the project are seen in relation to each other as they [took] shape at the head of the Peace River canyon.

The heavy segmented line shows how the hundreds of thousands of visitors … will travel in their viewing of these components:

From their first sight over the reservoir of 57 million acre ft. of water covering 640 square miles, to the 600 ft. high dam, the intake structure, the powerhouse, and the central control building.

Drawing of the Tourist Development Master Plan / planned tours and facilities for visitors over the entire project site.

Sketch: Rhone & Iredale Architects

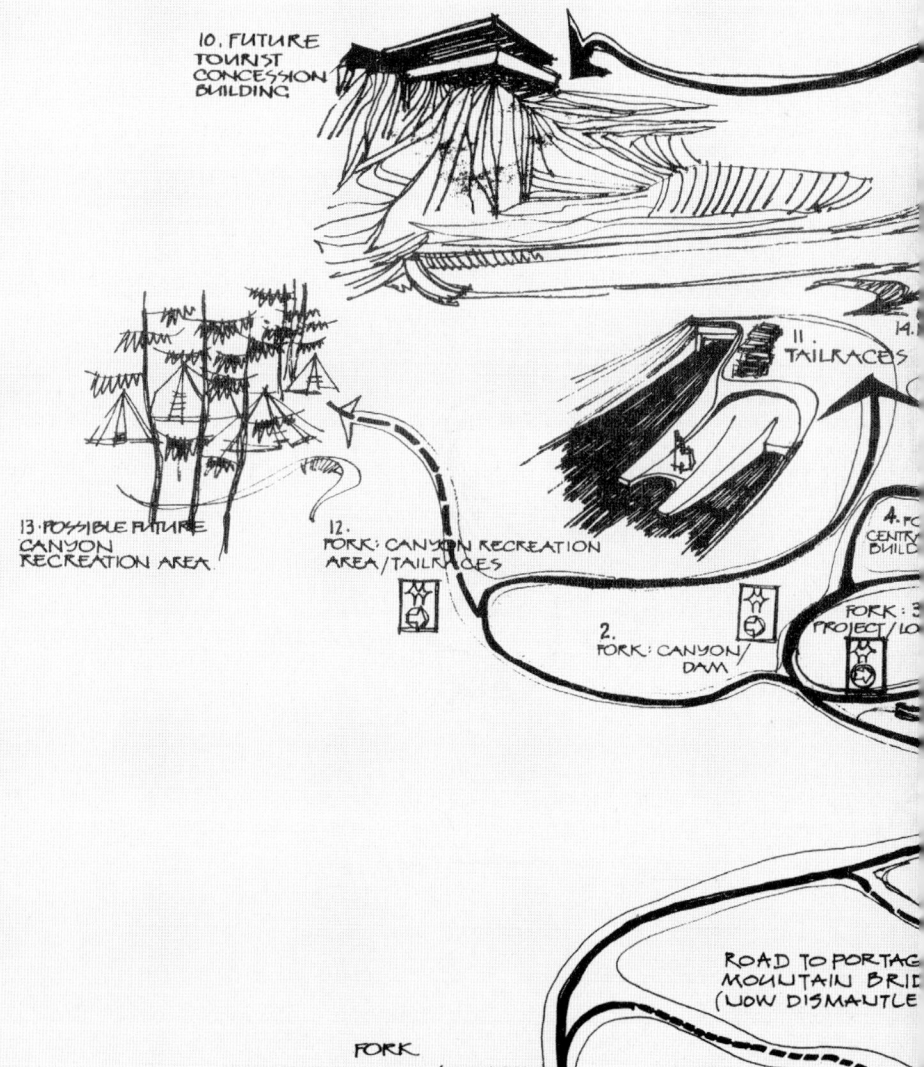

92 | Beyond Functional Necessity

Reprinted from *Industrial Architecture* (1967)

[This site] has yielded up relics of distant geological ages [and] the first recorded historical moment was ... Sir Alexander MacKenzie's arrival on May 24th, 1793. For engineers and architects of the twentieth century it is a site that embodies an inspiring challenge to create a fitting expression of the scope of human imagination and achievement.

The current tourists' look-out building, designed by the architects, is situated on the east side of the canyon. This location provides a comprehensive view of the total project during construction. Refreshment facilities are available there. A concession building is proposed for the west side of the dam above the spillway and from there, too, a view of the total project including the reservoir will be possible (IA, 585–86). ■

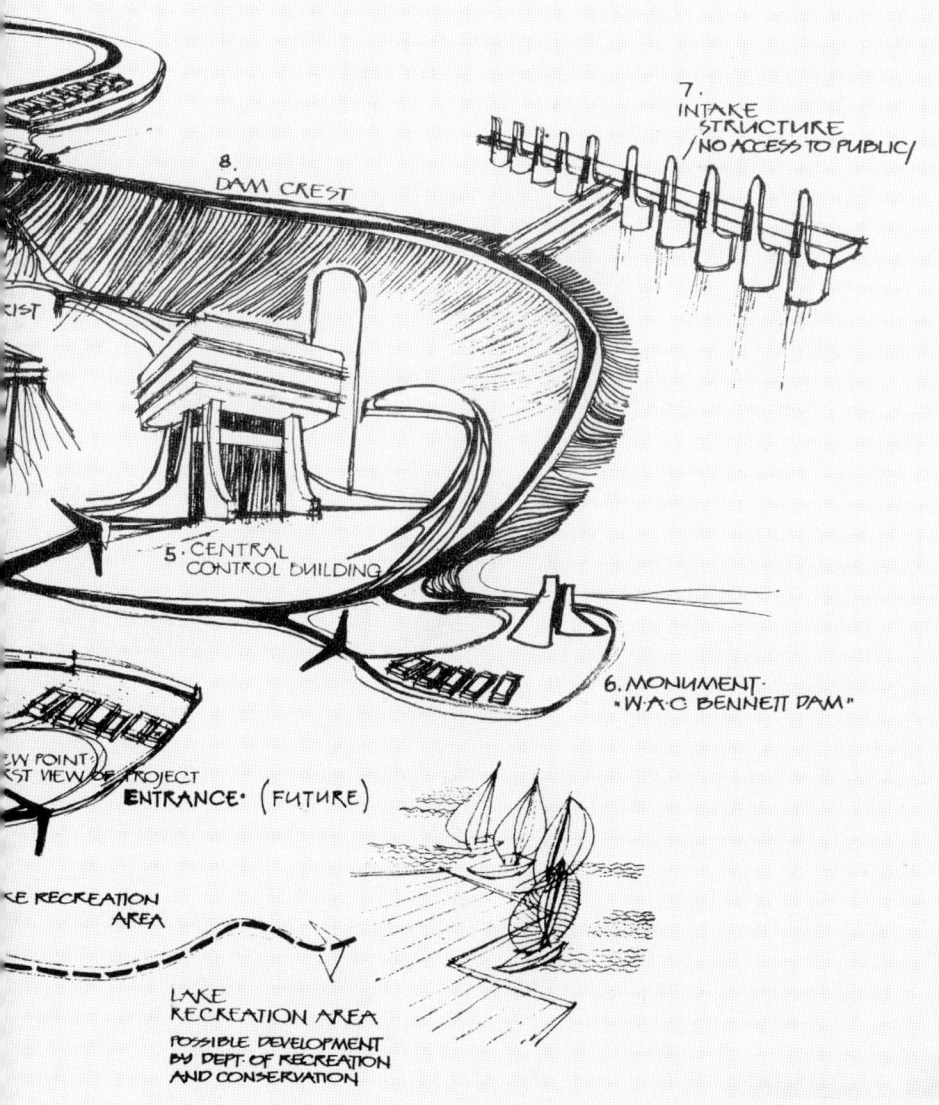

Legend to Sketch

1. View Point: First View of Project
2. Fork: Canyon / Dam
3. Fork: Project / Lookout
4. Fork: Central Control Building / Dam
5. Central Control Building
6. Monument / WAC Bennett Dam
7. Intake Structure / No Access to Public
8. Dam Crest
9. Spillway
10. Future Tourist Concession Building
11. Tailraces
12. Fork: Canyon Recreation Area / Tailraces
13. Possible Future Canyon Recreation Area
14. Existing Tourist Lookout

Artist's rendering of the Central Control Building, Peace River Development, on the front of one of BC Hydro's Christmas Cards (the original card was in colour)

Rand's Invitation to the "Official Dedication of the Portage Mountain Dam by The Honourable George R. Pearkes, VC, DSO, Lieutenant-Governor of British Columbia," on September 12th, 1967.

Rand and Dr. Shrum admire the Steel Industry Award for the Portage Mountain Project (1971)

Bennett to Pull Switch

PORTAGE MOUNTAIN — Today is the day a lot of people thought would never come. Today Premier W.A.C. Bennett stands in a powerhouse buried 500 feet beneath a massive dam that bears his name, and turns a handle that will transform a dream into reality. He will be officially switching Peace River power into British Columbia's electrical network. But he will also be signalling a victory in a seven-year controversy with critics who said it couldn't be done.

The occasion is the opening of BC Hydro's Portage Mountain generating station near this landmark, 10 miles upstream on the Peace River from Hudson's Hope. And the turning of the handle will start a chain of controlled force that will add 681,000 kilowatts to Hydro's generating capacity.

Water which has been building up since spring in the reservoir behind the 60-foot-high dam will surge down penstocks to spin three of the largest turbines in the world. The turbines, rated at 310,000 horsepower each, will drive three generators which will each produce 227,000 kilowatts of energy. The power will be transferred in switchyards on the surface, for transmission on the first of two 500,000-volt power lines to the Lower Mainland.

Arrival of the power at the coast will be proclaimed by the O Canada horns of the Hydro building in Vancouver.[1]

Engineers Okay Dam

PORTAGE MOUNTAIN — The Peace River Dam won't fall down. This is the word from the engineering review panel... Panel chairman G.M. Binnie of London, England said: "This has been an exceptionally successful project in inception and construction. It is extremely satisfying to be associated with such a project."[2] ∎

---

1 Ron Rose, "Bennett to Pull Switch: Mighty Peace Power Flows," *The Sunday Sun*, September 28, 1968: 1–2. Photo Caption: "HUGE POWERHOUSE of W.A.C. Bennett dam is hub of $700 million Peace River hydro-electric project which will send half a million volts surging through power lines to Vancouver today."

2 "Engineers Okay Dam," *ibid.*, 2.

> Our struggle resulted in the development of a new kind of function, what we called the *emotional function*.
>
> Form would still follow function, but with an added dimension: it must also express the aspirations and values of the builders.

THE EMOTIONAL FUNCTION

In the late 1960s, at the height of the Modern Movement, we followed the dictum 'Form Follows Function.' When we were selected as Architects on the Portage Mountain Project (Peace River Dam), we came to a project in which the programming had been done and the functions of Dam, Power House, Intake Structure, Control Building, Transformer Buildings, and Blast Walls were overriding. Like aeroplanes, their forms were defined by physical forces, which were firmly in the hands of the project engineers.

As architects we were to give 'form,' which was generally accepted as 'decoration,' for the engineering structures. As believers in the form-follows-function dictum of the Modern Movement, however, we faced a conundrum: these engineering structures already had their functional form, so what could we as architects contribute?

We struggled with this conundrum until we realized that, while the engineers had given each structure functional form, they fell short of architecture. We were staunch believers in the Modern Movement and we were not willing to retreat to William Morris's 19th-century notion that architecture is decoration.

Our struggle resulted in the development of a new kind of function, what we called the *emotional function*. We asked: What emotions did the building form elicit? Le Corbusier had taught us that planes and grain elevators were beautiful because they expressed the wonders wrought by 20th-century science. But the form he admired did not spring from function alone; it went beyond functional necessity to give expression—as does any great work of art—to the aspirations and values of their builders.

Form would still follow function, but with an added dimension: it must also express the aspirations and values of the builders. From this insight came our Mission Statement: To celebrate the wonder of the largest hydro-electric project in North America. We succeeded in this mission.

The project went on to win awards and was published in America, Britain, Germany, and Japan. We were not alone in our search; within ten years Venturi had published and the semiotics and postmodern movements were emerging.

Rand Iredale, Project Manager's Manual (1997)

5 The Earth on Which We Build

In January 1963 a report entitled "Higher Education in British Columbia and a Plan for the Future," by Dr. J.B. Macdonald, recommended the creation of a new university in the Lower Mainland. Two months later the establishment of Simon Fraser University received formal assent in the British Columbia Legislature, and in May of the same year Dr. Gordon M. Shrum was appointed Chancellor.

From the variety of sites offered, Chancellor Shrum recommended to the BC Government that the top of 1,200-foot Burnaby Mountain be selected for the new university. Located east of Vancouver, the site commands magnificent views of the mountains, Fraser River, Burrard Inlet and Vancouver Harbour. Architects were invited to compete in the design of the overall campus. Construction began in the Spring of 1964 and 18 months later, on September 9th, 1965, Simon Fraser University opened its doors to 2,500 students.[1]

Design for a University

The object of the contest was to choose architects for work that would total approximately 15 million dollars. The competition was directed toward obtaining conceptual ideas on layout of the campus, exploiting the natural advantages of the site, and grouping and sub-grouping of buildings, as well as creating architectural spaces and expression, traffic and pedestrian movements, and servicing. The overall character of the design had to be such that it could be maintained as the university expanded, over the years, to its declared target of 18,000 students. This program called for fluidity of imagination rather than precise solutions. Competitors were invited to make and state their assumptions.[2]

---

1 Source: http://students.sfu.ca/calendar (2006).

2 Warnett Kennedy, "Design for a University," *Report of the Board of Assessors: Simon Fraser University Architectural Competition* (November 1963).

Reprinted from *Report of the Board of Assessors: Simon Fraser University Architectural Competition* (Kennedy, 1963)

The Program

The programme comprised the design of buildings, the campus layout and the placement of the entire complex within a metropolitan park. Competitors were also asked to consider the growth of the University in two stages: for a 7,000 student population and a final 18,000 population.

The Building Program

The building programme consisted of Library building, Administration building, Cafeteria, Bookstore, Auditorium, Classroom buildings, Offices, Chemistry building, Physics laboratory, Biological Sciences laboratory, Gymnasium, playing fields, wind-sheltered architectural spaces between buildings, landscaping, outdoor sculpture, student residences (three dormitory units each for 800 students), Faculty housing, President's Residence, Student Union building, Faculty Club and Research institutes. The planning of each of these buildings did not form part of the competition.

The Board of Assessors

The Board of Assessors were as follows:

- Chairman, Warnett Kennedy (Professional Adviser – non-voting)
- Dr. Gordon Shrum (Chancellor, SFU – non-voting)
- Professor Henry Elder (UBC)
- Aaron Green (San Francisco)
- David McKinley (Seattle)
- Dr. Thomas Howarth (University of Toronto)
- Stewart Williams (Palm Springs)

The Awards

There were five Awards of $5,000.00 each, the awards being advances on fees for commissioned work; there were also five Honourable Mentions. The competitors were given approximately two months and had to submit three sheets of drawings.

Seventy-one entries were received from individual architects, firms of architects and special groups of architects. In these three classifications, almost 50% of the registered architects of British Columbia were represented.[1] ∎

---

1   Warnett Kennedy, "Design for a University," *Report of the Board of Assessors: Simon Fraser University Architectural Competition* (November 1963). Contents of the report are hereafter cited in this chapter as *'Report'* (no page numbers are listed in the report).

Reprinted from *Report of the Board of Assessors: Simon Fraser University Architectural Competition* (Shrum, 1963)

Simon Fraser University Competition

Award Winners
1. Arthur Erickson and Geoffrey Massey
2. William R. Rhone and W. Randle Iredale
3. Zoltan Kiss
4. Robert F. Harrison
5. Duncan S. McNab, Harry Lee and David C. Logan

Honourable Mention
1. R.A.D. Berwick, C.E. Pratt, Frederick S. Brodie, John M. Dayton, David A.D. Hickman, Roy Jessiman, Ronald J. Thom
2. Fred Thornton Hollingsworth and Barry V. Downs
3. Vladimir Plavsic
4. Alexander MacKenzie Webber
5. John Lloyd Kidd

Statement by Chancellor Shrum

On behalf of Simon Fraser University, I should like to thank all those who contributed so generously and effectively towards this very successful Architectural Competition.

Thanks are due to the 100 or more architects who gave unsparingly of their time to create new and imaginative designs for the campus and its buildings; to the assessors who studied the 71 submissions so conscientiously and competently, and to the Professional Advisor who successfully organized and supervised every detail of the Competition.

To all of these and many other public-spirited individuals, future generations of students at Simon Fraser University will be indebted for the creation of a well integrated campus in which the grandeur of the surrounding scenery is matched only by the quality of the planning and architecture.

This cooperative effort has ensured that Simon Fraser University will be one of the most beautiful and best planned universities of our time.[1] ∎

---

1 Dr. Gordon Shrum, "Statement by Chancellor Shrum," *Report, ibid.*

Reprinted from *Report of the Board of Assessors* (1963)

Architectural Competition

An event involving many persons is by nature important; when, however, the event forecasts changes that might easily affect established concepts, history is made. We feel this is precisely what happened with the architectural competition for the new Simon Fraser University in the Province of British Columbia, Canada.

The architects in the Province (the competition was limited to their participation) responded readily to a challenge laid down by the University's chancellor, Dr. Gordon Shrum, and in consequence some 71 schemes were submitted for adjudication by the appointed Board of Assessors.

The architectural opportunities were as great as they were unique.

The site, on the very top of Burnaby Mountain (just outside the city of Vancouver), commands extensive views over mountains and water; the climate is for the most part mild, although the rainfall tends to be heavy and occasionally the snow in winter may become a serious problem. If one adds to the strikingly romantic site a program of architectural requirements which invited the designers to concern themselves not with details but with broad concepts of what the image of this new university should be like, a heady mixture is produced. This is potent enough to seduce any architect away from his menial tasks into the creative fields that belong to man's more imaginative moments.

That such a procedure should be essential seems unreal, but there was no alternative. The university, already in possession of the site, did not possess a teaching policy and therefore the more finite conditions common in architectural competitions could not be the determinants. It is true that certain overall assumptions had to be made, but these were centered around an expanding student body eventually to reach a maximum of 18,000 to meet the correspondingly expanding population of British Columbia, and a certain precedent that had been set already by the nearby University of British Columbia. Beyond this little could be known.

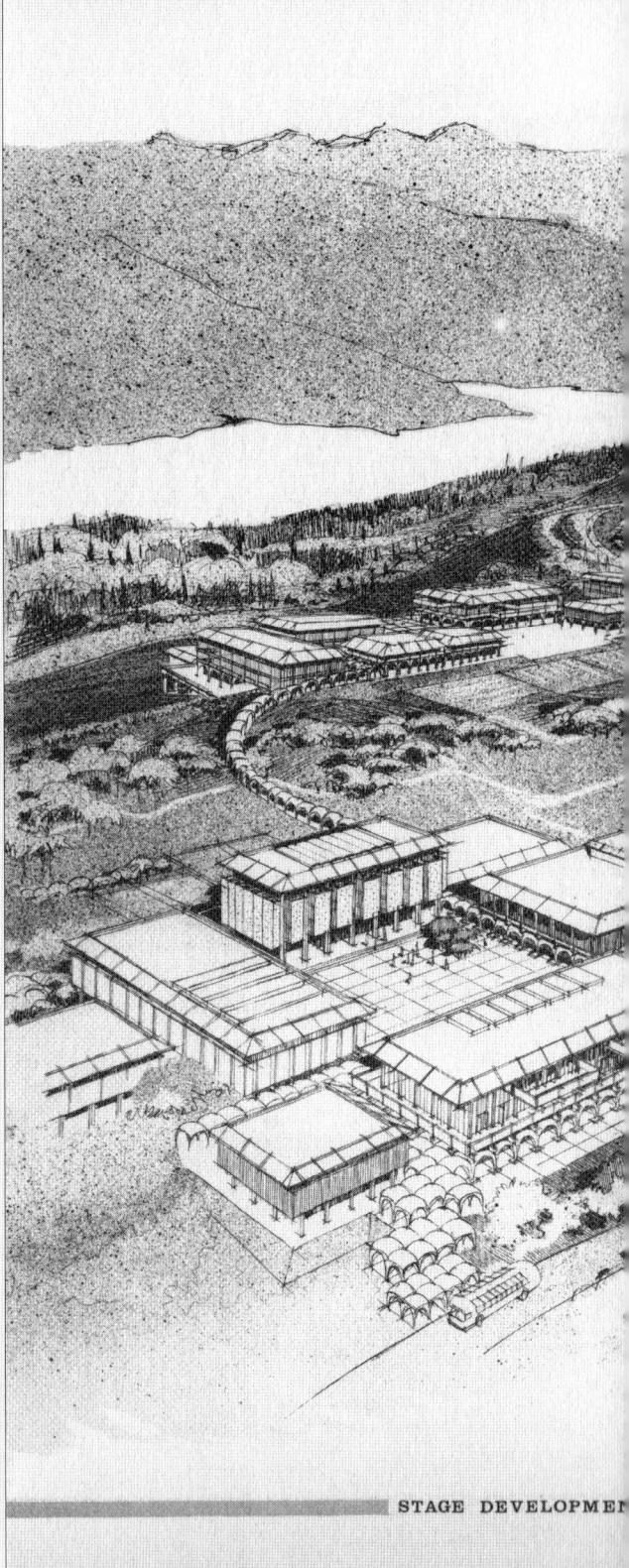

STAGE DEVELOPMEN

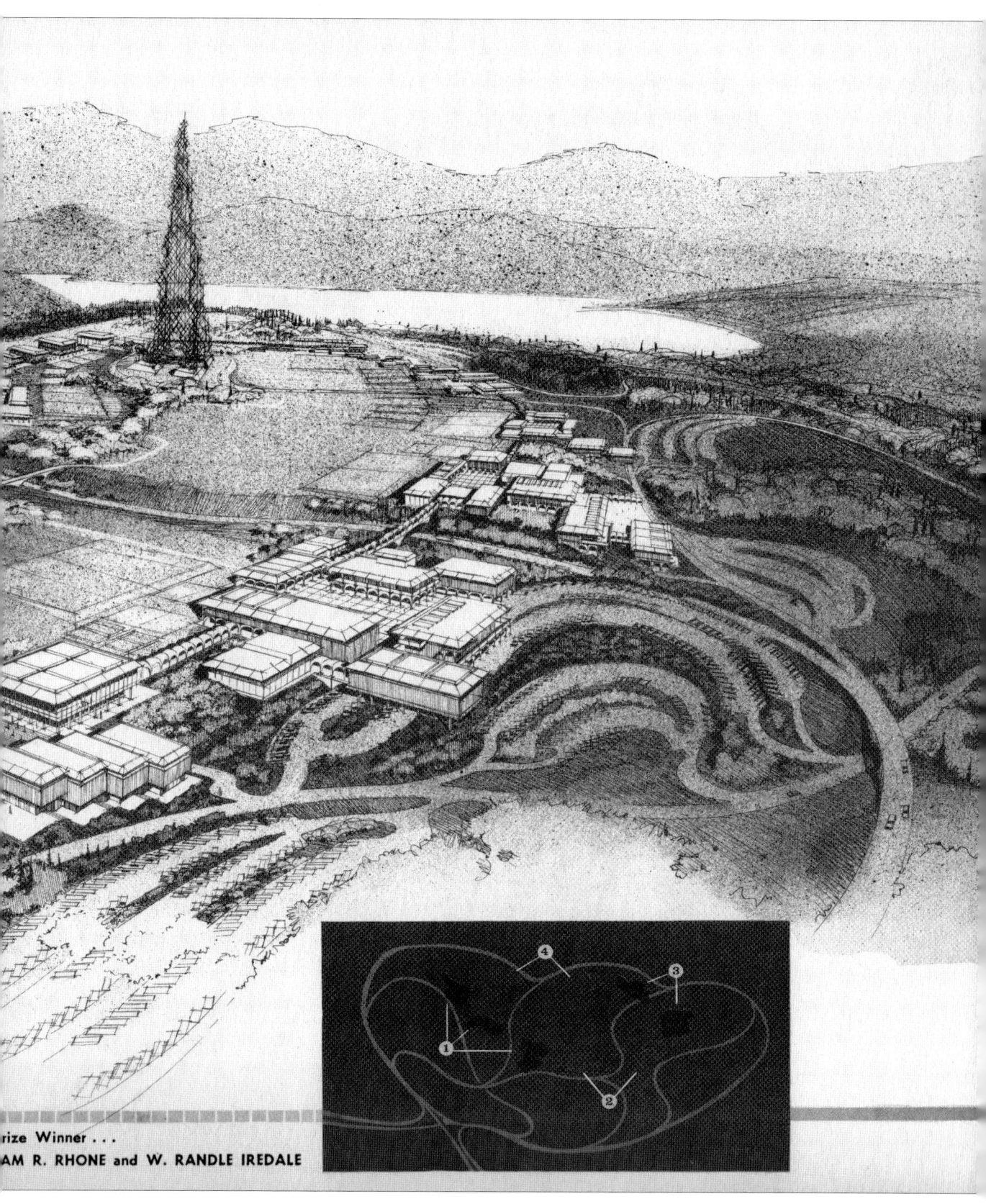

rize Winner . . .
AM R. RHONE and W. RANDLE IREDALE

The Earth on Which We Build | 103

Reprinted from *Report of the Board of Assessors* (1963)

Although this combination of circumstances turned out to be of great attraction to the architects of British Columbia, the task for the Board of Assessors was difficult, the absence of finite terms of reference placing them in a slightly invidious position.

The variety of submissions was considerable, embracing a diversity of thought through fine competence to utter dullness. Occasionally, but only occasionally, there was revealed the singular example which suggested that really profound architecture might be born should the opportunity be given. Eventually, it was found possible to select ten schemes from those submitted and place them in some kind of order of merit. . . . There is a need to record that complete unanimity was reached among the assessors in awarding the First Prize [to Erickson Massey], for it was thought to be an outstanding contribution in the field covered by the contest. The assessors went further than their appointed task in recommending to the Chancellor that every effort be made to see that the first prize-winning design be built without destroying the overall concept. . . .

The Board of Assessors is of the opinion that a useful purpose has been served by this particular competition in which the search has been for ideas and concepts rather than precise architectural solutions to a tightly organized programme.[1] ■

---

1   Comments by the Board of Assessors, *Report, ibid.*

Previous Page:
Stages of Development

Overleaf:
Typical College

Adjacent:
Traffic Pattern & Parking Areas / Topographical & View Analysis

Drawings: Rhone & Iredale Architects

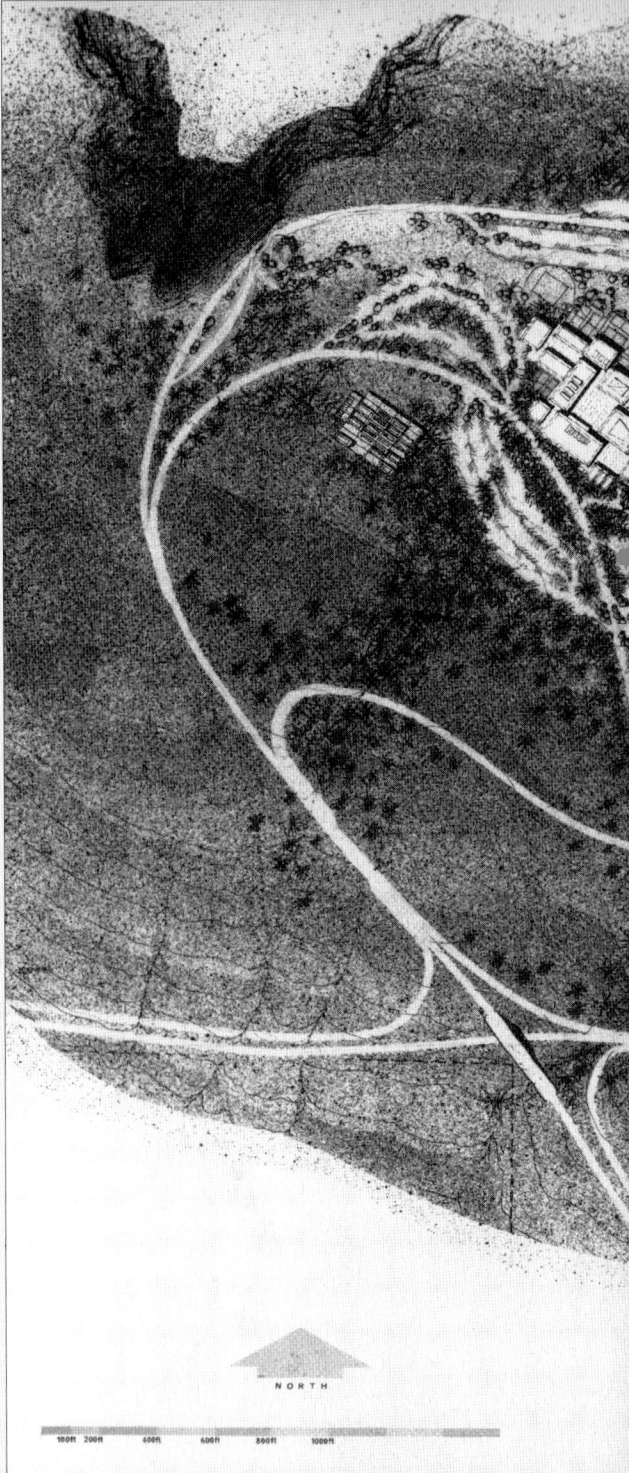

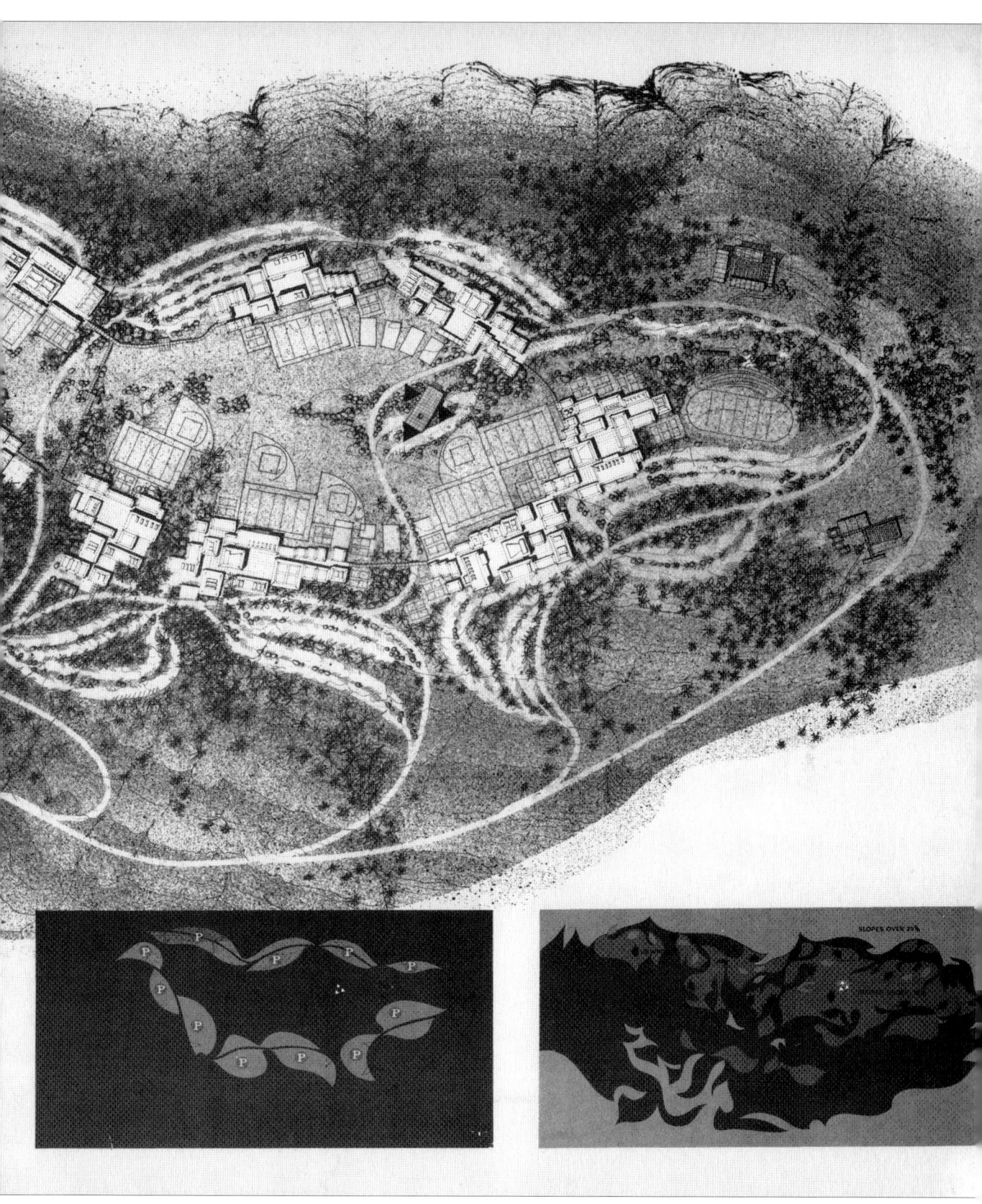

The Earth on Which We Build | 105

Reprinted from *Report of the Board of Assessors* (1963)

Second Prize Winner

It is a matter of debate as to how far an architect should formulate the operational policy of his client through the layout of buildings. In some cases the architect's ideas have been disastrous. When no policy is offered, and the search is for ideas, the architect frequently can give an insight into new directions upon which to determine policy.

The Rhone and Iredale submission had the courage to enter into this arbitrary field, and the assessors welcomed this courage. After all, the Conditions of Competition had invited competitors to state their assumptions. The basic concept was to divide the eventual student body of 18,000 students into nine colleges, each being autonomous. The nine colleges are shown grouped around the top of the mountain at a convenient contour level, creating a pattern loosely analogous to the Athenian Acropolis. Certain advantages are immediately recognizable: the sense of human scale is easily controlled; providing one can subscribe to the policy of education, expansion is simple and straightforward; car parking when related to each college is easier to handle and obviates the usual large inhuman areas devoted to the automobile.

There are, however, economical and practical limits to this form of thinking which demand the constant repetition of facilities such as libraries, auditoria, etc., for each college. The assessors were of the opinion that the scheme had gone beyond the point of usefulness in this respect, but were impressed by the ideas, which in themselves were simple and logical. Such simplicity appeared to be absent in the traffic circulation as it approached the university: it was thought that the motorist would have to make too many decisions in the course of his journey before he arrived at his choice of destination on the campus. Criticism was also aroused when we came to consider the spaces between buildings.[1] ■

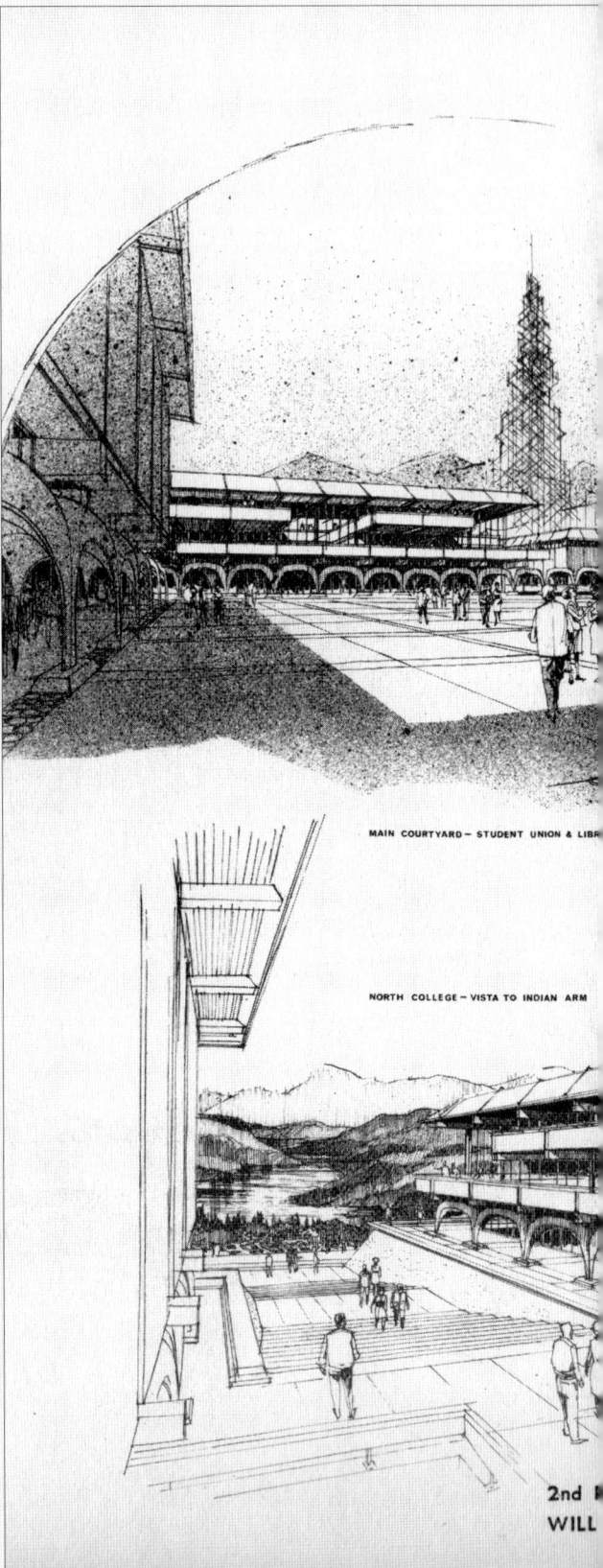

---

1   Comments by the Board of Assessors on the scheme submitted by Rhone & Iredale, *Report, ibid.*

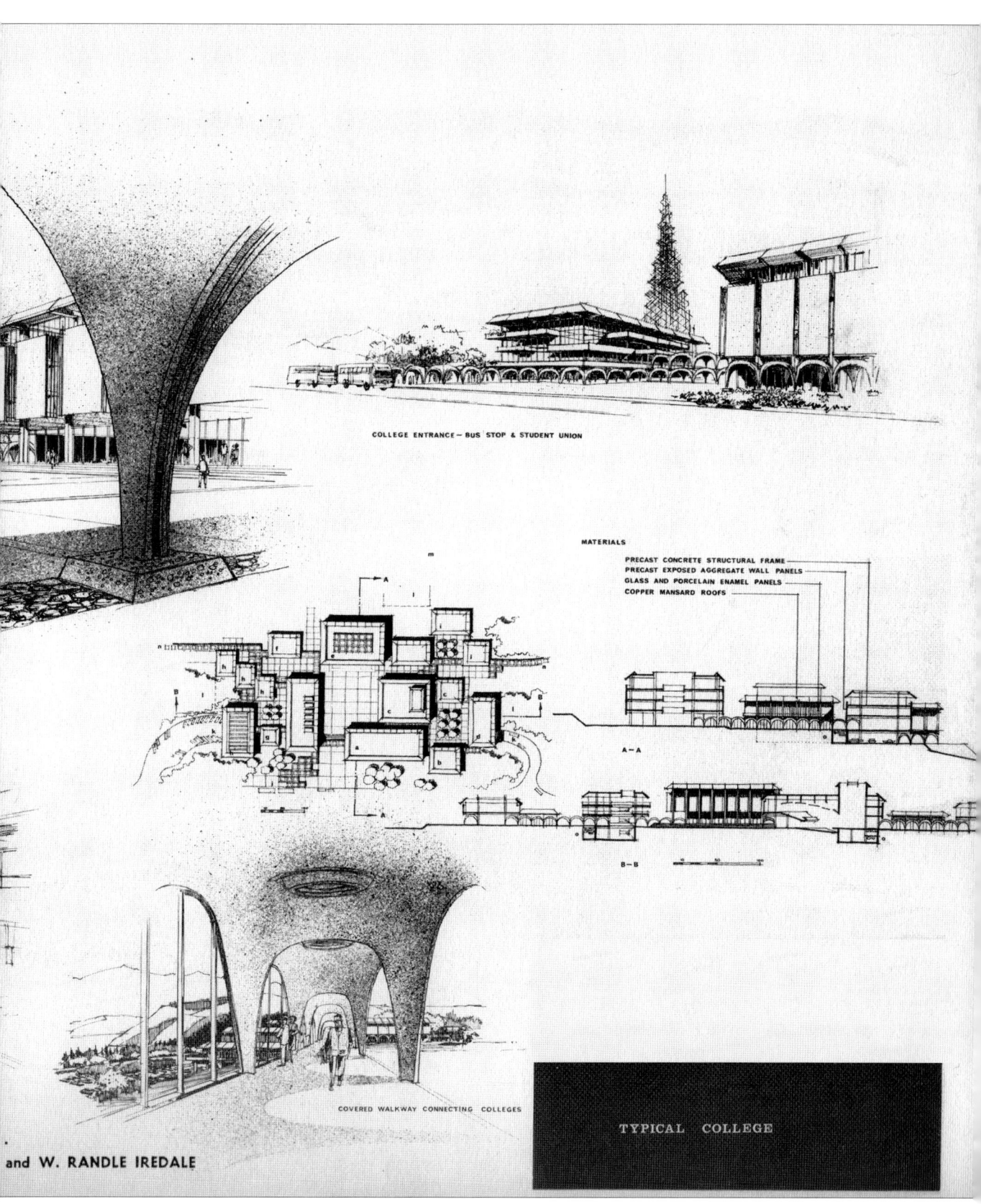

A Contest of Ideas

From an interview with Bill Rhone.

It was announced that there would be a competition to design Simon Fraser University (SFU). While we were working on the BC Hydro project, Dr. Shrum talked to both of us and said he wanted to have a contest. At that time, Thompson Berwick & Pratt (TBP) was larger than McCarter Nairne—those were the two principal firms at the time—and TBP virtually had a monopoly on the UBC campus. They had won a competition in the 1920s for the UBC campus (when they were Sharp & Thompson); Sharp & Thompson was a partnership in those days.

So they designed the mall system, the campus grid, and the Irving Building, the Main Library, which was stone-clad, the early Chemistry building, and so on. And then Berwick & Pratt joined the firm right after World War II and it became Sharp & Thompson / Berwick & Pratt. And, of course, the university just blossomed and grew and grew and they had designed all of these buildings.

And so TBP were pretty much the local 'experts' in university construction and buildings for education. There was no question that they knew a great deal about it. Anyway, I think they made a pitch to the Department of Education to design SFU, and the Department of Education informed Dr. Shrum, who was going to be the first Chancellor of Simon Fraser. But Dr. Shrum wanted to take a different approach and he thought, "Well, I think we'll have a contest and get some new ideas."

So that's how the competition was fostered. It was Dr. Shrum's idea to have this competition, open to BC architects only. He said there was no point in extending it nationwide and then having somebody in the East designing our university; "I don't think that's going to work at all. We'll have this competition and we'll give local architects the opportunity to design this university."

Dr. Shrum had two fundamental ideas: first, that it would be a competition; and second, that it would be limited to British Columbia. He approached Henry Elder, who was Head of the School of Architecture at UBC at that time, and Warnett Kennedy, who was the Executive Director of the AIBC, to both come on board. Warnett Kennedy was the professional advisor who wrote the guidelines with Dr. Shrum, and Henry Elder was also a kind of advisor at that time.

It was to be a 'general ideas' competition as opposed to a specific competition where you design the building right down to the last janitor's closet. So it was presented as a contest of ideas.

Continued

Anyway, everybody in the province was really excited about it, and we worked day and night. It was a real collaboration. We had a guy who worked for us at that time, Glen Cividin; Glen is retired and lives up near Courtenay now. Laurie Redpath worked on it. Rand and I both worked on it. We worked our butts off on that one!

We got Rudy Kovach from Hopping Kovach Grinnell to come in and advise us. He helped us out on renderings and drawings. He decided to draw the whole thing with pen and ink. In those days—before you had pens that were self-loading—you had to actually put a nib in the pen and dip it into a bottle of ink and draw like that. So it was really something.

I think there was a two- or three-month period between the time the competition was announced and the program was available to be picked up and the deadline. Anyway, it wasn't too long a time. The contest criteria called for a non-specific, conceptual design. Site sections were provided, but they didn't even say how many thousand square feet the various buildings had to be. It was pretty general.

Arthur Erickson's firm won the competition, and we were lucky enough to win second prize. Zoltan Kiss was third, Bob Harrison was fourth, and Duncan McNab was fifth. So those were the five guys. We thought, gee, if we just get in the top five, we're doing okay! And so we were ecstatic! It was great!

Sure, we were second, but second is very close to being first! But it's also like losing the Kentucky Derby by a nose! Still, we were delighted to be there and we thought, well, we can certainly build on this opportunity, starting with the SFU Science Complex. ■

Rand Iredale and Zoltan Kiss flank their winning submissions in the Simon Fraser University 'contest of ideas' (1963)

Project: The Science Complex

The Science Complex is a major element in the total university concept. Based on a spine and tributary arrangement of circulation and services, three buildings—physics, chemistry, and biology—are joined by glazed bridges that also serve as student lounges and study areas. The complex was constructed in three phases and each successive stage 'cascades' from the top of the mountain. ■

Project Team

Partners in Charge:
Rand Iredale & Bill Rhone

Project Architects
Andrew Ross & Alan Scott

Structural Engineers
Bogue Babicki & Associates

Awards

Massey Medal for Architecture (1967)

Architectural Institute of British Columbia Award of Merit (1966)

Publications

Canadian University Magazine
(May / June 1967)

Architecture Canada
(October 1966)

Also, see Gene Waddell Manuscript titled, "The Design for Simon Fraser University and the Problems Accompanying Excellence," prepared for the Canadian Centre for Architecture (1998)

Adjacent & Below:
Exterior views of the SFU Science Complex

Overleaf:
Interior view of the Science Complex Theatre

Photos:
William Dekur, North Vancouver

A 'School' for Architects

From an interview with Bill Rhone.

Rhone & Iredale was a great 'school' for young architects, as it turns out, though I didn't see myself as a mentor. I was just a guy doing interesting stuff. But we attracted good people and the kind of people we liked were people who would argue with us. Like, in some firms, absolutely not, you did not argue!

'There's the front office, and there's the boardroom, and there's the back office,' and decisions are all made in the boardroom and the decisions are sent out and nobody questions anything, because it's all run in a hierarchical, military way where people do not question the orders. Their job is to follow orders.

Well, we didn't do things that way.

A Highly Spirited Firm

We used to have very interesting sessions and discussions, and we'd put all of the projects up on the board, and we'd all sit around and we'd pick them apart and have arguments in those sessions, on the basis of a bunch of very interesting equals talking about the project. And it fostered a great spirit within the firm.

It was quite remarkable that we got critical feedback from our staff. Sometimes it affected the direction the project went in and sometimes it reinforced the direction that was already established. Rand was a major part of those sessions. He really loved that kind of milieu.

I must admit, it was a very exciting time. I wasn't the most successful participant because after a short time I didn't want to talk anymore, I wanted to draw! But that type of operation fostered a kind of intellectual-architectural ferment that was going on in the office, looking at new ideas in new ways, and so on. And that had a great deal to do with the spirit of the firm and we were a highly spirited firm at that time.

Coming of Age

So, it was in this environment that we came second in the SFU competition. We thought we would get just one building, but we got five buildings. That was great! We did pretty well out of the Science Complex, and those buildings were a collaboration. It was a real meeting of the minds, but Rand played a major role. I have to give credit to Rand on those lecture theatres. They were really quite nicely done. He devoted a lot of energy to them and it was really great.

Continued

Bill Rhone

Out of that opportunity we were growing very well as a firm, as a practice, as architects. With the university buildings you have to spend more time on detailing, and the longevity of the building becomes an issue. So you get into all kinds of new areas. You can use and explore better materials and you can talk to other people who are designing university buildings and developing better ways, and the technology of the building comes more to the front.

When we first got started on the Science Complex we were more enthused about design and image and all of this kind of stuff. But the university buildings had kind of a maturing effect on both of us, because we thought about the building's longevity and how it's really going to mold perceptions and how people are going to use this building for decades to come, and this kind of stuff. So we were thinking more long-term.

It was part of our coming of age in practice.

A Rather Elegant Structural Solution

Bogue Babicki did the Simon Fraser University buildings for us. He has a most interesting mind and a whole range of interesting ideas. The first job he did with us was a series of dressing rooms. There was some nice concrete work, a truss system with openings expressed around the perimeter of the building and the roof. They weren't big buildings, but it was a rather elegant structural solution, and that's why we were attracted to Bogue. ∎

A New Structural System

From an essay written by Bogue Babicki.

The competition to design Simon Fraser University provided my office with an opportunity to collaborate on a project that was the largest and most spectacular undertaking in British Columbia at that time. I was invited by Rhone & Iredale to be part of a team working on the design competition for this project. Our team was awarded the design of the Science Complex, which was built in four stages throughout the 1960s and 1970s.

The structural system of poured-in-place, post-tensioned concrete and pre-cast, pre-stressed concrete beams was used to minimize the depth of the large-span beams of the laboratory and classroom buildings. This structural system—especially the poured-in-place, post-tensioned system—was new in Vancouver at that time. ∎

Reprinted from the Internet (SFU Archives, 2006)

SFU Archives

W. Randle Iredale is one of the contributors to the architecture of Simon Fraser University. He and his partner, William R. Rhone, were responsible for designing and building the Science Complex according to design specifications outlined by Erickson and Massey (the architects responsible for the overall design of the university). Rhone and Iredale built the Science Complex in three phases based on preliminary drawings by Erickson and Massey, but added their own ideas and innovations to the building.

In 1963 Rhone and Iredale submitted an entry to the contest to design the new university that would be built on top of Burnaby Mountain. Their design finished in second place. The top five winners were each contracted to build a section of the campus according to the winner's overall design. Originally, Rhone and Iredale chose the Academic Quadrangle, but changed their minds and picked the Science Complex, which Chancellor Shrum had assured them would be expanded on a regular basis. The Science Complex was built in three phases: Phase I was substantially completed by August 1, 1965, Phase II was completed September 7, 1966 and Phase III was completed in 1971. Rhone and Iredale also designed and built several other SFU facilities (see opposite page).[1]

The files of W. Randle Iredale—publicity records, photographs, negatives, and slides—were donated to the SFU Archives in 1999, as follows:

Date Range	File Title
1964–1970	SFU Publicity
1965	Photo Album – SFU Science Complex – Phase 1
1965	Negatives – SFU Science Complex – Phase 1
1966	SFU Science Complex – Phase III Concept Presentation
1966	SFU Science Complex – Phase III Design Presentation
1966	SFU Science Complex – Phase III Lecture Theatre
1967	SFU Science Complex – Phase III Working Drawings
1967	Burnaby Mountain System Control Centre, BC Hydro, vol. 2
1970	SFU Centre No. I Pre-Design Study
1970	SFU Centre No. 1 Programme Report
1970	SFU Centre No. 1 Programme Amendment A
1978	SFU Physical Plant Building
No date	SFU photographs and reprints
No date	Slides – Central service, centre #1, Science Complex, pub
No date	SFU photographs (paper copies)

The Architectural Drawings (as bound reports) were added by the Archivist in 2006.[2]

---

1 Source: BC Archival Information Network at http://aabc.bc.ca/www.aabc.archbc/display.SFU-122 (2006).

2 Source: www.sfu.ca/archives (2006).

Reprinted from the Internet (SFU Archives, 2006)

SFU Building Chronology

Date[1]	Building	Architect
1965/67	Academic Quadrangle	Zoltan S. Kiss
1965	BC Hydro Building	**Rhone & Iredale**
1965/76	Chancellor's Gymnasium	Duncan S. McNab & Associates
1965	Convocation Mall	Erickson Massey
1965/70/72	East Campus Trailers	-
1965/94	Fire Pump House	Erickson Massey
1965/76	Library	Robert F. Harrison
1965	Madge Hogarth Residence	Erickson Massey
1965	SFU Theatre	Duncan S. McNab & Associates
1965	Shrum Science Centre	**Rhone & Iredale**
1965	Terry Fox Field	Erickson Massey
1965	Transportation Centre	Erickson Massey
1966	President's Residence	Zoltan S. Kiss
1967	Shell House Residence	Zoltan S. Kiss
1969	Louis Riel Residence	Erickson Massey
1970/78	R.C. Brown Hall	**Rhone & Iredale** / Erickson Massey
1971/82/90	Greenhouses	Lord & Burnham
1971	Strand Hall	Robert F. Harrison
1972/90	Facilities Management	**Rhone & Iredale**
1973/96	Maggie Benston Centre	**Rhone & Iredale** / Aitken Wreglesworth
1977	Animal Care Unit	Ronald Howard
1977/95	Day Care Centre	Bruno Freschi
1978/83	Education Building	Downs Archambault
1982	Bee Research Building	**Rhone & Iredale**
1982	Diamond University Club	R. Yoneda Associates
1985	McTaggart-Cowan Hall Res.	Howard / Yano
1989	Applied Sciences Building	Waisman Dewar Grout Carter
1989	Halpern Centre	Dalla-Lonal / Griffin
1991	East Academic Annex	Howard / Yano
1991	Shrum Classroom Building	Thompson Berwick Pratt
1992	South Science Building	Thompson Berwick Pratt
1993	10 Student Residences	Matsuzaki Wright
1994	Alcan Aquatic Building	Busby Bridger
1994	Science Research Annex	Pentland Management Court
1994	West Mall Centre	Aitken Wreglesworth / Arthur Erickson

---

1 Dates include expansions. Source: www.sfu.ca/mediapr/test9/campus/ca_chrono.html (2006).

Ian McHarg describes his book, *Design With Nature*,[1] as "a personal testament to the power of sun, moon, and stars, the changing seasons, seedtime and harvest, clouds, rain and rivers, the oceans and the forests, the creatures and the herbs. They are with us now, co-tenants of the phenomenal universe, participating in that timeless yearning that is evolution, vivid expressions of time past, essential partners in survival and with us now involved in the creation of the future.

"Our eyes do not divide us from the world, but unite us with it. Let this be known to be true. Let us then abandon the simplicity of separation and give unity its due. Let us abandon the self mutilation which has been our way and give expression to the potential harmony of man-nature. The world is abundant, we require only a deference born of understanding to fulfill man's promise. Man is that uniquely conscious creature who can perceive and express. He must become the steward of the biosphere. … He must design with nature." ∎

---

1   Ian McHarg, *Design with Nature* (NY: Doubleday / Natural History Press, 1971).

Source of Quote: Internet (2006).

Photo: Jack Lindsay, Vancouver

SITE ANALYSIS

The term 'site' is taken in its widest sense, as the complete context in which we are designing. At the broadest, it considers the culture in which we build; at the finest, the micro-climate and texture of soils.

In between are all of the factors impinging on the site, including its history and its connections to the surrounding world, including water courses, transportation, views, and regulations affecting use of the site. Obviously, much of this data cannot be recorded but is implied and taken for granted as understandings of the culture common to everyone.

Nevertheless, sifting through the various factors to identify key elements will pay handsome dividends in growing a solution that truly fits the needs of time and place. It is this fit that makes a great work of art resonate. Michelangelo's *David* continues throughout history to convey to us the Renaissance ideal of man founded in the idealized view of ancient Greece.

Great endeavours start with simple actions. In this case the simple action is to order a survey and soils tests for the property!

A book that will really turn you on to the potential of site analysis is *Design with Nature* (1971) by Ian L. McHarg.[1] When we know the earth on which we build, we will understand the motion of the tectonic plates that have made it steep or flat, the fault lines that will grind in earthquakes, and the glacial tilt left from the last ice age. All of this 'data' is present when we stand on the site.

As the poet William Blake put it:

> "To see the earth in a grain of sand
>
> and heaven in a wild flower,
>
> to hold infinity in the palm of your hand,
>
> and eternity in an hour."

Rand Iredale, Project Manager's Manual (1997)

---

1   Ian McHarg studied landscape architecture and city planning at Harvard University after WW II. He is founder and professor emeritus in the Department of Landscape Architecture and Regional Planning at the University of Pennsylvania. In 1960 he hosted his own television show, "The House We Live In," on CBS. His autobiography, *A Quest for Life*, was published in 1996. Source: Internet (2006).

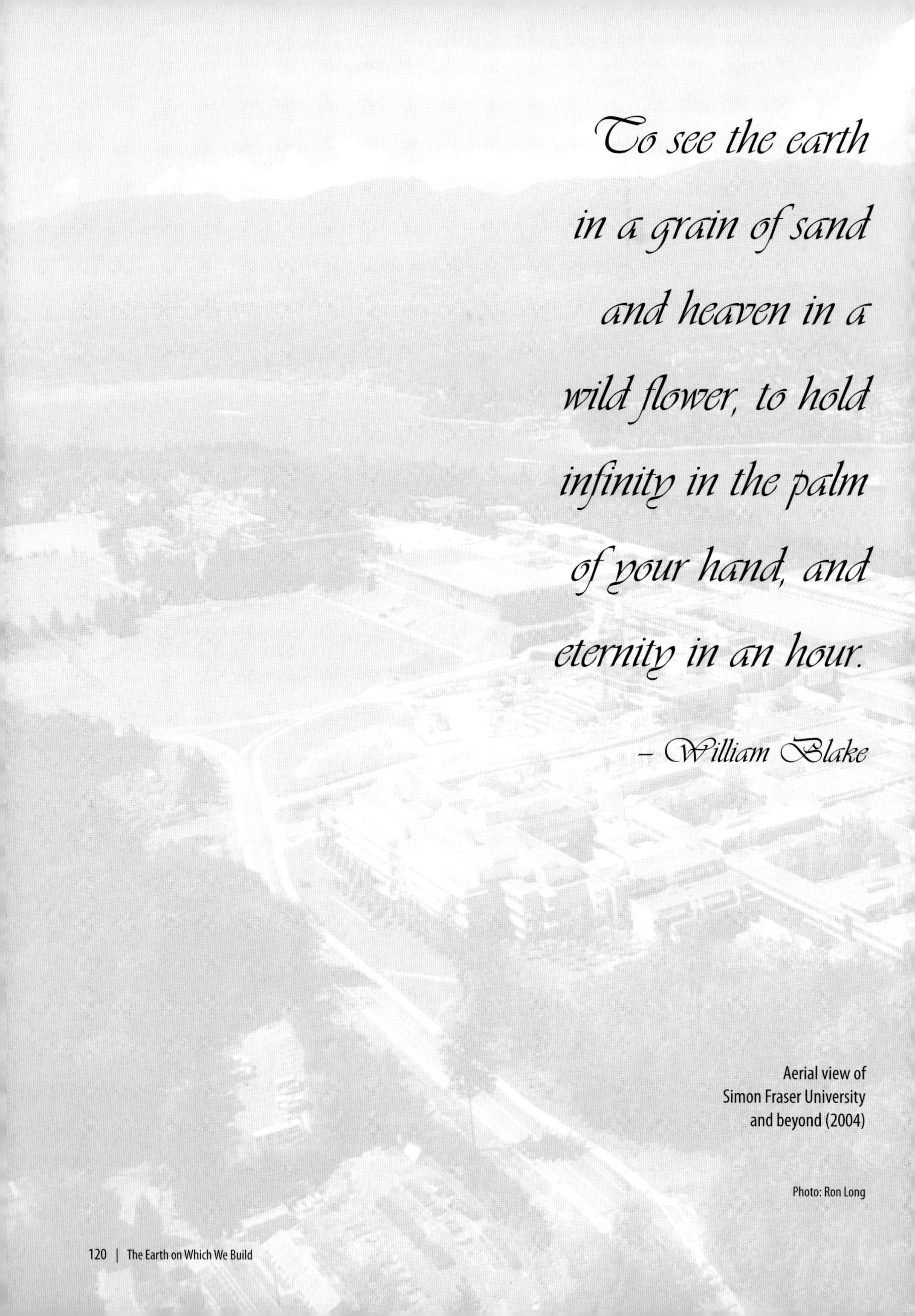

To see the earth in a grain of sand and heaven in a wild flower, to hold infinity in the palm of your hand, and eternity in an hour.

— William Blake

Aerial view of
Simon Fraser University
and beyond (2004)

Photo: Ron Long

6 Generosity of Spirit

Two significant projects designed by Rhone & Iredale in the late 1960s were the Westcoast Transmission Building in Downtown Vancouver and the Sedgewick Undergraduate Library at the University of British Columbia. The Westcoast Transmission Building was structurally suspended around a concrete core and the Sedgewick Undergraduate Library comprised an underground complex of interconnections. These diverse projects, one a vertical monolith 'hung from the sky' and the other a horizontal matrix 'embedded in the earth,' represent ground-breaking and award-winning examples of design excellence.

The Rhone & Iredale office had grown from two fledgling partners in 1960 to a professional practice by the end of the decade with over 300 projects in its portfolio and some 80–90 projects underway at any given time. Some of the top young talents were coming to work with Rand and Bill, people like architects Peter Cardew, Rainer Fassler, and Richard Henriquez, and landscape architect Art Cowie. All would have a hand and a voice in the firm's direction and development.

While completion of the projects at Portage Mountain and Simon Fraser was still underway, the new headquarters for Westcoast Transmission was commissioned in 1967, with Bill Rhone as Partner in Charge, and the new undergraduate Sedgewick Library at UBC was commissioned in 1969, with Rand Iredale as Partner in Charge. Both projects would be recognized as models of innovation and collaboration.

But time does not stand still. Just as the BC Hydro building that once dominated the downtown skyline (recall the view from the Fairview Slopes) was converted to strata offices and apartments and aptly renamed The Electra in 1995, so the 12-storey Westcoast Transmission Building and the two-level Sedgewick Undergraduate Library would be renovated and transformed in the late 1990s. The former is now an exclusive condominium complex called the QUBE and the latter is an unnamed underground extension of UBC's new five-storey Walter C. Koerner Library. ∎

Reprinted from *The Canadian Architect* (1971)

Project: The Westcoast Transmission Building

Designed for the Westcoast Transmission Co. Ltd., a British Columbia based natural gas pipeline company, the Westcoast office building provides approximately 138,000 sq. ft. of commercial office space in twelve office floors (the first office floor is suspended 36 feet above plaza level) and covered parking for 185 cars. Total building area is 156,035 sq. ft., and the construction cost was $5,100,000, including loft office space, plaza deck and landscaping, parking garage and fees.

The building is possibly the first in the world to employ the concept of suspension bridge techniques, where all major stresses are basically resolved into simple tension and compression forces.

Following selection of a site within Vancouver's "Golden Triangle" business district, a project team was organized comprising specialists from the consultants and general contractor. This team was responsible for the analysis of the client's present requirements, construction completion date and projected space requirements to 1975.

This team analysis, together with specialist technology, site requirements, and by-law extracts, established design limits within which the team pursued its investigations. The team's subsequent solution—a suspended structure—solved the problem of a column-free garage, provided open plazas with the magnificent mountain backdrop visible from Georgia Street and produced a structure considered to be more resistant to damage by earthquake shock than conventional columned buildings. . . .

Finishes for the project are designed to show the strength of the structural components and the lightness of the total structure. The structural core is exposed aggregate, allowing the natural texture of the solid concrete core to express compressive strength; hangers are of black aluminum to express tensile strength. The curtain wall is glazed with LHR 140 solar glass—a heat and light reflective glass [that] reflects the surrounding city buildings and mountains in a mosaic pattern. The plaza and main entrance to the building are paved with exposed aggregate panels and are landscaped to soften the concrete walls and provide a pleasant foreground to the harbor and mountain backdrop.[1]

Photos: John Fulker, West Vancouver

1 "Westcoast Building," *The Canadian Architect* (October 1971): 33. Content submitted by Rhone & Iredale.

Generosity of Spirit | 125

"Westcoast Transmission today revealed plans to build [their] company headquarters in downtown Vancouver. Construction of the futuristic office building, at Georgia and Broughton, will begin in May . . . chairman Frank M. McMahon announced.

"The new building—which will house its own energy system using natural gas to provide heat, power and air-conditioning—will be one of the first of its kind in North America to use a core-supported floor suspension system.

"Because of the unique design, the building will appear to 'grow' from a 37-foot-square concrete stem . . . All 12 storeys will hang from the central concrete core on steel cables, or 'hangers' . . . Four high-speed elevators . . . will be located in the core. Entrance to the building will be through an outdoor, terraced plaza . . ."[1] ∎

---

1 "Futuristic Office Building to Use Novel Floor System," *The Vancouver Sun*, March 15, 1968 (author unknown).

Reprinted from *The Vancouver Sun* (Kemble, 1969; Chow, 2004)

The Most Significant Building in Canada Today

Architects Rhone and Iredale are to be complimented not only for the design but for talking their client into trying something new and engineer Bogue Babicki for attempting what has never been done before. ... For the public—it will leave the street level open, which can then be used for anything. When finished in reflective glass it will be compatible with any building that goes up beside it; [it] might even reflect the mountains. ...[1] ■

The Landmark Westcoast Transmission Office Building

Considered by architects to be one of Vancouver's most earthquake-resistant structures because of its unique design [it] will undergo a $20 million redevelopment to convert it into an upscale residential tower. Spurred by the current hot demand for luxury condominium living along the city's Coal Harbour waterfront, building owner Anthem Properties announced Wednesday it plans to replace the office space inside the existing 12-storey facility with 180 state-of-the-art condos.

Anthem president and CEO Eric Carlson said when his Vancouver-based company purchased the Westcoast building ... in 1998, it originally intended to keep it as rental office space. ... [But] "when Westcoast merged with Duke Energy and restructured, we lost our major tenant ... [and] Coal Harbour just isn't a good location for renting premium office space."

Cognizant of the area's attraction as a high-end residential community—in the past year, Coal Harbour condos have been selling at prices ranging from $400,000 to $6 million—Carlson said Anthem decided to transform the location from a drawback into a marketing opportunity. "Just look at the quality of life," Carlson noted. "An area that used to be railway tracks and welding sheds is now seaside bistros and bike paths." Prices are projected in the range of $450 to $600 per square foot, meaning a 1,000-square-foot unit would cost about $600,000. ...

Anthem's decision to maintain the building's exterior was applauded by Vancouver architect Robert Lemon, who is among the founders of a local group dedicated to preserving what it considers B.C.'s modern architectural treasures.

"The hanging pedestal design made it a modern classic from the day construction began," Lemon said. "There are less than half-a-dozen like it around the world. Now the classic is being rejuvenated; the investment in this conversion will keep it modern and vital."[2] ■

---

1   Roger Kemble, "And Now, the Architect as a Reviewer: Westcoast Transmission Building," *The Vancouver Sun*, August 22, 1969: 5A.

2   Wyng Chow, "Unique Office Building Now Condo Project: Westcoast Transmission Building Sits on Prime Coal Harbour Site," *The Vancouver Sun*, February 5, 2004: F1–F2.

"A 12-storey office tower is hung from a central mast. Floors are carried by high-tensile-strength steel cables looped over top of concrete core ... Core was poured from bottom up, steel floors installed from top down. Method is said to have saved 20 per cent in material costs, 40 per cent in erection time. Curtain walls are of heat-rejecting insulating glass."[1] ∎

---

1   James Marston Fitch, *American Building: The Environmental Forces That Shape It* (2nd Edition, 1975).

Above:
The sloped streetscape / site accommodates a multi-level landscaped plaza

Below:
The street-level view—looking across the plaza from West Georgia Street, through the central core—opens to the harbour and mountains beyond

Photos: John Fulker, West Vancouver

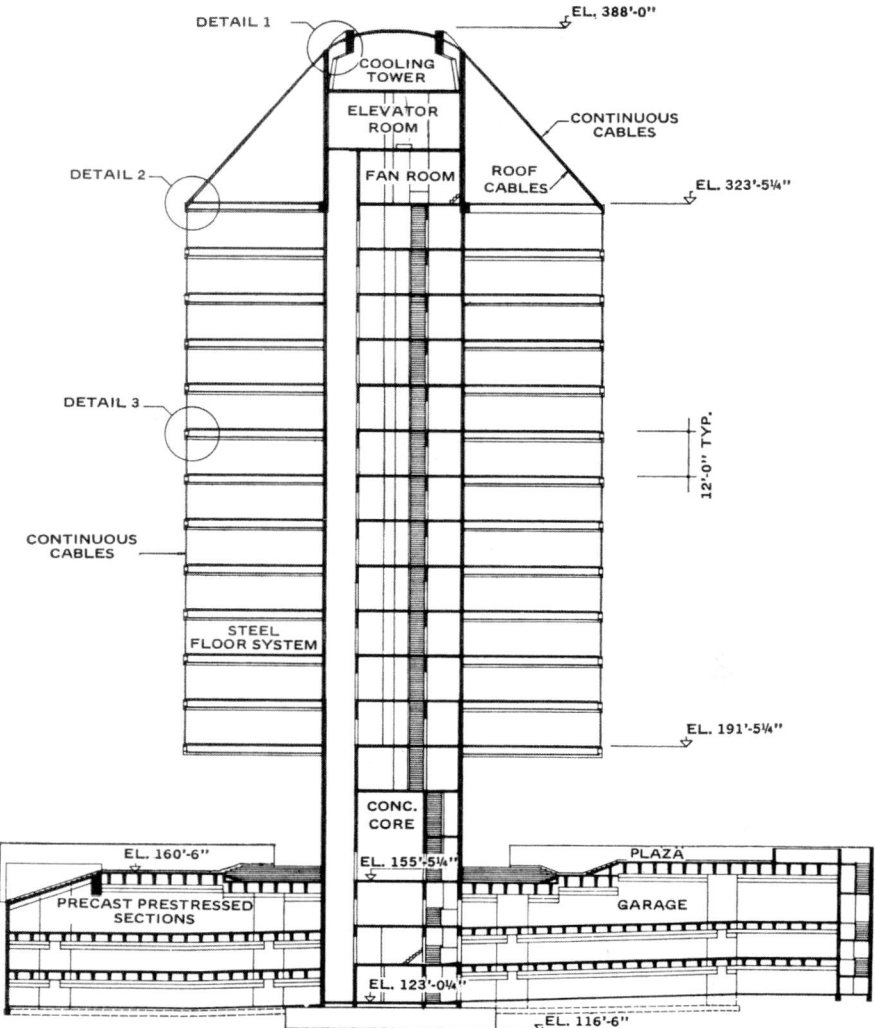

An Interactive Design Process

The design of the Westcoast Transmission Building evolved through an *interactive design process* developed by Rhone & Iredale, which incorporated the input of clients, colleagues, consultants, and other stakeholder groups in the early stages of conceptual design.

Urban design studies revealed the importance of the view across the site to Vancouver's Coal Harbour waterfront. This fact, combined with the optimum floor plan to meet the client's needs (accomplished by the central core) and the real estate analysis indicating that there was no retail market for ground floor space at that location, led to the building's unique structural form and resulted in the open street level plaza. It had a higher ratio of usable floor space than any other building in Vancouver at that time. ∎

Can We Build This?

From an interview with Bill Rhone.

Ross Fitzpatrick, who is now Senator Fitzpatrick, was an executive assistant to Frank McMahon, who was the President of Westcoast Transmission at the time. Ross interviewed about eight architectural firms and he interviewed me and what happened was quite interesting. We had just finished a small office building for Weldwood Canada on their mill site at the foot of Fraser Street. It was designed to last for about five years and then it was going to revert to a warehouse and Weldwood was going to move downtown. But we did a very interesting building, put a big skylight on it, and put a big hole in the centre, with gravel and benches inside. Then the offices within the concrete block wall on the outside looked into this central space. And people loved it. And then there was an executive office wing that poked out.

So I took Ross out to see this building we had just finished and it couldn't have been better timing! We ran into a guide there and I said, "This is Ross Fitzpatrick, and I brought him out to see the building." And this guy said, "This is the greatest building in Vancouver!" I couldn't have written a better script myself! And he went on and on about how he loved the building and how everything worked perfectly. Jeepers creepers, I didn't even know it was this good! And so Ross was really affected by this and, gosh, he said, "You've really got a client who's happy. I think you've got the job!" So that's how we got the Westcoast Transmission Building. We had one satisfied client who we just happened to run into on the site; not the President of Weldwood, but a junior department head who gave us a great recommendation.

I would say that I played a major role in the Westcoast Transmission Building. Rand played a less active role but a crucial one. He was working on other projects but he was very, very interested and made extremely interesting comments and design critiques. And we got Bogue Babicki on board. It was kind of exciting how the thing evolved because—you know, you design an office building, you try things out, you build a team—we had some really good guys. Rainer Fassler was with us, and the chief Project Architect was an Australian guy named Errol Bullpitt, who's since gone back to Australia; Terry Williams, who's still here. So there was Errol and Terry and Rainer and Tao Chang, who has since retired from the federal Department of Public Works.

We put this thing together and it ended up being a square tower. We built scale models of it and it had columns down the outside. A real estate consultant was going to lease out the building, and he told us there was no market for ground floor space in that area

Continued

of town. The typical pattern at that time was to have some shops or a bank on the ground floor and office space above, but he said that "we can't lease anything down there because there's no pedestrian traffic."

And so we all looked at each other and somebody said, "Well, let's start the building three floors up." So we had these long columns around this cardboard model and Bogue came in and we said, "It's too bad we can't get rid of the columns." And Bogue said, "Well, you might be able to. We could hang the building from the top."

I think it was Rainer who reached over and grabbed all the little pieces of balsa wood at the ground level and took them out and asked, "Can we build this?" And Bogue said he would go back to his office and look at it. And that's how the suspended structure came about: a few casual comments and some real estate stuff.

Anyway, it's a bit out of proportion. I wish it wasn't quite so squat and thick. You know, it just needs another four floors to be a more elegant shape. You always like to go back to your buildings and redo them after they're done! But it was a successful building and, from a real estate standpoint, it was 100% leased six months before the construction ended. I like to think that people liked the building and that had something to do with it, but it was also a hot real estate market at the time. ▪

Structural Efficiency

From an essay written by Bogue Babicki.

The Westcoast Transmission Building was designed to maintain views of the ocean and mountains from West Georgia Street and, most important, to minimize the destructive effects of an earthquake.

The vertical reinforced concrete core enclosing the stairs and elevators is used to its full structural capacity, eliminating the need for conventional columns. Because the floors hang on continuous steel cables supported on the rounded top of the central core, the weight of the building acts as a pre-stressing force on the core, improving the building's stability and structural efficiency.

This project provided me with an opportunity to conduct research and physical testing on how the structure would behave in an earthquake—research that subsequently allowed me to complete my Doctorate of Science (D.Sc.). ▪

Open to the Ideas of Others

From an interview with Bogue Babicki.

Bill and Rand did not try to separate themselves on projects; of course, one of them would be in charge, but it didn't exclude the other one from contributing. When we had a design meeting, both of them would be there to provide input.

Rand had a technical and mathematical mind and was more interested in technology than beauty or 'beauty for the sake of beauty.' Bill had a different approach. He was a better illustrator than Rand and produced beautiful drawings. They complemented each other: Rand was more science oriented, and Bill was more of an artist.

There was a very responsive attitude in the office, especially in Rand. He was waiting for ideas. He was producing ideas himself but, at the same time, he was open to the ideas of others. And this is how his personality was different from many other architects. ▪

A Powerful & Innovative Idea

From an interview with Rainer Fassler.

When I first came to Rhone & Iredale one of the more significant projects they were working on was the Westcoast Transmission Building. It was actually one of Bill Rhone's projects but, of course, every project was also the firm's project and the design was challenged by everyone in the office. There were some intense discussions!

The design revolved around a powerful and innovative idea that started with a simple structural notion and culminated in a concert of structure, architecture, and urban design. It was a real team effort.

A Height Restriction

The client was faced with a height limit for the building; it could only go so high and his office was to be located on the top floor. No architectural concept was yet in place, and those early discussions involved how to gain more height (these early discussions took place a bit before my time).

At the same time, driving down West Georgia Street, there is that wonderful view of the North Shore. And, so, ultimately, a proposition was put forward: We could preserve the view at street level if the City would allow us to build a little bit higher.

Well, asked the City, "How would you do it?"

A Design Solution

There was a structural way of accomplishing this feat. We could actually design a building that was totally free at ground level, apart from the elevator core, and the City could have its public views and the client could have a higher building with greater views and greater prominence.

And, so, a great part of the story of the Westcoast Transmission Building is that it was driven, not by a singular notion of structural or architectural ingenuity, but by bigger issues: by the collaboration of city, client, and design team; and of urban planning, downtown setting, and public perception.

Slowly, it all came together. The construction was incredibly exciting because the building was basically built upside-down. Of course, we all bemoaned the fact that, aesthetically, it should have been higher. It always felt a bit stubby, but those were the limits of zoning at the time. ■

Tao Chang, Rainer Fassler, and Errol Bullpitt

Project Team

Rhone & Iredale Architects
William Rhone, Partner in Charge
Randle Iredale, Consulting Partner
Errol Bullpitt, Project Architect / Job Captain

Structural Engineer
Bogue Babicki and Associates

Mechanical & Electrical Engineers
Phillips, Barratt, Hillier, Jones & Partners

Landscape Architect
Canadian Environmental Sciences Ltd.

General Contractor
Dillingham Corporation Canada Ltd.

Awards

American Iron and Steel Institute, Design Award in Best Engineering High Rise Construction, 1971
Canadian Consulting Engineering Award of Excellence, 1971

Publications

Roger Montgomery, "Skyhook Tower: Mirrored prism on the Vancouver skyline is a sure blend of several disciplines," *The Architectural Forum* (May 1972)

"Westcoast Building: Vancouver" in *The Canadian Architect* (October 1971)

"Cable-Hung Building Needs Only One Column" in *Engineering News-Record* (June 1969)

Generosity of Spirit | 133

Reprinted from *The Architectural Forum* (Montgomery, 1972)

Skyhook Tower

Mirrored prism on the Vancouver skyline is a sure blend of several disciplines.

Technical innovation, responsible urban design, and sure handling of architectural detail seldom come packaged together. When they do it is always worth paying attention. This explains taking a close look at the mirrored glass box Rhone & Iredale have hung in the Vancouver sky for Westcoast Transmission, a Canadian gas pipeline company.

Several factors converged during the early stages of the project to favor the extraordinary tension structure used for the building. Everyone had become sensitive to walling off the central area of the city from its magnificent visual setting of sparkling bay waters and forested mountains. A building which would not block views from Georgia Street, the main drag downtown, would score high points for environmental responsibility. But this point may stand out more clearly in an observer's hindsight than perhaps it did in the minds of the owner and the architects during preliminary design. Other factors determined the decision.

Economic consultants for this project told the designers and their clients that the first three floors would not produce office rents comparable to those from higher floors. Neither would such space find a strong market from prospective retail business. The site lies too far from the city's shopping core, and pedestrian flows past this corner are too small. A feasibility analysis set the stage for a design without any enclosed floorspace except the core below the third floor.

Programming and site studies of various alternatives, along with the cost analyses, suggested twelve office floors of 10,000-plus square feet gross, laid out symmetrically about a central, vertical core. The final plan, a grid of perfect squares, has 36-foot-square steel-framed bays ranged around the 36-foot-square concrete core. The architects and their engineer, Bogue Babicki, also of Vancouver, obviously had been thinking for some time about hanging a steel frame office building from cables slung over the top of a slipformed concrete core. Such a clear generic idea demanded to be built.

They felt it offered structural and constructural advantages that would offset the costs of its pioneering novelty. They were right—its final cost was comparable to others in the area. Among the advantages, the core resolves horizontal and dynamic earthquake forces efficiently because the hanging weight of the twelve-story steel box compresses (or prestresses) the core enough to resist buckling. This was important because the city lies in a seismic danger zone.

In developing their design, Rhone & Iredale have handled the idea expressively yet with a nice restraint. They have produced a good-looking building that neatly tells the story of its structural system. From the outside it could not be clearer. A slender concrete tube, visible both top and bottom, holds up the office space volume and, at the same time, obviously contains the vertical services. Taut black tension members spring diagonally downward from its top to carry a nearly weightless-looking mirrored prism. The top of

Reprinted from *The Architectural Forum* (Montgomery, 1972)

the core is rounded to spread the load from the cables. Expressive fittings mark their point of springing. Fireproofing and a black metal cover substantially increase the visual weight of these tension members. At the bottom they hang down just a bit below the mirrored curtainwall; to my eye they should have been left another foot longer.

Inside and close-up its architectonic qualities read nearly as well. This seems a considerable achievement given our late Twentieth Century predilections for such visually homogenizing demands as totally controlled working environments and office spaces smoothly adapting to any organizational changes. To enter the building from the street the visitor walks into the one small hole in the bottom of the core. This puts him in a necessarily tiny lobby; as it is within the core it cannot be larger than the elevator landings on the office floors above. The skimpy dimensions here represent one of the costs of achieving formal clarity with this scheme.

From the lobby the visitor enters a hot orange elevator cab to ascend to the office floors. There he emerges again into the confined area of the core (see above). A distinct portal marks the passage from the elevator landing to the office areas. These, totally columnless

Photos, above & overleaf:
John Fulker, West Vancouver

"Technical innovation, responsible urban design, and sure handling of architectural detail seldom come packaged together. When they do it is always worth paying attention . . . [and] taking a close look at the mirrored glass box Rhone & Iredale have hung in the Vancouver sky for Westcoast Transmission."[1]

---

1   Roger Montgomery, "Skyhook Tower," *The Architectural Forum* (May 1972): 36.

and panoramically open to Vancouver's scenic splendors, offer a welcome contrast to the tight core space. In detailing, the architects have enhanced the contrast. While it was still green they had the concrete of the core-tube wire-brushed to expose the aggregate. This heightened the sense of structural strength and space containment within.

Given the small size of the floors, an office landscape approach to their layout and furnishing would have further strengthened the tension between the tough concrete supporting core and the light work areas open to the far-off mountains. This explains why in this building, as in most headquarters office buildings, the executive floors come off best spatially: their openness and lack of clutter gives the architectural design a chance to show through. Does this mean that careful attention to architectonic matters has little or no place in the design of ordinary office space?

Viewed as urban design Rhone & Iredale's building displays some other positive qualities that flow from its constructional idea. For instance, it adds a distinctive silhouette to the Vancouver skyline without looking the least bit "googie." Like other megamirrors it moves throughout the day reflecting every change in light and clouds. Built as it is, it comes out looking even more reflective than if it were conventionally framed. Hung mirrors really look diaphanous.

From the ground level on Georgia Street no one can miss the openness below the main volume. Someday when it is walled in by other structures, as it surely will be, the effect should prove spectacular. At the moment it occupies a position sufficiently away from the actual heart of the city that only parking lots and low, nondescript older buildings surround it. This diminishes the impact of the missing bottom stories.

The plaza created by the absence of these enclosed areas poses a few problems. The site slopes sharply, necessitating steps down into, or up onto the space. These get pretty complicated at the principal corner where the steps first go up quite a long way only to go down a bit before finally getting to the plaza. Ideally the back corner should have provided a fine viewpoint from which to overlook the scenery. But no clear path pulls strongly on the passerby; and, once there, he finds a micro-scale pollution problem. The "total energy package," which makes the climate for the building by using WTC natural gas, exhausts its fumes at plaza level. Too bad. Underneath, another of the benefits of the hung structure becomes apparent: it permits a column-free, three-story garage.

The appearance of imitators testifies to the intrinsic value of Rhone & Iredale's work. They have made a handsome and sensible architecture, at the same time that they and Babicki have realized a very intriguing structure. It makes a worthy addition to the small but growing list of fine buildings in downtown Vancouver.[1] ∎

---

1   Roger Montgomery, "Skyhook Tower: Mirrored Prism on the Vancouver Skyline is a Sure Blend of Several Disciplines," *The Architectural Forum* (May 1972): 36–39. At the time of writing, Roger Montgomery was Professor of Urban Design at the University of California, Berkeley, and a member of the Forum's Board of Contributors.

Below, left:
Vancouver's skyline with the new Westcoast Transmission Building, as viewed from Stanley Park (circa 1972)

Below, right:
The view from downtown, facing northwest, toward the mountains

Photos, below & opposite:
John Fulker, West Vancouver

Generosity of Spirit | 139

The adjacent photos were submitted for inclusion in the awards booklet, *Design in Steel 1971*, published by the American Iron and Steel Institute. The entry, titled "Starting at the Top," is for the Westcoast Transmission team's 'Design Award in Best Engineering High Rise Construction 1971.'

Bogue Babicki, Consultant
Structural Engineer

William Rhone, Architect
Partner in Charge

Randle Iredale, Architect
Consulting Partner

DESIGN EXCELLENCE

It is sometimes argued that design is, by its nature, a creative process not suitable for a disciplined and orderly approach.

Certainly, no amount of organization will ever replace the creative insight that leads to brilliant solutions. But an orderly process has proven effective in supporting the design of award-winning projects.

By listening carefully to our clients' needs and by working together at all stages of the design process, we succeed in finding imaginative solutions to our clients' building needs and we achieve design excellence.

To us, achieving design excellence means providing aesthetic quality, well-considered utility, and technical soundness, while simultaneously meeting all budget and time constraints.

Rand Iredale, Project Manager's Manual (1997)

> By listening carefully to our clients' needs and by working together at all stages of the design process, we succeed in finding imaginative solutions to our clients' building needs and we achieve design excellence.

Project: The Sedgewick Undergraduate Library

The jurors of the The Canadian Architect Yearbook 1970 Award of Excellence commented on the new undergraduate library at UBC: [1]

> "Possibly the most interesting and prescient of all the projects submitted. The difficult problem of infill is handled with imagination and sensitivity. Many projects and problems could benefit from the lesson of this solution—beyond that it needs little comment." *(Juror James A. Murray, FRAIC, MTPIC)*

> "A most impressive solution to a very complex problem. The very simple structure of the building totally integrated with the landscaping produced the least possible interference with existing buildings or surroundings and yet improves the function of each. This is a very superb example of architectural ingenuity and humility." *(Juror Professor Douglas Shadbolt, FRAIC)*

> "The most sophisticated of several entries of this nature, the scheme provides, in addition to the required library, lecture rooms, etc., an imaginative linkage between buildings on the campus while preserving elements of the existing landscape. A most sensitive development of the non-building prototype." *(Juror Douglas C. Rowland, FRAIC, P.Eng.)*

Photos

Below:
John Roaf, Vancouver

Overleaf:
Selwyn Pullan, North Vancouver

1   The text on these two pages is adapted from the Rhone & Iredale texts published in *The Canadian Architect Yearbook 1970* and submitted to the RAIC Festival of Architecture Awards Program.

The program called for a new undergraduate library and general university space for study, lectures, seminars, and lounges. A concept was developed to integrate the required accommodation with a matrix circulation system that would link the major campus buildings. The $3.8 million, 113,000 sq. ft. complex includes the library and a part of the matrix on two levels.

The upper level combines the matrix (circulation, lounge, study rooms) and library facilities (catalogue and reference areas, periodicals, offices); the lower level consists of library stacks in the centre with reading areas on both sides that look out onto the landscaped courtyards. The pin oak trees on the Main Mall were considered by the university community to be extremely precious, and they were preserved by encasing them in eight large drums.

"The expression of the building seeks to mold itself with surrounding earth banks and landscaping. Sloped planter boxes cascade down from the upper level into enclosed courtyards."

The design team, comprising consultants, librarians, and students, identified characteristic environments for study, which were thus provided while also maintaining an intimate and non-institutional environment. An extensive sunken garden between Sedgewick Library and the original Main Library provides outlook and sunlight to this innovative facility.

The project received considerable press coverage and several design awards, and was featured in at least nine architectural and landscape design articles published in Canada, the United States, Britain, Germany, and Japan. One journalist aptly describes the library's "quiet horizontality and almost non-existence … [as] it snuggles below ground level" (reference unknown). ∎

A Great Deal of Weeping & Wailing

From an interview with Bill Rhone.

UBC was considering Rhone & Iredale for a new administration building on campus. They showed us this rather grey-looking, heavy concrete building they had built, and we were not too thrilled!

There was another architectural firm getting a project at the same time—Toby Russell Buckwell Partners (TRBP), who were going to do an extension on the back end of the existing library—and what transpired is that Rand and I expressed dismay at doing an office building that was just plunked down on campus. TRBP said they'd rather do the office building and we were a little more turned on with doing the library.

So they took the office building and we took the library. Originally it was going to be an addition to the Main Library. The idea was to build an undergraduate library where students could come in and study. There was quite an interesting young librarian there [Basil Stuart-Stubbs], and as the program developed we got excited by his ideas and we realized very early on that tacking an extension onto the existing library was the wrong approach.

And so a site study was done, which was quite interesting. Rand was instrumental in getting the site study done, and it turned out that the best place for the library was smack-dab in the middle of the Main Mall, where people walked to classes. There was a great deal of weeping and wailing by the powers that be, but that was definitely the place to put it. It ended up being below ground to preserve the view down the Main Mall. That's how it evolved, and it was very successful and it sure got used.

Rand was very skillful at meetings and agendas and dealing with faculty, and he liked that phase of the work tremendously. He played a major role in the development of that location and how the whole thing worked out. ∎

A Whole Lot of Gyrating Around

From an interview with Rainer Fassler.

Richard Henriquez was working on the site studies regarding what to do with the library, and it took a whole lot of gyrating around that university precinct to present the courageous notion of locating it underground! ∎

Project Team

Rhone & Iredale Architects
Partner in Charge: Randle Iredale
Project Manager: Robert Todd
Project Planner: Richard Henriquez
Project Detail & Interiors: Ke-liang Chang & Andrew Nothiger

Structural Engineer: C.Y. Loh / Canadian Environmental Sciences (CES)
Mechanical Engineer: John Campbell / D. W. Thomson Consultants Ltd.
Electrical Engineer: S. Mahanti / D.W. Thomson Consultants Ltd.

Landscape Architect: Art Cowie / Canadian Environmental Sciences (CES)
Illumination & Acoustics: Bolt Beranek & Newman Inc.

Awards

AIBC Festival of Architecture Award of Honour, 1980
Royal Architectural Institute of Canada Award, 1974
The Canadian Architect Yearbook Award of Excellence, 1970

Publications

Process Architecture, Japan (February 1978)
Landscape Design, Britain (February 1978)
Landscape Design, Britain (August 1978)
PCItems (PreStressed Concrete Institute), USA (April 1978)
The Architectural Review, Britain (August 1976)
Progressive Architecture, USA (March 1973)
Baumeister, Germany (October 1973)
Architecture and Urbanism, Japan (1973)
The Canadian Architect (April 1973)

UBC Archives

The Rhone & Iredale collection (1969–1983) was transferred by Sedgewick Library to the University Archives in 1988. It includes original manuscript drawings, construction plans from the various contractors, proposals for alterations, and contractors' plans for alterations.

Site Plan
Sedgewick Library

Drawing prepared by
Rhone & Iredale

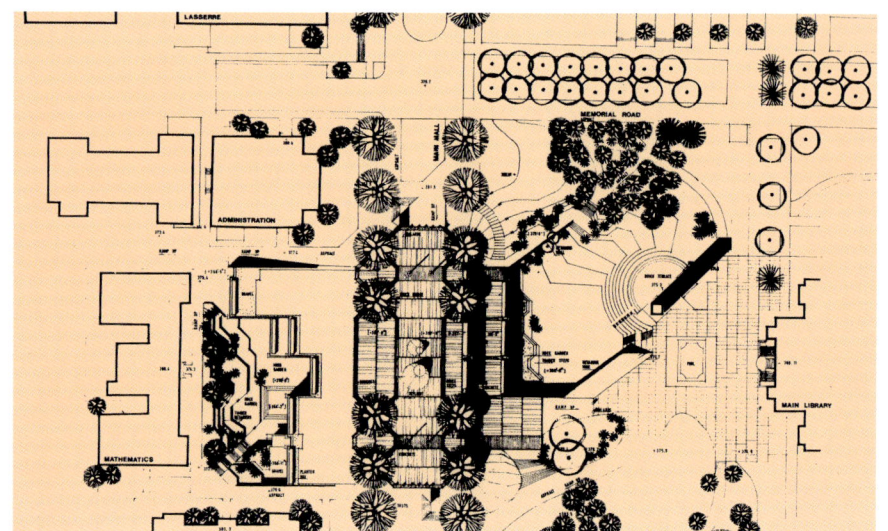

Elevations
Sedgewick Library

Drawing prepared by
Rhone & Iredale

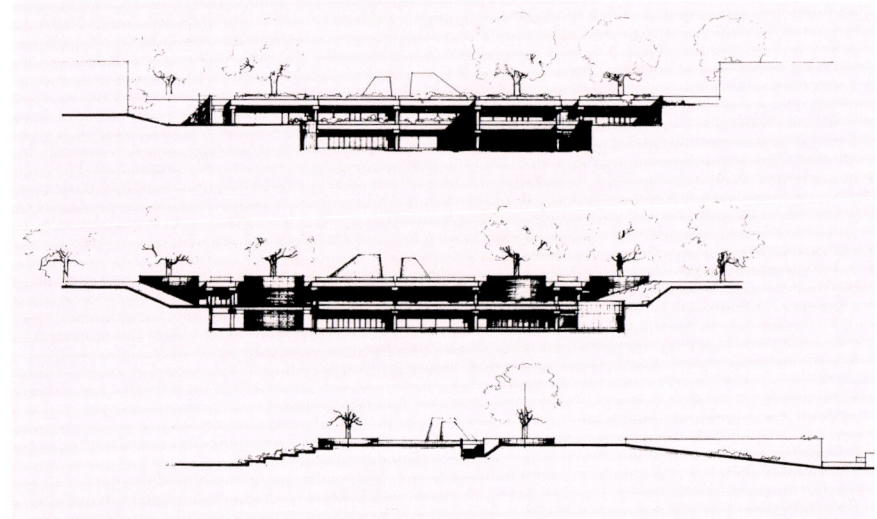

Desire Lines
Sedgewick Library

Drawing prepared for
Rhone & Iredale by Toby Russell
Buckwell Partners Architects

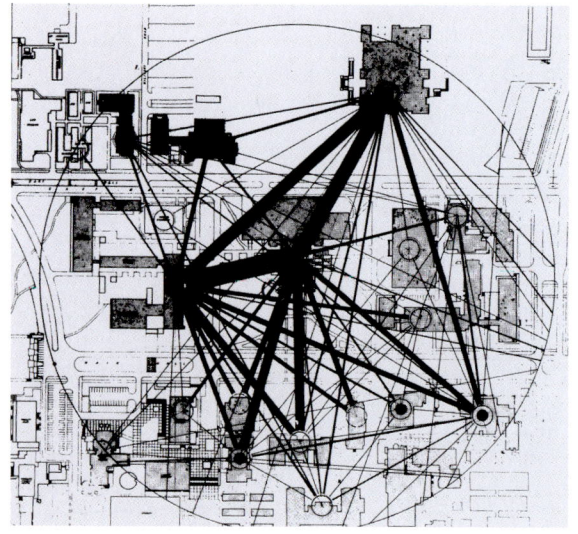

The adjacent site / space plan marks out students' intuitive and intentional pathways across campus, creating a map of what landscape architects call desire lines or the pathways of desire.[1]

---

1 Desire lines are discussed in the classic text by Christopher Alexander, et al., *A Pattern Language: Towns, Buildings, Construction* (NY: Oxford University Press, 1977).

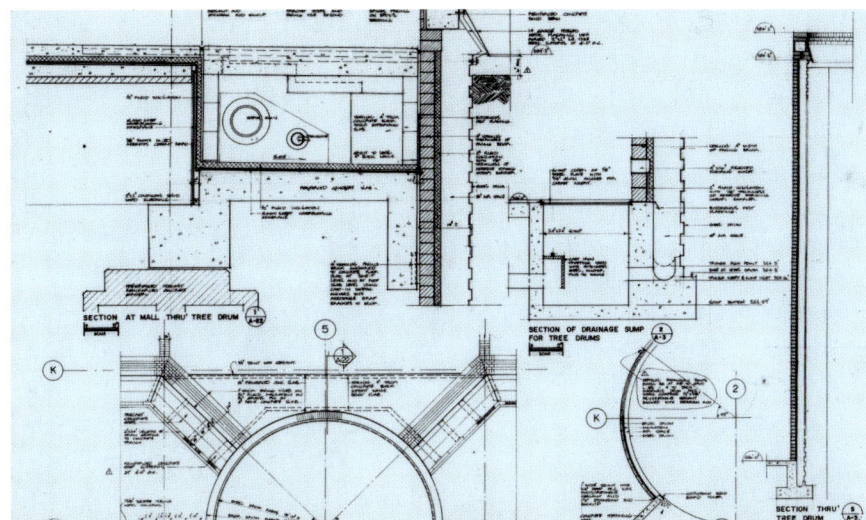

Tree Drum Details
Sedgewick Library

Drawing prepared by
Rhone & Iredale

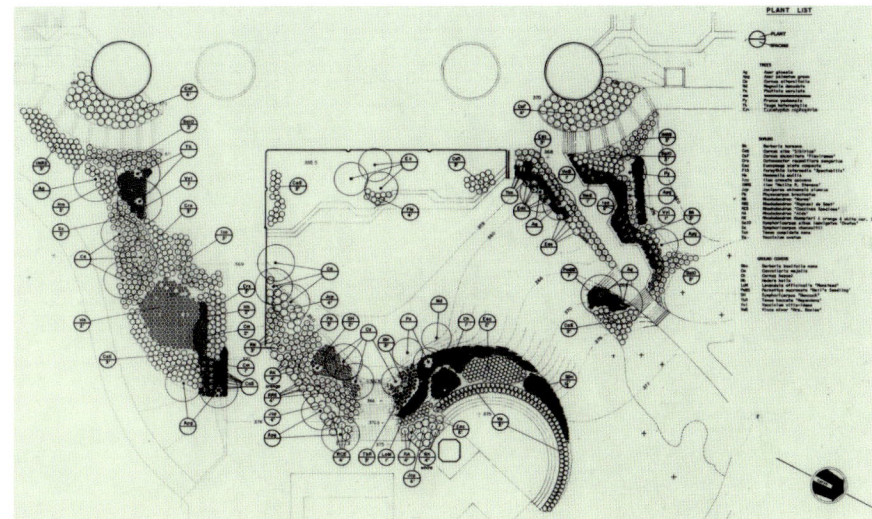

Planting
ground level – east
Sedgewick Library

Drawing prepared for Rhone & Iredale
by Canadian Environmental Sciences

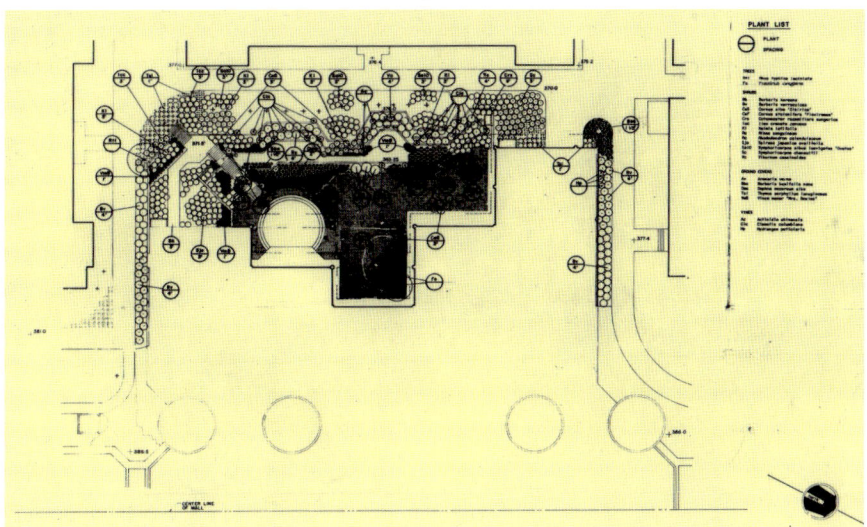

Planting
ground level – west
Sedgewick Library

Drawing prepared for Rhone & Iredale
by Canadian Environmental Sciences

SPACE PLANNING

The grouping of spaces for planning purposes is a critical step in the design process. The first step in developing a Relationship Diagram is the grouping of like spaces to reduce the elements to be considered. There is a strong tendency among designers to skip the Relationship Diagram in the design process. Two reasons are apparent: first, a desire to do it by planning the real building on the site and, second, a fear that the ideal relationships set out in the diagram cannot be accomplished on the site.

The problem with planning the real building on the site is that the ideal relationship is never determined; it is lost in the complexity of coping with site constraints and all of the other factors that give form to the building. Fear that the ideal relationship cannot be accomplished is well founded; however, the diagram at least tells us where we have had to compromise and, in many cases, leads to a synthesis that resolves the conflict between ideal relationship and real site constraints. A carefully considered and simple diagram at this stage will give direction to the emerging design. It is in these early stages that the concept design for the building begins to emerge. Have faith and keep an open mind.

It was at this stage that a key concept for the award-winning UBC Sedgewick Library became apparent. The Facilities Program called for a new 120,000 sq. ft. undergraduate library with 200,000 volumes. Why, we asked, do you need a new undergraduate library when there is already a 2,000,000 volume main library? Because we need a new central library for undergraduates where they can find 95% of the books they use in a building that, by its plan, will show them how to find the information they are looking for.

Our Relationship Diagram then became a diagram of how to research a subject to arrive at the books that have the information needed: from the entry, where library staff offer assistance to the student, to the reference library containing the encyclopaedias and digests where the search begins, to the 200,000 volumes arranged to demonstrate the index system. It was through these diagrams that the design team learned how a library works and the librarians saw how the space could be arranged to accomplish the goal of making the building itself teach.

Rand Iredale, Project Manager's Manual (1997)

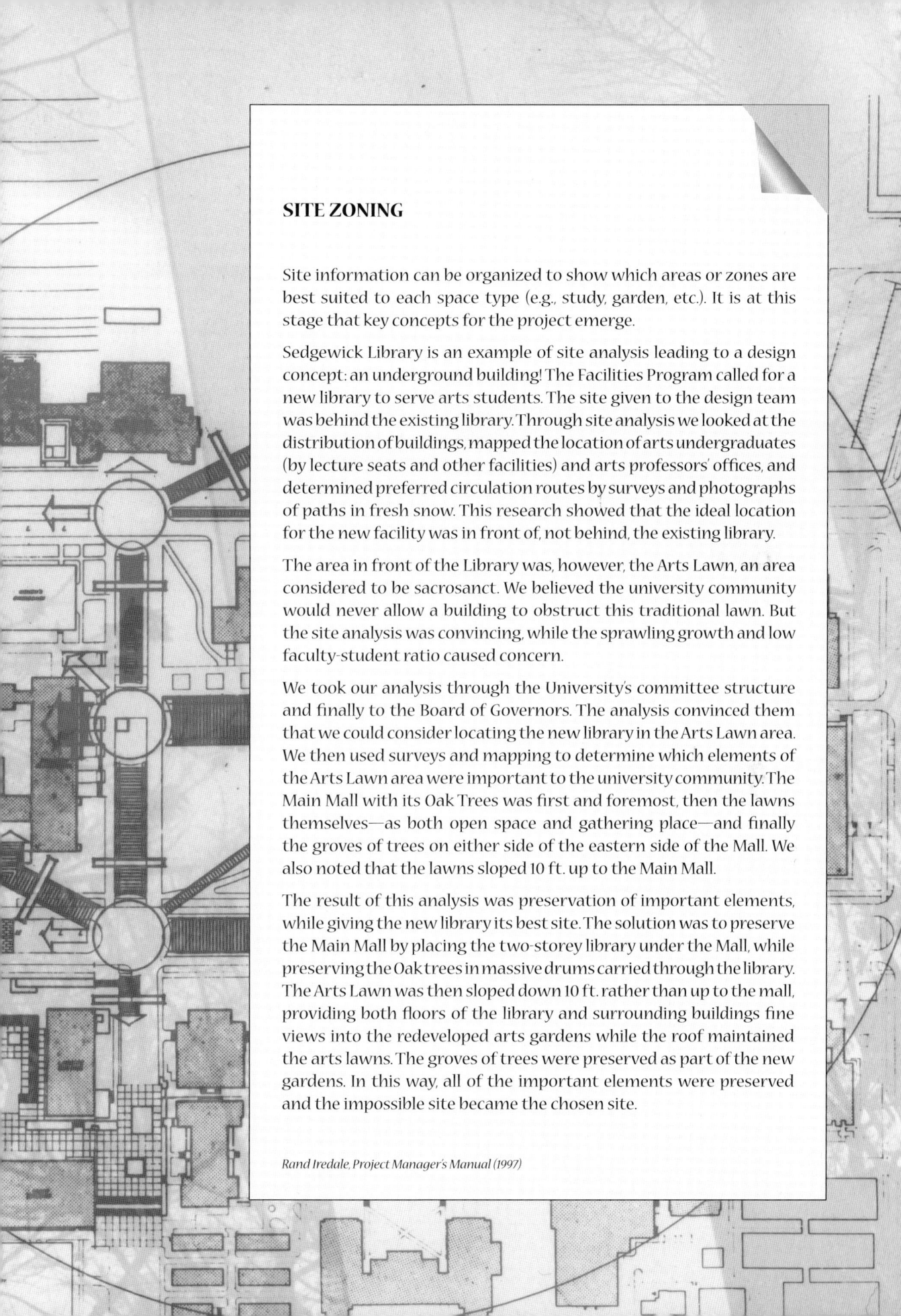

SITE ZONING

Site information can be organized to show which areas or zones are best suited to each space type (e.g., study, garden, etc.). It is at this stage that key concepts for the project emerge.

Sedgewick Library is an example of site analysis leading to a design concept: an underground building! The Facilities Program called for a new library to serve arts students. The site given to the design team was behind the existing library. Through site analysis we looked at the distribution of buildings, mapped the location of arts undergraduates (by lecture seats and other facilities) and arts professors' offices, and determined preferred circulation routes by surveys and photographs of paths in fresh snow. This research showed that the ideal location for the new facility was in front of, not behind, the existing library.

The area in front of the Library was, however, the Arts Lawn, an area considered to be sacrosanct. We believed the university community would never allow a building to obstruct this traditional lawn. But the site analysis was convincing, while the sprawling growth and low faculty-student ratio caused concern.

We took our analysis through the University's committee structure and finally to the Board of Governors. The analysis convinced them that we could consider locating the new library in the Arts Lawn area. We then used surveys and mapping to determine which elements of the Arts Lawn area were important to the university community. The Main Mall with its Oak Trees was first and foremost, then the lawns themselves—as both open space and gathering place—and finally the groves of trees on either side of the eastern side of the Mall. We also noted that the lawns sloped 10 ft. up to the Main Mall.

The result of this analysis was preservation of important elements, while giving the new library its best site. The solution was to preserve the Main Mall by placing the two-storey library under the Mall, while preserving the Oak trees in massive drums carried through the library. The Arts Lawn was then sloped down 10 ft. rather than up to the mall, providing both floors of the library and surrounding buildings fine views into the redeveloped arts gardens while the roof maintained the arts lawns. The groves of trees were preserved as part of the new gardens. In this way, all of the important elements were preserved and the impossible site became the chosen site.

Rand Iredale, Project Manager's Manual (1997)

Reprinted from *UBC Reports* (1969, 1973)

1969: An Ingenious Plan

Comment by Dr. Robert M. Clark, Director of Academic Planning:

"I think the plans, as amended to meet earlier criticisms, are the most imaginative building proposals I have seen presented on this campus since 1946."

The design proposed by the architects is an ingenious solution to a seemingly insoluble problem: how to create an attractive new library facility, located where studies show it ought to be—that is, immediately west of the existing library—without destroying the traditional character of the treed Main Mall and adjacent lawns. The solution: construct the new library *under* the mall. This makes it possible to preserve all but one of the 40-year-old pin oaks and the vistas they frame along UBC's main street. But the architects wanted to create a light, open environment for learning, not just an underground knowledge vault. They have accomplished this second objective by designing the new library in such a way that its east and west faces will open out onto landscaped courtyards in front of the Main Library and the mathematics building. Every room in the building will have an attractive view onto one or other of these garden courts.[1] ∎

Views of interior stair of Sedgewick Library, exterior skylights on Main Mall, and reflection of trees (centre) on one of the skylights

Photos

Exterior, Above:
Selwyn Pullan, North Vancouver

Background & Exterior, Opposite:
John Roaf, Vancouver

Interior Views:
(photographer unknown)

University Librarian Basil Stuart-Stubbs [has] a rich understanding of what a library should be:

"People have a poor image of libraries and librarians. Certainly a library is a place where serious work must be done, but that is no reason why it should be dreary. We have tried to make this place, frankly, a little joyous. This is a very human library."

1973: A Very Human Library

UBC's new Sedgewick Library is a repository for 130,000 volumes, 20,000 records, eight red oaks, 42 Shakespearean quotations lettered onto plate glass windows and sliding doors, and a vivid, purple, orange, yellow, and green supergraphic that dodges around corners, darts along the walls, and occasionally explodes in balloons of colour. [It's] a place for people to be comfortable, to sit back and relax, to stretch, to gossip, to drift off to sleep, to listen to Mozart, Moussorgsky, or Miles Davis or, if the spirit moves them, to study. The library is a bit of a shocker for those accustomed to libraries as funereal buildings with gothic arches, rows of dusty tomes, and female librarians in tailored suits and horn-rimmed glasses.[1]

---

1   Excerpts on these two pages are from "Board Approves New Library Plan: Ingenious Plan," *UBC Reports* (October 9, 1969): 1, and "A Very Human Library," *UBC Reports* (January 18, 1973): 6, respectively.

A Popular Place

The Sedgewick Undergraduate Library, which opened its doors in January 1973, was named after Dr. Garnet Gladwin Sedgewick (1882–1949), a Shakespearean scholar and the first head of UBC's Department of English. It was a popular place of study for new university students and a favorite tourist attraction for visitors. It was one of the largest branches in the UBC Library system, and—thanks to the architectural firm of Rhone and Iredale—one of the most innovative in design.

When the student population increased rapidly in the 1960s, UBC decided to construct a new library building devoted entirely to undergraduate needs. Students' traffic surveys indicated the best location would be the Main Mall, close to the Main Library. To preserve the area's open space, it was decided to build the new library partially underground. The eight magnificent oaks that had lined the Mall for decades were incorporated into the design. The name of the library ceased to exist when the renovation attaching it to the Koerner Library was completed in 1997.[1] ∎

Above:
Exterior view of the mirrored skylights, emerging onto the Main Mall and reflecting the surrounding trees and buildings

Opposite:
Interior view, looking up at one of the skylights

Photos

Above:
John Roaf, Vancouver

Opposite:
(photographer unknown)

---

1   Source: www.vancouverhistory.ca/chronology1973.htm (2006).

Reprinted from the *Journal of Commerce* (Sorensen, 1980)

Underground Library Has Many Advantages

Energy-conservation isn't the only reason for constructing earth-sheltered buildings, says one of the two Vancouver architects responsible for the University of BC's 120,000 sq. ft. (3,252 m²) undergraduate library.

Randle Iredale says the Sedgewick Library was recessed into a campus niche in 1970 to save three significant campus features.

They were a mall that students used for walking, eating, and lounging; a sloping garden bowl that provided greenery on the campus and provided visual relief from the stone grey buildings; and the presence of eight large red oak trees on the mall. At the height of the environmental trend, campus administration was not willing to let the trees be toppled.

The L-shaped library was slid into the bowl with the mall road rolling over the long side while the short end joins a walkway entrance down the garden slope. The cup of the bowl is virtually untouched.

The trees were the major challenge, says Iredale. Unfortunately, they are still posing problems a decade later.

The tall trees were root pruned on the mall one year before excavation, as corrugated metal was pushed 25 ft. (7.6 m) into the earth in a 30 ft. (9.1 m) ring diameter.

As a result, once the 140,000 cu. yds. (106,400 m³) of earth were removed from the site, eight "flowerpots" remained standing on the site. The library design incorporated the pots in the building plans and the drums were eventually bricked in.

Economical Building

The Sedgewick building was economical, despite the limitations of construction techniques at the time.

"The loading on the roof garden and the mall is higher but the cost was still equivalent to a conventional building that size—there is no exterior finishing on two sides," Iredale points out.

The two sides finished were done primarily in glass.

One aspect of earth-sheltered construction on a large scale that makes it more attractive today is the growing size of earth-moving equipment. The Sedgewick excavation took six weeks, and the material had to be trucked to a dump, Iredale says.

Method of construction was suspended-elevation slab pre-cast concrete construction with formed retaining walls on the two buried walls. The slab span was 25 to 30 ft. (7.5 to 9 m) between pre-cast girders with a span of 20 ft. (6 m).

Reprinted from the *Journal of Commerce* (Sorensen, 1980)

Waterproofing Problems

A Uniroyal rubber roofing method was used for water proofing; but there have been leakage problems, Iredale says. He doesn't blame the bonding material but rather those eight trees and the brick drums that surround the root columns.

Iredale believes that when it rains the water is transferred from the mall top through the very porous bricks to travel down the columns of earth into the library.

On the sidewalks, asphalt on concrete was used followed by gravel and drain tile at the bottom before back filling started.

Sedgewick has an air-change every hour.

"The library was built when energy conservation was not an issue," he says. However, it is well-insulated and "heat is not wasted."

Photo Caption

"Sedgewick Library at the University of B.C. is a prominent example of earth-sheltered construction in the Vancouver area."

Photo: John Roaf, Vancouver (a different photo was used in the article)

Iredale feels the library design was ideal for the slope and constraints on the campus site but sub-terranean public building sites are limited.

A well-drained area is needed; the area must be clear of rock—which can be expensive to remove, and cannot have fast-flowing ground water which can cool the concrete wall and rob heat from the building.

Assisting Iredale on the project was Vancouver architect Bill Rhone. Rhone says Sedgewick was not looked at as a complex building at the time. [We used] "warehouse (construction) techniques," he says.[1] ■

1 Jean Sorensen, "Underground Library Has Many Advantages," *Journal of Commerce*, September 22, 1980: 7.

Creative thought is critical to design ... [and] generosity of spirit is critical to creativity in a group endeavour.

The present reflects the past and the future.

UBC's old Main Library, mirrored in one of the skylights of the undergraduate Sedgewick Library, signals Rand's increasing interest in the history and heritage conservation of neglected buildings threatened with demolition. It also foretells the Heritage Building Study Rand will eventually undertake of the UBC campus.

FINDING A GOOD FIT

We believe that good design is a fit between the existing reality and the needs and aspirations of our clients and users.

This vision of the design process has led to a methodology that mobilizes the creative skills of our clients and users—together with the architects, engineers, and other specialists in environmental design—in a common search for the best fit between our perceived needs and aspirations and the physical world upon which our design will impact.

From this vision comes our commitment to thorough and careful programming. We need a shared understanding of the needs and aspirations for which we are designing and a firm understanding of the environment in which we will design.

The great nineteenth century American architect, Louis Sullivan, stated that "An architect must have a ten-fingered grasp of reality." It is this *ten-fingered grasp of reality*—given by a thorough understanding of the existing situation, including the site, bylaws, codes, budgets, and value system of the community—that maps our exploration for design fit.

In the schematic design phase of the design process our client, user, and consulting team undertake a joint exploration for fit. Creative thought is critical to design. It is nurtured in an atmosphere of trust and respect in which ideas from all participants are accepted as gifts to the common endeavour. Generosity of spirit is critical to creativity in a group endeavour.

Rand Iredale, Project Manager's Manual (1997)

7 Imagining a Different Reality

In the Fall of 1969 Rand, myself, and our three children had the good fortune of participating in one of the UBC School of Architecture's first four-month Studies Abroad Programs, organized by Professor Abraham Rogatnick and held in Venice, Italy. As a part-time lecturer in the School of Architecture, Rand was invited to join the Program and our children were at just the right ages (13, 11, and 8) to benefit from this exposure to Italian culture.

Venice is a fascinating city, having been a major trading centre for 700 years, up to the end of the 18th Century. The wealth generated in this active, historic, canal-linked centre resulted in the creation of many splendid palaces and churches, particularly around the Piazza San Marco: the Church of Santa Maria della Salute, the Campanile of San Marco, the Church of San Marco, and the Gothic façade of the Ducal Palace.

We left Vancouver on a chartered plane, along with about two dozen students and professors. We were travelling at student rates and waited at the airport until 2:00 am for the chartered plane to finally take off. We flew to Amsterdam with a few extra days before arriving in Venice. The family joined a boat cruise down the Rhine River and passed many old castles along the way to Koblanz, where we rented a car and drove through the Moselle Valley. Along this route we visited Paris and Versailles and saw several castles and palaces, such as Chateau Chenonceau, Chateau de Chambord, and Chartres Cathedral. The family then drove through Switzerland to Italy.

In Venice we lived with the students in the beautiful 18th-century Palazzo Sceriman, located on the Lista de Spagna, which originally housed the Spanish Ambassador. I had taken along schoolbooks, as my plan was to do schoolwork with the children in the mornings and then they would attend school in the afternoons and hopefully learn some Italian. Rand was one of the UBC program instructors and so we ate our evening meals with the students in a big cafeteria-type room in the palazzo. After dinner, while enjoying a brandy with the staff and students, there was much animated discussion about all that we were being exposed to in Venice.

Opposite:
The Church of San Marco, reflected in the *aqua alta*, the common condition of flooding in Venice in Winter.

The biggest impact on all of us was *Venezia* itself, a city of canals, where you travelled either by foot along the narrow lanes between the buildings or by *vaporetto* or gondola on the Grand Canal and the smaller connecting canals. The day was structured differently, as Italians had their big meal mid-day, followed by a two-hour siesta. Supper was served late in the evening. A big frustration was adapting to the shops being shut during the siesta!

We participated in stimulating lectures by visiting architects in and around Venice. During a major weekend study visit to the Renaissance town of Urbino, we listened to a lecture on its ancient history and modern developments by the world-renowned architect and planner Giancarlo de Carlo, who was acting as the Chief Planning Consultant for Urbino.

Other educational excursions included visits to Venetian country villas, a trip along the lagoon to Chioggia, a trip to Udine to meet with the architect Gino Valle, and visits to Milan and Turin.

Toward the end of our time in Venice Rand arranged for his mother to join the family on a boat tour of the Mediterranean. We left from Venice and travelled down the Adriatic Sea to Kotor and Corfu, Delphi, the Corinth Canal, Mycene, Cape Sunion, Athens, the Isle of Rhodes, and Knossos. As a finale to our grand journey we stopped for a few days in St. Moritz, Switzerland for a skiing holiday.

Charlotte Murray was also a member of the Studies Abroad Program in Venice, and it was there that we formed a friendship with her and her husband, Gordon. Charlotte would participate in those first architecture workshops and lamb bakes at Campbell Bay, and she and Gordon were to become good friends and regular visitors to Mayne Island. She would also work for Rhone & Iredale in the mid-'70s, then return to UBC to earn her M.Arch., and rejoin Rand in a new professional partnership in 1980.

During our entire trip we were exposed to ancient ruins and history and made so very much aware of how young our part of the world is here in British Columbia. The trip made a lasting impression on all of us. It contributed enormously to Jennifer's abiding interest in Canadian history and historic structures. It motivated Talbot to do a school project on Knossos. And it rekindled Rand's passion for urban planning.

Rand was as much influenced by what he saw and learned in Venice as the students were, perhaps more so. Though he had undertaken planning studies through Canadian Environmental Sciences (CES), the visit to Venice broadened his vision and invoked his desire to strive for a vital city centre in Vancouver that would be populated with people, not empty office spaces and abandoned buildings.

Further, the Venice experience, along with visits to other old towns and cities in Europe, made Rand conscious of the need to conserve some of BC's historic sites and structures. ∎

When a busy architect leaves his practice for three months there are bound to be good and bad ramifications. One negative consequence was returning to find the firm in dire financial straits. Accounting for a professional practice is by accrual and the consultant payables had not been accrued! As a result, the firm took a big loss that year, which caused Rand to become more involved in managing the firm.

Also, the firm was involved in the construction phase of Sedgewick Library and Rand's absence required that others take over the supervision. Egos got involved and credit for the project became a contentious issue, which was unfortunate and detracted from Rand's satisfaction with the job.

On the positive side, the trip was an especially stimulating experience for our children. No history class or architecture book could ever have provided them with such a realistic experience. It was a highlight of their education. They have always felt privileged to have been included in the program. Jennifer has many times expressed to Professor Rogatnick the influence this experience had on her decision to become a curator of heritage buildings.

Abraham Rogatnick and his students on various walkabouts through the canals, streets, and buildings of Venice

Is that a Coca-Cola sign? No wonder Venice is crumbling!

The Venice Venture

Venetians, especially a new group called Venice Island of Studies, invited UBC architectural students to study some of Venice's problems and perhaps offer some solutions. The students came to Venice to extend their experience with the urban scene; that is, to become acquainted with urban matters ... and to gain practice in dealing with these matters. In short, they came to Venice to do what they, as students of environment, might have done in almost any other city of the world—to learn and to develop their own capacities as decision-makers in ... whatever present or future urban environmental problems they may face in the practice of their profession.

Venice is repeatedly held up as a paragon among cities. Venice, we are told, has realized a human scale and a division of functions in its form which aid, abet and enhance human life and activities; it is a real urban utopia only dreamed about or weakly attempted elsewhere. For these reasons Venice is loved by all the world; Venice is wanted by all the world; Venice belongs to the world. Venice is beautiful. Venice is unique. Her area is small, her houses are underpopulated, and the problems of her preservation are monumental. ...

Venice is threatened with death from several directions: *Death by drowning*, the slow but obvious sinking of the entire lagoon region, which has led to a frightening acceleration of the frequency of tidal flooding in the old city. *Death by decay*, the moulding, crumbling, spalling, disintegrating state in which the city's surface decoration ... and structural fabric has fallen, a phenomenon that began centuries ago, but which [has accelerated] in recent years. *Death by depopulation*, the rapid emptying of the city from year to year of permanent residents who do not merely constitute the natural guardians and maintenance crew of an urban complex [that] is in itself a historic monument, but who also give an authenticity and richness to the character of life in the city, which a mere combination of tourists and non-resident commuters would fail to accomplish. ...

One of the themes of study ... [concerned plans] to construct a hospital designed by Le Corbusier at one end of the island group, and to construct near the other end a Congress Hall designed by Louis Kahn. These outlying districts of the Venetian historic centre happened to be among the historically poorest, least economically developed, and most neglected areas of the town. ... The students set out to investigate ... the effects [that] the construction of the two proposed public structures at the two far ends of the city might have upon the stimulation of economic and other activities between them. ...

If Venice can be thought of as the centre of the larger metropolis of which it forms a part ... it is clear that the historic centre, the ancient group of islands in the lagoon, like centres of so many old cities in the rest of the world, has been suffering a period of depopulation. Here was [another theme of study], one which should also have parallels elsewhere. ... The latter of the three threats [death by depopulation] was the one [that] most concerned the students of architecture, and for which professionals in architecture would be most prepared to tackle. ...[1] ■

The Venice Island of Studies group subsidized a large part of the program, which also received funding from UNESCO, UBC, and UBC's School of Architecture.

Faculty of the UBC School of Architecture Studies Abroad Program (1969–1970):
Henry Elder
John Gaitanakis
Helen Goodwin
Andrew Gruft
Donald Gutstein
Randle Iredale
Giuseppe Milanesi
Charlotte Murray
Abraham Rogatnick

The students came in two groups, each for an academic term (Fall 1969 and Spring 1970). The themes of study suggested themselves as the Venice project unfolded. "Many of the details of what was learned—much of it previously unpublished—appeared in the May 1971 issue of *Architectural Review*, dedicated entirely to the problems of Venice. It was largely the UBC program in Venice that, by bringing together an invited group of experts and doing some of its own research, inspired the composition of the *Review's* issue on Venice."[1]

---

1 Text excerpted and adapted from "The Venice Venture," *UBC in Venice, 1969–70* (undated): 1–7, a booklet prepared by UBC Professor Abraham Rogatnick.

Creating a Culture of Design

From an interview with Rainer Fassler.

Rainer Fassler graduated from UBC's School of Architecture in 1965. He worked at Rhone & Iredale for five years (1968–73) and then with Arthur Erickson for 19 years. Rainer joined Architectura, which is now part of Stantec, in 1992. He is currently Senior Associate, Architecture & Interior Design.

I Always Wanted to be an Architect

I always wanted to be an architect. In 1959 I started talking to people in the School of Architecture at UBC and, luckily, they encouraged me to enrol. Arthur Erickson was teaching in that first year. It was the transition of the old school of architecture and the five-year program into the three-year program with Henry Elder as Director. It was a real adventure, and everything was being questioned. It was an exciting time at the school and later on in the profession, too. We became more aware of the social implications of our work, and we brought broader issues and concerns to the table.

When I started working in Rand's office, for example, he had established Canadian Environmental Sciences (CES) in parallel to the architectural office. CES had a multidisciplinary team approach: C.Y. Loh was working there as a structural engineer; Eric Karlsen, an urban geographer, was working there; Art Cowie was there in landscape; and we often brought sociologists and anthropologists and economists into CES projects, too.

After graduating from UBC I worked and travelled in Europe for a few years. I could have gone to work for Arthur Erickson at that time (1968), but I looked around and there was this firm people were talking about, Rhone & Iredale. Peter Cardew was working there, and Richard Henriquez, and Terry Williams, and Alan Scott. I remember going for an interview and you could sense the energy in this place! I think there were about 25 people then; they had grown rapidly in the previous two years and it seemed to be an interesting collection of people, all in a similar age group. During my discussion with Rand it didn't take long to realize that both sides were interested. This was the place for me!

Office Culture

I worked at Rhone & Iredale during the formative years of my career, in a dynamic environment that combined a number of important influences: where I worked, the contacts I made, and the projects I worked on. And it was the times. The late 1960s,

Continued

early 1970s was a really vibrant, vibrant time. The office had collected a group of people all roughly at the same point in their lives. We didn't have kids yet and we had time to preoccupy ourselves with the question of architecture, with the profession in general, and with life in general, too, beyond work.

Looking back, I sometimes think that Rand had a lot of guts and courage. He had a bunch of energetic young people in the office who he entrusted with work; there weren't very many really experienced people around and he had enthusiastic, inexperienced people leading his projects! He encouraged us and gave us a lot of room, a lot of freedom, and he gave us unlimited support. He must have freaked out sometimes, but it was fundamental to creating this 'office culture' that he gave us an incredible amount of responsibility.

Design Process

Now, Rand had very cleverly established a safety net. In place was the notion of *process*, of how we approach projects and how we achieve milestones, so we couldn't go totally off the rails. The framework was there to catch you and Rand was there, too, but he certainly wasn't holding your hand! We became quite busy in those years and the firm grew rapidly over a relatively short period of time. So I think it was fundamental that Rand both gave us a lot of freedom and put a pragmatic safety net in place.

Rand was very design process–oriented, and I often talk at Stantec now about the framework of what is expected in terms of process. The issue in architecture isn't so much about managing the project as about managing the design. If you are a manager who only manages, who doesn't understand anything about design, all you can do is panic and crack the whip. You don't know how to help a design team when there is a real problem. As well as being a very good manager, Rand was very interested in the design process.

Rand developed a project architect's manual that was simple and understandable. It was down-to-earth and explained what was expected at various stages of design: concepts, schematics, design development, and so on. Today we tend to make this process too complicated. Architecture is partly an intuitive process, and if you try to define it too much you're just defining one particular person's process on one particular project. When the next project comes around with another person, the previous process doesn't work. So there is no sense in over-defining it. We need to know how much to define and how much room to leave for creativity.

Rand was interested in coming up with innovative solutions, and you can only come up with innovative solutions if you enter into the process without preconceptions. Rand was really keen

Continued

and very, very supportive of doing thorough research at the start of a project: *"Understand the opportunities of the program, understand the opportunities of the site, and beware of relying on your preconceptions and jumping too quickly to solutions."*

It wasn't critical that we produced great architecture but, rather, that we produced innovative architecture. We worked in a strong teaching and learning environment.

Design Culture

One aspect of this whole teaching-learning environment was the creation of a 'design culture.' Every other Friday we had an internal design panel. I often talked about it later on—first in Arthur Erickson's office and then at Architectura—but I've never known it to be as vibrant as it was at Rhone & Iredale. The office staff was just the right size to bring us all together in the conference room; someone would present their project and the whole office would critique it.

These were *real* events and they weren't always necessarily kind! There was a delicate balance between being brutally blunt about how good or how bad something was and being supportive. It was an interesting dynamic. And it wasn't just that these design panels improved the work; they got us talking to each other and becoming aware of each other's work. This vehicle toward creating a design culture—the semi-weekly design panel—is just one example of the teaching-learning environment that I remember so well.

When I talk about Rand's courage in supporting this interactive approach, I mean that you cannot control the outcome. The result of a design panel might mean that the design isn't good enough yet. What are you going to tell the client? The client thinks that we're there, and we're not there! It was courageous stuff.

It basically requires a lot of nerve and patience. Sometimes it's just easier to make a decision; it's much more difficult to say, *"We're not ready to make a decision yet; we're not ready to draw conclusions from our research."* It was a unique environment and it worked.

I don't think I ever saw Rand actually lose his nerve, in spite of having gone out on a limb by entrusting people with projects and seeing them taken in directions he probably didn't anticipate. He may have lost his nerve privately, but he had this incredibly calm sense of stability.

There was a level of kindness in Rand and a bit of shyness. Some of us might have wished to be a little closer in understanding the private man. He was a very generous and thoughtful person.

Continued

Social Life

This whole office culture / design culture at Rhone & Iredale also had a fun, social side. We had the greatest parties! It doesn't take long before anybody who reminisces about that time starts to talk about the parties at CES in the old house [at 1100 West 7th Avenue]. We had great Summer parties and great Christmas parties. The Christmas party was like a big family: it started in the morning with Rand talking in a very formal and fatherly way about how the year had gone. And then we would have a great party. There was the question every year of how we should decorate the attic. One time we clad it completely in silver foil!

The attic was also our coffee area. Coffee time was for 15 minutes, and often the office manager had to switch the lights off and on from the bottom of the stairs to remind us to get back down to work! We never stopped talking about important things; coffee breaks up in the attic were a great time to talk about life and work, and about anything and everything.

It wasn't uncommon on Fridays that we would all go out for a beer—the whole office, including Rand—and, over our beer, deciding what we were going to do for the rest of the evening and then bringing along our spouses and girlfriends. It was the kind of culture that was allowed, that just happened.

Summer Office

As to the social side of the office, I want to mention Campbell Bay on Mayne Island. Great optimism existed at that time about what one could do in one's professional life, and Rand talked about the idea of having a Summer office. We were all quite excited, and wondered what it would take to create such a place.

It was a hot topic of discussion, partly stimulated by Ralph Erskine, the Swedish architect, who came to Vancouver a number of times and spoke about his innovative office environment. Erskine had refurbished an old sailboat and turned it into a floating mini-office, complete with drafting boards. In the summertime his staff and their families all camped on one of the islands, and staff members worked part-time on the boat.

We thought Campbell Bay would be a wonderful place to have a Summer office. And it wasn't just a fantasy. Rand was intrigued with the idea, and we thought about what it would take so that the office culture could include families a bit more and become a sort of extended family.

Of course, we never quite accomplished this ideal, but we often went to Mayne Island for weekend picnics and camp-outs. Before one of our picnics—this was the time of Buckminster Fuller and his

Continued

It wasn't critical that we produced great architecture but, rather, that we produced innovative architecture. ... We worked in a strong teaching and learning environment ... [and] I had been given a fundamental set of values and attitudes that I could continue to carry forward.

— *Rainer Fassler*

geodesic dome—we decided that we had to build one of those domes! We figured out how to do it quickly, precut all of the wood, and put this structure together in a lovely location. It was a nice translation of an idea into a reality and into a setting.

The School of Architecture also had parties on Rand's property and staged incredible events that started in the afternoon and went into the evening. I remember the evening Henry Elder floated into Campbell Bay on a barge that we had made, with musicians playing, candles everywhere lighting the way, and Bruno Freschi walking out of the water like Neptune.

It shows the relationship between Rand and the School of Architecture and the importance of the profession being closer to the school. These events continued on for many years and were always part of the talk in town: stories of what happened at this or that event on Mayne Island!

Transition Time

Part of this whole design culture was Rand's view that, after five years with the firm, people should have a sabbatical, an opportunity to take some time out. But it was just at that point that Arthur Erickson got the job to do Robson Square—the government offices and the law courts—and offered me the position of Project Architect.

I told Arthur, "I haven't got the experience to do that!" And Arthur said, "Well, neither has anybody else, and we're building a very young team." Bing Thom was already there as the overall coordinator of this three-block project.

I really liked Rand's and Bill's office and all of the people there. I'd learned a lot and was torn about leaving, but here was this wonderful opportunity. It was both sad and exciting when I decided to leave Rhone & Iredale in 1973.

I took with me, however, that attitude toward the process of design: searching for innovation, thinking about the questions one should ask in the beginning, being patient and not jumping to conclusions too quickly. And some of those very fundamental issues that Rand talked about were also very much what Arthur talked about when he approached his work: that you need to understand your site, to do your research, to innovate. So it was a wonderful transition for me.

Though I didn't have the practical experience to take on such a significant project as Robson Square, I had been given a fundamental set of values and attitudes that I could continue to carry forward. ■

Rhone + Iredale Brochure

Promotional Text

Rhone & Iredale Architects, in response to this era of rapid change, which has deeply affected man's relation to his environment, practices as a multidisciplinary team of specialists—a team because no one person can handle the complexity of today's problems alone, specialists because the people involved are highly competent in their fields, and inter-disciplinary because in dealing with environmental problems it is necessary to apply more than one point of view.

A team from **Rhone + Iredale** can effectively undertake research, feasibility studies, physical planning, design and execution of any environmental project. In addition, it is possible to draw upon a large group of consultants in related fields with whom close liaison is maintained.

The management involved in creative endeavour is critical to any organization dealing with today's problems. Rhone & Iredale has developed effective techniques for the organizing of time and creative energies for problem solving, to produce effective answers to specific environmental questions.

These factors are instrumental in producing advanced concepts in dealing with environmental problems. **Rhone + Iredale** is a firm whose specialty is the synthesis of all factors affecting environment into an effective solution. [1] ∎

---

1 Text above, staff list, and background graphic are reproduced from the Rhone + Iredale brochure (circa 1970).

Key Personnel

Principals

Randle W. IREDALE B Arch (UBC) MRAIC

William R. RHONE BA (Arch) (Univ Calif) MA (Arch) MRAIC

Associates

Andrew GRUFT B Arch (Capetown) MRAIC

Ralph MEYER Dip Arch (Birmingham) ARIBA MRAIC

Senior Personnel

Ferruccio ALFELD Dip Arch (Munich)

Errol M. BULLPITT B Arch (Queensland) ARAIA ARIBA

Peter J. CARDEW Dip Arch (Kingston)

Ke-liang CHANG BArch (Manitoba) MRAIC

Glen E. CIVIDIN B Arch (Notre Dame Ind.) MRAIC

Arthur R. COWIE B Sc (Forestry) (New Brunswick) AILA (Britain) BCSLA M Sc (Planning) UBC Cert. of Landscape (London, Eng.)

Rainer J. FASSLER B Arch (UBC)

Brian A. FISHER B Arch (UBC)

Jerry C. GLOCK Dip Arch Drafting, B Arch (Manitoba)

Robert E. GUTHRIE

Terrance R. HARRISON B Arch (UBC)

Richard G. HENRIQUEZ B Arch (Manitoba) M Arch (MIT) MRAIC

Alexander LANDSKRON Dip Eng (Linz) Dip Arch (Vienna)

Donald E. MATSUBA B Arch (UBC) M Arch (MIT) MRAIC

Claude H. MAURICE B Arch (Manitoba) MRAIC

Horst W. MESSER B Arch (Toronto) MRAIC

Hugh F. MOWAT

Andreas NOTHIGER Dip Arch (Zurich)

Neil J. PELMAN B Arch (UBC) MRAIC

Donovan REEVES B Arch (UBC) MRAIC

Andrew R. ROSS B Arch (McGill) MRAIC

Alan B. SCOTT

Hanna SKAPSKI M Arch (Cracow)

Michael R. STEBBINGS P Eng B Sc (London) MICE

Charles W. G. TAYLOR Cert General Accountant Deg MCGAABC

Robert J. TODD B Arch (Manitoba) MRAIC

Anthony S. WATTY B Arch (UBC) M Arch (UBC)

Terence J. WILLIAMS B Sc (Bath) ARIBA

Anthony S. WILSON ARIBA MRAIC

A Historic Hike Up the Chilkoot Trail

From an interview with Rainer Fassler.

An example of Rand's approach to the design process was when Parks Canada put out a proposal call in 1972 for a preliminary planning study of the Chilkoot Trail International Historic Park. I was working with the urban geographer, Eric Karlsen, at the time and we were both pretty inexperienced. But Rand suggested we go after this study, even though it was far removed from architecture, and Eric and I thought about how we could approach it.

I recall asking Rand, "What if we recreate this historic hike up the Chilkoot Trail? And Pierre Berton has written this book, *Klondike*, and what if I phone to see if he wants to come along?" And Rand said, "You're crazy! He's not going to do that!" And I remembered Abe Rogatnick, our school history professor, talking about his work in Venice, in this historic setting, and I thought, what a bizarre thing it would be if we could talk Abe into coming on the hike, too. I mean, Abe is the urban man! What if he got some hiking boots and came along? And we brainstormed a lot and thought we should have somebody who could look at the whole landscape of the Chilkoot Trail. "What about Jack Shadbolt?" [1]

So I went out on a limb and phoned these three guys. I did not get through to Berton, first talking to his secretary and saying, "I've got Jack Shadbolt quite interested, and Abe Rogatnick." And then turning around and telling Abe, "Pierre Berton is going on the trip!" And before long we had them committed to hike the Chilkoot Trail with us. Rand's son, Talbot, came along, too.

That's what I mean by Rand taking on projects that were really out there and letting us take a chance. It was just amazing. We got the Parks Canada job, we hiked the Chilkoot Trail, and we worked hard on the preliminary plan. In the end, it was declared a national historic site. It was an exciting project and it was also exciting in all of its failures! We arranged for helicopters to drop supplies and materials so that we didn't have to carry everything with us, but it was totally disorganized. The group got separated and there were people that first night with tents and food, but no tent poles and no stoves; others had the poles and the stoves, but no tents and no food!

---

1   Pierre Berton, *Klondike: The Last Great Gold Rush, 1896–1899* (Toronto: Random House, 1972). Professor Emeritus Abraham Rogatnick is an architect, patron of the arts, playwright, and actor. The artist Jack Shadbolt was a major contributor to the development of abstraction and modernism in Canada; his paintings are represented in all major public collections in Canada and in numerous corporate and private collections. Source: Internet (2006).

Continued

We were recreating this great hike and, ultimately, the question was, "How do we deal with this historic site?" We were basically walking across historic garbage dumps. People had discarded stuff along the way.

At the top of the path we found folding boats and steam engines that were to be fitted onto boats when they reached Bennett Lake, which were carried up in bits and pieces and just left there. All along the way we encountered these remnants of human tragedy, these leftovers of that whole history. And what were a bunch of architects doing there, anyway?

But it all fit with Rand's notion that we can do more when we bring a whole bunch of disciplines—urban geographers, artists, historians, architects—into a team environment and when we set aside our preconceptions and start asking questions.

Disciplined Adventurism

Rand was able to create and sustain a great sense of adventure. He was probably one of the first Vancouver architects who ventured to the Middle East for work. We didn't, in the end, do the work, but we looked at a project in Dhahran in Saudi Arabia, and we were in Beirut, Lebanon for a while, and then Cyprus, where the contractor was located. Rand encouraged this sort of 'disciplined adventurism,' and flying over there, looking at that project opportunity, was really, really exciting.

Umbrella Company

Rand had a dream of building Rhone & Iredale into an 'umbrella company,' and I wish he had succeeded. I believe he had this idea, when Richard Henriquez and Bob Todd went out on their own, that there could be a kind of franchise and that Rhone & Iredale could be an umbrella.

There were the guys in Seattle, Miller / Hull, for example, who have become one of the really great small firms in the Pacific Northwest.[1] They basically started a Rhone & Iredale office in Seattle. This event transpired after I left the firm, so my view may be too vague. But there was definitely this notion that the office in Vancouver could become an umbrella, and under this umbrella you would have people who had a certain amount of independence but were still connected to Rhone & Iredale. ∎

---

1   Founded in 1977 by Dave Miller and Bob Hull, Miller / Hull received the American Institute of Architects architecture firm award for 2003. This award is given annually to a single firm that has consistently produced significant work. The firm's work is documented in *Miller / Hull: Architects of the Pacific Northwest* by Sheri Olson (Princeton Architectural Press, 2001).

Project: Chilkoot Trail

"In 1897 two ships, the *Excelsior* and the *Portland*, arrived in San Francisco and Seattle laden with Yukon gold. The Klondike Gold Rush was about to begin. Today, the Chilkoot Trail—historically, a First Nations trade and travel route—commemorates the mass movement of people to the Yukon during the Klondike Gold Rush. Extending from Dyea AK to Bennett BC at the headwaters of the Yukon River, the Trail offers a superb hiking experience of spectacular natural beauty steeped in history. This national historic site was designated as an International Historic Park in 1998."[1]

---

1   Source: Parks Canada / www.pc.gc.ca (2006).

In conjunction with Canadian Environmental Sciences (CES), Rhone & Iredale undertook a Master Plan Study in 1972 for the proposed Klondike Gold Rush International Historic Park. They prepared a Concept Master Plan for the Chilkoot Trail between the historic points of landing at Skagway and Dyea at the end of the Lynn Canal in Alaska and the head of river navigation at Bennett Lake in British Columbia, a distance of over 30 miles. The concept integrated historic and natural aspects of the Trail to interpret the events of the 1897–1899 Gold Rush for today's visitors.

The Klondike Gold Rush was multinational in scope and involved men from many nations. The Chilkoot Trail itself spans the international boundary and today involves federal and local levels of government in British Columbia, the Yukon, and Alaska in planning for the commemoration of this historic period. The final report was prepared with the assistance of several agencies from each of these governments and resulted in eight recommendations for implementation of a Master Plan. ∎

Photo: www.answers.com

"Never will I forget it, there on the mountain face,
Antlike, men with their burdens, clinging in icy space;
Dogged, determined and dauntless, cruel and callous and cold,
Cursing, blaspheming, reviling, ever that battle-cry—'Gold!'" [1]

---

1   Stanza from the epic poem by Robert W. Service, "The Trail of Ninety-Eight" in *Ballads of a Cheechako* (1909). He was often referred to as 'the Bard of the Yukon.'

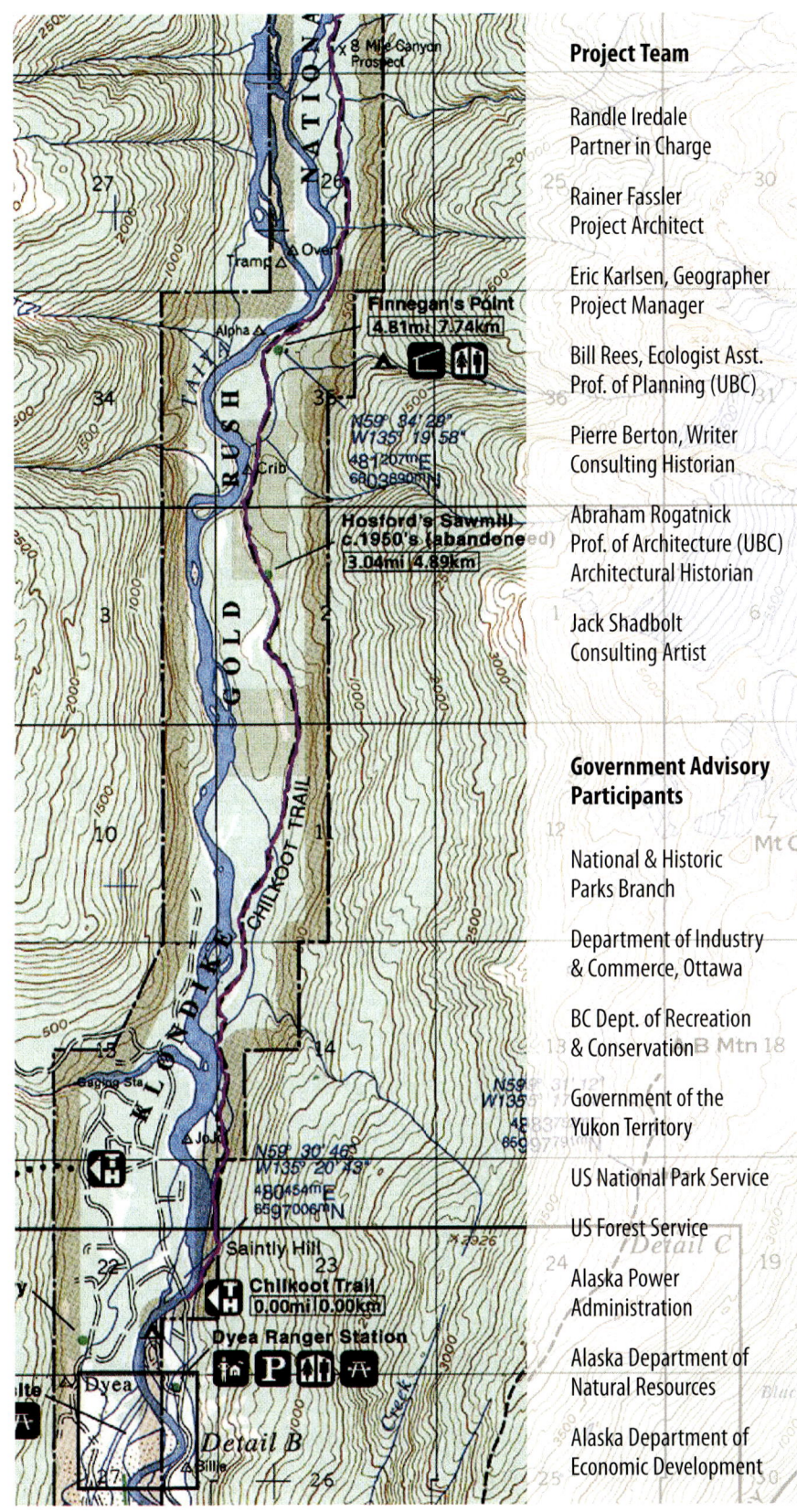

Map: www.n2backpacking.com/
maps/alaska/chilkoot/Chilkoot

Project Team

Randle Iredale
Partner in Charge

Rainer Fassler
Project Architect

Eric Karlsen, Geographer
Project Manager

Bill Rees, Ecologist Asst.
Prof. of Planning (UBC)

Pierre Berton, Writer
Consulting Historian

Abraham Rogatnick
Prof. of Architecture (UBC)
Architectural Historian

Jack Shadbolt
Consulting Artist

Government Advisory Participants

National & Historic
Parks Branch

Department of Industry
& Commerce, Ottawa

BC Dept. of Recreation
& Conservation

Government of the
Yukon Territory

US National Park Service

US Forest Service

Alaska Power
Administration

Alaska Department of
Natural Resources

Alaska Department of
Economic Development

Imagining a Different Reality | 177

HE LET YOU SHINE

From an interview with Rainer Fassler.

Rand entrusted me with the Seymour Medical Clinic when I was young and inexperienced. Here was a group of doctors who talked about practising as a collective, as a clinic. And how does one translate that kind of practice into an architectural setting? I went with the doctors on field trips and we talked at length.

I have remained friends with some of these doctors, and Dr. Jim Ironside, long-retired and now in his eighties, still recalls the intensity of those early discussions about architectural concepts and medical practices. He often talks about how exciting it was to participate in that experience and to undertake that project. He wasn't just the client across the table listening to us tell him, "Trust us, we'll give you something that you'll like." Rather, it was searching together and panicking together and struggling together. It was a collaboration.

This project is an example of how Rand's approach to design not only had a huge impact on the immediate culture of our own office but, also, on the clients who participated in this adventure. Working on the medical clinic was a really important experience for me. I still go to this clinic, and I often bemoan how it has changed. *It is the tragedy of projects that they are eventually renovated, and you wonder, why couldn't they be more sensitively renovated? They become very precious; they are your kids!*

Following the Seymour project, another group of doctors was impressed with our approach and asked us to do the Burrard Medical Building, which made it into *The Canadian Architect Yearbook* as an innovative project. I don't want to make these projects seem more important than they were; my point is that they were very important for me and for my relationship with Rand. They demonstrate the innovation that can come out of the collaborative environment that Rand had a key role in creating.

When you are given a lot of opportunity and a lot of leeway on these projects, your ego inevitably comes into the picture. Over the years I have often thought that it must have been tricky for Rand. He played a supportive role and gave you the opportunity. He was very generous in that sense and he let you shine. At the opening of the medical clinic I was allowed to be the star. Being young and full of oneself, I probably wasn't sensitive enough to the fact that here was this generous man who had given me this opportunity. Being supportive of others requires both modesty and generosity. Looking back at those events, I could have been a little more generous myself, but this was Rand. ∎

Rand at the pegboard / blackboard in the office at 1100 West 7th Avenue, perhaps reviewing the status of a project or facilitating a design panel (1973)

Reprinted from *The Canadian Architect* (1976)

Project: Seymour Medical Building

The concept of a medical clinic is to bring together a variety of medical specialists, encouraging the sharing of knowledge and experience. Seymour Medical Building provides facilities for thirty doctors, along with an x-ray department, a laboratory and a pharmacy. Allowances have been made to expand the structure to accommodate up to fifty doctors and to increase parking areas.

Criteria for design involve creating an efficient working environment for doctors, as well as maximum clarity of patient circulation systems, waiting areas with a mixture of intimacy and distraction, and personal contact between patient and nurse. The criteria were met by grouping doctors into clusters of examining and consulting rooms. The cluster provides each doctor with a private consulting room and eight examining rooms shared with four other doctors. Nurses and supporting facilities are also shared.

Paired clusters are served by mutual waiting areas. These waiting areas are located along an interior pedestrian spine and separated from each other by landscaped courtyards. This concept offers a clear patient circulation system and pleasant small waiting rooms. Nurses' stations are strategically located allowing the nurse to establish visual contact with both patient and doctor.

The structure and enclosure system is of concrete, which forms a major element of all interior spaces. Concrete surfaces are either sandblasted, plywood-formed or board-formed. Concrete, wood and plants were chosen as finish materials for a simplicity of expression and the tranquility of environment required for patients suffering from the stress commonly associated with illness.

The use of natural light in all major public spaces and substantial planting areas bring out the texture of concrete and create an ever changing background to waiting areas and public circulation spaces. The moss green carpet, bleached ash furnishings and plain white partition walls work to make grey concrete warm and reassuring.[1] ∎

---

1 "Seymour Medical Building, Vancouver BC," *The Canadian Architect* (September 1976).

Photo:
Selwyn Pullan, North Vancouver

Project Team

Randle Iredale
Partner in Charge

Rainer Fassler
Project Manager

Ray Lacktman
Project Architect

Publications

The Canadian Architect
(September 1976)

Adapted from *The Canadian Architect* (1976)

Project: Burrard Medical Building

This building incorporates offices for thirty doctors (mostly specialists practising singly or in groups of two or three) and a 1,200 sq.ft. pharmacy. Easily accessible patient parking is provided. The average floor space per doctor is approximately 400 sq. ft. Each doctor is provided with his own consulting office and shares business offices and examining rooms with a small group of cohorts. Waiting areas are shared on a floor by floor basis.

As 70% of the patients arrive by car, the design integrates the pedestrian and automobile entry in a landscaped forecourt with a pedestrian ramp up to an entry at the base of a vertical garden and an automobile ramp down to an elevator lobby and parking. The garage provides one patient parking place per doctor. The clarity and directness of the movement pattern and a combination of intimacy and distraction in the waiting areas are intended to reassure the patient. Generous waiting areas relate directly to the nursing stations and open to the visual interest of the vertical garden.[1] ∎

Photo:
Selwyn Pullan, North Vancouver

1 Adapted from *The Canadian Architect* (September 1976): 64.

Project Team

Randle Iredale
Partner in Charge

Rainer Fassler
Project Manager

Publications

The Canadian Architect
(1976)

The Canadian Architect
(1974)

The Canadian Architect
(1971)

Award

The Canadian Architect Yearbook
Award for Excellence in the Design Stage
1971

"An ingenious arrangement of pedestrian and automobile entry involving a carefully worked out section which establishes the main lobby as a bridge spanning the cars and equally accessible to motorists and those arriving on foot. The integration of pedestrian and vehicular access, particularly on a confined site, is a frequently encountered problem in the urban scene. Here it is skilfully accomplished. . . ." (James A. Murray).

"A very restrained and delightful architectural understatement utilizing a highly efficient and well-disciplined plan form related with a section of undeniable clarity, interest and scale" (Peter Webb).

"A handsome and ingenious configuration . . ." (R.J. Thom).

In the 1970s Rhone & Iredale conducted numerous facility planning and land development studies. One such study that Rand shepherded through Canadian Environmental Sciences is briefly summarized here. Following the trip to Venice, and with several significant projects 'under his belt,' Rand's attention increasingly turned to issues concerning the redevelopment of downtown Vancouver, highlighted in the next chapter.

Project: Manning Park Housing Study

This 1971 study presented the findings of background studies undertaken by Rhone & Iredale / Canadian Environmental Sciences (CES) for the Parks Branch of the Department of Recreation & Conservation. It involved the preparation of a staff housing program for a park services community in Manning Provincial Park.

Several policy issues were raised in this study concerning housing requirements that related to the development of the Park Centre and in turn to the park as a whole. Specifically, the study dealt with the summary analysis of Manning Park, its facilities, and its present and future use; the proposed development of a recreational and service village; and the proposed housing for a park services community. ■

Architecture is not a solitary art like painting or writing. You cannot do it alone.

ARCHITECTURE IS A TEAM SPORT

Architecture is not a solitary art like painting or writing. It is more akin to theatre or movie making. You cannot do it alone. First you need a client who, like the movie producer, supplies the money and picks the team; then you need a director, the role that is closest to architect. The specialists akin to sound technician, set designer, and cameraman are our engineers and other specialist consultants.

Architecture is a team sport, so get your team organized and working together before you start designing. You have hopefully had the consultant team participating in the Program and Site Analysis Phases, but the first design meeting is where we start asking for input. Inviting the whole team may seem wasteful of time, but they are going to work together on your project. They need to know each other and share a common vision and commitment to the project.

Leadership to get the commitment of creative people requires a special style. Share the vision and expect each team member to respond creatively in his area. Authoritarian, top-down management, often associated with the military, won't work here. Leadership takes many forms, from dictatorial to consensual. But the leader must always carry the overall responsibility. A short story illustrates this point:

After a great victory at the battle of Austerlitz, the General was honoured at a banquet. A rumour had circulated that the victory was really due to the brilliance of a certain Major and later it was rumoured that the real author of the victory was a Captain on the Major's staff. A lady with more physical charms than tact fluttered up to the General and asked, "General, after all of these rumours about the Major and the Captain, who was responsible for the victory?" The general replied, "Madame, I am not sure who is responsible for our victory; however, I am sure who would have been responsible if we had lost."

Rand Iredale, Project Manager's Manual (1997)

Manning Park was one of Rand's favourite places. As Kathryn wrote in her Preface, he "died suddenly and unexpectedly on August 20th, 2000 from an aorta aneurism. He died 'with his boots on,' having spent the previous week hiking and camping in Manning Park …"

Photo: www.mottie.com/albums/manning/IMG_0635.jpg

A Lifelong Friendship

From an essay written by Charlotte Murray.

At my first encounter of Rand, I knew who he was; most people connected to the world of architecture did. The well-known architect, Randle Iredale, was a visiting lecturer at the UBC School of Architecture when I was a student in the 1960s. His subject was the business of architecture and its management, which was *not* what the starry-eyed students wanted to know!

Once in Venice

My second encounter was a few years later, just after I graduated. At my husband Gordon's insistence, I managed to get a job as a teaching assistant with the School of Architecture's Studies Abroad Program in Venice in 1969. During our much delayed flight to Amsterdam, the four Murrays—Charlotte, Gordon, Joyce, and Gordie—and the five Iredales—Rand, Kathryn, Jennifer, Talbot, and Hardy (Richard)—found that we at least had our frustration in common.

Once in Venice, however, and comfortably settled in the *palazzo* provided for the UBC group, our daytime duties and desires were quite disparate and we crossed paths only occasionally. We sat at our appointed family tables during dinner, so it was only after dinner that Rand, Kathryn, Gordon, and I discovered an important common interest, which was, for the few weeks that we were actually together, to enjoy a *caffè corretto* or two served at the *palazzo* bar. Over our relaxing libations we would tell of our experiences and important discoveries of the day. Sharing visions of beautiful paintings, incredible glass objects, intriguing warrens of *calles*, the romance of the canals, and even the antics of students, as they were led on unique explorations of the Venice environment, cemented a lifelong friendship.

Teaching & Interning

Back in Vancouver I carried on working as a teaching assistant for a few more years before deciding it was essential to work in an architectural office, no matter which direction my career took. I trudged the streets of Vancouver's business district and knocked on every architect's door—36 in total! *No, I did not type. No, I did not do interior decoration. No, there was not a job.* I did have a private commission to do a school playground in Williams Lake, and then a second one to do an adventure park in the same city.

With this second commission in hand, I finally knocked on the door of Rhone & Iredale and asked to see Rand. Gracious as usual,

Continued

he saw me right away. Without much preamble I told him that I had a little job and that, as he was an MAIBC, it was his duty to hire me to do the job with his firm so I could work toward my registration. He did not even blink before answering, "I think we can arrange that. And, of course, we will expect 50% of the fees for office expenses." Then he added, "If things go right and we have work, we may keep you on as a regular employee." So that is how my four-year internship with Rhone & Iredale began.

True to His Word

Rand was an amazing person to work for. His apparent level of trust in me seemed to be several notches above my own level of confidence. Rand came to me not too long after I had finished the adventure park job, for example, which had extended to the level of building expertise required to design swings and a couple of climbing structures, and said he had a project for me to do. Naturally, I was pleased, but very surprised when he explained that it was a house renovation job for a client who wanted a new library extension and a large deck over a new two-car garage, plus a complete kitchen renovation. I demurred, as it seemed huge to me, but Rand urged me not to worry and assured me that, as the Partner in Charge, he would be right there if I needed help.

Well, he proved true to his word in a way I would never have dreamed. To prepare for our first meeting with the clients I had to copy some plans of the house to use in discussing the project. I drew these up in good time, but when I attempted to get the print off of the old office diazo printer in the basement it would only produce blanks. I needed help, so I went to Rand! He immediately responded and tried to work the printer with no greater success. It was 4:30 and we had to be ready for a 5:30 meeting, so it was already too late to send the drawing out for printing. Down on his knees, Rand laid the exposed print paper on the concrete basement floor, poured ammonia into a sponge, and waved it back and forth over the paper as the drawing emerged. We got to the meeting, not too late, and from there the project moved successfully to completion. That was my first of many observations of Rand's ingenuity as an active problem-solver.

On Time & On Budget

In 1971 or 1972 Rand went to Boston and took a management course at MIT; it was shortly after that time that I started my internship at Rhone & Iredale. Rand was keen on orderly and well-planned management. The firm was very busy and, by the last year of my internship, had grown to a staff of about 20. I was put in charge of the smaller projects and asked to manage a group of four or five interns. In this capacity I was invited to join the Monday morning management meetings and, thus, was given the opportunity to learn how this complex organization of prima donnas and neophytes actually got the work done profitably! It was an impressive lesson.

According to Rand, the key was to complete projects "on time and on budget"—his favourite phrase. This premise required planning the progress of the project, building a budget appropriate for the job, and managing the job according to the plan. It was all tracked on a big chart on the blackboard: projects, people, stages, budgets, and resources.

It was at this time that Rand started the Ri-Rite system. He was the keener, the planner, and the initiator; Bill Rhone was a designer and he recognized the value of Rand's approach. By combining their talents, the firm prospered. The difference between them was that when Rand had a job he would give it to you and say, "do it," and when Bill had a job you would work for him.

The Lamb Bake

During these years of internship, I continued to teach part-time at the School of Architecture. Bill Rhone did not entirely approve of my mid-day moonlighting, but Rand considered it all to be good experience. In fact, he learned something from it that became an important family tradition lasting until this day: how to set up a spit and barbecue a whole lamb, Greek-style.

It started during a pre-term, first-year workshop run by our mutual good friend from the Venice days, Professor John Gaitanakis. Knowing Rand's established relationship with the School of Architecture and how generous and hospitable he and Kathryn were with their large undeveloped Mayne Island property, I suggested to John that we deposit the 25 or so new students on Mayne Island for a lesson in the natural environment.

So it was that, while the students followed the rhythms of sun, moon, wind, and wave, we provided a great common evening meal prepared over a large open fire. The focal point of the feast was a whole lamb roasted on a spit and lovingly tended by John for the entire day. It happened that Rand and Kathryn came over to Mayne Island that weekend to observe the goings on. There was a bit of a to-do over the open fire, which Rand soothed with the constabulary who showed up to 'put the fire out'.

Much more important, we realized that we had no retsina to go with the Greek lamb, and Rand, ever the problem-solver, jumped into the breach! Rand phoned the airport on Vancouver Island and learned that a float plane was returning to Vancouver in the late afternoon. Somehow he got in touch with the pilot and

Continued

arranged with him to stop at a liquor store on his way to the plane to pick up a case of retsina and drop it off at the north end of Campbell Bay during his flight to Vancouver. And it happened just like that! The lamb was roasted to perfection, the wine was a noble complement and, all in all, it was a great success. The lamb bake tradition continues, unto Rand's children's children. ∎

THE WAY WE WORKED

From an interview with Bill Rhone.

Rand was very creative, but we worked in different ways. I like to draw stuff and sit and be quiet and solve things in a graphic way, and I feel that I had some graphic skills and that's the way I liked to work. But Rand worked in a different way. He was much more verbal than me, and he liked to explore ideas by talking them through.

I usually reached my verbal limit relatively quickly and would want to go off somewhere and concentrate. But Rand liked to talk! It was always extremely interesting, extremely interesting, but I had a limit! We brought different things to the table, though there was always a degree of overlap. We weren't total opposites; there was maybe a 25% overlap. And that's the strength of an organization, because you want a balance of different skills and personalities.

So that worked very well; the two sides came together. We collaborated. It wasn't like, who drew that line, and who thought of this idea? It didn't work that way. We'd hash it out together and I'd draw something and he'd draw something and somebody else would draw something, and we'd pull it together and say, okay, let's go. And that's the way we worked.

There are other ways of running projects, where you have a lead designer who's the common thread throughout the project. That's a very successful way to go, and I tend to work that way now. As our practice grew we both had other projects, and you have to assign the job to somebody else. Then you can come in and you can participate in the job, but somebody else has to carry it through. That's always a part of financial growth.

Later on we started to grate on each other, which was a mistake, a real shame. There are ways of getting around that, but egos get involved. I made my mistakes and Rand made his, but you can't go back. You just have to focus on what was positive. ∎

Project: BCIT Master Plan

The success of student programs at the British Columbia Institute of Technology (BCIT), which first opened its doors in 1964, made it necessary to expand the campus in 1973. Rhone & Iredale was commissioned to undertake a Master Plan to rationalize the campus and add to it.

Existing facilities at that time served 3,000 full-time students and 4,000 evening extension program students. Projected enrollment for 1975–76 was approximately 4,300 full-time students, with extension classes increasing by approximately 25% per year. BCIT growth was to be limited to a maximum of 5,000 full-time students.

Two contrary campus plan concepts were evident in the existing layout. The 1962 and 1967 buildings combined to form a single academic structure; however, the Boiler House, which also contained educational facilities, and the Library, Student Activity Centre, Food Service Building, and Department of Education Building were sited in the traditional campus form with gardens and lawns between the buildings. Circulation through the campus and between these buildings appeared to have been developed on an ad hoc basis as each building was added.

Some of the recommendations included in the new Master Plan were to:

- adopt the superblock concept in locating future utilities, road, parking, and buildings east of Willingdon Avenue;
- undertake a further planning study to consider the physical planning implications of growth on the BCIT campus, based on minimum and maximum growth scenarios; this study would produce a plan for growth based on normal ratios of academic, service, athletic, parking, and other uses, and the intention of such a study would be to:
  - indicate the site area required for various levels of BCIT growth;
  - establish order of development of sites for parking, temporary buildings, residences, and future academic buildings; and
  - provide a basis for consideration of site area to be reserved for current and future needs of BCIT.
- request the Provincial Government to undertake a planning study of the total site to:
  - establish the pattern of development (zoning road and utility easements) for the undeveloped site west of Willingdon as a basis for decisions with regard to the future use of the site; and
  - determine areas to be reserved for expansion of BCIT and other organizations (such as the BC Vocational School) now located on the site. ■

Project Team

Randle Iredale
Partner in Charge

Alan Scott
Project Architect

Project: BCIT Campus Building

Completed in 1975, this project comprised over 100,000 sq. ft. of laboratory, research, classroom, and administrative space. The project was conceived as a major link between an existing classroom building, the library, and the south end of the campus. A central courtyard with a student lounge, cafeteria, and activity centre forms a node on the major circulation system and acts as a focal point between the new construction and the existing building.

Our design approach was framed by the following criteria: BCIT is devoted to training in technical skills; thus, the character of the new building should reflect the precision, efficiency, and concern for economy associated with high technology. In contrast to a liberal arts college, the BCIT building should provide a suitable environment for a two-year course, during which time the average student obtains the technical skills he or she requires to take their place in industry, business, or the health services. ■

THE NATURE OF CREATIVITY

A Project Manager's Manual with check lists and design aids contains no recipe for Schematic Design. You are now in the difficult uncharted area of the search for fit. Previous phases built the logistics for this great adventure, our base camp is in place, and we are at the foot of the mountain, ready to scale the peaks. Our site analysis and program objectives have mapped the terrain.

Our most likely route should be visible. If not, go back and sift through phases one and two again in search of the issues and concepts that will inspire the project.

Creating New Patterns

The first two phases, Program and Site Analysis, were information gathering and sorting. They required analytical or linear thinking. Now the Design Phase requires what Edward de Bono has termed 'lateral thinking' (as opposed to linear thinking).[1] His work on lateral thinking defines methods for creating the new patterns that change our world, such as designs and inventions. Actually, our first two phases have used two of de Bono's techniques:

First, if a problem is solved sequentially, the first pattern introduced will obscure many possible solutions. To discover a creative solution he recommends assembling all of the patterns involved in the problem before attempting a solution, which is what we have done during the Program and Site Analysis Phases.

Second, it is useful to divide the patterns that are to be recombined in our solution into their constituent parts so that the largest and best established pattern does not overwhelm the opportunity to discover a fresh solution. The pattern that our minds bring forward in response to the idea of *home*, for example, is a complete house.

In the Program Phase we have taken this larger pattern apart by programming separately each of the activities that will take place in the specific house we are designing. With these subdivisions of the larger *home* pattern, we are free to rearrange the traditional pattern and to consider combinations and divisions that would never occur if the larger pattern were allowed to dominate our thinking.

---

1   Edward de Bono is regarded by many to be the leading authority in the world in the field of creative thinking. He is a prolific writer and teacher and the originator of the concept of *lateral thinking*. Source: www.edwdebono.com (2006).

Avoiding Fear of Failure

Another idea that is important as you begin the Schematic Phase is [to avoid] the fear of failure syndrome. Fear is the greatest enemy of creativity. I believe most of us suffer from fear that we are inadequate, that our tentative solution will appear ridiculous in other people's eyes, that we are not brilliant enough to find a building form that fulfils the stated needs and aspirations, not to mention one that is on time and on budget within the regulations.

Imagining a Different Reality

Synectics, Inc. is a Boston organization that studies the nature of creativity.[1] They point out a simple truth: that creative solutions come from imagining a different reality, of imagining *what-if?* What-if there was no gravity? What-if the budget was infinite? It sounds easy until you play the *what-if* game. It is very unsettling when you truly let your imagination create a different world.

With your imagination you have distorted rules that govern your world and leave you lost in a crazy house. As you explore a world without gravity or without budget constraints, your normal world is unsettled and you are at sea. And, like someone after a shipwreck, you will grasp at any floating object to rescue you from confusion. You naturally grasp the first solution you see. But wait! Mark it with a sketch and swim on.

Have faith, assume you will survive, swim through the debris to find a raft, a solid life boat that will survive the rest of your journey. Grasping at the first possibility too often misses the really great idea that is just a few minutes of struggle away. By having the confidence to share our first iterations, no matter how inadequate, we open the way to assessing many solutions until we arrive at the sturdy scheme that will carry the program home to a great building.

A synectics idea that has served me well is that all ideas have value, no matter how inadequate they may seem at first hearing. Suggested solutions can be evaluated on a scale of 1% to 100% usability. No idea has zero value and no idea is going to score 100%. If you recognize this truth, you can expect a sympathetic hearing for your tentative solution and you will be open to the criticism that will improve it.

Rand Iredale, Project Manager's Manual (1997)

---

1 Synectics, Inc. is a global consulting and training firm dedicated since 1960 to helping organizations create and foster innovation and to implement breakthrough ideas "by harnessing the creativity and energy of [their] own people." Source: www.synecticsworld.com (2006).

8 The Heart of the Design Process

❧ Rand was a person of great courage, enthusiasm, and generosity of spirit. He was a problem-solver with an inventive mind and a lively curiosity. He always wanted to know how things worked. Having recognized the 'vacuum at the centre' of his professional practice, he took on the tasks of managing the partnership and developing office systems and computer programs for managing projects. Rand was an expansive thinker who foresaw the computer revolution and who enthusiastically persisted in his vision for the Downtown Stadium and the redevelopment of False Creek. And he was a great believer in sharing credit with all who worked on a project.

Planning was a major area of interest for Rand. In the early days of the Rhone & Iredale practice, several planning studies were done in conjunction with Canadian Environmental Sciences (CES). After CES folded Rand continued to pursue this area of interest in the Rhone & Iredale practice and, later, in The Iredale Partnership practice.

The most exciting project was the Vancouver Centenary 1886–1986 Study, which included the Downtown Stadium Study. This study was completed in 1978 and became the basis for much controversy in the downtown community, as it required finding creative solutions for multiple vested needs and interests. It also became the concept plan upon which Expo '86 was ultimately built.

At the time, Rand did not receive much acknowledgement from various political and business interests. Despite the controversy, however, he never gave up on his vision; he kept pushing it forward. A Provincial Government commission finally reported back, and the Stadium and Expo '86 were built. Premier Gordon Campbell has since credited Rand with having had a great vision for the City of Vancouver.

Rand enjoyed working with people and addressing the challenges of long-range planning issues. This chapter introduces his urban planning, heritage restoration, and condominium development projects of the 1970s. ∎

Reprinted from Internet / *Canadian Government EXECUTIVE* (2002); Leadership Summit (2004)

The Strength of a Good Idea

Remarks by Premier Gordon Campbell.

One of the great things about Canada is that it is a place where an individual can help shape the future with the strength of a good idea that gets the ball rolling. For example, when Rand Iredale came forward two decades ago with a plan to rejuvenate Vancouver's False Creek with a stadium, most of the vested interests said that this was crazy. But he persisted because he knew what could happen if the City and Province would just take the right steps. It was his initiative and drive that brought us the downtown stadium and that brought us what was first called Transpo and what then became Expo '86. Because of Expo, we then got the Trade & Convention Centre and the SkyTrain and the redevelopment of False Creek. All of those changes came because one citizen would not give up on his idea for making his City and Province a better place for all of us.[1] ∎

Vancouver Board of Trade Leadership Summit

Remarks by Premier Gordon Campbell.

... It is important to take time out from the challenges we face on a day-to-day basis to think about where we want to go in the long term—to think about what our horizons are and to think about what we can accomplish when we work together. We live in an exceptional place, with exceptional opportunities for everyone who lives here. We must work together, looking for areas of agreement and building on those areas, on the foundation we've inherited from those who went before us.

One of the challenges we have is to recognize how fortunate we are to live in a part of the world that has not only incredible natural resources but also a truly exceptional package of human resources. Many people visit British Columbia and Canada, and can't believe the diversity we have in our communities. ...

As we've had wave after wave of immigration coming from all over the world, the commitment of those immigrants to their vision of Canada has helped our country grow stronger. A few days ago we celebrated Remembrance Day—a day that gives us a chance to think about the incredible commitment a generation of British Columbians had creating an open and free world—a world where people could pursue their dreams and where democracy had an opportunity to flourish.

We should never take our freedom for granted. We should never take for granted that we live in a place where an individual can make a difference. Where the vision, drive and commitment of an individual can draw people together, using the strength of community to achieve results.

---

1 "Premier Gordon Campbell: E-Government in British Columbia," *Canadian Government EXECUTIVE*, Issue 4 (2002): 11. Source: www.bcpublicservice.ca/awards/quotables/innovation.htm (2006).

Let me give you an example. In 1978 I worked ... with Marathon Realty. A fellow came into my office that I knew from when I worked ... [for Art Phillips] the Mayor. His name was Rand Iredale. He had a vision for our city. It was a vision that nobody else had for the city at the time. His vision was that we would build a new stadium downtown. His vision was also that the stadium would be moved out into the middle of False Creek and float. Sometimes you have to amend visions to get them accomplished.

But he did have a vision that we would have a new stadium downtown. Everyone said: "Well, Rand, that's crazy." He said: "Well, look, you know, if we put the stadium downtown, the parking spaces are already built, the hotel spaces are already there. Surely, this is something that makes sense. Instead of putting a stadium in the middle of a single-family neighbourhood, why don't we take it and put it in the middle where the action is, downtown?"

I know the powers that be at the time said: "Well, that's crazy. It's not going to happen." He kept on it. And that one person became five people. Actually, it was at the Board of Trade. I can remember this day—I think it was in about June of 1980—where there was a presentation by the Downtown Stadium Committee. And ... they showed the meeting a picture. It was a picture of how the stadium could fit into the downtown.

Rand Iredale never gave up on his vision. He kept on pushing it, and the next thing that happened was that a Provincial Commission reported back and said: "Actually, this is not a half-bad idea. Why don't we have a World's Fair, and use those resources to help build this stadium? We'll call it Transpo. And actually, while we're thinking of it, why don't we have a transit line that goes by it, and we'll call it SkyTrain?" And everyone said: "Well, it's the Province. They can spend money, I guess. Let's do that."

Transpo became Expo, and Expo became an entire generation of building the public's vision of Greater Vancouver, of British Columbia. Expo was a vision that went beyond Vancouver. Expo was a vision that reached out first to the province, then to the country and then to the world, and it was a vision we all shared. As Expo was moving down the road towards completion, there were a bunch of people saying: "Oh, we shouldn't do Expo. Boy, there's going to be problems with Expo. Gee, we're not sure if we want Expo."

We went ahead and hosted Expo, and we had a transforming event in our city. I would suggest it was a transforming event for our province, and it was because of one person's vision and commitment and persistence. We are one of the few countries in the world that have empowered our citizens to shape their world and future if they're willing to stick with it. That's leadership, and that's what every one of you in this room is all about. On behalf of everyone in the province, let me say thank you for your commitment to the future of British Columbia. ... [1]

---

1   Premier Gordon Campbell, Vancouver Board of Trade: Leadership Summit, November 19, 2004. Copyright © Province of British Columbia. All rights reserved. Reprinted with permission of the Province of British Columbia. www.ipp.gov.bc.ca. Source: www.bcliberals.com/premier's_speeches/ (2006).

Excerpted from "A Preliminary Study..." (Rhone & Iredale, 1978)

Project: Vancouver Centenary Study

Vancouver: Canada's Gateway

This study presents the seed of a concept that has grown from a small commission given to our firm by the Minister for Recreation & Conservation, The Honourable Sam Bawlf. It is intended to present conceptual ideas of the events and facilities Vancouver could establish to celebrate its Centennial year in 1986.

Our Centenary can be a catalyst, a catalyst to create permanent facilities that Vancouver as a major Pacific Rim city needs: a catalyst for investment in a flagging economy: a catalyst for the redevelopment of a part of our city that no longer functions effectively.

This study focuses on the celebration of the founding of a great city: a city with one of the most beautiful settings in the world, a city with 100 years of history on the north Pacific, a city founded to trade. Vancouver's centenary is back-to-back with the centenary of the completed Canadian Pacific Railway (CPR). In 1987 it will be 100 years since Canada was connected with the Pacific Ocean by railroad, making it a time to remember our national heritage.

The Vancouver / CPR centennial celebration can generate a Pacific Gateway Exposition to celebrate 100 years of our history. Our Pacific Rim trading partners are a key reason why Vancouver exists. Japan, China, Hong Kong, the Philippines, and our sister dominions New Zealand and Australia have a special relation to Vancouver. Such exhibitions have contributed to the vitality of such sister cities as Montreal in 1968, Seattle in 1962, and Spokane in 1972, to mention a few. If properly conceived, such an exhibition becomes a key element in the continuing growth and quality of the city.

If a Centennial Exposition gained the support of the Federal Government and our Pacific Rim trading partners, many millions of dollars of redevelopment funds would flow into the site at no cost to the taxpayer of Vancouver. In response to this opportunity: this study presents a concept for the redevelopment of a depressed area of the city and a shopping list of facilities that are appropriate to the event and to the site.

The study is not intended to demonstrate whether the ideas are practical or to create a controversy over the site for major facilities that Vancouver has not as yet decided to build. It is intended to create awareness of an opportunity and recognition of the fact that now is the time to plan our Centennial events and the facilities which will house them, and that we can minimize the costs and maximize the benefits by comprehensive planning.[1] ∎

In 1978 the Honourable Sam Bawlf, Minister for Recreation and Conservation in the Bill Bennett government, approached Rand Iredale to do a study concerning the celebration of Vancouver's 1986 centennial. Sam's idea arose from his heritage responsibilities as a conservation minister. It would prove to be an exciting and controversial study.

The study's proposed features included the construction of a Museum of Science and Technology, a 60,000-seat stadium, and a 1986 International Exposition in an Amsterdam canal-like setting.

This Centenary Study was implemented by others and went on to become the concept for Expo '86. With the attendance of Prince Charles and Princess Diana, Vancouver officially welcomed the world to its doorstep.

---

1   Rhone & Iredale Architects, "A Preliminary Study of Various Opportunities to Mark the Centennial Celebrations of the City of Vancouver" (March 1978): 2.

Excerpted from "A Preliminary Study..." (Rhone & Iredale, 1978)

How Redevelopment of this Site Can Contribute to the City Fabric

It is surprising that a half-mile radius from [the intersection of] West Georgia and Granville Streets reaches this site as well as the Burrard waterfront. Because this site is the back door, the undeveloped industrial fringe with no destination, it seems much further from the centre of the city than the end of Granville Street or the end of Burrard Street. But it is, in fact, the same distance from Georgia and Granville.

Georgia Street needs a termination. We have the Queen Elizabeth Theatre, the new CBC building, and plans for a new Federal building. If this scheme were to relocate the bus terminal, we would regain Larwill Park and turn Georgia Viaduct into a new gateway (now a misplaced segment of the throughway). Visitors to the new facilities and those using the waterfront walkways will be able to reach the restaurants and shops of Gastown and Chinatown with ease.

The Georgia Gateway area is the 'hole in the doughnut' of our city fabric. Chinatown, Gastown, the Financial District, the Golden Triangle, Georgia Street, Granville Street, and Theatre Row are vital and alive. They can be further strengthened and linked together by this new development; at the same time, the depressed area bounded by Beatty, Hastings, Richards, and Georgia will be revitalized.

The proposal also provides stimulus to Yaletown by bringing the waters of False Creek to the ends of the existing streets. This form of development does not compete with the high-rise office towers or with the residential development of the West End or the city lands of False Creek. Piers and canals are most appropriate for the continuation of Yaletown into the commercial area of the Marathon Realty (CPR) lands and down to the Creek.

While the north end of False Creek extends into the city fabric to Chinatown as a revitalizing influence, we see the land south of the Roundhouse as being [suitable for residential development] in the way that Marathon has planned during recent years. This [approach] would salvage much of the investment in plans already made for the area and would restore a downtown housing market to the City of Vancouver.[1]

༺

This study shows that while there may be apparently insurmountable difficulties in bringing such a plan to fruition, it has the potential to contribute in many vital ways to Vancouver's next 100 years of being a city worthy of its site, worthy of its history, and worthy of its people.[2] ∎

Project Team

Randle Iredale
Partner in Charge

Simon Richards
Project Architect

Paul Bridger
Project Manager

Opposite, above, & overleaf:
Thumbnail Image of the Dome and downtown Vancouver

Source: Internet (2006)

1 *Ibid.*, 6.

2 *Ibid.*, 18.

Adapted from "A Preliminary Study ..." (Rhone & Iredale, 1978)

Based on his planning study, Rand's redevelopment scheme included:

- a 60,000-seat enclosed multi-purpose stadium on False Creek at the foot of Georgia and Robson Streets, at a cost of $50–100 million;

- excavation of the northeastern corner of False Creek, under the Georgia Viaduct and back to Keefer Street in Chinatown (once False Creek water, the area had since been filled in);

- convention and eating facilities to accompany the stadium;

- five canals excavated at right angles to the shoreline between Robson and Davie Streets and extending as far back as Homer Street; mixed commercial and residential space would be developed between the artificial canals;

- a BC Museum of Science & Industry that would be created by converting the CPR Roundhouse at the foot of Davie Street in False Creek;

- eight or more national exposition pavilions created between a proposed twinned elevated highway along the shoreline and over the canals;

- a transit centre for long-distance buses just north of the proposed Stadium.

Comments in the press hint at political controversy:

Mary McAlpine wrote in the *Vancouver Sun* that the Iredale scheme "offers vitality and beauty" to the city, that Rand received a small fee from Sam Bawlf, and that he was asked to come up with a plan that could turn this no-longer-young city into a great and beautiful metropolis.[1]

Sam Bawlf commented in the press that Rand "developed all these ideas for the site and pulled all the threads together." There was strong opposition from PNE President Erwin Swangard and others, who wanted the new stadium to be built at the PNE. Backers of the Downtown Stadium formed The Downtown Stadium Committee to promote ... [this] location.[2]

Columnist Jim Hume quoted from Rand's study and commented that, though Premier Bennett mentioned many cabinet ministers who played key roles in the history of Expo '86, he never mentioned Sam Bawlf or Rand Iredale's original concept study. He observed that to read Rand's report was to read the text of 100 speeches since delivered by Premier Bennett and members of his cabinet; to view the maps was to view the Expo site almost exactly as Sam and Rand saw it; to view the critical path charts was to view the step-by-step procedures followed precisely by those who picked up the concept and ran with it. Jim Hume's article was a tribute to the authors, who seemed to have been forgotten in the Expo glow.[3] ∎

---

1   Mary McAlpine, "How to Create a Beautiful Metropolis," *The Vancouver Sun*, April 10, 1978.

2   Alan Merridew, "Stadium, Convention Centre Seen in False Creek Dream," *The Province*, March 9, 1978.

3   Jim Hume, "Thank You Sam, For a Job Well Done," *The Times-Colonist*, July 5, 1986.

Excerpted from "A Preliminary Study . . ." (Rhone & Iredale, 1978)

Recreation & Entertainment

The scheme will extend and enhance the existing recreational and entertainment facilities in the immediate vicinity: hotels and restaurants on Granville, Robson, and West Georgia Streets; in Chinatown and Gastown; the Queen Elizabeth Theatre; the new Chinese Cultural Centre; and False Creek Marina, with its associated boats and sailing activities.

The proposed additions are a Museum of Science and Technology, national displays from many Pacific Rim countries, a public sports facility, the restoration of Larwill Park, a new hotel, more areas of water for boating and sailing, and a stadium that could be the venue for concerts, tattoos, spectator sports, and boat and motor shows, to name but a few.

All of these facilities would be linked by the scenic waterfront roadway, the LRT, and a street-car route, with immediate access from the transportation interchange.[1] ▪

Below & overleaf:
black & white aerial views of Vancouver, (circa 1978)

Source:
Rhone & Iredale Planning Study

---

1 Rhone & Iredale Architects, "A Preliminary Study . . . ," 12.

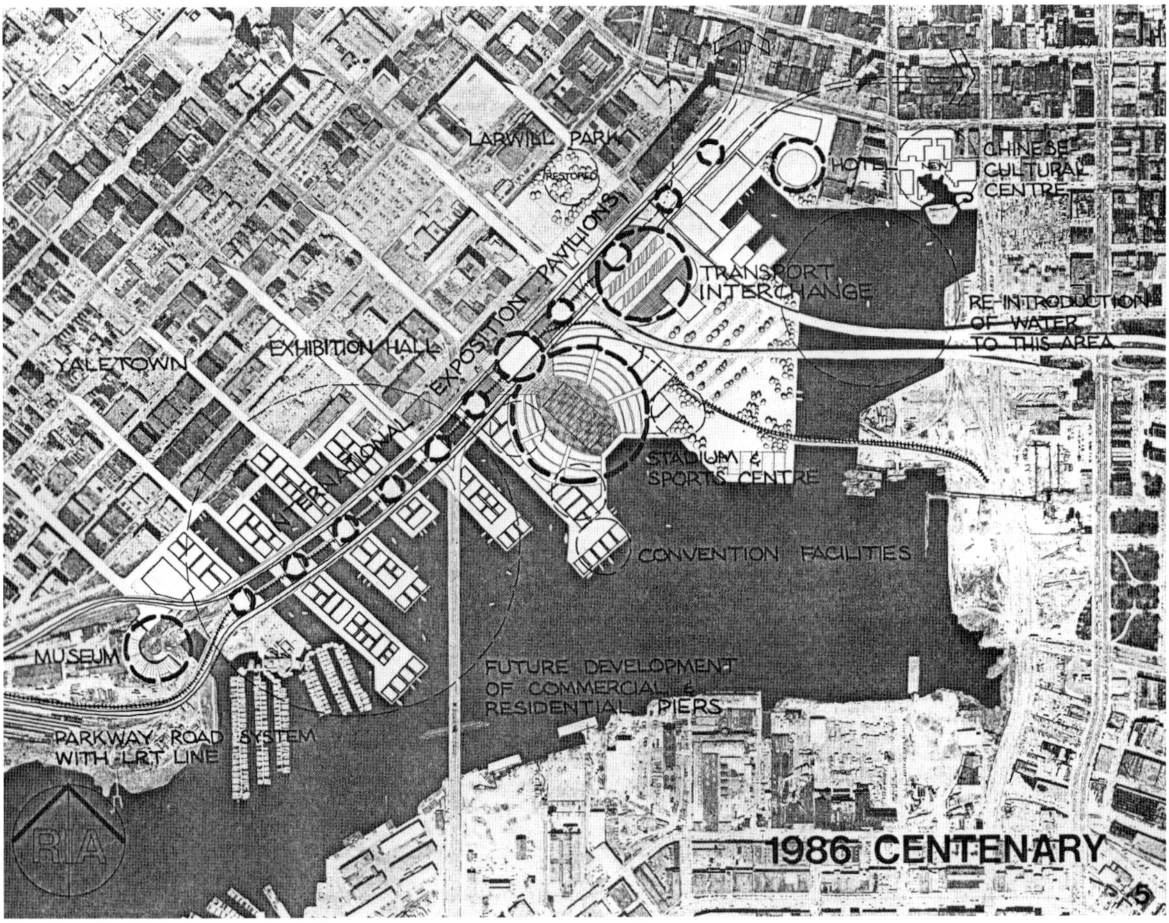

Excerpted from "A Preliminary Study..." (Rhone & Iredale, 1978)

City Fabric

"It is surprising that a half-mile radius from [the intersection of] West Georgia and Granville Streets reaches this site as well as the Burrard waterfront. Because this site is the back door, the undeveloped industrial fringe with no destination, it seems much further from the centre of the city than the end of Granville Street or the end of Burrard Street. But it is, in fact, the same distance from Georgia and Granville."

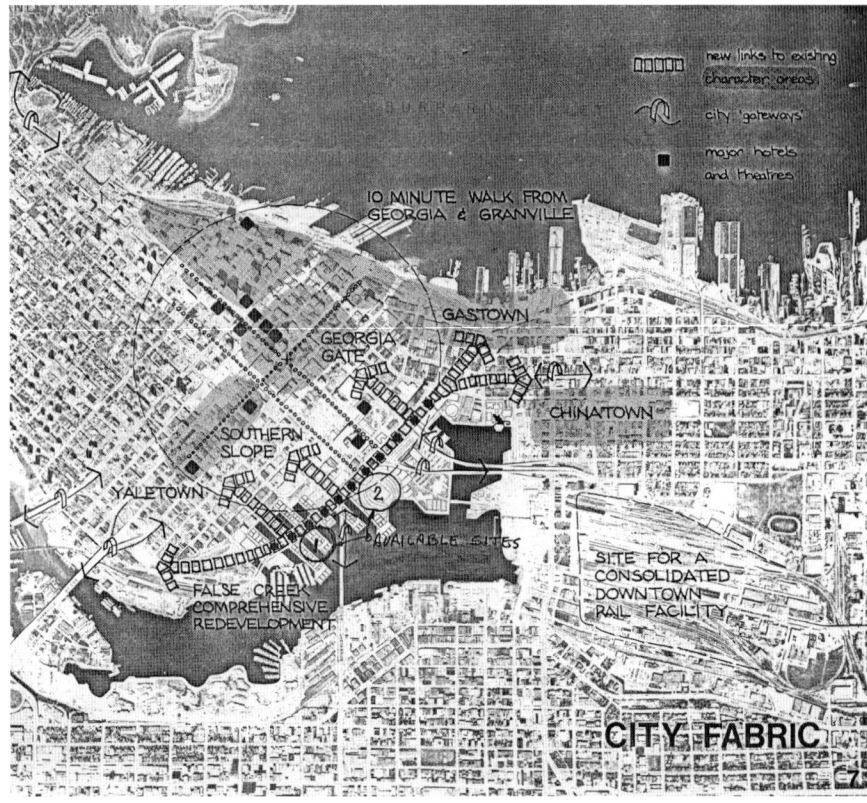

Site Access

"Vancouver is renowned for its Marine and Beach Drives along so much of its beautiful waterfront. We believe an extension of Beach Drive as a parkway could form the spine of redevelopment in this part of the city. ... [It] provides not only another traffic by-pass for the Downtown and a new entry to Gastown and Chinatown, but also a pleasurable experience for businessmen, citizens, and visitors alike who are moving through the city."

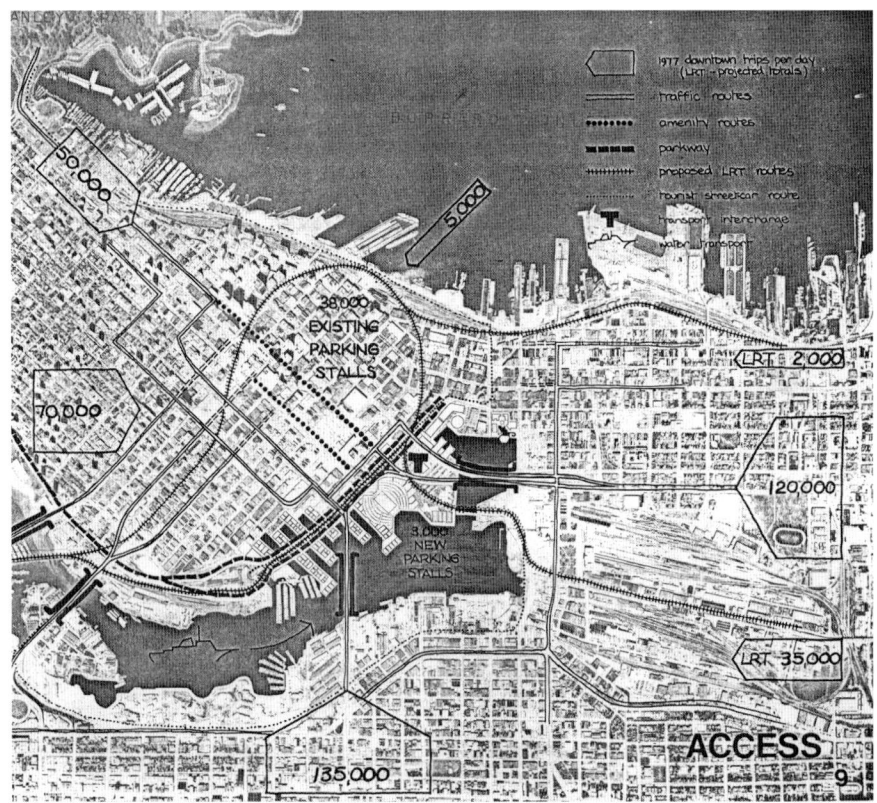

Excerpted from "A Preliminary Study..." (Rhone & Iredale, 1978)

1986 Exposition

"A Parkway road and LRT system on the waterfront would link a series of exposition pavilions, each built by one of Vancouver's Pacific Rim trading partners. Following the centennial celebrations these national pavilions would encourage commercial development ... and the direct influence on Yaletown would be dramatic."

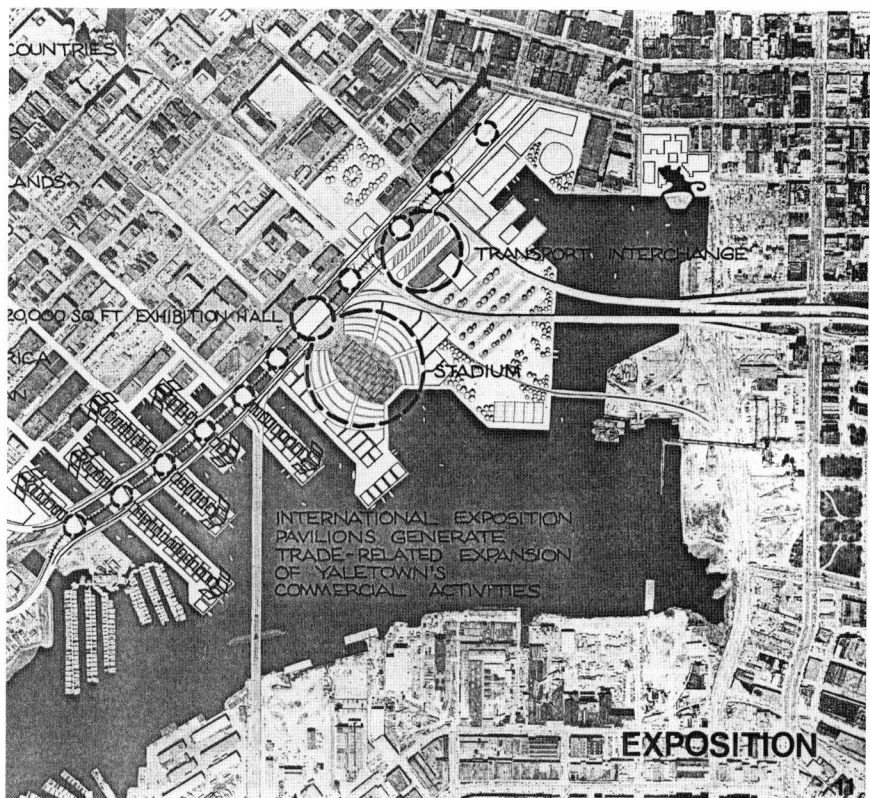

Recreation & Entertainment

"The scheme will extend and enhance the existing recreational and entertainment facilities in the immediate vicinity: hotels and restaurants on Granville, Robson, and West Georgia Streets; in Chinatown and Gastown; the Queen Elizabeth Theatre; the new Chinese Cultural Centre; and False Creek Marina ... The proposed additions are a Museum of Science and Technology ... a public sports facility ... and a stadium that could be the venue for [multiple events]."

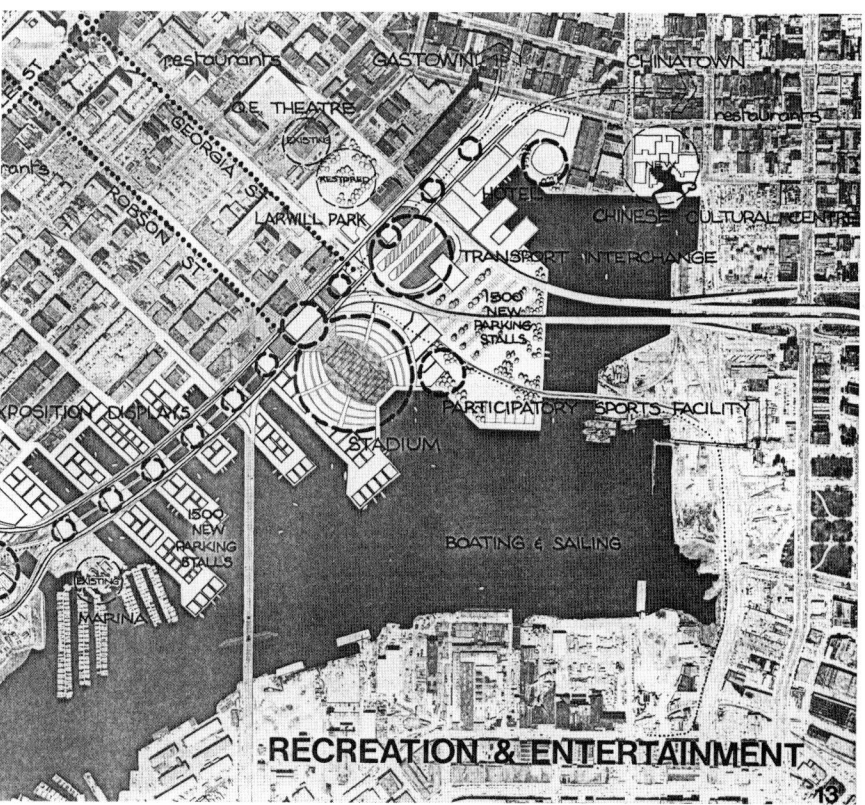

This study shows that while there may be apparently insurmountable difficulties in bringing such a plan to fruition, it has the potential to contribute in many vital ways to Vancouver's next 100 years of being a city worthy of its site, worthy of its history, and worthy of its people.

— *Rand Iredale*

A Major Contribution

From an interview with Bill Rhone.

False Creek

Rand was a member of the Board of Trade and a committee was struck to look at False Creek. He got very interested in False Creek. Here was all of this industrial land. So he looked at the pattern of ownership, and the majority of the land around False Creek was owned by the City of Vancouver. In those days the Board of Trade was fairly instrumental in making contact with the City of Vancouver and expressing their opinions … and Rand became very involved in that [process].

And then, out of the blue, through some sort of connection, I don't know where it came from, but Sam Bawlf—the senior Sam Bawlf who wrote the book on Sir Francis Drake—phoned Rand and they got together. The Provincial Government was interested in doing something with False Creek. So we did some planning work as a result of that call and we produced some concepts as to how the whole False Creek area could be developed. It's part of what you do as an enthusiastic participant in the overall scheme.

The Stadium

The stadium was an interesting idea.

There was a move afoot to build a new stadium. At that time the only stadium in town was the Empire Stadium, which was built for the 1958 British Empire Games, and it was located out at the PNE, which was okay at the time.

Thompson Berwick & Pratt had a monopoly on all of the work at the PNE and they built this stadium. It was a fairly low-budget structure with big steel columns every 50 feet coming down the centre of the seating. So you had to look around the columns, but it was all that could be afforded at the time.

But it was obvious that every city in North American that was coming of age had a proper stadium. And the thinking was, well, let's put the stadium downtown where everybody can use it. A special committee was formed, and Rand was very active on that committee. As a result, we were instrumental in influencing the location of the new stadium. We did some drawings at the time of what the stadium could look like downtown.

I don't think we got paid any money, but Rand's service on the Board of Trade and on their special committee made a major contribution to what eventually took place. ∎

Reprinted from *The Province* (Taylor, 1979)

Bennett Wants $50-Million Promise from Clark

But electioneering PM won't say yes or no on stadium

Premier Bill Bennett asked Prime Minister Joe Clark for $50 million Thursday. Clark said he'd think it over. Bennett wants Ottawa to pay half the $100-million cost of a domed stadium-amphitheatre in downtown Vancouver because its construction would be tied to an international exposition on transportation (Transpo '86) tentatively set for Vancouver in 1986.

Clark, campaigning in Vancouver, was just as reserved toward a request for another $4.5 million to help the Vancouver Art Gallery renovate the old court house. "We have not seen it (the stadium study) and we haven't judged it," Clark said during a news conference. "The other question (art gallery) is being pressed upon me by my members of Parliament, but we have not taken a decision yet." Then he added, apparently referring to both questions: "I don't know that we will."

Later in the day Clark took a softer stand on the stadium issue. "I want a look at the report that has gone to the government of B.C.," he said. "The premier and I have discussed that subject in general terms, and I would imagine the government of B.C. will be announcing their response to it before the federal government will. Naturally we want to look at the nature of the proposal and in[to] the federal role that might be influential."

Gallery director Luke Rombout took Clark's words to mean that the gallery's request is merely stalled until after election day, Feb. 18. "The prime minister has been made aware that there is a lot of public support which is both symbolic and tangible," he said. "We have raised $4.5 million and the city has put up $5 million. We're not in a stadium situation."

Bennett said Expo '67 set a precedent for a 50–50 cost-sharing between a province and the federal government. "I plan to put party leaders in the current federal election campaign on the spot and get a commitment for funding the amphitheatre and Transpo," Bennett said. He added he was "99.9 per cent certain" that the International Bureau of Expositions, which has given its tentative approval to Transpo 86, will give final approval next spring.

The stadium report released Thursday recommends construction of a multi-use facility on the north shore of False Creek, noting that the location would complement the planned Pier B-C convention centre and that together they are logical sites for Transpo.

Bennett said his cabinet won't decide until next month whether to support or reject the recommendations in the report.

From Hawaii where he is vacationing, Vancouver Mayor Jack Volrich said the report, written by Paul Manning, 34, an unsuccessful Liberal candidate in the last federal election, was "one man's opinion."

Reprinted from *The Province* (Taylor, 1979)

Highlights of the amphitheatre plan:

- *Designed for soccer, football and baseball. Could also be used for large rock concerts, religious and other large gatherings, consumer shows, rodeos and exhibitions. Would not duplicate facilities at proposed harbourside trade and convention centre at Piers B-C.*
- *Construction time: Four years.*
- *Operation would be under a provincial authority.*
- *Capacity: 60,000*
- *Cost: Estimated at $100 million.*
- *Land: Owned mainly by Marathon Realty and the CPR. Priced at $500,000 an acre, it could be leased or swapped for other property.*
- *Size of site and parking facilities to be determined by planners.*

Photo Caption:

"Vancouver architect Randle Iredale explains the facilities of the $100-million False Creek stadium proposal with the aid of a model."

Photo: Dave Paterson

Volrich, who has always supported the PNE site, said such an important planning decision should not be "based on a kind of 'crash' report," a reference to the 112 weeks Manning spent studying possible sites. Volrich said he thought the hotel industry wouldn't be overjoyed at the suggestion contained in the report of a hotel or entertainment tax on downtown businesses which the report says would gain considerable economic benefits from a nearby stadium.

The mayor was gratified that Manning recommends the stadium be funded and run by a provincial corporation, freeing Vancouver residents from the prospect of paying for part of it. Manning said his mandate was to define the type of building and the location, and suggest a funding formula.

"The province already has $25 million, not just committed, but already in the bank," said the premier. He implied the province might put up $50 million in order to get the job done. "The province is very healthy ... ," he said at one point. And later: "I want to emphasize my personal determination to see the facility built. ... I don't want to get bogged down in allowing other areas (of governments) to slow down the facility."

At the press conference Manning said bottlenecks at the bridges ruled out Richmond and Surrey; lack of public transport went against Coquitlam; the PNE has no room for further expansion; and experience of other multi-use stadiums elsewhere have shown the advantages of downtown sites. He suggested "people carriers" between the amphitheatre and the trade convention centre might be installed—perhaps like the Expo transit methods.

Mayor Jim Tonn of Coquitlam, who has fought hard to have the stadium in his municipality, called the False Creek recommendation, "crazy, really crazy," because of access and parking problems. "Anyone who thinks stadium visitors can utilize existing parking in downtown Vancouver is dreaming. Have you ever tried to park your car on a Friday night?"

The report includes a "special thanks to Mr. Erwin Swangard, President of the Pacific National Exhibition," for his long history of contributions to the building of stadiums and encouragement of sports events. A somewhat subdued Swangard said he would not comment until the cabinet reaches a decision. [1] ■

---

[1] Jim Taylor, "Bennett Wants $50-Million Promise form Clark," *The Province*, December 21, 1979: A4.

It is interesting to note the parallels between then and now: then, the Art Gallery's request to renovate the old Court House, the debate about downtown recreation and entertainment facilities, and the anticipation of hosting an International Exposition in Vancouver; and now, the plan for a 'cultural precinct' in the City that includes relocation of the Art Gallery, development of the Athlete's Village on the south shore of False Creek, and the anticipation of hosting the Olympics in 2010.

Model of
Downtown Stadium

Georgia Street Promenade

Robson Street Promenade

Project: Downtown Stadium Proposal

In 1979 Rhone & Iredale was invited to submit a proposal to the Downtown Stadium Association. Their proposal was instrumental in the City of Vancouver's decision to locate the new covered stadium (to be called BC Place) on the North Shore of False Creek.

By locating the facility at the base of the escarpment, the height of the new structure would be kept at a scale compatible with the existing buildings and, at the same time, would provide mid-level entries from Georgia and Robson Streets. The Rhone & Iredale proposal resulted in a strong integration of pedestrian and transportation routes to the downtown core.

As was stipulated in the proposal, BC Place has a seating capacity of 60,000 and is covered with an air-supported Teflon roof. The estimated cost of designing and constructing the stadium was $100 million. ∎

Project Team

Randle Iredale
Partner in Charge

David Osbourne
Project Architect

(Note: Rhone & Iredale did the proposal only)

Entry Concourse

Artist's Drawings

Adjacent & opposite:
Robert McIlhargey

A Multidisciplinary Practice

From an interview with Peter Busby.

I started working at Rhone & Iredale at a summer job in 1976. I worked on a project called CanCel, which was an office building in Prince Rupert for the Canadian Cellulose Company, and then I went back to UBC for my final year. I had formed a friendship with Rand, and he sat on my thesis committee in the Spring of 1977. My thesis was a proposal for a 'sustainable heart' in the City of Vancouver. After graduation I worked again at Rhone & Iredale (from May 1977 until I left to go to Europe and work for Foster in December 1979).

I continued working on the pulp mill up in Prince Rupert, and it really was the most polluted environment you could ever imagine. In those days pulp mills spewed smog and dioxin. We were working on the gatehouse, and the previous building was this rusting, rotting place where visitors come, where employees work, where people have meetings. So we turned it into a nice, simple, clean building; we clad it all in stainless steel so it wouldn't rot, and we created visibility from the president's office through to the secretary and other staff so that there was a kind of democratization [of space]. We even proposed methods to clean up the hog fuel dump that was next to it.

CanCel was the main project I worked on. I took it through to working drawings; it never got built, but I did the entire project. It was a great experience for me. I took that project to Europe to get the job at Foster and I said, "Here's what I can do." It was actually published in *The Canadian Architect* way back then.

I also helped with the design of the Crown Life Building, though Peter Cardew was the lead architect. That was a very important project in the city; it was a European James Sterling design aesthetic being brought to the city. I worked with Peter Cardew only for a short period of time. And with Bob Morton. But I principally worked with Rand, and not as much with Bill.

We worked on a couple of planning studies for downtown. One of them was the Lagoons project at False Creek, next to Granville Island. That early planning study showed the opportunity, arranged the form, proposed the idea of the waterways, and so on. At that time Granville Island had come together and False Creek was just being developed. We also did the planning and constructed a couple of buildings for the Burnaby Lake Sports Complex. Other people in the firm did the working drawings. There were lots of smaller projects, too, but I can't for the life of me remember them. I did the washroom details!

Continued

— Peter Busby —

Sustainable Design

We were definitely thinking about sustainable and environmental issues in the 1970s. It was there in the School of Architecture to a certain extent, and it was there at Rhone & Iredale. We thought about it, you know; we definitely thought about it.

There was a serious oil crunch in the mid-'70s; oil was very expensive and so people were aware of the issues. The response to the first oil crunch was a book called *The Autonomous House*.[1] And I know Rand read it because everybody did. And so he took some of those ideas and built his geodesic dome on Mayne Island and tried to create a 'back to the woods' settlement there.

It was a special piece of property. I went to two of the lamb bakes on Mayne Island and they were quite magical. They engendered a sense of community in the office. We took the ferry over, some people sailed over, and we camped on the property and smoked dope and stayed up late. I remember that moon coming up and into the Bay ...

A Man About Town

I first met Rand in 1975. He was a personality, a larger-than-life character. He drove a Jaguar and was well known, a kind of 'man about town.' Even then, he had his white hair! He was gregarious and outgoing. He could be very bombastic. He had some bad habits, he slept in, and then he expected you to work late with him! *[Actually, interjects Kathryn, he typically went for an early-morning jog, then sang pop songs in the shower, and then ate breakfast with his family!]* He had a temper and he could use it.

But it was a thoroughly enjoyable experience. I enjoyed working for him very much and I learned a lot from him. I learned about the opportunities to be entrepreneurial, because Rand was clearly an entrepreneur. And I learned about business and about thinking holistically. I don't regret a day that I worked there.

---

1 In 1975 Brenda and Robert Vale published their revolutionary book, *The Autonomous House*, a manifesto offering down-to-earth suggestions for building homes that neither pollute the earth nor squander its resources. Their book received tremendous praise around the world and was seen as a significant move toward green architecture. Nearly 20 years later, in the early 1990s, the Vales turned their groundbreaking ideas into reality: their latest book, *The New Autonomous House: Design & Planning for Sustainability* (2002), records their building of a house on the principles of sustainable resources in the small town of Southwell in the British Midlands. The Vales provide a thought-provoking, practical solution to the environmental problems caused by the houses in which we live, a blueprint of green architecture for future generations. Brenda Vale is Professor of Architectural Technology and Robert Vale is Senior Research Fellow at the University of Auckland, New Zealand. They are also the authors of *Green Architecture: Design for a Sustainable Future* (1991). Source: www.thamesandhudsonusa.com/new/fall02/528287.htm (2006).

— Continued —

I remember Rand as a person who encouraged you to do your best work. He had high standards and wanted to be as good as he could be with his clients. When I think about it, the diversity in the firm came from Rand. Bill Rhone was a beautiful sketcher, a felt-pen-and-paper guy; he could draw up a building in an afternoon. And Rand was a broad thinker with a vision of creating a multidisciplinary practice. He was a great guy to work for, an interesting person who would be critical of your work and challenge you to do better.

'Good People Make Good Practice'

Rhone & Iredale had the tradition of a Friday afternoon 'pin-up,' where you pin up your project and people kick it around. It's a tradition that I continue today; I've always done it in my practice. Every Friday at 4:30 we have a design charette. We pin up a project in the office and critique it in a social setting.

Rhone & Iredale was a good practice that attracted good people and 'good people make good practice.' That's what we try to do here; we have a good reputation so good people come here and, in turn, they enhance our reputation. That's what was going on at Rhone & Iredale. They weren't seen as the leading design firm—that was Arthur Erickson—but people wanted to work there. I met Paul Bridger there; Paul was my first partner and we practised as Busby Bridger Architects from 1986 to 1996. It was a place where you made friends and went on to work together.

They were one of the pre-eminent firms in the city. There was Thompson Berwick & Pratt (TBP), and there was McCarter Nairne (MN), and there was Rhone & Iredale, and there was Arthur Erickson, and that was essentially it. TBP did the university stuff, MN did the downtown stuff, and Rhone & Iredale did commercial buildings, institutional buildings, and planning studies. Erickson did all of the high-powered stuff.

But Rhone & Iredale had a very interesting group of people; you know, Richard Henriquez had been there, Terry Williams had been there; Art Cowie was there. They were doing landscape design and environmental design. They did a brilliant environmental study for the White Pass and Yukon Trail. So it was a broad, diverse practice. There were some star designers and there were some good people. It was attractive to be there!

Tough Times

By 1979–80 it was tough financial times and the market tanked, which is why I worked in Europe for a few years. In those days there would be too much work and then there would be no work, and then too much work and then no work. It was tough. ∎

Project: False Creek Housing (The Lagoons)

Commencing in the late 1970s, and with a large injection of money from the Federal Government, the City of Vancouver undertook to redevelop the south shore of False Creek. The zoning was changed from industrial to mixed residential-commercial.

Rhone & Iredale were commissioned by the Daon Development Corporation to produce a planning study of a site known then simply as Area 10B. This waterfront site is bounded on the east by the Granville Street Bridge and on the west by the Burrard Street Bridge.

An urban redevelopment scheme was proposed to replace what had become an industrial wasteland with inner-city housing. The residential buildings were to be terraced toward the water and mountain views, with existing and new streets and pathways converging on a central plaza at the waterfront.

It was deemed necessary to remove all mill waste soil, which would allow 2,600 feet of waterfront bays and canals. It would also increase the privacy of homes and create recreational possibilities, as well as allow for cost savings in landscape and maintenance of the development.

The proposed density of housing—over 100 units per acre—could be accomplished in low-rise construction by using stepped terrace forms over basement parking. All houses would have private exterior front doors and open views of the bay, city, and mountains. The project team, along with members of Daon Development, visited California to research such developments in the area north of San Diego.

The economic recession of the early 1980s precipitated Daon's acquisition by Bell Canada in 1985 (an investment written off in 1989); however, 'Area 10B' is now developed with housing ('The Lagoons') that conforms to the concepts laid out in the original Rhone & Iredale planning study. ∎

Project Team

Randle Iredale
Partner in Charge

Robert Hull
Project Manager

Simon Richards
Project Architect

Project Team

Randle Iredale
Partner in Charge

Charlotte C. Murray
Mike Hill
Project Architects

Awards

Canadian Housing
Residential Design Award,
1975

The Canadian Architect
Yearbook Award Citation,
1975

Publications

The Canadian Architect
(February 1976)
The Canadian Architect
(April 1975)
*Canadian Housing
Design Council* (1974)

Adjacent:
Fairview I – east side
(front corner of Steamboat
House is visible on left side
of photo)

Opposite:
Fairview II – west side
(view from W. 8th Avenue)

Project: Fairview Townhouses I & II

These two townhouse projects are located in the 1100 block of West 8th Avenue on the Fairview Slopes of Vancouver. Fairview I, built in 1974, and Fairview II, built in 1976, comprise two L-shaped clusters that frame the restored carpenter gothic Steamboat Heritage House, which was converted to Professional Office use in 1980.

The townhouses are designed around a generous, multi-leveled, landscaped courtyard that steps down to the commercial floor and parking below. An upper level pedestrian street surrounds the south-facing courtyard, which opens all spaces to sunlight, and gives access to the front doors of the townhouses. In this way, the commercial and residential activities are separated by a change in level while sharing the common courtyard.

According to the awards jury, "This project has several features which combine to make it outstanding. Of major significance, the architect was able to incorporate an office and residential mix which is an extension of the street character despite a lengthy battle with the City of Vancouver. This is very significant, as the architect provided a means of reintroducing housing to this historic neighbourhood on a sound economic basis.

"The courtyard and siting of building mass achieved a number of benefits. First, the stairs make walking up and down the three levels a pleasurable experience. Second, the complex does preserve, and indeed mutually complements the historic carpenter gothic frame house next door; this is especially important to this area of the city which is facing extreme pressure to redevelop by indiscriminately pulling down the old. A third strength of this design is the inclusion of significant loft/storage space." [1] ∎

---

1   *The Canadian Architect Yearbook Award* (April 1975).

216 | The Heart of the Design Process

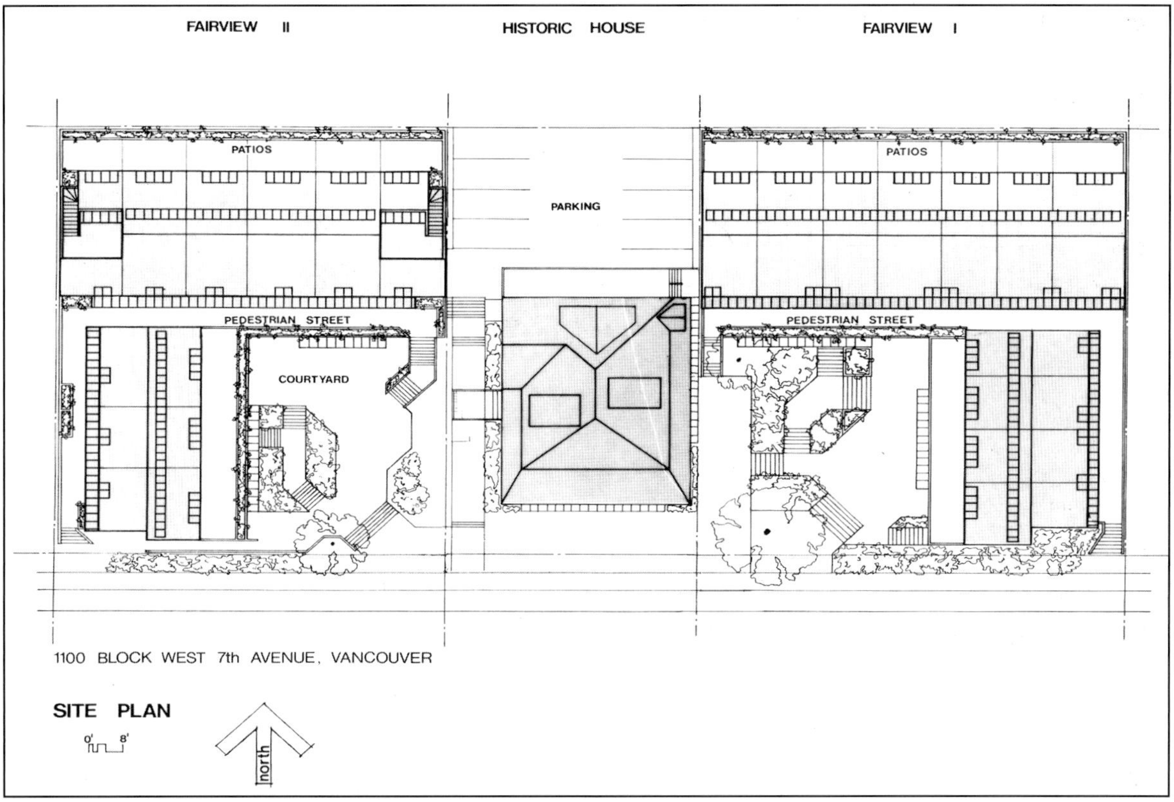

| FAIRVIEW II | HISTORIC HOUSE | FAIRVIEW I |

1100 BLOCK WEST 7th AVENUE, VANCOUVER

SITE PLAN

The Heart of the Design Process | 217

Project: Steamboat Heritage House

Restoration of the Steamboat Heritage House is presented in greater detail in the following chapter. It makes its first appearance here, however, as the centrepiece around which the Fairview Townhouses were developed.

Rand purchased the property in 1979 to develop an economically viable scheme for restoration in conformance with the desires of the Vancouver Heritage Board and other municipal authorities. This strategy was proven correct, as the building was fully leased within two months of completion.

The 1980 restoration and adaptation to professional office use of the Steamboat House, together with the adjacent Fairview I and II residential and commercial complexes, pioneered mixed-use development and heritage building adaptive reuse in the Fairview Slopes area of Vancouver.

The Iredale Partnership occupied the main floor as their offices from 1985 to 2000, and the successor firm, Iredale Group Architecture, with Richard Iredale as one of the studio partners, continued to occupy the space from 2000 to 2006. The Iredale family sold the house in 2006. ∎

Opposite:
East side of house

Below:
West side of house

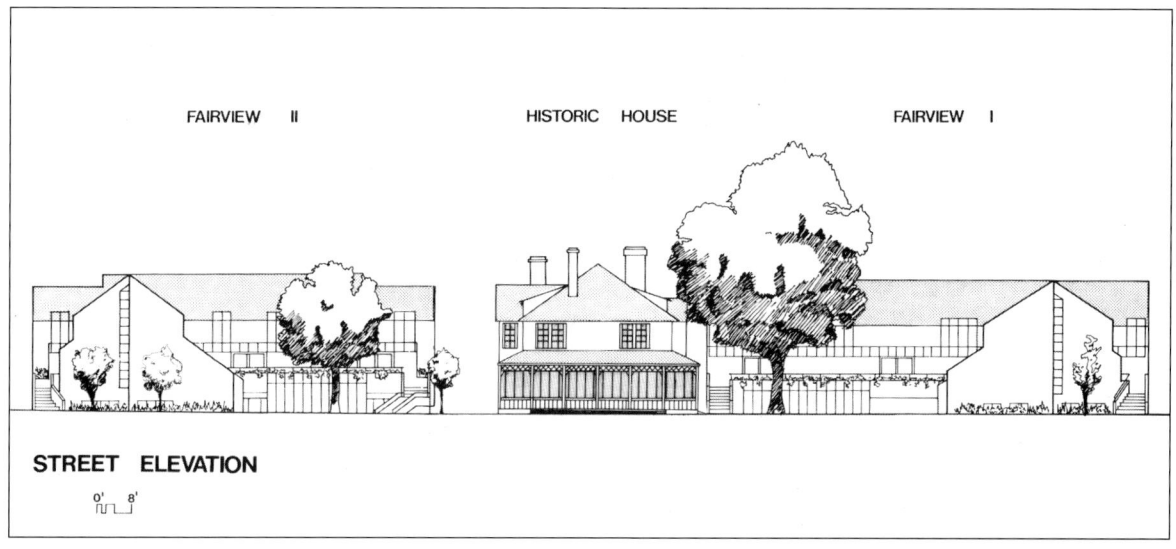

FAIRVIEW II HISTORIC HOUSE FAIRVIEW I

STREET ELEVATION
0' 8'

AN ITERATIVE DESIGN PROCESS

The next task is the heart of the design process. It is complex, interactive and impossible to manage without some exploration in directions that turn out to be blind alleys. By building the program and site-related constraints we have done what we can to identify the right issues and solve the right problems. Now we immerse ourselves in the design phase, accepting the chaos and lack of control this phase requires, with faith that we will emerge with a great scheme.

While a diagram can appear to be straightforward, the truth of the process is that some early directions will have to be modified, as we admit that we have gone up a blind alley and problems will arise that cause both conflict and creativity among members of the team. Accept such conflicts as positive evidence that the proponents are so committed to the project that they will fight for it. Resolution can usually be obtained by focusing your team on the problem (not the egos involved) to find the synthesis that comes when the different ideas are rubbed together.

In other cases, it is better to have the conflicting parties meet separately to resolve the issue. As a manager, accept conflict as positive: it is evidence of the fire that is driving the project, but ride it until it is resolved or you run the risk of losing the commitment of one or both of the team members who have the fire.

In managing the process, try to maintain a strategic overview so that detailed studies are not undertaken until the general direction and principles are established. Try not to smother far-out notions. Allow them enough effort to evaluate them on that 1% to 100% scale: "Okay, let's give it a one-day study and bring it back tomorrow." Encourage imagination and creativity. The schematic design phase should be open to all possible solutions that may contribute to finding a good fit between project aspirations and constraints.

Rand Iredale, Project Manager's Manual (1997)

> The schematic design phase should be open to all possible solutions that may contribute to finding a good fit between project aspirations and constraints.

THE SCHEMATIC DESIGN PHASE

Design Panel

In addition to creative interaction among team members, we have found that our internal Design Panel provides a productive forum to test schemes with fresh eyes. All projects should come to the Design Panel at the schematic phase for two basic reasons: first, to keep everyone in the office informed about the projects we are doing; and second, to elicit comment that may improve the quality of our design. While the quality of our service keeps clients coming back to us, it is the quality of our design that stands in bricks and mortar.

In presenting projects to a Design Panel it is important to present the Program and Site Analysis so the Panel understands what the project is trying to accomplish and the constraints under which the team is working. In receiving comment try not to be defensive. The comments are offered to help you improve the project. All suggestions have some value. Respond by summarizing the suggestion to be sure you understand it. Then note three positive things it offers (this can be difficult). If you want to explore the suggestion further, note the factors for which you don't yet see a solution.

The Design Panel presentation is also a useful dry run for presentation of the schematic drawings to the client. Note the points in the Program and Site Analysis that are unclear to panel members, as they will probably also be unclear to members of your client group. Consider the form of presentation in terms of the Panel's reactions, too, so that you can improve it for the client.

Design Freeze

After two or three iterations, an acceptable scheme will begin to emerge. ... We have scaled the first major peak in our quest. We have a design! Now we will proceed to build it. To do this effectively, however, we must commit to the scheme we have; we must freeze the scheme and stop Schematic Design. The next phase, Design Development, provides the opportunity to develop details that polish the quality of the building, but we must avoid the natural tendency to have new ideas that take us back to the design phase. Now is the time for execution. Develop the scheme! Beware of brilliant ideas that come too late; they will have to wait for the next project. Remember the old military strategist's maxim: *'a poor plan well executed is better than a good plan poorly executed.'*

Rand Iredale, Project Manager's Manual (1997)

Changing Times

While Rand was busy running his practice, I was busy bringing up the kids. And whenever anybody spoke to me they had to say "Mom" because I didn't respond to the name Kathryn! That was quite funny. I suddenly realized, my identity is MOM! But the kids grow up in about 18 or 20 years, and then they start fleeing the nest.

So I was looking around for something to do. I was 50, it was the mid-1970s, and I didn't really want to stay at home. I was trying to figure out what I wanted to do with the rest of my life. Rand was successful as an architect, but money was always tight. It costs a lot of money to bring kids up to begin with, and we had to educate them.

I took some courses at UBC. And I worked as a volunteer at the Museum of Anthropology, which I enjoyed, except that typing envelopes seemed like a waste of my time. Rand had done this development, Fairview I, and the condos sold well. That was in 1974. At that time I took the real estate course, still fishing around, trying to figure out what I wanted to do. But I'm not extrovert enough or people-oriented enough to be a successful real estate person. You learn a lot about yourself taking these courses!

Kathryn Iredale

Photo: Schiffer, Vancouver (1975)

Then in 1976 Rand did Fairview II. The condos weren't moving and I said, "Well, Rand, you've got to rent them," and he and I talked about it and agreed that we'd rent some of them and I'd try to sell some of them. And I did move some of them, and we rented the rest.

And then Rand wanted to buy and fix up the Steamboat House, which was in *awful* condition. The lady who owned it had no money and was running it as a boarding house. We bought the building from her, and the first thing we did was call the SPCA to get rid of the raccoons living in the attic! We renovated the house and went through the whole process with the City of Vancouver Heritage Committee about what you can and cannot do.

About that time the partnership of Rhone & Iredale broke up. Inflation was terribly high. That was around 1980 and we knew a lot of developers who were suffering. Projects would start and then stop because the developers couldn't afford the high interest rates. Homes and lots just sat for a while. Developers had been land-banking and perhaps had a lot of leveraged money. Some of them didn't survive. ∎

Where did the time go? After many happy years together—and with our children now in university—Rand and I were becoming empty-nesters!

Celebrating our 25th Wedding Anniversary 1978

PEOPLE PLACES

9 'God is in the Details'

> The early 1980s was very hard economically on an awful lot of people. I had friends who went bankrupt; it was really sad, and some of them didn't survive. One friend of Rand's lost all of his contracts because of the high interest rates. He turned up in the office one day and asked, "Rand, could you give me a job? I'm down to my last $2,000." It was a bad time for a lot of people. I don't think Rhone & Iredale would have survived had they stayed together; there was no work because of these high interest rates. When we went for financing on the Steamboat House our interest rate was 18%. It was a killer.

One Door Closes . . .

When Rhone & Iredale broke up they owned the house at 1100 West 7th jointly, but they had a buy / sell agreement. The agreement was that, in front of their lawyer, they would each write up an offer of what they thought the building was worth and put it in an envelope. Then they'd each pull a card from a deck of cards and the person with the highest card would offer their envelope to the other person. The other person then had the choice of accepting or rejecting the offer.

Their lawyer, Paul Beckman, was quite amused by this method. As it happened, Rand got the high card. I've forgotten the details, but the end result was that we bought Bill out. We got the building and Bill got the money. Bill moved into offices downtown with Peter Cardew and Bob Morton. In retrospect, it was a good thing that the firm broke up. At the time it was very upsetting, but with that economic climate in the 1980s they wouldn't have survived. *There was just no work.*

Rand was 50 when the practice was dissolved, and we still had to earn a living. We had worked together a fair bit because I'd helped him sell some of his units, and I said, "Well, we've got to keep the office going." So we set up practice at 1100 West 7th, which Rand had won in that unusual lottery.

Adjacent:

1100 West 7th as it looked in 1912.

This wood-frame house was built in 1908 by Robert Stewart as a family residence overlooking False Creek. During the 1920s the area, called Fairview Slopes, was a middle-class suburb of the growing City of Vancouver.

During the Depression and WW II these large houses were divided into suites and rooming houses.

By the 1950s the Fairview Slopes had become a slum area and was designated by the City as part of the 'downtown fringe' requiring redevelopment.

Adjacent & below:

1100 West 7th as it looked when Rhone & Iredale purchased it in 1965.

Notice the enclosed verandah on the front and side; the broken glass and boarded-up windows; the complete absence of vines, shrubs, and flower boxes; and the television antenna on the roof next door.

Photos: William Dekur (1965)

1100 West 7th Avenue

At the time of purchase, the house was divided into several sub-standard suites and had fallen into a serious state of disrepair.

The house was restored and renovated to accommodate an architectural staff of 30 to 35 people. Approximately 600 square feet was rented to Nanson & Dyer, graphic designers.

The restoration work involved relocating the front entrance, regrading the site to provide parking, and removing partitions to create open spaces for office use. The total cost of these renovations was $50,000.

(In 1965–66 the house had most likely been more 'modernized' than 'restored.')

Photos: William Dekur (1966)

… And Another Door Opens

Rand invited Charlotte Murray to join him. She had another commitment to finish first, and then she arrived in the Fall of 1980. We stayed at West 7th and rented out Steamboat House, which we owned through our family holding company, Kara Resources. It held that humongous mortgage at 18%. It was a tough time.

When Rand set up the new partnership, I joined him as Office Manager. I ran the office, did the accounting, and answered the telephone. I did everything: typed specs, prepared change orders, whatever I could to help. It was fun working together. We'd have our disagreements, because all couples do, but I enjoyed working with him. And I felt useful, too. I think that's important. When you've been at home bringing up kids I think you need to feel useful. I didn't have any particular training; I had taken a BA, but what can you do with a BA? I had taken the real estate course, but I wasn't cut out to be a real estate agent. I contemplated teaching, but I don't know if I would have been a very good teacher.

We went for lunch together almost every day, and other people often joined us. Rand didn't boss me around; he didn't act as my boss. As I said, we didn't always agree. It wasn't Eden, or whatever you want to call it. But we worked well together and he had always discussed things with me, like when he was figuring out how to get the stadium downtown. I remember in our bedroom at night there were long discussions about, "What should I do?" He would use me as a mentor and I used him as a mentor, too.

Though I knew everything that was going on, I did not get involved in design; I had my opinions but never expressed them because I wasn't an architect and that wasn't my role. But I expressed myself about other things. My favourite word in the '80s was 'no': People in the office would ask, "Can we have this and can we have that?" "No! We don't have enough money!"

It was tough starting over again, but many new adventures awaited us. Rand had a new practice and a new partner. He and I could begin travelling together; Rand had travelled to many places while I brought up the kids. He attended conferences and he went to China. He promoted work in Beirut, which perhaps was a bit of a pipe dream. And he went to England; his mother wanted him to go to England with her brother to visit his grandparents. I couldn't go because I had small kids and, also, we didn't have the money.

But we did a lot of travelling after the kids left home. Not so much in the '80s, because we were just barely surviving. That's when we'd done the Mayne Island (Bell Bay) Strata development and the lots wouldn't sell! Oh, it was a tough time. Eventually they were sold, but nobody had any money. Expo '86 brought us all out of it. Vancouver went from being a small town to being a big town. And that was Rand's era. He and Bill had designed the original stadium. Rand's planning study laid the groundwork for the future developments of Expo '86, the SkyTrain, Yaletown, and False Creek. ∎

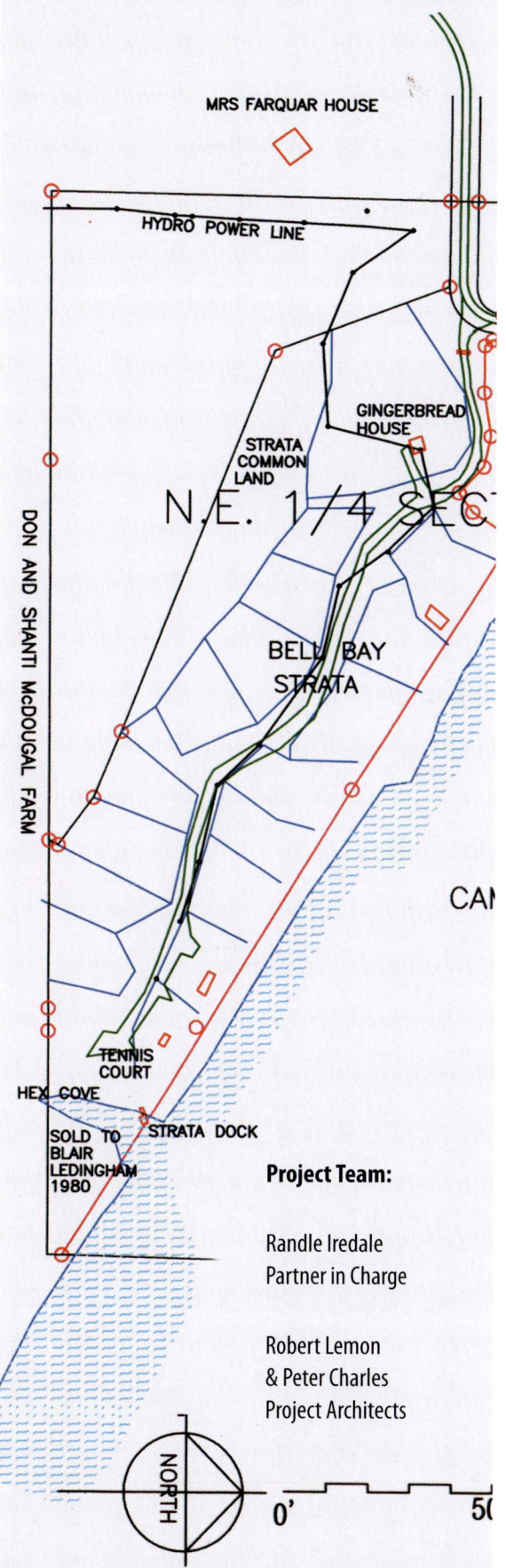

Project Team:

Randle Iredale
Partner in Charge

Robert Lemon
& Peter Charles
Project Architects

Project: Bell Bay Strata Plan

In 1958 Rand and his parents had purchased a quarter section of land (which included the water of Campbell Bay) on Mayne Island in the Gulf Islands of British Columbia. This property, which at that time was quite inaccessible and wild, was the summer playground for our growing family, and over the years many improvements were made to cope with our housing needs.[1]

Mayne Island became more accessible in the early 1980s and, though it was still a sleepy little island, property taxes were becoming expensive. We wanted to sell some of the land, but the Mayne Island Community Plan had zoned our property to allow only one lot per 10 acres. Rand was of the opinion that dividing the entire property into 10-acre lots would make it too expensive to service. As a planner and a conservationist, he felt that the higher, hilly area should be used to build somewhat clustered cottages and the lower valley area should remain as a green space and be used for sheep farming.

Rather than dividing the property into 10-acre lots, in 1979 Rand decided to subdivide 20 acres and create a Bare Land Strata of 2.5-acre lots that cross a common private road and share a dock and a tennis court. The subdivision was titled the Bell Bay Strata Corporation, to which Rand transferred development rights on the full quarter section (minus Campbell Bay). The new lots were sold as bare land strata lots.

Careful ecological study produced a method of preserving existing trees, views, and landforms, while allowing for a high degree of privacy on each lot. Rand prepared and administered a set of Design Guidelines to ensure that development by individual owners would be compatible with the surrounding structures and the landscape. The remaining lower valley area is now a 30-acre farm and the mountainous hillside is a managed forest. ∎

---

[1] Chapter 3 covers the story of Iredale Place on Mayne Island.

A project that fell between the cracks of past and present—the break-up of Rhone & Iredale—and also foreshadowed a future dedicated to heritage conservation was Rand's feasibility study in 1979 of downtown Vancouver City Block 15, later named the Sinclair Centre.

Project: Vancouver City Block 15

Project Team

Randle Iredale
Partner in Charge

Bill Rhone
Project Architect

Peter Busby
Project Manager

Opposite:
Sinclair Centre Clock Tower after seismic upgrade, envelope repair, & heritage restoration in 2003

Photo: Justin Adam

Below:
Original Post Office & Clock Tower, circa 1910

Photo: Vancouver Archives

Public Works Canada, Pacific Division, commissioned a detailed Feasibility Study for the downtown Vancouver City Block 15, bounded by Granville, Hastings, Howe, and Cordova Streets. Four buildings of heritage merit occupy the site: the old Post Office, the Winch Building, the Customs Examining Warehouse, and the Post Office addition.

The concept developed would stabilize and restore major heritage elements, modernize interior layouts, and create a heated, glass-roofed atrium space in the central area of the block between the four structures, connecting them in one continuous environment.

Following completion of the study, Public Works Canada solicited bids for architectural services. Six firms, including Rhone & Iredale Architects, were invited to tender and were screened with uniform criteria. It was Public Works Canada's intention to bind the selected firm to a four-year, fixed-fee contract, which was a harsh condition in an unstable economic time.

Though Rhone & Iredale had been awarded the contract, the firm's dissolution in late 1979 resulted in Public Works Canada reassessing the awarding of the contract, which then went to Henriquez and Partners Architects and Toby Russell Buckwell Partners Architects. When it was decided to execute the project, these firms implemented the original Rhone & Iredale study.

The project, now known as Sinclair Centre, received an award for Henriquez and Partners and Toby Russell Buckwell Partners in the RAIC 1990 Governor General's Awards for Architecture. The write-up in the 1990 Awards program describes the project:

> "Vancouver's Sinclair Centre is a classic example of Canadian Heritage architecture. It consists of four of the country's historic landmarks, occupying an entire city block.

> "The original, baroque Post Office, with clock-tower, at Granville and Hastings Streets (1910), with its 1936 extension; the R.V. Winch Building (1911), to the west; the brick-faced Customs Examining Warehouse (1919), north of the Winch Building; and the Federal Building (1937). The Winch Building and Customhouse are both Renaissance Revival in style."

Some 25 years later Iredale Group would undertake the seismic upgrade, envelope repair, and heritage restoration of the Sinclair Centre Clock Tower, with Kendall B. Jessiman, MAIBC, MRAIC, as the Partner in Charge. ∎

The Sinclair Centre Clock Tower is a dramatic architectural landmark in Vancouver. It crowns a cohesive grouping of early 20th-century stone-clad buildings that are without parallel in the city. The Tower was at one time an icon of federal presence and the highest point in the city's skyline. It is recognized today by the Heritage Council of Canada as one of the most prestigious heritage features in Western Canada. Vancouver's citizens and visitors can now enjoy its restored splendour for many years to come.

Reflections

In May 1980 Rand revisited UBC's Sedgewick Library. He gazes directly at us through his reflection in the mirrored skylight of an earlier time. The old Main Library in the background is now a heritage treasure on campus. Rand stands at the threshold between past and future, between old and new, lingering momentarily between the ending of his 20-year partnership with Bill Rhone and the beginning of his 20-year partnership with Charlotte Murray.

If this moment marked a break from what went before, it also formed a bridge to what lay ahead. Rand's increasing interest in heritage preservation would be reinforced by his daughter Jennifer's growing passion for rescuing old houses and his new partner Charlotte's studies in adaptive reuse of existing buildings.

The adjacent photo captures the crossroads where a career built on designing larger public places intersects with a commitment to creating smaller-scale people places. Rand's future would unfold amidst family collaboration, heritage conservation, and cultural revitalization—as his expertise in master planning and his fascination with computer technology would also flourish.

THE HERITAGE PARTNER

Excerpts from an essay written by Charlotte Murray.

After four years of working with Rhone & Iredale in the 1970s, I got my AIBC registration and then decided I needed a higher degree. I accepted a scholarship and returned to UBC in the Master of Architecture program. My thesis topic presented a rationale for encouraging repopulation of Vancouver's inner city. In the course of doing the research, and with the help of Jennifer Iredale, I determined that over 70% of the buildings in the study area were constructed before 1940, at a time when small wood structures were considered to be without value after 40 years. This finding led me to write a chapter on the true value of preserving and improving these buildings to provide more housing.

It was a great surprise and a pleasure to see Rand at my thesis presentation. It was an even greater surprise when he came up to me after the presentation and asked, almost without preamble, if I would be interested in joining him as a partner! Rhone & Iredale had just split up, and Rand was carrying on as Randle Iredale Architects. Well, I had to think about it—but not for long! We met to discuss the terms, which I considered most generous and, as they say, 'the rest is history.' Within not too many days, in June 1980, I was an official partner in the fledgling firm of Randle Iredale Architects.

During the first few months of my partnership with Rand there were only five of us in the office: Rand and Kathryn, their daughter Jennifer, and Martin Cruise and me. Our chief activity was promoting the new firm. We agreed that Rand was the Planning Partner and I was the Heritage Partner, which always gave Rand a giggle because it suggested that I was 'old,' when in fact he was one month older than me! We would each take responsibility for the promotion of and, if successful, be the Partner in Charge of, projects in our respective areas. It should be said, however, that Rand had long been a supporter of heritage preservation.

The Neophyte & the Pro

Rand and I got along very well; I was the neophyte and he was the pro, and I was very grateful for his mentorship. Certainly, at first, I had no idea of how to set up a partnership and he explained everything. We didn't formalize our agreement until 1983 but, looking back, he probably wanted to work with me for a few years before formalizing things! We had many agreeable discussions about all facets of setting up our partnership, which basically reflected our working arrangement over the previous two years.

Continued

Charlotte Murray

The Roundhouse

An early project that came to Randle Iredale Architects was for Expo '86. Rand became Project Leader for renovation of the Roundhouse complex, which was to be the location for an exhibit featuring the history of the City of Vancouver. Our team got right to work producing measured drawings and studying the significant history of the buildings. From the upper windows in our office we could survey all of False Creek and watch the daily changes as clearing progressed for the Expo development.

One day Rand came roaring up the stairs and exclaimed that a bulldozer was knocking down one of the Roundhouse buildings. A quick glance out of the window confirmed the worst. Rand tore out of the office, jumped into his car, raced down to Expo headquarters, and walked straight into the President's office. "A bulldozer is knocking down the Roundhouse buildings! They can't do that! I'm the architect and we have not decided what buildings, if any, are to be demolished!" The President's reply was swift—"I am in charge of the Expo development, and you are fired!" When we heard the news from Rand, we were all in shock. But that was that. Somebody else got the job.

The Desktop Computer

It was about this time that the desktop computer was introduced. The computer was another of Rand's enthusiasms from way back. Before I ever came into the office he had designed a program called Ri-Rite that computed all of the information needed to produce the firm's month-end statement. When I joined Rhone & Iredale in the 1970s, pressure already permeated the office to get all of the required information together for the monthly run to the downtown mainframe computer. By the next day the firm's financial performance was there for all to see.

Now, in the 1980s, the desktop computer promised in-house miracles in the form of processed data produced right in the office. After Expo '86 there was ample time to ponder how this new tool could serve the office activities. One thought was to create an indexed address book that would instantly produce a list of names for any purpose we could imagine. I'm not sure where that list went, as I must have scored a job that diverted my attention!

A Level of Trust

How we all worked together depended on what work came into the office. When I joined the firm as a partner the only project we had was Barclay Heritage Square, for which Jennifer Iredale and I wrote the proposal (Rand's activities for heritage preservation had already been recognized by Heritage Canada in the 1970s).

Continued

Charlotte Murray

In 1974, with Rand's guidance, Jennifer had been instrumental in the relocation and renovation of Hodson Manor (on the Fairview Slopes), which is now home to the Vancouver Early Music Society. And Rand gave her the opportunity, in 1980, to act as Project Manager for relocation and restoration of the Gingerbread House, which was moved somewhat precariously from the Fairview Slopes to its new 'home' on Mayne Island.

In 1985 the economy had been in a recession, so Rand and Kathryn sold the double lot the office stood on and moved into the Steamboat House. It had been built around the turn of the century for the captain of a local steamboat. When I first came to Rhone & Iredale it was a boarding house, and then they restored it and converted it to offices. It stood between the two Fairview condominium complexes designed and built by Rand shortly after my initial internship began. In fact, Rand had the nerve to allow me to supervise construction of the first one!

An amazing thing about Rand was his level of trust in you to take on a job and do it from scratch with no experience. It was incredible! And he kept doing that to me. What a wonderful way to make people grow. ∎

An amazing thing about Rand was his level of trust in you to take on a job and do it from scratch with no experience. It was incredible! And he kept doing that to me. What a wonderful way to make people grow.

— Charlotte Murray

Project: Hodson Manor

The William Hodson residence, built on Vancouver's Fairview Slopes in the Queen Anne Style in 1894, was one of the principal homes in the area for many years. By 1974, however, gentrification was taking place on the Fairview Slopes, and Hodson Manor was dilapidated and in immediate danger of demolition. At that time it received Vancouver City's first-ever Heritage Designation.

City land one block away was made available, and on April 30th, 1974 Vancouver City Council approved the relocation of Hodson Manor from its original site to 1254 West 7th Avenue. Rhone & Iredale was appointed to assist in this project and to prepare a report for Council on the work required to restore the house and make it usable once again.

Jennifer Iredale was a major advocate of saving this historical house. She has since worked as a Curator of Historic Sites in the Coastal Okanagan Region, and is currently a Senior Heritage Curator for the BC Government.

According to Robb Watt, then Curator of the Vancouver Museum, "The stained glass above the door is the earliest heraldic glass that survives in Vancouver. … It is presumed to be the work of the Blomfield Company, the outstanding art glass firm in Victoria and Vancouver whose shop was in Mount Pleasant in the early 1890s."

The exterior was completely restored above a new stone foundation. Historically important interior spaces and details were restored and new elements sensitively added to equip the building for new uses. It is now leased by a variety of community arts and social services organizations, providing office space and music rehearsal and performance space. ∎

Reproduced from Unpublished Report (Kara Resources, 1980)

Project: Gingerbread House

Fairview Cottage

Fairview Cottage, or the "Gingerbread House" [as it would become known], was an elaborately ornamented cottage built on Vancouver's Fairview Slopes around 1900. Mr. Burnett was a cabinet maker who worked for Williams & Hackett on the False Creek Flats and later for the Canadian Pacific Railway in the manufacture of railway cars. His work would have given him access to the variety of architectural pattern books published in the United States. Having purchased his lot at 1301 West 7th Avenue with its commanding view north over False Creek, he built his house, Cottage Design No. 1748, from *How to Build, Furnish and Decorate* (1900), published by the Co-operative Building Plan Association, Architects, 203 Broadway and 164–6–8 Fulton Street, NY.

This firm was the publisher of *Shopell's Modern Home Quarterly*, a series that appeared over a number of years; Cottage No. 1748 may have appeared in an earlier number and been reprinted in the 1900 collected book of designs. The design was modified by the addition of a bay window facing the street and a small conservatory, relocation of the staircase, and the addition of the distinctive wooden 'gingerbread' of the gable ends, eaves brackets, and porch detailing.

The house was continuously occupied as a residence until 1975. Considerable change had taken place on the Fairview Slopes, having suffered a decline in desirability as a residential neighbourhood and a shift to industrial uses. The area was rezoned in 1971 as a mixed-use residential / commercial zone to promote inner-city housing, take advantage of the spectacular views, and preserve some of the older houses.

The Fairview Cottage was identified by the Vancouver Heritage Advisory Board as a building of architectural value, but increased land values and higher density zoning determined its eventual demolition. When the owners offered the building for removal so that they could develop the property, Jennifer Iredale persuaded her father, architect Randle Iredale, that the building was worth moving. Their offer for removal was denied when the owners decided to use the house as their offices.

Future Use

The owners removed the fretwork and stored it in the basement and used the house as their office until 1980. In September 1980 Jennifer noticed that the house and its neighbours were vacant. The owners confirmed that the property was going to be developed as condominiums. The Iredales' proposal to remove the house to Mayne Island was accepted and the elaborate and newsworthy moving process was underway.

The Gingerbread House was moved to Mayne Island where it has been restored as a residence on the 20-acre bare land strata development that was being created by Kara Resources Ltd. (owned by the Iredale family).

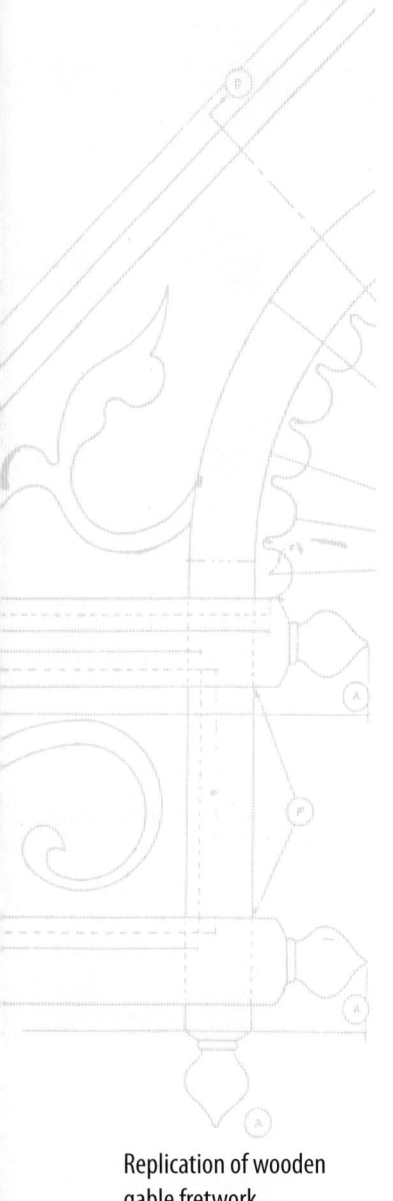

Replication of wooden gable fretwork

Drawing: Don Grant

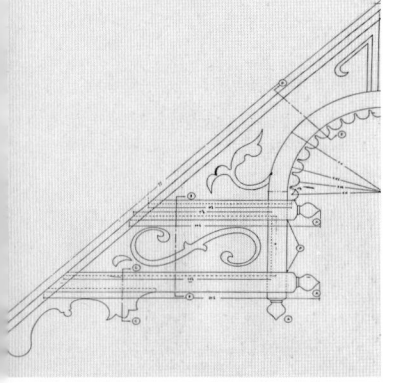

Reproduced from Unpublished Report (Kara Resources, 1980)

Rescue & Restoration

Rescue

In the Fall of 1980 the house was purchased by Kara Resources Ltd. for the sum of one dollar. Nickel Bros. was hired to undertake the complicated house-moving process. Just one week before the move, the carved wooden gingerbread that had been removed for safekeeping and stored in the basement by the previous owners was stolen. Such architectural components are valuable as interior fittings. The reward offered did not aid in the return of the most distinctive feature of the house. It would be necessary to have the gingerbread replicated as part of the building restoration.

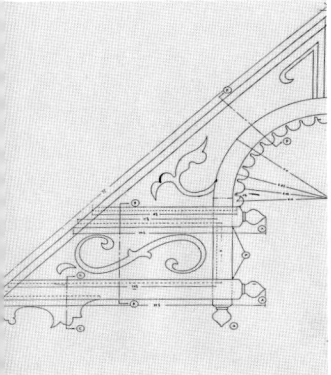

With the initial preparation complete, the house was lifted from its foundations and attached to steel 'I' beams and wheeled 'bogies' on which it was manoeuvred down the steep streets of the Fairview Slopes to a barge docked at nearby Granville Island. The logistics of the move were complex, involving coordination of the temporary removal of utility lines and [relocation] of several construction sheds along the route to Granville Island.

Despite careful planning, there were some complications. A communication problem with the telephone company resulted in the house being stranded on the Birch Street hill overnight until the overhead lines were removed. The headline, "Salvaged House Stalled in Middle Of Street," created considerable attention on Hallowe'en with [newspaper] coverage in the *Vancouver Sun*.

After reaching the barge, the house was floated some 40 miles across Georgia Strait to the Gulf Islands, where it was unloaded from the barge at David Cove on Mayne Island. The house was then wheeled across the Island to its new location on the Iredales' property at Campbell Bay.

Below, left:
Front of Fairview Cottage in original location (1974)

Below, right:
Rear of Fairview Cottage in original location (c. 1910)

Photos: Courtesy of G. Colchester

"Call it Victorian picturesque or carpenter Gothic but a little bit of Vancouver history that was slated for the wrecker's ball is about to set sail for the Gulf Islands. . . .

"Project manager Jennifer Iredale said she talked her father, architect Rand Iredale, into saving the house as a favor to her because of her interest in heritage buildings. 'But in return, he made me project manager, which he said was a fair exchange.' . . ." [1]

Photo: Don Scott, Vancouver Sun

---

1   "Salvaged House Stalled in Middle Of Street," *The Vancouver Sun*, October 31, 1980.

"Parked home . . . stalled on Birch between Sixth and Seventh while en route to Mayne Island"

1. loading house onto barge at Granville Island

2. house on barge in False Creek

3. house on barge near Mayne Island

4. unloading at David Cove

242 | 'God is in the Details'

Reproduced from Unpublished Report (Kara Resources, 1980)

Project Team

Randle Iredale
Partner in Charge

Jennifer Iredale
Project Manager

Publication

The Canadian Architect,
September 1982

Below:
Front and back views of Gingerbread House, as restored

Photos: Jennifer Iredale

Restoration

A new road was cleared through the wooded property to the building site overlooking Campbell Bay. The terrain of the site allowed the house to be positioned on its new foundations with a basement that had grade access toward the water.

A new cedar shingle roof was installed, the shiplap siding repaired, and some of the later windows replaced with antique ones purchased in Victoria. The gingerbread, balustrades, porch posts, and brackets were carefully replicated by a craftsman on Mayne Island. The exterior was painted shades of yellow and white, based on research of pattern book cottages of the period.

The interior was refinished with new drywall, the original floors and wooden moulding were retained, and a new fireplace mantel was installed based on period designs. The staircase was relocated to gain easier access to the partially finished upper storey. Few problems were found in locating period fittings and details for the house.

Shops in Victoria and Vancouver were scoured for the interior doors, replacement windows, and other components. All of the work on the house was done by young craftsmen who chose to live and work in the quiet rural setting of Mayne Island. The Gulf Islands are home to a significant number of artists and craftspeople.

A well was drilled and a septic field located according to the regulations of the Gulf Islands Trust. The grounds of the house were landscaped in sympathy with the scenic, wooded surroundings and its prominent position at the entrance to the bare land strata development.

In its completed state the setting and appearance of the Gingerbread House is similar to that of its first location on the newly settled slopes above False Creek at the turn of the century and the idealized rural setting of pattern book picturesque cottages.[1] ■

---

1   This text on relocation and restoration of the Gingerbread House has been reproduced from an unpublished report prepared by Jennifer Iredale on behalf of Kara Resources Ltd. and Randle Iredale Architects (circa 1980). Relocation of the Gingerbread House to Mayne Island is also recounted in Chapter 3.

Memories of Dad

Essay written by Jennifer Iredale.

We were a small and close-knit family: Dad, Mom, me, my older brother Talbot, and my younger brother Richard. Dad had no siblings, and though Mom had a sister, our cousins lived in faraway places. Our closest relative was my dad's mother, who we called Nana. I remember that her garage had a curious sign posted inside that read, "No Beach Fires Allowed." As a teenager, Dad had removed the sign from the beach at Spanish Banks where, of course, he and his friends were stoking a good, big fire. This story, and a few other personal experiences with my father, helped shape my perception of him as someone who liked to push boundaries and question authority.

Actually, though, Dad was the authority in our household and we kids gladly followed him to many places we would not have otherwise gone. Mom did, too. Fires were definitely a favourite game with Dad. Ours was the house with the Hallowe'en fireworks—one time burning down our neighbour's tree. Another deliciously scary event was the time Dad didn't appreciate some boaters who were burning a big fire in a hollow log rather close to our dry forest on Mayne Island. After chasing them off the beach, he pushed the log into the water and it proceeded to float over to the sailboat, still burning, and bumped up against it. We kids watched in awe from the safety of our cabin as the sailboat turned tail and fled our bay.

Dad had his kids building things with shapes and blocks from an early age, and as we grew older he and his passion for architecture led all of our vacations and family time. I still remember being given tile and linoleum samples to play with when my brothers and I visited the office on the Fairview Slopes. Dad would bring home models of the projects he was working on, and talk at the dinner table often focused on whatever architectural issue he was grappling with at the time: location, massing, and circulation systems; preservation of existing elements or structures or trees in a new design; how people used buildings, colour, light, sunshine.

We kids had a say in many projects that we later saw being constructed. We were certainly raised to believe that architecture was the noblest profession and that buildings were the most interesting topic of study! Dad's influence on his three children was manifest in our choices of university study and, to some extent, career paths: me in historic preservation, Tab in structural and then software engineering, and Richard in structural engineering and then architecture.

Continued

Jennifer Iredale

Our Trip to the Arrow Lakes

I remember the summer in 1966 when our family vacation was a trip through BC to visit the Arrow Lakes and a portion of the Peace River that was going to be flooded by dams being built for hydro-electric power. During the previous year, Dad had been up north in the Peace Country working with BC Hydro to design a visitor centre, power house, and school for a new community to support the new Peace River Dam. Our road trips were long and fun, with lots of singing in the car and around the evening campfire in different provincial campsites. Mom did a great job of keeping us all fed, cooking on an old Coleman stove.

There is a photo of Mom and I beside our 'valiant' Valiant, with gear spilling out of the trunk and the Coleman burbling away. Standing in the background is an old wooden lodge building, somewhere on the Arrow Lakes. I remember being enthralled when Dad took me to visit its elegant lobby. Together we examined the lovely building and Dad told me it was one of the buildings that would be 'drowned' in the flood. I was about 10 years old and this was probably the first time—but not the last—that I 'fell in love' with an old building.

Our Trip to the Historic City of Venice

A significant event in our family life was Dad's decision in 1969 to take us all to Europe when he was offered a four-month teaching job in Venice with UBC's School of Architecture. It meant he had to leave his very busy architectural firm. It was probably not the wisest business choice, but from a personal and family perspective it changed our lives.

Jennifer and Talbot observe first-hand and up close, as they listen to UBC's Professor Abraham Rogatnik introduce his students to some interesting detail of Venice's built history.

Continued

Jennifer Iredale

We became part of an excited and exciting group of students and faculty focusing on architecture in Europe, particularly the incredible historic city of Venice. Imagine being a 13-year-old girl transported from Vancouver to Venice to live in a gracious old Italian *palazzo* across from the Grand Canal! And imagine joining a group of post-graduate students in their study of Venice, focussing on how to preserve and enhance the city.

Throughout the trip Dad urged us kids to participate in as many student activities as we could. Sometimes I resisted, but he would make us go on their walking tours with eminent professors (from UBC) and join in their drawing workshops, where I felt too self-conscious and insecure to actually draw anything. At dinner we would sit with students and faculty and be part of the discussion about what we had seen that day or theorize about modern versus historic architecture. During one of these walking tours—in and around the historic Italian town of Urbino—I began to realize that old buildings and streetscapes fascinated me.

My Passion for Old Things

Dad encouraged me to pursue my interest in architecture all through high school and university. My school projects on different architects or architectural history gave me a strong connection with my father. We would walk together in the evenings and discuss what I was learning. Those walks took us through the UBC campus where Dad was involved in a project designing and building the undergraduate Sedgwick Library. We discussed the books we were reading, such as William Gordon's *Synectics* (1961), Ian McHarg's *Design with Nature* (1969), and Christopher Alexander's *A Pattern Language* (1977). Dad was a supportive confidant as I imagined my future, and it was inspiring to share ideas about his projects.

At this time in my life I was forever falling in love with old buildings and old furniture. One time I was quite smitten with a badly beaten-up old wooden desk that someone had discarded outside of their fence, which I passed on my way home from school. I desperately wanted to redesign my room and incorporate this 'beautiful to me' desk, so that evening my parents walked six blocks with me to see this 'antique' that I was so excited about. I think they were both appalled when they saw it and really did not want me to have it. On the way home Dad kept asking me what it was that I loved about this desk and, after much discussion, we agreed that it had a very nice bit of gingerbread on the backboard.

We retraced our steps and removed the gingerbread, which then became part of the door to my room. This experience taught me to critically examine my choices to get to the root of an issue. Even

Continued

though my Victorian tastes didn't fit with the modern décor of our house, Dad always walked that extra mile to make something work. Starting with this single piece of the desk, we went on to design and build a desk, bed frame, and bookshelves out of large pieces of fir for my room. Both the design and the activity were very different from what most of my girlfriends were doing with their dads! The desk itself was left in the lane until it gradually just melted into the ground. Over the years, as I continued to walk past it, I would marvel at my parents' patience with me.

In 1970, our family built a dome as our summer cabin on our Mayne Island property. Though we kids were just 14, 12, and 9, we were part of the labour pool on this construction project. Mom and I peeled the log posts that the dome hung on, my brothers put together the struts, and we all lifted and hauled and screwed and hammered. We discussed what kind of door this dome should have and, when I passionately argued for a door from a Victorian house, Dad and I set out to find one in Vancouver.

We soon found a beautiful old Victorian panel door with lots of dentils and details, which became the entry door to our very modern dome! In this way, Dad continually supported my interests and validated my passion for old things. I stored the door when we took the dome down, and now it graces my new 'Arts & Crafts' style cabin on Mayne Island. Every time I look at that door I recall Dad's support of my crazy notions and how it led me to pursue a career in heritage preservation.

When I was in grade 11, I fell in love with an old house on the Fairview Slopes that was threatened with demolition, and Mom and Dad encouraged me to do a school project using the City Archives to research the building. They went even further than that and encouraged me to phone Vancouver's City Planner to bring the building to their attention. When I was in tears because the building was on the brink of being demolished, my parents encouraged me to call the *Vancouver Sun* and talk to a reporter about the project. This call led to a front page newspaper article and the City agreeing to move the building to a safe location. Hodson Manor still graces the Fairview Slopes, and I went on to study building preservation.

Together, Dad and I saved another building on the Fairview Slopes, the Gingerbread House, which we moved to our property on Mayne Island in 1980. Dad 'employed' me as the Project Manager on that job, giving me the experience of both failures and successes—a bit like jumping off the deep end—in designing and contracting, as well as doing the labour myself with the help of a small crew.

Continued

Jennifer Iredale

Model, Mentor, Maverick

Dad wasn't always sympathetic to my needs and wants. He could be overbearing, opinionated, and strong-minded, and he had no time for my complaints, especially when I didn't want to do the things that he wanted me to do. He would make me ski down mountains that were too steep for me, hike hillsides when I had asthma or blisters (I once walked a rocky five-mile mountain trail barefoot without any sympathy from him), and get up at four in the morning to fish for salmon in the rain and then gut the rock cod I invariably caught.

On the one hand, Dad was a great one for doing things—and doing them his way—and he brooked no complaints or laziness from his kids. On the other hand, if we had big dreams he was always the first to encourage and support us and was always willing to help us if he could. His model as a leader and a bit of a maverick—as someone who was willing to buck the trend and think outside of the box—has influenced me tremendously. He was my mentor and the audience to my successes, and I am deeply appreciative. ■

Adjacent & Opposite:
Rand and Kathryn attending Jennifer's graduation from Columbia University (1983)

He was my mentor and the audience to my successes, and I am deeply appreciative.

Reprinted from *The Canadian Architect* (1981)

Project: Steamboat Heritage House

Renovation & Restoration

The Heritage Canada Foundation 1980 Regional Award of Honour for the restoration and adaptive reuse of Steamboat Heritage House brings to full reality the vision of architect Randle Iredale that began in 1973. At that time, there was a mix of deteriorating turn-of-the-century houses and a smattering of small industrial operations on the Fairview Slopes overlooking downtown Vancouver. Its future as a mixed residential-commercial zone was in the early planning stages. This was also a time when the preservation of Vancouver's heritage was slowly gaining public attention.

Iredale, who was then involved in the design of Fairview Place (*The Canadian Architect*, April 1975), the adjacent property to the east, recognized the historical and architectural value of Steamboat House. He designed Fairview Place (a 1974 Canadian Housing Design Award winner), the first new mixed-use development, as part of a setting to complement and frame the old house.

Iredale was not the only one to recognize the value of the house. In 1974 the City of Vancouver Heritage Preservation Committee reported, "The `Fairview or Steamboat House' is the only old structure in the 1100-block of 8th Avenue and there is no question that it is one of the most historic houses in Fairview and in Vancouver. The Fairview House is a 'must' for preservation."

Steamboat Heritage House is an early Vancouver wood-frame mansion in the carpenter Gothic tradition built by Sir John Watt Reid between 1889 and 1891. In 1903 it became

The Steamboat Heritage House features new dormers that take advantage of the downtown view, while the wraparound sunporch gives the house three fronts. In his critique, Norman Hotson says the sunporch is an area of great controversy, particularly with the Heritage Committee.

An aluminum storefront system comprises the new skin enclosure. The courtyard is an extension of street space, yet with its own degree of privacy. A mature tree (seen in perspective) has since been removed.

Project Team

Randle Iredale
Architect

C.Y. Low Associates
Structural Engineer

Eric Thrun & Associates
Electrical Engineer

B.C. Comfort Ltd.
Mechanical Engineer

Don Vaughn Associates
Landscape Architect

the home of Walter C. Nichol, owner and publisher of the *Vancouver Province* newspaper and later Lieutenant-Governor of BC. With the development of Shaughnessy prior to World War II, the Fairview Slopes area lost its popularity and by 1970 the building had fallen into disrepair and was used as a rooming house.

In 1975 the property to the west of Steamboat Heritage House was scheduled for redevelopment with Iredale as architect. The second half of the frame for the house was completed at this time (it was awarded a Canadian Architect citation in 1976). The 1973 vision of a respectful contemporary setting for the old carpenter Gothic house materialized three years later when the house was officially designated as a Vancouver Heritage building.

Kara Resources Ltd. purchased the property in 1979. Guidelines provided by the Fairview Slopes plan allowed for the adaptive reuse of Steamboat Heritage House for professional offices. Key to its viability was the demand ... for such character-type office space.

The building lent itself to office use with minimal modification. The central location of the traditional main staircase allowed access to separate tenancies on each floor with the addition of one further flight of stairs to the top floor. The glass enclosure for the porch, while maintaining the traditional columns and porch-like atmosphere, resulted in a very attractive library for the lawyer-users. The necessity for new foundations permitted skylighting of the basement to create further attractive office space on the lower level. New dormers were also introduced into the roof to take advantage of the spectacular view and "original windows" were relocated where required by its new use.[1]

---

1   "Steamboat Heritage House, Vancouver," *The Canadian Architect* (May 1981).

"God is in the details."

Mies van der Rohe's dictum is still right. Unless the scheme is developed with details that express the design intention, we will lose the underlying concept in the final building.

"Ludwig Mies van der Rohe, along with Walter Gropius and Le Corbusier, is widely regarded as one of the pioneering masters of modern architecture. Like many of his post war contemporaries, Mies sought to establish a new architectural style that could represent modern times just as classical and gothic did for their eras.

"Mies created an influential 20th-century architectural style, stated with extreme clarity and simplicity. His mature buildings made use of modern materials such as industrial steel and plate glass to define austere but elegant spaces. He developed the use of exposed steel structure and glass to enclose and define space, striving for an architecture with a minimal framework of structural order balanced against the implied freedom of open space.

"Calling his buildings 'skin and bones' architecture, Mies sought to create a rational approach that would guide the creative process of architectural design. He is known for his use of the aphorisms 'less is more' and 'God is in the details.'" [1] ∎

---

1 Source: www.answers.com/topic/ludwig-mies-van-der-rohe (2006).

KEY DETAILS

"God is in the details."

Mies van der Rohe's dictum is still right. Unless the scheme is developed with details that express the design intention, we will lose the underlying concept in the final building.

During the Schematic Phase it becomes apparent which elements of the design need special attention if the design intention is to be achieved. Now is the time to go through the schematic drawings and identify which details need to be developed to assure that the design intent is met.

For instance, during the designing of Fairview I and Fairview II a key intent was to complement the Steamboat Heritage House, which is now our office. The concept was that the new buildings would provide a frame to complement the heritage building. This intent was done in plan by placing gardens around the old building and designing the new building to provide a simple frame to complement the elaborate fretwork and detailing of the Victorian house.

For this project it was clear that the Design Development Phase had to turn the design intent into an enclosure system that would express the simple form required by the concept.

The key enclosure system details developed to express the concept were a roof transition into the wall without an overhang, windows that turned the wall plane back into the roof, and balcony edges softened with planting.

Rand Iredale, Project Manager's Manual (1997)

Vancouver's Park Site 19

From an essay written by Charlotte Murray.

One of the new firm's first prospects was the request for a proposal issued by the Vancouver Parks Board for the planning of Park Site 19 in the West End.

Rand did not think we should put in a proposal for that job because another firm had already done a preliminary scheme. But Jen and I reasoned that the call for proposals was open because that scheme had not been approved. So Rand agreed that we should go ahead and see what happens, and we worked away at it until Rand felt that we had a credible proposal to submit.

It was a very exciting day when our proposal was accepted!

As the planning partner, Rand was to be in charge of the project. I remember sitting at the board room table and brainstorming the details of our approach for getting the large group of users and other interested parties in the site to agree.

Rand's idea was to have a roundtable meeting with all of the stakeholders: the Parks Board, the City Planning Department, the Heritage Association, and the Roedde House Committee; owners, renters, and the social housing tenants in Barclay Manor; and members of the local Rate Payers Association. All were to be included.

Rand also invited Martin Weaver of Heritage Canada to address the group about the importance of celebrating our heritage and the many ways it could be done. Every group had a say about its connection and aspirations for the site.

Finally, Rand put forward our idea of an Edwardian theme park that could keep the best of the existing houses in their original locations to be used for public benefit. The open spaces in between would be designed for public recreation and enjoyment. The Parks Board, however, wanted to clear the site and create a playing field, while the Heritage Committee wanted to save every house with no changes.

Perhaps it was a compromise but, with little apparent reserve, everyone agreed that we had presented the best use of the site for everyone's benefit.

At about this time Jen left to continue her studies and Robert Lemon joined the team. The whole office contingent worked on that project for over a year. When completed, Parksite 19 became Barclay Heritage Square, a jewel that rests proudly in the centre of the West End. ∎

Project Team

Randle Iredale
Partner in Charge

Charlotte Murray
& Richard Iredale
Project Architects

Project: Barclay Heritage Square

The City of Vancouver, in the late 1960s, commenced the purchase and assembly of Block 45, District Lot 185, in the West End with the objective of creating a park in an area of the city that had been rapidly increasing in population density through the '50s and '60s. The block—bounded by Nicola, Barclay, Broughton, and Haro Streets—was designated as Park Site 19. The block was home to an assortment of 17 residential structures erected between 1890 and 1927, and it was the city's intention to demolish these structures to make way for needed green space. Early in the 1970s, however, the citizens of Vancouver were becoming increasingly aware of the importance of retaining their built heritage.

The crusade to save buildings such as the Orpheum Theatre was led by the Heritage Committee of the Community Arts Council. This same committee became aware of the endangered status of beautiful Roedde House at 1415 Barclay Street on Park Site 19 and, with the help of the Heritage Canada Foundation, commissioned studies of Roedde House and the heritage value of all other structures on this block. Through the persistence largely of volunteers like Janet Bingham and supportive officials such as Art Langley, Director of Civic Buildings, the City and Parks Board eventually agreed to develop Park Site 19 for mixed civic, residential, and park uses, retaining nine of the original houses on the block *in situ*.[1] ■

---

1   Excerpt from the 1992 Heritage Award submission made by the Iredale Partnership to the City of Vancouver.

The restored historic buildings and park, here juxtaposed against the modern Vancouver skyline. Amid the bustle of modern life, a fragment of a more gracious past is preserved (1983–93).

Heritage Park Plan

Context

Park Site 19 is located amid the high-rise apartment buildings of Vancouver's densely populated West End. The West End is fortunate to be bounded by beaches and parks along English Bay to the south, Stanley Park to the west, and Burrard Inlet to the north. These amenities serve the whole Vancouver region, while the amount of neighbourhood park space for West End residents is deficient.

Aerial view of Barclay Heritage Square

"The site was acquired because of its central location in the West End and its mature vegetation. There is an established network of both shade and flowering street trees throughout the West End. Those few older houses that survive near the park site will soon be replaced by high rise residential buildings."

Concept

Notable features of the concept plan for the park design include:

- a village green for the West End in the form of a large Edwardian-era formal lawn area bordered by brick-paved and arbour-covered walkways, rose gardens, and flowering trees;

- the preservation of a turn-of-the-century streetscape, including the renovation of six houses for the heritage housing co-operative in a period front lawn and garden setting; and

- the extension of the park at its four corners, using the Dutch Woonerf system, which widens and landscapes the pedestrian street corners and narrows the vehicular portion of the street.

These components have been brought together in a unique park design concept that integrates green park space, heritage building preservation, public-use facilities, and a housing co-operative.[1] ■

---

1   Excerpt from "Park Site 19: Heritage Park Concept Plan," a summary report prepared by Randle Iredale Architects and submitted to the Vancouver Board of Parks & Recreation (January 1982).

Reprinted from *Historic Preservation* (McLean, 2003)

A Heritage Community

If past city officials had won the day, a playing field would have obliterated the block where heritage buildings stand in the densely populated West End of Vancouver. Instead, the assembly of historic buildings in an Edwardian style garden setting has become a successful melding of park space and housing served by a hospice, a senior centre, and a museum. Over 15 years in the making, Barclay Heritage Square is the result of diligent efforts by volunteer groups such as the Roedde House Society, the Garden Club of Vancouver, the West End Seniors' Network, the Friends for Life Society, and individuals who donated time, plants, wrought iron gates, and wood.

An all-female heritage carpentry class getting job training constructed a gazebo in the style of the cupola for the Roedde House garden. . . . The view from the cupola is to the lawn at the centre of the site that serves as a gathering place for sunbathers, a heritage picnic, and croquet matches. Spectators find seating on the lawn's granite walled edges. The Roedde House garden, designed by Jane Durante, features a small orchard and rosemargin beech trees, along with magnolia, and is framed by hibiscus, lilac, rhododendron, and other large specimen plants donated from estates in Vancouver.

The scent of roses and lavender pervade the site, especially around Barclay Manor, a former hostel and hospital which is now a senior centre. The Iredale Partnership's Rand Iredale and Charlotte Murray played a major role with the site design and architecture. Charlotte's attention to detail created warm, inviting spaces in the heritage building. Stained glass windows, a tile-lined fireplace, and incandescent lighting evoke a home-like setting for seniors who may have left larger homes for small apartments and senior residences. The design for the grounds around Barclay Manor by Larry Diamond, ASLA, features porches framed with roses, Ilex crenata, and lavender, with granite steps, mica flagstone paving, and ramps carefully integrated into the period style garden.

The community buildings are complemented by heritage buildings converted into low-income housing with front yards edged by picket fences and granite walls. Walkways of flagstone and crushed stone lead to small sitting areas throughout the site, including a small passive park edged by trees and shrubs, with a playhouse in the style of Barclay Manor. The Weeks House on the corner of the site was the last part to be restored, and now serves as a hospice for the Friends for Life Society. The porch of this house, and others on the block, allows visitors to enjoy the garden setting into the evening in the glow of the heritage style lighting, locally produced based upon old City of Vancouver molds.[1] ■

---

1 Nancy S. McLean, "Barclay Heritage Square, Vancouver British Columbia," *Historic Preservation* (the newsletter of a professional interest group of the American Society of Landscape Architects), *Vol. XIII, No. 1* (Spring 2003): 6–7. Nancy McLean, ASLA, CSLA, CLARB, is currently the Landscape Coordinator / Senior Planner for the Parks, Recreation & Culture Department, Corporation of Delta BC.

Reprinted from *Canadian Heritage Magazine* (Dalibard, 1984)

Vancouver's Model Park

Managing Change at Park Site 19

Preservationists find it difficult to accept the process of urban growth and change. But I, for one, not only accept the process but even find it exciting and challenging. Instead of trying to ignore it, I believe that preservationists should seek out ways to accommodate it, to harness and manage it.

Urban growth and change in North America have generally followed two lines of development: *substitution* (new buildings have replaced old buildings, new districts have replaced existing ones) and *extension* (suburbia, shopping malls, new towns). The preservation movement has developed its strength over the past 20 years as a reaction to these approaches. But it has failed, until now, to suggest a viable alternative to them. Yet there is, I believe, another way of approaching the question. Whether we call it "incremental design" or "additive transformation" or some other buzzword, the best way to define it is to illustrate it with an example.

The example I've chosen is a Vancouver project with the rather prosaic name of Park Site 19. It is a square block of real estate—bordered by Barclay, Haro, Broughton, and Nicola streets—in the city's West End.

At first glance, it could be an ordinary residential block in any number of North American cities: it has a regular assortment of large- and medium-size houses, small apartment buildings, garages, gardens, and alleys. The block's surroundings, however, make it unique; and the plans that are being formulated for the area suggest it could someday become the model by which inner-city parks are developed.

It was at the turn of the century that Vancouver's West End enjoyed its apogee. Built after the fire of 1886, it was populated at first by newly-prosperous businessmen, professionals, and CPR executives who were attracted by the area's panoramic views of English Bay, Burrard Inlet, and the mountains. The splendid homes which were constructed there were, typically, two and one half storeys high, were clapboard clad with a front or side porch, had wide bargeboard trim, and sported interesting details such as turrets and finials.

The West End soon underwent a transition. By 1909, many of the city's wealthier residents were drawn away to the CPR's newly-constructed and even more fashionable neighbourhood of Shaughnessy Heights. By the 1920s, the West End's mansions were joined by homes of a modest nature and by multiple family residences. By the 1960s, many of the area's older buildings had become dilapidated. The area's central location made it a natural focal point for developers. Properties were bought up and torn down. Highrises took their place. Parking lots covered greenery. Owner-tenancy rates fell. Transient residents replaced the permanent ones. Density rates skyrocketed.

Reprinted from *Canadian Heritage Magazine* (Dalibard, 1984)

In the midst of these changes, four or five West End blocks managed to retain more or less the character they had enjoyed in the pre-highrise era. These blocks survived because local politicians became concerned that, without some form of intervention, highrises would soon claim every corner of the West End. In the late '50s, the city, through its Parks Board, wisely acquired a number of blocks, among them Park Site 19. Zoning laws were later passed, restricting construction heights. Park Site 19 came to the attention of the Heritage Canada Foundation in the late 1970s, when the Parks Board began in earnest to formulate plans to turn it into a small community park.

That the West End needed more green spaces was undeniable. As it became the country's most densely populated square mile, the area's ratio of open spaces to population dwindled dramatically. The 25-year-old city standard of 1.3 acres of parkland per 1,000 population was largely ignored: local residents, who should have had about 37 acres to enjoy, had to make do with 24.

There were two major problems with the future development of Park Site 19. First, it would probably have called for the demolition of all the buildings on the block. Such wholesale destruction would have been a loss: from the flamboyant Roedde House, which is thought to have been designed by the great B.C. architect Francis Rattenbury, down through a hodge-podge of styles and building techniques, the block's houses reflect nothing less than the structural evolution of the West End. Equally worrisome was the prospect of what would replace the original block: most city-designed parks, after all, tend to be sterile. Nearby Nelson Park, for example, is a wasteland: it is a bare, unimaginative field bordered by a sparse collection of recently-planted trees. ...

Park Site 19: Concept Plan of The Iredale Partnership

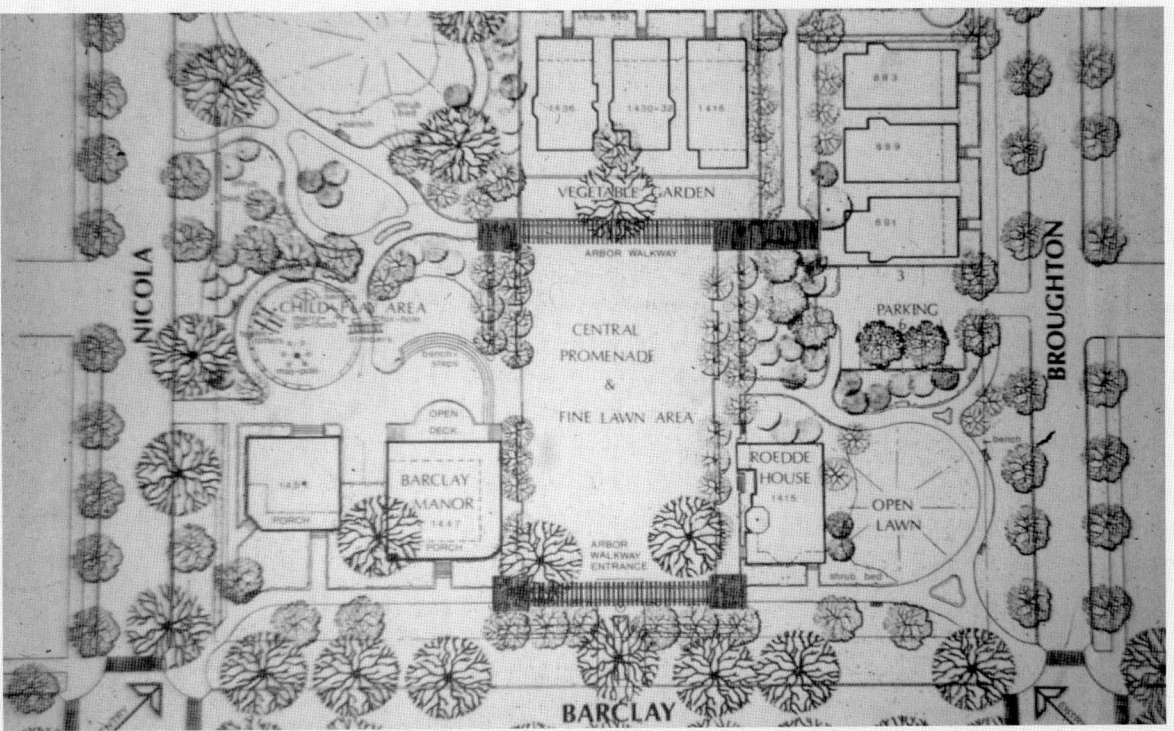

Reprinted from *Canadian Heritage Magazine* (Dalibard, 1984)

Incremental Change

The important distinction to make ... is between two kinds of change—the *cataclysmic* and the *incremental*. Cataclysmic change (the sort that ruined Nelson Park and which would have been the fate of Park Site 19) means a sudden and dramatic shift in an environment's direction. Such changes are not organic: they do not develop naturally from the environment itself but are the result of some outside force imposing itself upon the environment. Incremental change, on the other hand, takes into account an organism's natural blueprint. Incremental development is slow, purposeful, natural, organic. It is a change which has a wholeness to it: the various parts grow in their own way but contribute at the same time to the cohesion of the whole. It is also a change which has the advantage of allowing a process of trial and error, a process that often minimizes both social and material costs.

Could Park Site 19 be developed in an incremental way? Could the block fulfill the city's need for extra green space while retaining much of its eight-decade-old character? In 1979, the Heritage Canada Foundation approached the city to discuss these questions. To its credit, the Parks Board (which was under no pressure to consider alternate planning) proved willing to listen. The Foundation consequently committed $25,000 to study the feasibility of a new form of park.[1]

The study recommended several revolutionary steps. First, against all conventional wisdom, it advanced the idea that the block could be converted into a public garden while most of its buildings were retained. The idea was to focus attention upon the interior of the block, a space which currently consisted of a lane, garages, sheds, fences, individual gardens, and telephone poles. The lane would be closed. The garages, sheds, fences, and even some large additions to buildings would be eliminated. The wiring would be buried. Grass and new trees would be planted in harmony with the mature trees and shrubs which already exist in the private gardens. The effect of these modifications would be the creation of an inner court, a kind of leafy quadrangle in the spirit of a London square or of some university campuses. Access to this interior park would be via green passages created by the elimination of two or three of the houses in the block.

---

1   There have been many players in the Park Site 19 story: *Robb Watt, Leonard McCann, and the Vancouver Historical Society drew attention to the Roedde House in the mid-'70s. Janet Bingham, the late Peter Cotton, and the Community Arts Council were early supporters of Park Site 19. The Heritage Canada Foundation's $25,000 feasibility study was undertaken by Barry Downs with Graham McGarva. The 1981 "live-in park" study was undertaken by Randle Iredale Architects with a number of consultants, including the Foundation's Martin Weaver. Other key supporters of Park Site 19 have been the Vancouver Parks Board, Arthur Langley, the BC Heritage Trust with Martin Segger, the West End Community Centre, the Park Site 19 Tenants Association, and the Heritage Advisory Committee with Rhonna Fleming.*

These Edwardian Interior Details were reproduced by the Heritage Committee of the Community Arts Council of Vancouver (1983)

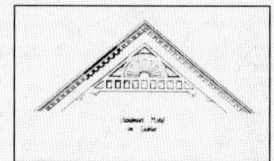

Sketches: Peter D. Charles (1982)

Reprinted from *Canadian Heritage Magazine* (Dalibard, 1984)

The virtues of this new kind of park are numerous. Vintage buildings, which would otherwise have been demolished, would be retained, some used for community purposes and the rest for housing. Housing would gain multi-directional vistas, looking out to the street and in to the park. The established trees and shrubbery would help create, on a domestic scale, an aesthetically attractive space, one that offers a pleasing combination of older buildings and greenery. A safer park would also be the result: the fact that it would be the ultimate "people park" (since people would actually live in it) would make it a secure place for a mother to walk her baby or for older people to stroll unconcerned. A park of such a human scale and with such links to its surroundings would encourage a sense of proprietorship, a sense that this park belongs to us.

Of course, some people may object that houses which stand in a park such as this lack privacy, the land about them insufficient to separate them from public areas. While it would be pleasant if all houses could boast fine, private gardens, land values in the West End are so high that only the very wealthy could expect to own such houses. What Park Site 19 offers, therefore, is realistic housing similar to the kind that can be found in Vancouver's False Creek or along Ottawa's public Rideau Canal, both very desirable areas in which private and public spaces merge and yet are distinct.

Over the next few years we'll know whether this new kind of park works as well as I envision: the Vancouver Parks Board has adopted the feasibility plan's proposals and has begun work at Park Site 19. In adopting this approach, the Parks Board has proved willing to learn a lesson that nature itself teaches—that the best kind of environmental change is slow, and careful, and sensitive to those elements which, both spatially and temporily, connect us to something greater than ourselves. This sense of continuity also has precedents in the man-made environment. Many districts in the historic cities of Europe owe their character, charm, and identity to structures that are now isolated, or in a state of ruin, or long forgotten. Whether they are or were ancient palaces, amphitheatres, triumphal arches, medieval walls, churches or castles, these structures have dictated forms, established constraints, or inspired designs that have made subsequent buildings or urban fabrics richer and more aesthetically pleasing and meaningful.

The great failure of contemporary designers and decision-makers when they approach urban growth and change has been to forget that people react emotionally to their environment—and one important aspect of this emotion is the need to relate to past experiences. By building on what exists or existed, by gradually changing rather than by starting again with a clean slate, one has a better chance to fulfill people's need for continuity.[1] ∎

---

1   Jacques Dalibard, "Vancouver's Model Park: Managing Change at Park Site 19," *Canadian Heritage Magazine* (Heritage Canada Foundation: Winter 1984): 3–5. At the time of writing this article, following an influential career with Parks Canada, Jacques Dalibard was the Executive Director of Heritage Canada. He was also a founding member and the President of ICOMOS Canada (International Council on Monuments and Sites). Source: Internet (2006).

CONSERVATION THROUGH ADAPTIVE REUSE

The firm has been a leader in the conservation movement since we established the Canadian Environmental Sciences Group in 1969.

The *limits to growth* concept has led us to propose conservation through adaptive reuse rather than new construction. In a sense, it has given us a new appreciation of Mies van der Rohe's dictum that "less is more" in all of our designs. The establishment of our Heritage Studio under Charlotte Murray in 1982 made this form of conservation part of the structure of the firm.

Today [1997], this commitment to conservation infuses all of the work of The Iredale Partnership. Planning and design, by their nature, change the world through human intervention. The overwhelming power of late 20th-century technology and the institutions who are our clients require design that maintains the ecological and human balance of our environment.

As designers we are committed to improving the fit between human intervention and the ecological systems in which we live. We believe that this can best be accomplished by considering the design process a search for fit.

Rand Iredale, Project Manager's Manual (1997)

> As designers we are committed to improving the fit between human intervention and the ecological systems in which we live. We believe that this can best be accomplished by considering the design process a search for fit.

10 Each Step of Our Exploration

The Iredale Partnership was a small practice, unable to undertake the large-scale projects of the Rhone & Iredale years. Moreover, with high interest rates imposed on the economy in an effort to control rampant inflation, the early 1980s were difficult years for architects, engineers, contractors, and developers, among many others. The Provincial Government's implementation of Expo '86, however, gradually provided jobs and greatly improved the economy.

In this context of revitalized economic environment, along with shifting social sensibilities, the firm necessarily directed its energies toward more community-oriented projects. The move from larger 'public places' to smaller 'people places' was emphasized by the firm's commitment to conservation and by its focus now, not on universities, but on schools; not on power stations, but on heritage houses and civic parks; not on stadiums and roundhouses, but on community churches and railway museums.

Rand's energies turned from visionary proposals for downtown Vancouver to planning Heritage Harbour in Ladysmith and Still Creek Park in Burnaby. Numerous small projects populated Rand's portfolio: designing townhouses for Choklit Park at 1095 West 7th Avenue, renovating and expanding the elementary school on Mayne Island, and restoring St. John's Anglican Church in Sardis. Though Rand had worked on several churches throughout his practice, church buildings were aging and congregations were starting to view heritage restoration as both a practical and a spiritual means of preserving cherished traditions.

One of Rand's favourite projects during the 1980s was the renovation and adaptive reuse of The Old Territorial Administration Building in Dawson City. He continued to do renovation work for BC Hydro and UBC, and he undertook a comprehensive study of heritage buildings on the UBC campus. With his professional stature well established—he had been elected a Fellow of the Royal Architectural Institute of Canada in 1977—Rand accepted an RAIC appointment as Professional Advisor for the 1986 Governor General's Medals for Architecture Award Programs. ■

Reprinted from *Royal Architectural Institute of Canada: 1986 Awards Program* (Eldred, 1986)

About the RAIC Award Competition

The Iredale Report

As the national organization for the profession, The Royal Architectural Institute of Canada has long recognized the contribution an effective awards program makes to the quality of Canadian Architecture. The Massey Medals Award program founded in 1950 was a major factor in the development of Canadian Architecture until the support of the Massey Foundation expired in 1978. Since then, the R.A.I.C. has operated a "Festival of Architecture" Awards program in 1980 and 1981 and a Governor General's Medals for Architecture Award Program in 1982 and 1983.

In 1984 R.A.I.C. Council decided to review its Governor General's Medals for Architecture Awards Program. They appointed W. Randle Iredale Professional Advisor to review past programs and advise on methods to strengthen this important element of the R.A.I.C. responsibility to Architecture in Canada.

The Iredale Report, based on a review of past programs and discussions with R.A.I.C. Council, Staff and former Professional Advisor to the Massey Medal Program Henry Elder, was accepted by R.A.I.C. Council in January 1985. The Iredale Report recommended:

- That the program operate every fourth year to allow time for the construction of projects worthy of recognition.

- That the jury be chosen from internationally recognized architects and critics who bring to the Awards Program an overview of Canadian Architecture.

- That the comments of owners and users be solicited to assist the jury in recognizing, not only the form of the projects, but also the commodity, firmness and delight which Vetruvious defined as architecture.

- That the effectiveness of the Program depends on wide recognition of the award winners. As well as a well publicized Awards Ceremony and Traveling Exhibition the program requires a first class Publication.

- That an effective Awards Program requires adequate funding to accomplish these objectives. The necessary level of funding requires support from outside the profession. The sources of this support must not prejudice the importance or independence of the Awards Program.

This support has been forthcoming. The R.A.I.C. wishes to thank the Canada Council, and the Department of External Affairs, Export Information Division, for their support of this important Canadian endeavor and to recognize the travel assistance given by Canadian Pacific Airlines for Jury Travel. . . .[1] ▪

---

1   Brian E. Eldred, "About the Competition," *Royal Architectural Institute of Canada: 1986 Awards Program, Governor General's Medals for Architecture* (1986): 3. At the time of writing, Brian Eldred, FRAIC, was President of the Royal Architectural Institute of Canada. Excerpts are hereafter cited in this chapter as *RAIC 1986*.

Reprinted from *Royal Architectural Institute of Canada: 1986 Awards Program* (Iredale, 1986)

Governor General's Medals for Architecture

The Professional Advisor's Comments

The program has been organized from Vancouver in recognition of the City's Centennial and Expo '86. Vancouver's Pacific Rim connection was reflected in the selection of the jury: John Andrews from Australia, Fumihiko Maki from Japan and Kurt Forster from Los Angeles. The fourth member of the jury, Moshe Safdie, has a special Canadian connection, as does John Andrews. Moshe Safdie's first major building was "Habitat," built for the Montreal World's Fair of 1967, while John Andrews began practice in Toronto with such buildings as Scarborough College. These projects were both recognized with Massey Medals.

The jurying for the first phase was done in Ottawa on January 23, 1986. The jury selected 26 award-winning projects from the 162 entries received. The Governor General Medalists ... were selected in the second phase [of] jurying during the 1986 R.A.I.C. Convention in Vancouver.

The program, and this publication, have been organized to provide a review of contemporary Canadian Architecture. As well as the usual project description by the architect, this catalogue reproduces the actual architects' presentation material, showing presentation techniques and attitudes. It also provides owners' comments, which express their concerns and response to the project.

Above & overleaf:
Postcard printed for Canadian Architecture 1986:

"The Governor General's Medals for Architecture competition is held every four years, carrying forward the tradition of the Massey Medals, which began in 1953. ...

"Sponsored by the Royal Architectural Institute of Canada and the Vancouver League for Studies in Architecture and the Environment."

Left to right:

Moshe Safdie, Fumihiko Maki, Kurt W. Forster, John Andrews, & Rand Iredale

The Jurors (1986)

John Andrews

After receiving his Bachelor's degree in Architecture in Sydney, Australia, Mr. Andrews completed his Master's degree at Harvard in 1958. He came to Canada and taught at the University of Toronto, School of Architecture from 1962–1969, including a term as Chairman of the department. In private practice, his major projects include: Scarborough College Arts Centre, Kent State University; Weldon Library, University of Western Ontario; Harvard Graduate School of Design; King George Tower, Sydney, Australia. Mr. Andrews' entry was selected as a winner of the International Architectural Competition for the Intelsat Headquarters, Washington, D.C. in 1980.

His work has been recognized with numerous awards including the Royal Australian Institute's Gold Medal, 1980, the Massey Medal for Architecture (Scarborough College), Centennial Medal, 1967, American Institute of Architecture Honour Award, 1973. Mr. Andrews is a life Fellow of the Royal Australian Institute of Architects, an honourary member of the AIA, and a Fellow of the Royal Architectural Institute of Canada.

Kurt W. Forster

Director of the J. Paul Getty Centre for the History of Art and the Humanities, Santa Monica, California, Kurt Forster was educated in Zurich, Switzerland, and obtained his Ph.D. in the History of Art and Architecture there in 1961. Prior to taking a position with the Getty Centre, he was Professor of History of Architecture at the Massachusetts Institute of Technology and Professor of History of Art and Architecture at Stanford University. As an Architectural Historian he has been editor of *Oppositions: a Journal for Ideas and Criticism in Architecture*, published for the Institute of Architecture and Urban Studies by MIT Press, and has published in such architectural journals as *Journal of the Society of Architectural Historians, Architectura, Architectural Record,* and the *Harvard Architectural Review.*

Fumihiko Maki

Mr. Maki's practice in Tokyo, Japan, has been responsible for such major projects as the Osaka Prefectural Sports Centre, 1972; Tsukuba University, The School of Art and Physical Education, 1974; Toyota Memorial Museum, 1974; Embassy of Japan Brazilia, 1975; The National Aquarium, Okinawa, 1975; and the National Museum of Modern Art, Kyoto, 1986. His awards and prizes include: "Low Cost Housing in Lima, Peru," 1969, sponsored by the United Nations; Mainichi Art Prize, 1969, for Rissho University Kumagaya Campus; and the 24th Art Prize, 1969, from Minister of Education for "Hillside Terrace Apartments," 1973; as well as the International Invitational Competition for design of the Headquarters of DOM Co. in Koln, West Germany, 1980. Mr. Maki has also been Associate Professor at Washington University and Harvard University as well as visiting critic at Harvard, Berkeley, Columbia, U.C.L.A. and the University of Vienna.

Moshe Safdie

Mr. Safdie, F.R.A.I.C., conducts his architectural practices from a main office in Boston, with branch offices in Montreal and Jerusalem. He has been responsible for such major projects as "Habitat '67," Montreal; "Western Wall Precinct," Jerusalem, Israel; "Old Port Montreal," Quebec; "Renovation of Jewish Quarters," Jerusalem; "Musee Nationale De Civilization," Quebec City; "Colegio Hebreo Maguen David," Mexico City; "National Gallery of Canada," Ottawa; and "Cambridge Centre Master Plan," Cambridge, Massachusetts.

He has received numerous design awards, including the Massey Medal for Architecture, Lieutenant Governor's Medal, AIRA Architect of the Year, and the Urban Design Concept Award from the U.S. Department of Housing and Urban Development, 1980. Mr. Safdie has taught at McGill University, Yale University, and Ben Gurion University, Israel, and is a professor of Architecture and Urban Design, Graduate School of Design, Harvard University. His publications include *Beyond Habitat*, 1970, *For Everyone a Garden*, 1974, and *Form and Purpose*, 1982. ∎

Reprinted from *Royal Architectural Institute of Canada: 1986 Awards Program* (Iredale, 1986)

Very few projects are photographed with people. John Andrews commented, "there is a tendency towards presenting the project as a piece of art as opposed to a piece of architecture and to me these two things are very different. At the same time you need a dictionary to understand some of the words that they have used." Kurt Forster noted, "there are very few analytical sections and there is hardly any attempt to give to the entire project a kind of cohesion and quality in the presentation."

It is notable that in the period reviewed by the competition the predominant and most common building types were commercial buildings, office buildings and shopping centres. The jury had to stretch to recognize projects in these categories. This raises a fundamental question about the quality of patronage, of developers as Clients and whether the conditions for good work are there. If, as the jury concluded, the profession performed better in institutional buildings and in housing, the lack of award-worthy buildings in these categories must be due to a combination of factors [that] transcend the profession.

There is also a lack of high rise buildings. Moshe Safdie noted, "one feels the impoverishment of the profession in dealing with this building type, which is more and more the most dominant building type."

Projects done by Canadian Architects outside the country were also not well represented. Future programs should encourage the submission of foreign work by Canadian Architects.

The question of whether the present procedure of voluntary submission of the architects' own work is adequate to search out and identify everything worthy of recognition was also raised. Supplementing the submissions by nomination by others, such as owners, could fill in the gaps.

The 1986 R.A.I.C. Governor General Awards Program has been given a new level of support to re-estabish the tradition of excellence of the Governor General Massey Medals Program. I wish to express the appreciation of the program to all those who [gave] their enthusiasm and dedication to this important endeavor in Canadian Architecture.[1] ■

---

1   W. Randle Iredale, "Professional Advisor's Comments," *RAIC 1986*: 8. The adjacent biographies of the jurors were reprinted from *RAIC 1986:* 9–12. Rand's roles included those of Professional Advisor & Publication Editor.

Map of Canada

Dots indicate the location of 1986 RAIC Award Winners across Canada

Source: *RAIC, 1986:* 13

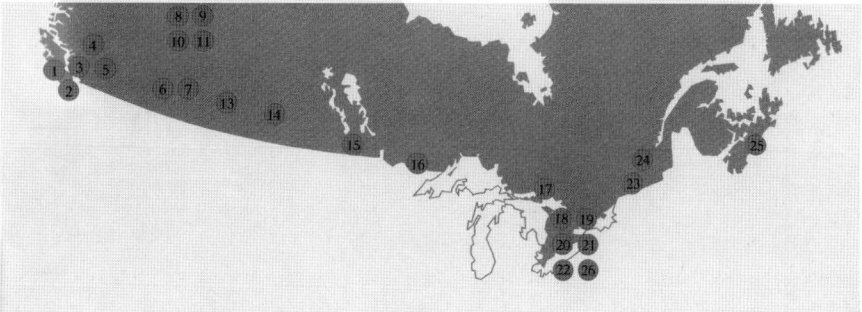

Church Buildings

Gothic Style Architecture

Rand's architectural philosophy regarding churches is best expressed in the following excerpts from an article he wrote for the *Anglican News*: [1]

> "How often have you heard it said of a new church, 'But it doesn't look like a church'? This criticism arises because most of us still associate the beautiful Gothic forms of Europe with our concept of a church. …

> "However, we must realize that many of the forms of the Gothic period were created in stone and cannot be re-created in wood, which is the common local building material of today. It must be remembered that the function and place of the church in our society has changed greatly. Today's parish church—with its large Sunday School hall, meeting rooms, and administration office—is a far cry from the parish church of even 30 years ago, and is vastly different from the church during the greatness of the Gothic period. …

> "While recognizing these changes, we must also remember that the underlying religious principles of Gothic architecture are still valid today. …

> "If the architect keeps these facts in mind, many of the attributes of Gothic churches can be maintained—the soaring height, the regular structural progression toward the sanctuary—without copying the superficial symbols (pointed arches just don't belong in a wood frame wall), and by using the underlying concept developed by the Christian Church over the centuries."

Design & Restoration

In the early days of the Rhone & Iredale practice, Rand designed several churches in and around Vancouver. The most noteworthy was St. Helen's Anglican Church, located at the corner of West 8th and Trimble on Vancouver's West Side. Additional church projects included St. Martin's Anglican Church Hall in North Vancouver, St. Cuthbert's Anglican Church in North Delta, and St. Catherine's Anglican Church in Port Coquitlam.

Given the heritage focus she shared with Rand, it warrants mention that Charlotte Murray designed and restored several churches during her years with The Iredale Partnership (and later with Iredale Group). Of particular note are her award-winning heritage restorations of the St. Francis of Assisi Rectory (1998) and the interior of Christ Church Cathedral (2005). ■

---

1   W. Randle Iredale, "Gothic Style Architecture is Valid for Churches Now," *Anglican News*, October 1964.

Project Team

Randle Iredale
Partner in Charge

Rainer Fassler
Project Architect

Project: St. Helen's Anglican Church

St. Helen's Anglican Church was designed in two phases, in 1962 and 1972. Having built the church hall, meeting room, and kitchen for the congregation in 1962, Rand was retained to design and build a new church when the original 1912 structure was lost to a fire in 1970.

The church and parish hall were constructed on opposite sides of a courtyard containing the parish bell tower and a sacred garden. The new building has increased seating capacity and includes a chapel, located to handle overflow crowds for special celebrations.

The new church also maintains the timber quality of the original church, which was typical of early Anglican churches constructed in British Columbia. Exterior materials include timber beams, cedar shingle roof, and rough stucco, creating a warm and inviting impression. The interior is framed in heavy timber, reminiscent of traditional ecclesiastical architecture. ▪

St. Helen's Anglican Church

Parish Bell Tower and Sacred Garden

THIS BEAUTIFUL TIMBER STRUCTURE

From an interview with Rainer Fassler.

I cannot remember a single negative scene with Rand, and yet I must have done some things that really caused him problems! When St. Helen's Anglican Church burned down, Rand had a relationship with the church community and an opportunity to rebuild the church. The issue was simple: How closely do we rebuild it to what it was before? The original church was a timber frame building, somewhat gothic inside, and very dark.

We came up with a new design, not for rebuilding the original church, but for rebuilding the essence of the church. One of the biggest features was this beautiful timber structure, which looked spectacular in its natural colour. The church community, however, was expecting it to be painted dark brown! I was convinced that you could not paint these beautiful timbers dark brown. The client committee was really upset; here is this young architect who had sort of snuck it past them.

Rand had not been watching things too closely and he said, "Rainer, we should have talked about this!" He was quite upset, but he also came to my defence and told the committee, "Maybe the way this happened wasn't quite the way he should have done it, but it's right." And he let me know that it was an uncomfortable situation and it was a bit of a problem, but it was still the right thing to do. He was always there to support you. ■

St. Helen's Anglican Church

Adjacent:
exterior view (1972)

Opposite, below:
interior, after 1972 redesign & rebuild

St. Helen's before 1972 redesign & rebuild

St. Helen's after 1972 redesign & rebuild

Project Team

Charlotte C. Murray
Partner in Charge

Randle Iredale
Planner

Randy Cleveland
Project Architect

Project: Burnaby Village Museum

Rand was engaged as the Planner on Charlotte Murray's project to expand the Burnaby Village Museum as an open-air living museum.

Burnaby Village Museum is dedicated to providing visitors with a hands-on experience of life in the early period of the settlement of Burnaby. A concept was devised for expansion of the museum site from five to ten acres.

The Master Plan included retention of the natural features on the site, convenient traffic and pedestrian circulation patterns, and the development of six distinct character areas. Each area works as a setting to display and interpret the museum collection.

A settler's cabin, an early berry farm, and a logging camp were grouped amidst the natural flora of Deer Creek to form the new rural display area. The new Administration Building was sited to provide a strong presence on Canada Way. The building rests comfortably in the natural setting and affords an intimate introduction to the museum experience. ∎

The original village, one of six character areas

The new rural display area

Burnaby Village Museum

The new administration building and museum entrance are prominent on Canada Way

Excerpted from "A Proposal for a Family Fitness Park" (1983)

Project Team

Randle Iredale
Partner in Charge

Michael V. Geary
Project Architect

Project: Still Creek Park

Still Creek Park was an innovative recreation park proposed for the Burnaby Sports Complex. Unique to Still Creek would be its integration of fun and fitness activities for the whole family, with an emphasis on providing enjoyable and confidence-building activities of graduated difficulty.

Facilities would range from those of a recreational nature—such as a water slide and a wave pool, to those of a more traditional nature—such as field and racquet sports [unfortunately, the park was never developed].

The Iredale Partnership was commissioned to produce a feasibility study that selected a site from three possible locations within the Burnaby Sports Complex. A schematic design was then developed to integrate all activities into the park and, concurrently, the park into the existing Sports Complex.

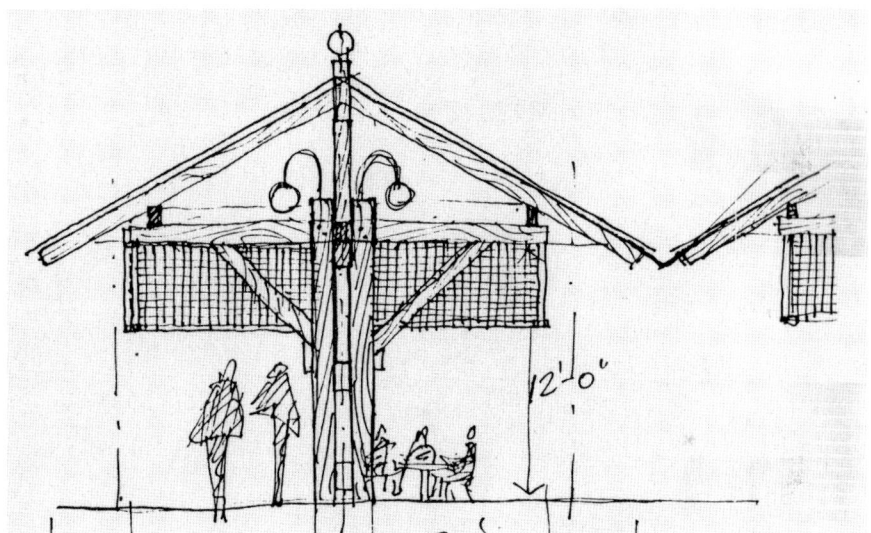

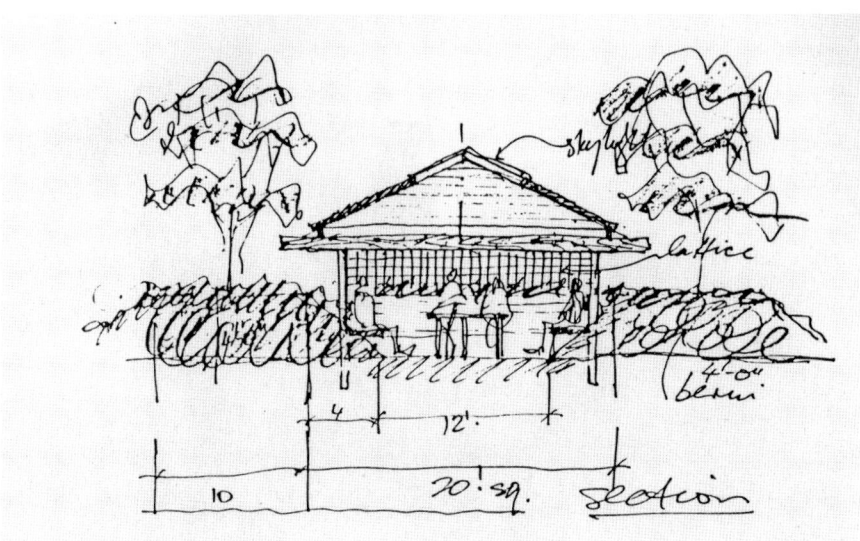

Sketches, adjacent & overleaf: these sketches are believed to have been created by Michael Geary

Excerpted from "A Proposal for a Family Fitness Park" (1983)

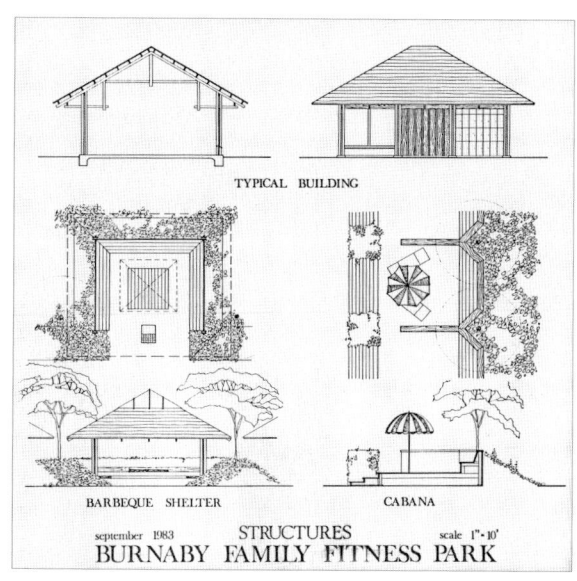

The Site

The site was chosen for its location and topography. It contains both high and low ground, suitable for summer and all-weather activities. The high knoll of the northwest corner is an ideal location for the summer activities. By sculpturing the ground into two separate hills to accommodate the water slides, combined with careful landscaping of trees and ground cover, an integration of slides, pools, paths, bridges, streams, and waterfalls achieves a hillside of fun and delight.

The remaining site is flat ground on which the games courts and fields, 'beach,' barbecue, paved areas, and support buildings will be located. The existing vegetation of alder, salal, bullrushes, wild grasses, and ponds will be retained wherever possible with new landscaping recognizing the native vegetation to create a park as natural as the existing area.

Working with the Burnaby Planning Department, we determined that the park would utilize 9.6 acres, with an additional 5.0 acres to be developed or reserved for parking.

Excerpted from "A Proposal for a Family Fitness Park" (1983)

The Concept

The architectural concept will develop the park theme with careful landscaping and comfortably-scaled, low-rise wood structures to complement the existing buildings in the Sports Complex. Covered areas with heated slabs and overhead radiant heat lamps will link key activities, providing comfort even on winter days.

A mixture of activities—exercise classes, running, weight-training, and court sports—will surround a water slide and a series of activity pools. Activities will be carefully chosen to appeal to all ages and to those with few athletic skills as well as to the accomplished athlete.

The Fitness Park is designed to provide year-round variety, instruction, and supervision in an attractive social setting. Except for roller skates and float rentals, all sports equipment will be provided free of charge.[1] ∎

---

1   Text excerpted from "A Proposal for a Family Fitness Park," prepared by Burnaby Lake Management and The Iredale Partnership (1983).

Excerpted from "The UBC Heritage Building Study" (Iredale, 1986)

Project: UBC Heritage Building Study

Rand Iredale was commissioned in 1986 to undertake a heritage building study of the UBC campus. This text, comprising edited excerpts from his final study submission, demonstrates his growing sensitivities to heritage restoration.

Intention of This Report

This Report has been prepared by Randle Iredale as a member of a study group for the UBC Alumni Association Heritage Committee. The Report identifies certain campus features that could be considered to have *Heritage Merit*.

The Report has been undertaken in response to the continuing erosion of older buildings, landscapes, and vistas on the campus and the decisions required by the recently completed "Facilities Audit," prepared by Neville Smith, Director of the UBC Physical Plant, which states: "Decisions must be made to determine which buildings have heritage merit and where there is justification to spend the cost of preservation."

The Audit establishes the planned life of the Auditorium and the Mathematics, Mathematics Annex, Geography, and Administration Buildings at zero to six years. The fate of these original campus buildings is of concern to alumni, faculty, staff, and students.

In selecting those elements of the campus to be preserved and those to be replaced with new construction, we must identify those we consider worthy of preservation. This choice is based upon three factors:

- **Heritage Values**: The importance to the University Community of the buildings, monuments, vistas and landscapes on the Campus and the locale of events of historic significance to the University.

- **Campus Development Pattern**: The Development Pattern of the Campus to establish the pattern of growth which will conserve and enhance the existing (heritage) character of the central Campus.

- **Current Utility**: The practicality and cost of maintaining heritage buildings, considering life cycle cost and functional obsolescence.

This study makes a preliminary assessment of these three factors, from which a discussion plan for a *Heritage Precinct* is developed. This plan illustrates the planning concepts required to conserve the character and quality of the historic campus while adapting to the changing needs of the University.

Campus photos in the study included these views from Main Mall:

Left:
View from Main Mall, facing south (the roof and skylights of Sedgewick Library are in the foreground)

Right:
View from Main Mall, facing northwest to the mountains

Excerpted from "The UBC Heritage Building Study" (Iredale, 1986)

Heritage Values

Our history is embodied in our buildings and places as surely as it is recorded in our history books. The University of British Columbia—like Harvard, Cambridge, or any other university—presents its sense of values by what it builds, what it preserves, and what it demolishes. The physical form of a campus, its 'hallowed halls of ivy,' imbue its students with the values of a great institution as surely as its teaching.

When questioned on the cost of preserving the eight oak trees on the Main Mall when Sedgewick Library was built, Randle Iredale, the Architect, responded that the cost of preserving each tree was equal to one year's salary of an intermediate faculty member, and that each tree would continue to impart its lesson of concern for our heritage and respect for the environment to generation after generation of students.

During the past 40 years expediency and the historic discontinuity of the modern movement in Architecture have resulted in insensitive additions to building form and landscape as well as dilution of the spatial concept of the original University of British Columbia campus plan.

This section of the Report identifies places, buildings, and monuments that have historic significance on the campus ... [see list of historical sites together with a location map on the next page].

Campus Development Pattern

The significance of heritage buildings, monuments, and places depends upon a suitable context. This section of the Report analyzes the changes in planning concepts that have affected the campus so as to identify those planning concepts that must be maintained in the Heritage Precinct planning.

Heritage character is not just a matter of building preservation. Pattern of development—with its gates, set-backs, heights, landmarks, and open spaces—is equally important in maintaining heritage character as the preservation of individual buildings.

Only by a thorough understanding of the essential planning elements can changes, which are inevitable over time, enhance our built heritage. This section identifies the planning patterns that have affected the campus and their significance to future development.

Heritage buildings on UBC campus (circa 1986)

Excerpted from "The UBC Heritage Building Study" (Iredale, 1986)

Historical Sites on UBC Campus

The following list of places, buildings, and monuments that have historical significance ... must be considered open-ended and subject to additions and deletions as the university community changes over time:

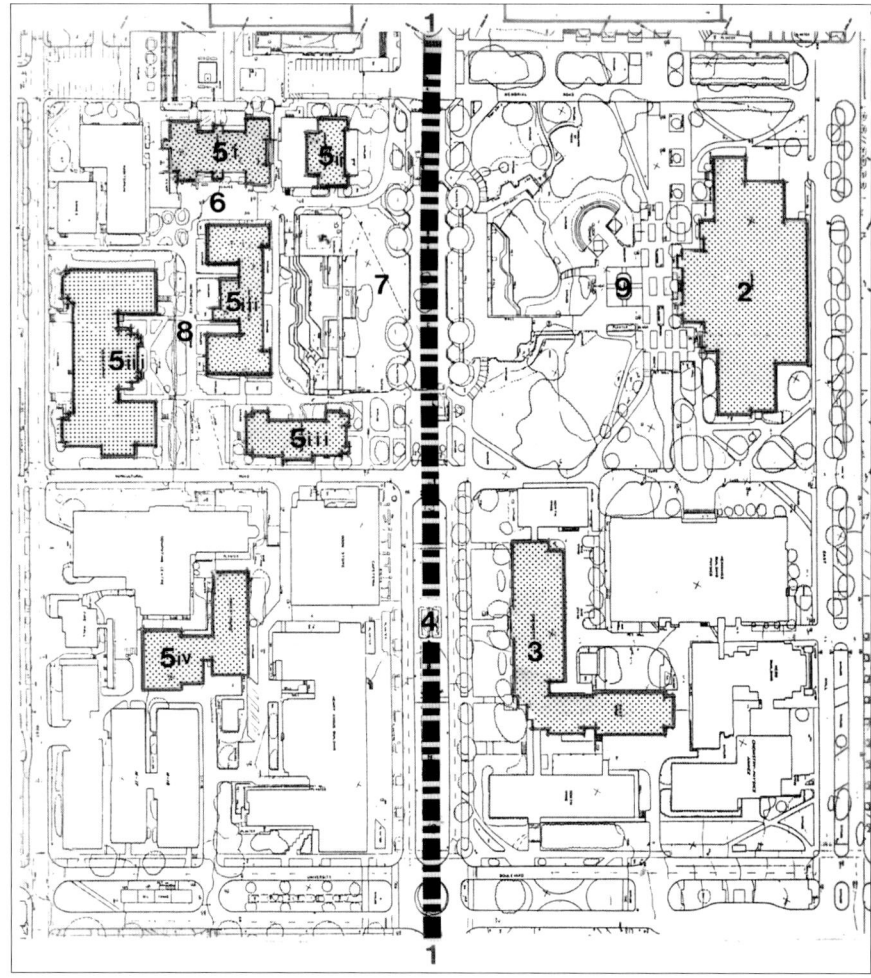

Location map of features of historical importance, including places, buildings, & monuments (1986)

1 the sense of spatial organization given by the Main Mall and the gardens surrounding Sedgewick Library;

2 the Main Library, with its Collegiate Gothic façade facing the main gardens;

3 the Collegiate Gothic stone façade of the old Chemistry Building;

4 the Cairn, created in commemoration of the Great Trek of 1922, which moved the government of the day to continue construction of the Point Grey Campus after WW I;

5 several of the stucco and wood frame buildings constructed in 1925:

 i. Auditorium / Cafeteria

 ii. Administration Building

 iii. Teaching & Academic Office Buildings (Geography, Mathematics, & Mathematics Annex)

 iv. Campus Heating Plant

6 original Quadrangle, south of the Auditorium;

7 Arts Lawn (on the roof of Sedgewick Library);

8 Mathematics Road, with its memorial trees; and

9 the Library Pond.

Excerpted from "The UBC Heritage Building Study" (Iredale, 1986)

Sharp Thompson 1914 Plan

The Master Plan for the Point Grey site of the University of British Columbia was based on a competition held in 1914 and won by the Vancouver architectural firm of Sharp Thompson.

This plan is formally set out along the Main Mall flanked by the East and West Malls and connected with cross-axes defining super blocks in which are located quadrangles of buildings set in broad lawns. The first phase of construction developed the four blocks north of University Boulevard on the Main Mall. By mid-1925 UBC had an impressive stone library and science building plus nine semi-permanent buildings.

Over time the organizing influence of the Malls has been compromised and new buildings have become part of departmental complexes, each with a style and an identity of its own. As a result, the form and spirit of the 1915 grand plan is visible only through the vestiges of the 1925 quadrangular superblocks and the surrounding wood frame buildings.

Douglas Shadbolt, Head of the UBC School of Architecture, wrote in the recent publication "Vancouver Arts and Artists, 1931–1983":

> *It now appears that the original Master Plan, based on quadrangular superblocks along a Central Mall, may be salvageable. The plan may have the flexibility to provide the framework for the next phase of expansion, which will effect consolidation and make sense out of the apparent confusion of the past 30 years [of] work.*

Other Plans

[Several other plans are detailed and illustrated in the Report. These plans are omitted here but they include:

- the Wurster Bernardi 1968 Plan
- the Rhone & Iredale / Toby Russell Buckwell Buchanan / Library Matrix 1969 Circulation Plan
- the Department of Physical Plant Campus Development 1976–1980 Plan

Rand goes on to discuss his concept plan for, and implementation of, a Heritage Precinct at the University of British Columbia.]

Heritage buildings on UBC campus (circa 1986)

Excerpted from "The UBC Heritage Building Study" (Iredale, 1986)

Concept Plan for Heritage Precinct

The following concept plan illustrates a pattern of growth based on the assumed heritage priorities developed in this Report.

It is subject to modification as the detailed studies (recommended in the following section on Implementation) establish the importance of each element and the economic viability of the heritage option.

The magnitude of growth required is not known at this time. As President Strangway stated in his address to the Board of Governors in October 1985, "It is necessary for the University to determine its mission."

Until such determination is accomplished, this Concept Plan provides for incremental growth to the density possible without major change to the heritage values of the central portion of the campus.

Based on the current input the Concept Plan:

- allows for 440,000 square feet of potential new construction within the Heritage Precinct; 60,000 sq. ft. extends the matrix concept of the Sedgewick Library at a level beneath the Main Mall and 380,000 sq. ft. is new building within the set-back lines and massing of the Sharp Thompson plan;

- preserves the Auditorium, Mathematics, and Mathematics Annex buildings as heritage buildings;

- restores the Administration Building and removes the 1950 addition to restore the entrance area in front of the Old Auditorium;

- upgrades the overgrown landscaping in the Heritage Precinct by removing overgrown trees, such as those in front of the Chemistry and Mathematics Building, as well as replacing ground cover and paving with traditional lawn; heritage landscaping will bring back to this area of the campus the sense of fine buildings set in broad lawns of the original plan;

- designates the Geography and 1970 Auditorium Annex buildings as subject to replacement after the vacant building sites have been developed, allowing construction of most of the space proposed by the Campus Development Plan 1976–1980 while preserving the heritage buildings;

- upgrades and restores the Places and Monuments identified as important by the University community, which are likely to include the Great Trek Memorial Cairn, the Auditorium Quadrangle, and the Memorial Avenue of Trees on Mathematics Road.

Excerpted from "The UBC Heritage Building Study" (Iredale, 1986)

Implementation

If the Heritage Precinct Concept Plan developed in this study is accepted, the following procedures for implementation are recommended:

- Establish an open planning process to develop the Heritage Precinct Concept Plan using surveys and a broad-based committee structure to obtain the input of the university community in identifying those buildings, monuments, and places that are of heritage value to the University community.

- Undertake detailed studies to confirm the utility of each of the 1925 wood frame buildings. This undertaking involves establishment of a Code Conformance Committee charged with the responsibility of establishing the cost benefit of alternate means of code conformance, as well as detailed analysis and establishment of priorities for the upgrading of buildings to be preserved.

- Give heritage designation to those 1925 buildings chosen after detailed study and feedback from the planning process.

- Designate a Heritage Precinct encompassing the buildings, monuments, and places identified in the process of the first recommendation above.

- Develop heritage design guidelines for restoration of heritage buildings and for all landscaping and new construction within the Heritage Precinct.

- Undertake restoration and new construction projects as required to fulfill the mission of the university and to maintain the heritage values established through the planning process.[1] ∎

---

1 W. Randle Iredale, "The University of British Columbia Heritage Building Study" (August 1986). Edited excerpts are taken from pp. 1–3, 6–7, 12, & 14.

Old Main Library, looking north from the Main Mall (the 'roof' of Sedgewick Library), in between the Sedgewick skylights

Pushing the Boundary of Technology

Essay written by Talbot Iredale.

Even though Rand's focus was primarily on architecture, for as long as I can remember he had a fascination with technology and a special interest in computers. He was always trying to understand how things worked, what made them tick, and whether he could make them better.

When something broke he had no fear about taking it apart to see if it could be fixed or, at least, to find out how it functioned. I remember a story about Dad as a young child taking a watch apart, but after putting it back together he seemed to have a problem getting it going again!

Another tale about Dad's early exploration of 'technology' was when he decided to find out what electricity was all about. He wrapped a wire around his arm and then stuck the two bare ends into a plug. Fortunately, his mother—my grandmother, Nana—found him and unplugged the wires before any serious damage could be done.

From a very young age, I was always interested in construction, in building things. Even as a baby I apparently took things apart to see how they were built. And I've heard tales about myself unscrewing the neighbours' light bulbs and bringing them home.

By the late 1970s, when I was about 20 years old, I began to show an aptitude and an interest in computers. Rand had been interested in computers since the late 1960s, long before I even understood the concept. But once he had a computer and I was able to start playing with it, his curiosity allowed my curiosity to develop and grow.

Micro-Computers

As a young teenager I remember sitting at the dining table and listening to Dad talk about the Ri-Rite computer program—a project management and billing program—that he had created. I still have his original manual for the Ri-Rite program. This spreadsheet program was created long before the days of PCs or even mini-computers.

The Ri-Rite program ran on a mainframe computer in Calgary or Edmonton, as I remember it, because there were no mainframe computers in Vancouver at that time. Dad had a teletype terminal in his office, which was connected by a phone line to the mainframe in order to enter the data.

Continued

Micro-computers first appeared on the market just after I graduated from high school in 1975. Dad immediately purchased one for his office. This computer was state-of-the-art for that time. It used a Zilog Z80 8-bit processor running at 4 MHz (as compared to today's computers that are 32-bit processors running at over 2,000 MHz), two 360KB floppy disk drives, and no hard drive. Dad and I spent hours together learning how to use this computer. He was primarily using it for accounting, word processing, and project management, with the first spreadsheet program ever created.

This computer was a kind of nirvana for Dad, as it came with manuals that described all of its internal workings. Inevitably, we had to take it apart to see how it worked! The manuals also included information about how to 'program' it and descriptions of things called 'registers,' which neither of us understood at the time, along with listings (printouts) of the programs that came with the computer, information that was to become invaluable to us. It was during these many hours that I developed my fascination with computers, which would eventually lead me toward becoming a software engineer.

Computer Programs

Over the next few years Dad and I spent time learning more about how computers worked and how to write programs for them. Finally, we actually began writing some programs, including games, a dis-assembler, and a project estimating program.

My interest in construction continued, however, during and after high school and I pursued a career in engineering. I graduated from UBC in 1982 and worked as a structural engineer for a few years. But the economy was in recession and I left engineering in 1985. I had taken a few university courses in computer programming and decided to move into computer technology, which was really starting to develop at that time.

These early computers were not as sophisticated as today's models, and they would 'crash' at the most inopportune times, losing all of the day's work. I remember one extreme instance, which occurred near the end of my second year at university when I was studying for final exams. I had been at home preparing for a three-hour physics final that I was to take at 9:00 the next morning.

Dad did not make it home for dinner because he was working at the office to get a proposal completed for the next day. Late in the evening he phoned to say that his computer had crashed and he had lost all of his work—was there anything I could do to help him? Having studied the program he was using, including the program listing that came with the system, I thought there might be something I could do. So I headed down to his office.

Continued

Talbot Iredale

As I have found from many subsequent hours working on computers, time seems to stand still when trying to solve a computer problem. You seem to be in a constant state of thinking that the next thing you do—and, of course, it will only take a few minutes—will be the step that solves the problem. Inevitably that is not true, and by the time you check to see what time it is, many hours have passed.

In this case, Dad and I worked almost the whole night trying to recover the data he had lost, and by the time we finished and headed home it was time for me to go for my morning exam. I don't even remember whether we succeeded in recovering the lost data. I do remember Mom being extremely concerned about my lack of sleep before such an important exam—which I succeeded in passing with good marks.

Computer-Aided Drafting

As computers became more powerful and sophisticated, including introduction of the IBM PC in the mid-1980s, Dad started to think about using them for CAD (Computer-Aided Drafting). In his typical well-organized manner, he undertook a project to research and evaluate various CAD systems on the market and he asked if I would help him, which I was more than happy to do.

Together we researched all of the CAD systems to determine what they could do and whether they would be appropriate for use in Dad's architectural practice. We even investigated the possibility of developing our own system that used a large tabletop display, with the ability to draw directly on the display, rather than using a tablet, which was the common interface for all CAD systems at that time (mice had not been invented yet!).

Thinking back on this research project, I am struck by how much technology has changed the way we do things. When researching the CAD systems, we did most of the initial work via magazines, as there was no Internet to use to determine what CAD systems even existed. We attained more detailed information by then sending letters to each of the companies and requesting literature about their products—fax machines were still not in widespread use at that time.

Once we had narrowed the field to a couple of potential systems, Dad believed that we needed to see demonstrations of these programs. Now, this was before there were any CAD systems in Vancouver, or anywhere else close by! So he decided we should go to the CAD offices and, therefore, Dad and I headed off to Los Angeles—where both of the companies we were interested in were located—to see their products.

Continued

Talbot Iredale

This trip was memorable for me, only partly because we met with the developers of these two CAD systems (both systems would become very popular: they were AutoCAD and VersaCAD).

It was my first trip to Los Angeles and, in particular, to towns south of Los Angeles such as Irvine and Laguna Beach. I was struck by how warm, sunny, and pleasant these places were. The office complex in Irvine where VersaCAD was located reminded me of a university campus, with lots of green grass and trees around the buildings. We stayed at a very nice hotel in Laguna Beach—reminiscent of something from the 1920s—that overlooked the beach and ocean. I remember having dinner at the hotel and being impressed by how easy life seemed to be there; the air was warm and fresh and the people were polite, pleasant, and happy. Before breakfast in the morning Dad and I went for a run along the long sandy beach that stretched out below the hotel.

When we returned to Vancouver and completed our analysis, Dad decided to purchase AutoCAD, and his practice used it from then on.

Working with Dad on this project gave me insight into his organized methodology for running projects. We put a project plan together, executed the work, and compiled the results of our research in a final document. This experience has had a great impact on the methodologies of project development I employ in my work today as a software development manager. ∎

Rand and Tab loved to tinker with technology and find out how things worked; here they are measuring the water when the well ran dry on Mayne Island (1999)

The technology

for preserving

and manipulating

knowledge is expanding

and changing at an

unprecedented rate

during our time.

APPLYING NEW TECHNIQUES

As architects and engineers, we deal in knowledge. The technology for preserving and manipulating knowledge is expanding and changing at an unprecedented rate during our time.

For this reason, we are committed to applying new techniques of computer-aided design wherever they will improve our ability to contribute to better design.

As the computer replaces the paper and pencil on which our creative process is based, we are challenged to develop new skills—to interact with the new medium in writing, counting, and drawing.

We embrace the new technology, secure in the belief that it will improve the quality of our design.

Rand Iredale, Project Manager's Manual (1997)

We embrace the new technology, secure in the belief that it will improve the quality of our design.

Project Team

Randle Iredale
Partner in Charge

R. Martin Cruise
Project Architect

Project: Greenwood Village Townhouses

Greenwood Village is a four-building townhouse development of 23 units. The buildings are wood frame with stucco cladding, arranged around a central courtyard. The 100 x 110 lot has the highest density of units per acre to date in the Fairview Slopes area, resulting in affordable housing units in the vicinity of Vancouver.

The townhouses were developed in 1983 in response to demographic studies that indicated the type of housing desired by the consumer. They are the 'Baby Boom generation,' now over age 30, who want to reside close to the city centre but have the amenities of a single-family dwelling in the suburbs.

One- or two-bedroom units, with one- and two-storey floor plans, range in floor space from 750 to 1,060 sq. ft. Each unit has a private entry and private outdoor space (either a garden or deck). Laundry facilities, workshop areas, and parking for two cars are standard amenities. Fireplaces are provided in many units, and the rear buildings take advantage of the view of the city. ■

Greenwood Village is in the foreground, looking from the Fairview Slopes toward downtown Vancouver

Notice the Dome / BC Place Stadium in the upper right-hand corner (completed in 1983)

Project Team

Randle Iredale
Partner in Charge

R. Martin Cruise
Project Architect

Project: Bennett Road Townhouses

This 1984 project is a family rental development in Richmond of 19 ground-related townhouses that achieves a density of 27 units per acre. Each townhouse has 1,425 sq. ft. of living space, private garage, and fenced garden. The three-storey configuration provides entry, garage, utility, and common room on the ground floor, with farm kitchen and dining, living, and powder rooms on the main floor. The master suite and two bedrooms are located on the top floor. The rear garden is elevated to provide direct access from the main-floor rooms. ∎

Project Team

Randle Iredale
Partner in Charge

Catherine Campbell
Project Architect

Project: Ladysmith Heritage Harbour

Since the turn of the century, the Ladysmith waterfront had been devoted to logging, first using oxen and then steam railroads to penetrate the Vancouver Island wilderness. Changing logging technology had left a collection of historic industrial artifacts and buildings.

The Iredale Partnership was commissioned by the Town of Ladysmith in 1986 to undertake a planning study of the waterfront site. Their study recognized the opportunity for Ladysmith to develop an historic attraction for the burgeoning tourist industry of Vancouver Island.

With the aid of Expo Legacy Funding, the Ladysmith Heritage Railroad Museum and the Tall Ships Society were housed in restored industrial buildings to become anchors for the development. To create a sense of place, a heritage square with an amphitheatre was developed as a centre for such visitor services as restaurants, craft shops, and tourist information.

To ensure that the new development contributed to business in the existing town centre, a new access between the main street and the harbour was key to the new Heritage Harbour development. ∎

Ladysmith Heritage Harbour and the Amphitheatre

Project Team

Randle Iredale
Partner in Charge

Randy L. Cleveland
Project Architect

Project: Kamloops Indian Centre

The plan for development of the Kamloops Indian Centre (1988) on the Yellowhead Highway was based on three years of interactive planning with Chief Clarence Jules, Band Council members, and 22 Native organizations that would occupy the site, as well as the Band professional staff.

A Facilities Management Inventory of the existing buildings provided the basis for a restoration plan to adapt the historic 1927 brick residential school to offices for Indian Government in the region. Conversion of the 1955 annex to a museum and other cultural uses, and the salvaging of earlier wood buildings as character elements on a commercial street, served visitors as well as members of the Band.

The Centre is designed as a place of pride in the Indian culture, to develop recognition of the importance of the historic Indian ways in the wider community. The business plan element of the master planning process identified the potential for visitor facilities and commercial enterprises that would provide employment for Band members and a return on the Band's investment in land and buildings. ▪

Kamloops Indian Centre
on the Yellowhead Highway

LETTING EVERYBODY SPEAK

"A number of years ago when I was dealing with public consultation, Rand Iredale, an architect friend of mine, said: 'You know, Art, sometimes it takes less time to get something done if you let everybody speak and have their say.' It does. That is a truism.

"Over the years I have taken that advice whenever I have had any consultation and tried to get through any projects. I have tried very hard ... to make it a plan that everybody could feel a part of ..."[1]

---

1 Art Cowie, *Official Report of Debates of the Legislative Assembly* Vol. 12:5 (1993). Art Cowie worked with Rand in the 1960s in Canadian Environmental Sciences (CES). Source: Internet (2006) Art is a community planner and landscape architect, and a former Vancouver Alderman, provincial MLA, and Parks Board Chair.

One time Rand was putting in a proposal for the Old Territorial Administration Building in Dawson City. It had to get there by courier before the deadline.

We had a new computer and had just switched from WordPerfect to Microsoft Word, but neither Rand nor I knew how to work it! Here we were struggling to get this darn proposal out. It was awful.

I was exhausted at the end. But we succeeded. Rand was always right there. He didn't walk off and leave you. No, no, no, no, no. ∎

—*Kathryn Iredale*

DEEP-FREEZING & BRAIN-STORMING

From an essay written by Charlotte Murray.

In 1985 Rand was given a job by the Federal Government to renovate the Old Territorial Administration Building in Dawson City, to provide a museum and offices for the RCMP. He really enjoyed the trips to Dawson and the challenge of working on a project with extreme weather conditions.

Martin Cruise did the drawings for the project, and later I was called on to analyze the original paint colors and provide a paint schedule for the project. The project had lots of problems because of the extreme weather conditions, the deep-freezing of the earth, and the challenge of keeping the building warm. There were a lot of technical problems, too. This heritage project was technically out of my range, so I didn't mind that it was Rand's project!

In those days we still had the vestiges of the old design panels. It was a regular event in the office, and when a project came forward everyone had the chance to look at it and have input. It became more than just a small team; it became the whole office.

With this Territorial Building, Rand re-initiated the design panel approach, and we met several times as a group to brainstorm ways of dealing with some of the technical problems and the establishment of the new museum space. ∎

Adapted from text prepared by The Iredale Partnership (1985)

Project Team

Randle Iredale
Partner in Charge

Robert Lemon
Project Architect /
Conservation

R. Martin Cruise
Project Architect /
Contract Documentation

Project: The Old Territorial Administration Building

The Klondike Gold Rush of 1898 brought some 50,000 fortune seekers from all over the world to Dawson City, Yukon. The romance of this last great gold rush, as conveyed in the writings of Robert Service and Jack London, lures visitors to Dawson City every summer.

Parks Canada began the task of restoring the City in the 1960s and, in 1986, the Yukon Government and Parks Canada jointly determined to restore the Old Territorial Administration Building as a visitor attraction and a source of local pride.

Historic Preservation Challenges

The Canadian tradition of Law and Order was maintained by the Northwest Mounted Police and supported by government and courts. The Old Territorial Administration Building, designed by the Federal Architect Thomas W. Fuller, was constructed in 1901 as the seat of government symbolizing this Canadian tradition of frontier Law and Order.

"The Yukon Administration Building – Dawson, Yukon"

Sketch: Charles Simpson (1934)
(this sketch is housed in the Provincial Legislative Building in Dawson City; original sketch was done in colour)

Adapted from text prepared by The Iredale Partnership (1985)

Due to the existing building's historic significance, the Yukon Government required its thorough and careful preservation. The new uses of Museum and Government Offices, however, have demanding functional needs in conflict with full restoration, as well as the common problems of introducing modern mechanical and electrical services into an historic structure. Wood frame buildings, particularly in the severe northern Canadian climate, are not suited to the controlled environment required for Museum Galleries and Artifact Storage.

Restoration *vs.* Renovation

The following scheme addresses these problems of historic preservation:

- First, placing the areas requiring the most intervention in a new wing: This addition houses those uses requiring plumbing and mechanical and electrical services.

- Second, equipping the Museum Galleries and Artifacts Storage areas with humidistatically controlled heating currently under development by National Museums of Canada: This system controls humidity rather than temperature, allowing the galleries to cool to freezing during the winter season when the galleries are closed. It necessitates insulation between the galleries and all-weather uses.

- Third, separating the modern construction interventions from the original fabric of the building: The insulation, fire separations, vapour barrier, and window interventions are contained completely within the historic enclosure system. Historic finishes are then replaced within this intervention.

Image reproduced from a coloured photo / postcard (circa 1905) of the original Administration Building

Image lent to Dawson City Archives by John Grainger of Ketchikan AK

Restored Old Territorial Administration Building
(1986)

Above:
front elevation, restored

Below:
rear elevation,
new construction

Adjacent:
Restored Building

Background:
Antique Locomotives
in Dawson City

Background Photo: Hunter (1985)

Adapted from text prepared by The Iredale Partnership (1985)

Northern Environment & Construction

Given its construction in the north and at the turn of the century, this major government building is wooden from its foundations in the permafrost to its roof structure. The northern climate and permafrost, together with the building being unoccupied for almost 20 years, placed this completely wooden structure under extreme stress. Foundation movement due to the permafrost caused deformations within the structure of up to two feet, which only the resilience of wood could survive without structural failure. The restoration maintained this use of wood, including wooden foundations and finishes.

Programming

The building occupies an important site flanked by a formal axial garden commemorating World War I. The Dawson City Museum was to be located within the building. To maintain the viability of the building as an active part of the community and to involve visitors in the day-to-day life of Dawson City, government offices—including the circuit courts and community uses—were also included in the programmed uses.[1] ■

---

[1] This text has been adapted from the draft text and final award presentation prepared by The Iredale Partnership and submitted to *The Canadian Architect* (1985).

Old Territorial Administration Building

Louis Sullivan (1856–1924) was an American architect, often called the 'father of modernism.' Considered by many to be the creator of the modern skyscraper, he was an influential architect and critic of the Chicago School, and was a mentor to Frank Lloyd Wright.[1] ▪

ೲ

"However thoroughly Louis Sullivan's work was eclipsed by his Eastern contemporaries [McKim, Mead, White], he for one had fused the vital impulses of the vernacular into what he liked to describe as *organic* architecture (a word he loved for its sense of 'a ten-fingered grasp of reality').

"The vision he had caught from the great Eads Bridge at St. Louis was given concrete expression in his buildings. 'With me,' he wrote to Claude Bragdon, 'architecture is not an art, but a religion, and that religion but a part of the greater religion of Democracy.' Here, close to the vernacular roots, was the first flowering of an architecture indigenous to modern civilization." [2] ▪

---

1   Source: Internet (2006).

2   John A. Kouwenhoven, *Made in America: The Arts in Modern Civilization* (1948).

Quality control by means of checking never makes up for "doing it once, doing it right, doing it now." Creative design is an iterative process that grows from imagination to built form.

QUALITY CONTROL

We are committed to the quality dictum "do it once, do it right, do it now." If we are to succeed in creating designs that provide the fit we aspire to, our designs must be based on Louis Sullivan's "ten-fingered grasp of reality." Each step of our exploration for fit must be founded on accurate information and careful analysis.

Dr. W. Edwards Demming, the inventor of Total Quality Control (based on his background in statistics), recognized that quality is variable; you can improve only if you have measured standards to improve upon. He understood that training and education for all is an essential part of Quality Management.

As the Japanese manufacturing industry found from working with Dr. Demming, quality control by means of checking never makes up for "doing it once, doing it right, doing it now."[1] Creative design is an iterative process that grows from imagination to built form.

Thus, doing it once and doing it right can only be accomplished by knowing the appropriate level of detail for each document we produce and by having the courage to share first approximations, knowing they will evolve during our search for fit.

Rand Iredale, Project Manager's Manual (1997)

---

1   Rafael Aguayo, *Dr. Demming: The American Who Taught the Japanese About Quality* (NY, 1990).

Dr. W. Edwards Demming is the American industrial engineer whose radical methods were not accepted by US industry, but were so accepted by Japanese industry that they named their highest industrial award after him. He initiated much of the philosophy now known as *Kaizen* (meaning 'good change' or 'continuous improvement') while assisting the Japanese following WW II.

Demming's message was simply to focus more on *how* something is done, rather than on *what* is done. And to paraphrase one of his famous quotes, 'If you don't control the quality of input ... it is impossible to control the quality of output.' Considered to be the *father of quality*, he was a statistician as well as a music theorist and composer.[1] ■

---

1   Source: Internet (2006).

11 We Build a Shared Vision

The range of Rand's smaller projects took him into communities—urban and rural, new and old—that benefitted enormously from his planning expertise. His heartfelt commitment to heritage conservation was influential by example: working with Jennifer to 'rescue old houses' in the city, and partnering with Charlotte to restore existing buildings for adaptive reuse. And change was never far away: in the 1990s computers would make great strides, Richard Iredale would join the firm, and retirement would beckon.

Though Rand began winding down his architectural practice in the '90s and preparing to turn it over to others, his energy and curiosity still thrived. He was a man of many hobbies and activities. Equal to his love of computers was his lifelong love affair with cameras. I like photographs that you can put into an album, but Rand liked slides that he could project onto a screen. I never realized how many pictures he took until I started going through boxes and boxes of slides with Jennifer on my 75th birthday.

Over all of the years, from the earliest times, Rand took pictures. He had a screen at home and a screen at the office. He would present slide shows of the trips he took, like when he went to Beirut, or when he went to China the first time, or when he and the boys went skiing in the Bugaboos. When he got a camcorder he camcorded everything! He filmed our trips to France and to Cuba. He camcorded a music concert on Mayne Island when two of our grandchildren, Adam and Marlies, and Richard's wife, Lael, were performing. He stood in the small auditorium and didn't move a muscle. He camcorded for two hours and then made a tape of it.

Rand had an early interest in theatre. As a teenager he worked at the Banff School of Drama doing stage lighting. And he belonged to the Players Club at UBC. He wasn't an actor, but he liked to record events. He was intrigued with technology. Later he used a computer software program to edit and organize his tapes, and then he would run them through the television set. It was very much an activity of creating and documenting something. ■

THE PEG BOARD OF THE PAST

An email from Charlotte Murray.

During my last year working for Rhone & Iredale in the 1970s I was coordinating the work of a group of junior staff assigned to smaller projects and, therefore, was introduced to the weekly management meetings and the workings of 'the peg board.' I believe it was Rand's invention, inspired by his sojourn at MIT for advanced studies in business management.

The board, about 3' high and 6' long, was in a prominent framed assembly that included an equally large blackboard, mounted on the end wall of the main meeting room. It was on tracks that, with the simple pull of a chain, would cause the blackboard to lift to the top of the wall and thus expose the peg board with its significant array of bright multi-colored pegs, each purposefully placed in its appropriate hole. To the cognoscente, this array told the complete story of the progress of all work in the office.

Actually, when one got the hang of it, it was an ingenious method for monitoring ongoing and upcoming projects in the office. The projects were listed vertically on the left, with the size of the operating budget deciding the number of rows allocated to each project. The dates were listed by working days in each week horizontally across the top, with enough space to show three months. Each architect and assistant was represented by a different coloured peg. The simple process was to plug the appropriately coloured pegs in the holes for the assigned job according to the time and budget available for each phase of a project.

This function was performed regularly and in detail during the management meetings for about three weeks ahead, and only in outline for the remainder of the period on the board. At each weekly meeting the arrangement showing the work in progress was updated, needed adjustments were noted, and new projects were added. The group managers could then go back to their groups and assign each person their tasks as planned by the particular holes in which their personal pegs were placed for the next week.

It is not to be assumed that everyone was enthusiastic about the virtues of the peg board. It did apply a degree of discipline to the progress of work in the office, however, and provided an immediate view of how things were going overall and individually. But the biggest problem came on that inevitable day, after about six to nine weeks along, when every one of the pegs on the board had to be relocated to show the next three-month period. That was a drag!

Continued

Thank goodness for the desktop computer and Rand's eagerness to make full use of its ever-increasing capabilities. It did not take long for him to devise a single-page electronic format to record the planned and ongoing progress of each project, to be maintained by the Partner in Charge. The peg board moved with the office and was kept as an artifact (behind the still much-used blackboard assembly) in the Steamboat House. As time passed and the digital era dawned, it became an object of awe and wonder. When occasionally revealed to new staff or visitors, its labour-intensive ingenuity inevitably generated anecdote and amazement. ▪

THE FUTURE OF THE FIRM

From an essay written by Charlotte Murray.

For a while in the late 1980s there was almost nothing for us to do. I spent most of my days working on a CHMC-funded research project on seniors' housing. It was about this time that Rand and myself and Kathryn—who held down the front desk and did the bookkeeping—held a meeting to discuss the future of the firm. We were only a few years from retirement, and there were plenty of bright young architects coming along to compete for the few decent jobs that needed talent.

Then there was Richard Iredale about to finish his Master of Architecture degree at the University of Washington. Richard was an experienced engineer who loved painting in water colours and dreaming up exciting schemes. Rand proclaimed that he would do nothing to persuade Richard to join us but would be pleased if his son decided that was what he wanted.

For the next year or so we kept modestly busy. Computers were really moving forward with new programs for drafting, and Rand was keeping right up with the technology. Then Liz Scremin joined us as a draftsperson with computer know-how. Before long we had a computer on every desk but mine (I was in the middle of a sizeable heritage project for seniors housing—the Abbeyfield Houses—that was hand-drawn). Work had picked up and desks were filled.

Richard joined the firm, and we changed our name again. It had changed from Randle Iredale Architecture to The Iredale Partnership Architecture & Planning at the time that Rand and I wrote our partnership agreement in 1983, and now, in 1990, it was changed to Iredale Partnership Architects & Engineers. ▪

Grand Gestures & Simple Sketches

From an interview with Liz Scremin.

I started working for Rand in July 1988. I was taking an evening course in AutoCAD at Kwantlen College, and Rand was starting to use computers in the office. He had one computer then, and he called the college—the only accredited AutoCAD training site in Vancouver at the time—and asked if they could recommend anyone. I just happened to be the only person in the course with an architectural background; everyone else in the course at that time was an engineer. So they mentioned my name and I met Rand and Charlotte on my first job interview.

A Sense of Family

The good thing about working for Rand was that the office was always very family-oriented. Rand was the patriarch and so, for him, the sense of family extended beyond his own family; it extended to the office, too.

There was always a sense of camaraderie and Rand always tried to be inclusive. He had managed a huge firm in the past and, even though the office was much smaller now, he still had a sense of needing to manage the office and needing to keep people's morale up. There was always lots of understanding about people's personal needs. So that was one of the good things, and that was definitely because of Rand, because of his personality and his approach.

The design panels focused on the firm's direction and included everybody. The office was small but, of course, it was always growing. There were probably just five or six people, but it grew and during those times it was always, "What do we all want to be doing?" And that attitude was reflected in the annual staff reviews. We each filled out a form that asked, "What are your goals this year? What are your five-year goals?"

Rand always made sure that the firm was fulfilling your needs and providing opportunities. He would discuss your salary with you, and make sure that you got to work on a certain type of project that you wanted to work on, or got course experience or training in some area of interest. All of that mattered to him.

Rand believed that building a stronger team, which is ultimately to the benefit of the firm, keeps people happy. I think that's probably why I stayed so long; longer than I expected, that's for sure. When I started working here, I never dreamed I'd still be here today [1988–99 and 2001–06].

Continued

Liz Scremin

I know of friends who worked elsewhere and who jumped ship because they felt that they weren't getting opportunities. For a person who was just starting out, there was lots of opportunity working for Rand. He believed that everybody should be able to do everything. He didn't slot you into just being a draftsperson or just being a spec writer or just being a model builder.

And he was always proud of people. So he gladly took you along and introduced you to clients. He didn't belittle people; he wasn't condescending. Depending on your own level of confidence, you were encouraged to take on pretty much anything you wanted.

But Rand was always in a role of leadership, and he could sometimes be autocratic. He could sometimes be blunt. He spoke his mind. At design panels, for example, when somebody was drawing something, he might say, "That's just a pile of crap!" or "Get back to the basic concept!" or "You're going off in a different direction! It makes no sense at all!" So, yeah, he pushed you.

As a small 'family firm,' with Kathryn and Richard both working with Rand in the 1990s, they sometimes got on each other's nerves and there were words and tense moments until they got over it. And that wouldn't probably have occurred if they had not been related. But it occasionally happened where they would get into these family arguments and, as an outsider, you would just stay out of the way! Because they were family, they probably said and did things that others would think twice about if they were irritated or frustrated.

But there was a lot of love and devotion between Rand and Kathryn after all of those years of being together and raising a family. There was a strong bond between them and a mature kind of love. They walked up to the Village Green every day for lunch and sometimes I'd go with them.

A Certain Flamboyance

There was always a certain flamboyancy to Rand. He liked big gestures. Whenever new clients or consultants visited the office he would introduce them to everyone, and when it came to Kathryn—when she was working at the office—it was always, *"And this is my beautiful wife, Kathryn,"* with a *big* beaming smile and a *big* sweep of his arms!

Rand had a daily routine of doing a sweep through the office before sitting down to do his work; walking all through the office, all around the front porch. It was a habit from his days in the larger firm, making verbal contact with everyone. It was important to him to have a social presence and to make contact with staff.

There was a sense of Rand surveying his domain.

Continued

One time, Rand was doing a townhouse development and had employed a young man to turn out the drawings. Rand kept asking, "Are the drawings going to be ready on time?" And the guy kept saying, "Yes." The client was in the construction business and was furious because the drawings weren't ready. So Rand phoned the young draftsman and said, "You've got to come in over the weekend. We have to finish these drawings." And the guy hung up! Then Rand phoned Liz Scremin, who was up at Whistler, and she rushed down and they worked all weekend to finish those drawings and turn them out. On Monday morning, when the draftsman came in, Rand said, "I think I can accept your resignation." The irony was that he then applied for a job with somebody else and gave Rand's name as a reference!

—Kathryn Iredale

———— Liz Scremin ————

Rand was a Tinkerer

There was such a whirlwind of deadlines in the early years and we pulled many all-nighters, probably because getting drawings out was a more difficult task; printing times, assembly time, courier time, all of that was longer. There was no fax, there was no email. I remember Rand being tickled pink when he got his first fax machine. He had a client in Singapore and he was just so thrilled that he could fax a sketch or a document to Singapore and have a response the next day. That was amazing!

When we put together spec books, we photocopied them in the office; we would have a collating party with four or five people running around the table collating spec books. And corrections were done literally by cutting and pasting. We had all-nighters because it was a slow process and it was a group effort.

In those days the printers worked very slowly. It would take an hour to get a printout on the inkjet. Initially, there was only one computer, and then there were two, and because it took so long to print, Rand set up a little program where he could line up the plot in a file to run at night. And so you would print at night and you would work during the day, because at that time you couldn't work [at the computer] while the file was printing.

I can't remember why, but Rand had put the computer on a timer. We would be working away and we'd forget about the timer and all of a sudden it would shut the power off and if you hadn't saved your work you would have lost it. And that happened way too many times! You'd think we would be more sensible. And so you'd be working at 2:00 am and all of a sudden you would lose 45 minutes worth of work and you'd be pulling your hair out!

Rand was the kind of man who wanted to be able to do everything, and he thought that you should be able to do everything, too: an architect should be able to do electrical engineering and should be able to do mechanical engineering and should be able to do *everything!* He always had a Swiss Army knife in his pocket. He was always the one standing on top of the counter to reach up and change the fluorescent light bulbs; he was always the one who was taking a machine apart—the printer or the fax or whatever—to fix it; he was always the one who was replacing a door or fixing a doorknob. Whatever needed to be done, he would do it. He enjoyed it, and he thought it was important to be practical.

And Rand's approach applied to computers, too; learning the programming, learning the computer language. He developed the Ri-Rite program. I don't know what the origins of it were, but he certainly customized it for the firm's use. And he hired an architectural technician to assist with computer systems; someone

———— *Continued* ————

who was trained as an architect but who was teaching computers to architects. He helped Rand develop a program for managing architectural projects. Then Rand contacted AutoCAD to become a third-party developer. He loved doing that. Of course, the software soon became more sophisticated, but he gave it a good shot for a person who had so little training and background.

Rand was a tinkerer. He was always fixing things, and I think he even viewed his interest in heritage restoration as being environmentally beneficial: you make something last, you adapt it, keep it purposeful, and work on it, and that saves resources and makes it sound in every way, in terms of both history and environment. He always wanted to make things last.

The Things You Remember

The things you remember about someone are not necessarily profound. I just remember his white leather loafers, which were so 1960s! A lot of Rand's clothes were from the 1960s and, I mean, that was his style. You fix things and you keep them going. And the Christmas parties, when he would enthusiastically lead the carol-singing in his deep voice, often wearing his silk Nehru-collar jacket. I'm going to guess it was made in Hong Kong, so it was also from the 1960s, and he proudly wore it on holidays.

And I remember his slightly long, flowing, silvery hair, white hair, and his sort of rumpled face. He always looked a little bit older than he actually was because he would go jogging along the beach in the morning with his dog, even in his seventies. People would be surprised to know that he was still jogging. Silver hair runs in his family and his skin was always kind of mottled and ruddy. Yeah, I remember things like that.

Stop Gilding the Lily!

I also remember him occasionally looking over my shoulder and commanding, "Stop gilding the lily!" It meant that I was fussing over a detail or adding too much detail. *Enough is enough!* His drawings were ruthlessly simple because he was used to working with tradespeople who had standards and he didn't have to draw every infinite last bit of detail (not like today). In those days it was kind of a master craftsman thing: you went on site and scribbled on an envelope and the person knew what you needed and they built it. And so Rand's drawings were really sketchy. Actually, he hated drafting. He often said that he loved computers because he hated bending over a drawing board and straining his back. Anyway, he would tell me again and again to "Stop gilding the lily," because I would be putting too much detail into something. "Good enough, good enough!" ∎

Project: Norquay Elementary School

Project Team

Prime Consultant
The Iredale Partnership

Randle Iredale
Partner in Charge

Stanley Paulus
Project Manager

Richard Iredale
Structural Engineer

Jane Kinegal
Project Programming

Elizabeth Scremin
Technician

Sub-Consultants

Quadra Pacific
Mechanical Engineers

R.A. Duff
Electrical Engineers

Gage Babcock
Code Consultants

Award

City of Vancouver
Heritage Design

Built in 1913, Norquay Elementary School is a City of Vancouver Heritage Building of the Classical Revival style. In 1991 the Vancouver School Board commissioned The Iredale Partnership to analyze the options of replacing or renovating this building.

The decision was made to upgrade the structure to preserve this proud heritage landmark, and to adapt the building to suit contemporary teaching and learning requirements.

The project involved the addition of two classrooms, a new library resource centre, and a modernized mechanical / electrical plant. New washrooms were installed at each floor level to replace antiquated basement facilities.

The centre of the school was opened up to provide a view into the new open plan library. Staff room facilities and student services and administration were grouped around this central 'commons' to create a welcoming space.

The 10" concrete walls of the library / addition were linked by means of new concrete slabs to a new concrete frame / elevator shaft to strengthen the heavy timber and masonry structure against lateral forces. ■

Front entry and one wing of renovated and expanded Norquay Elementary School

1995 City of Vancouver Heritage Award Nomination

John Norquay Elementary School (4710 Slocan Street), constructed in the formal Edwardian Style typical of early Vancouver school buildings, was built in stages, beginning in 1918 with the central core and stairwells, followed by additions in 1922, 1924, and 1956. Each of the early additions stayed true to the original brick tectonics and the formal axial plan, but the 1950s gymnasium and primary annex added to the south differ in style and are poorly joined at the basement level to the existing main corridor.

The Vancouver School Board commissioned The Iredale Partnership to plan yet another addition, which would join to and enhance the original formal axial plan of the building. In addition, seismic bracing was to be retrofitted into the non-reinforced masonry skin of the building and dovetailed with new state-of-the-art heating, ventilation, communications, and lighting in such a way as to leave the historic character intact.

The architect's response is a renovation / addition that develops a new cross axis and opens up the centre of the building to the play fields, using a formal structural grid juxtaposed with glass partitions arranged informally to reflect the child-centred style of modern education.

Exterior brick and cornice detailing of the new addition blends with the original building, while use of a carefully detailed curtainwall glazing system subtly articulates the transition between old and new.

An innovative system of concrete butterfly trusses and concrete floor slabs were retrofitted into the old timber structure at the main, second, and attic floor levels to connect into the new concrete addition and provide a rugged shear core able to resist seismic loads. The masonry facade was restored and epoxy-anchored into steel reinforcing elements retrofitted around the perimeter of the floor plates.

The 6,000 sq. ft. of additional space was constructed for about $800,000, while the renovation of the historic 42,000 sq. ft. building cost about $2.8 million, or about $66 / sq. ft. The project demonstrates that the restoration of an historic structure to modern standards is less expensive than construction of new equivalent space.[1] ■

---

1   Text taken from The Iredale Partnership Heritage Award Nomination / Submission.

A letter from the Board of School Trustees of School District No. 39 (Vancouver), dated April 7th, 1995 and addressed to The Council of Educational Facility Planners, International (nominating the project for another award) stated in part that it "recently received a City of Vancouver Heritage Design Award for its innovative approach to seismic upgrading and adapting an historic building to a modern educational program. The project was completed on time and on budget in 1994. Scheduling of the work was arranged to enable full use of the existing building while construction of the addition was underway. . . . A contingency sum of $308,000 based on the requirements of a renovation project was set aside. At completion of the contract the sum of $40,644 remained in the contingency allowance, demonstrating that the project was delivered for less than the originally anticipated budget amount."

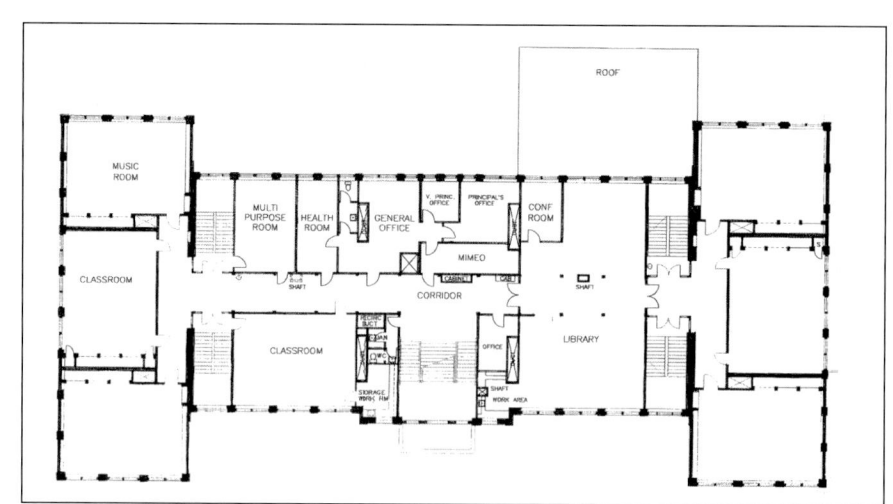

Above:
floor plan before 1994
changes to the school

Below:
floor plan showing all
added and renovated areas

Above, opposite:
east elevation, before
and after 1994 addition

Below, opposite:
examples of Rand's early
3-D computer modelling

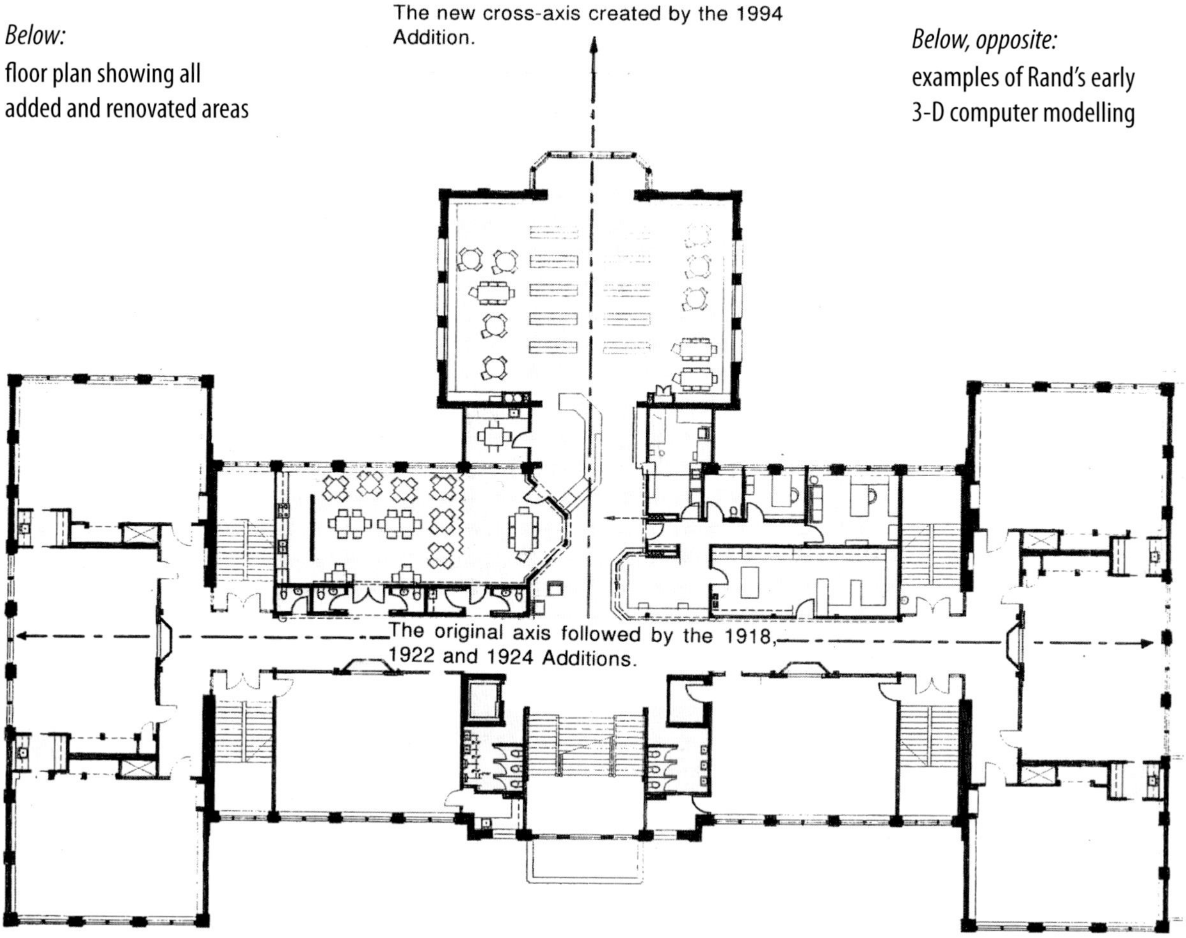

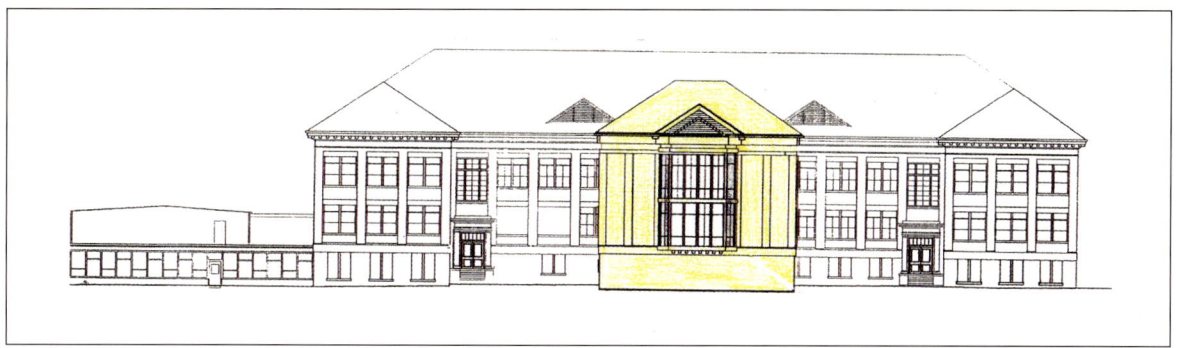

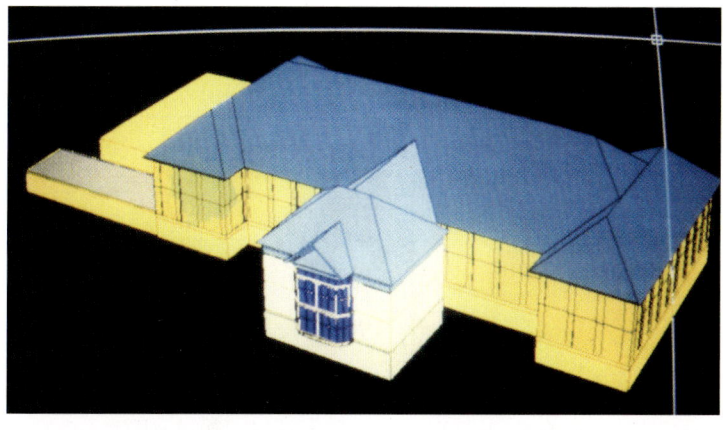

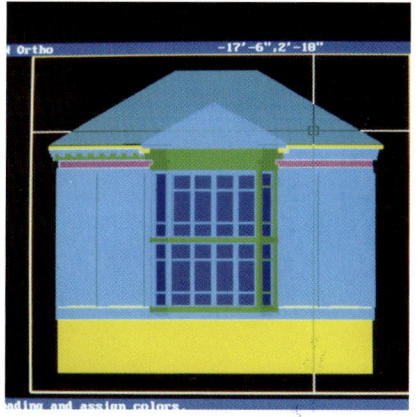

Reprinted from *The Courier* (Hill, circa 1995)

City Honours School With Heritage Award

Iredale Work Wins for Third Time

For Rand Iredale, a heritage building is a vessel of social history, a comment on the values of its era. If that building is a school, its stature and presence reflect the community's pride in education. So when the Vancouver architect began a renovation project at 82-year-old John Norquay Elementary School two years ago, he knew his work would have to respect the attitude with which the school was originally built.

"In 1913 (when the school was built), a three-storey classical brick school had to be the biggest building for miles around," says Iredale, of The Iredale Partnership, a firm hired by the Vancouver School Board to renovate and build an addition to the East Side school at 4710 Slocan. "It was wonderful to come back to a school built with such pride and that so strongly indicated great faith in education."

Two years ago, the VSB hired the [firm] to adapt the heritage building to meet seismic standards and add 6,000 square feet to it. "When we built the 1994 addition, we matched the brick with great care. We repeated the same form, so our addition would disappear in the main building." The architect's work "disappeared" so well [that] the city awarded the firm a 1995 Vancouver Heritage Award this month. The Iredale Partnership joins 16 other groups and individuals recognized for maintaining the character of existing heritage buildings across Vancouver.

The Norquay project is the first ever to receive a Vancouver Heritage Award for the Vancouver School Board. Having "so many heritage schools, the VSB have found them a mixed blessing," says Iredale. "They're heritage, but it can be difficult and expensive to make an old school work well."

The Iredale Partnership's work has been similarly honoured every year for the last three years. Partners [Randle Iredale and Charlotte Murray] have won Vancouver heritage awards for their renovations to Alexander House and to Abbeyfield Heritage House.

School principal Gwen Smith says she's relieved the renovations are over, for practical reasons. "The dust and the noise was absolutely horrendous," she says, "but (teachers and students) managed to survive and keep the upbeat atmosphere right through it. They deserve a great pat on the back." The inconvenience paid off: "You wouldn't know it was an addition. It fits in perfectly to the tune of the school."

The architects opened up the library, to "bring it to the more open style of education we have today, while still retaining that quality of pride in the classical form," Iredale says. The latest addition cost about $3.5 million, "where a replacement school would cost about $7 million, Iredale says.[1] ∎

---

1   Mary Frances Hill, "City Honours School With Heritage Award," *The Courier*, circa 1995 (date unknown).

CHECK & DOUBLE-CHECK

No drawing is to be issued for tender or construction that has not been checked and initialled by the Partner in Charge and a member of the firm who has taken the responsibility of completing the check.

The cost of errors that Owners have back-charged during the past three years, beyond what we could reasonably claim as 'normal,' is over $20,000. To this amount must be added our loss in reputation in getting Owners to approve Change Orders for errors that a reasonable check would have remedied.

On Norquay School for the Vancouver School Board, for example, the survey carried the note "OIL TANK COVER". Our drawing added the note "REMOVE". Of course, the contractor removed the cover; however, he claimed $60,000 to remove the tank itself and the contaminated soil around it. The claim was settled for $20,000 after many days of the partner's time in negotiation. The time spent negotiating the settlement exceeded the time required to check the whole set of drawings, and our reputation with the School Board was damaged.

Another even more outrageous example was our failure to catch, during checking, the fact that no heating was provided for the second floor of Place des Arts. The mechanical drawings noted that the second floor was heated under division 16 Electrical. But the electrical drawings and specifications contained no mention of electric heat, except in the parking level Elevator Lobby. The owner back-charged us $10,000 for this omission—enough to spend 140 hours in checking!

Rand Iredale, Project Manager's Manual (1997)

The addition to Norquay Elementary School

Reprinted from *AIBC Newsletter* (Fiss, 1994)

Norquay Elementary School: The Three R's

... When it comes time to build more classroom space the choice is often between sprucing up a tired and potentially unsafe older school building or settling for a prefabricated portable trailer parked in a playground. The monies are just not there for a high tech, state of the art ... learning module. Or are they?

The Iredale Partnership recently took on the challenge of rehabilitating the Norquay Elementary School in Vancouver's School District No. 39, and their results are instructive. The project team began their course of studies with a report analyzing the existing facilities and evaluating the options for full replacement versus renovation.

The existing school, built in 1913, a three-storey, classically composed, bilaterally symmetrical brick box suffered from both structural and programmatic shortcomings. Though solid enough looking in its strict institutional appearance, it nevertheless failed to make the grade in seismic performance, achieving only a rating of 20% of the requirements. The public spaces were dark and congested, and the typical placement of the washrooms in the basement was inefficient ... as well as unsafe and unsupervised.

Enter the architects. They have obviously been studying their 3 R's: Reuse, Recycle, and Reduce, the watchwords of the greening of contemporary design. In an ingenious reworking of the central stair in the building, they have been able to both seismically upgrade the building to meet 100% of today's standards, and as well, paradoxically, open up the central core to bring more daylight and outside views to the public areas.

On a recent tour, Project Manager Stanley Paulus, MAIBC, and Structural Engineer Richard Iredale, P. Eng., MAIBC, enthusiastically explained how they had introduced a concrete butterfly truss into the central core, allowing an opening up of the circulation space and an introduction of new windows into the main entry lobby and the stair landings. Additionally, this rejuvenated core also boasts the addition of an elevator, and cheerful, decentralized washrooms at each floor, with entry signage mosaics developed by an artist working with student art classes.

The existing classrooms were given fresh coats of paint and new carpets but otherwise remained largely unchanged, save for the addition of storage and additional counterspace in the art rooms. In fact, the old classrooms offer many luxuries unattainable by today's ministry standards: a larger floor area than would be allowed for a new classroom and generous 12' high ceilings. The proportion and height of the 'traditional' room can achieve better natural daylight performance and a more comfortable environment, both acoustically and in air quality, than its modern counterpart.

The reuse of the old classrooms and the generous nine-foot wide corridors should earn this project a few bonus points, not to mention the fact that the upgrading and recycling of a venerable old school resulted in a net savings of $3 million below the cost for building equivalent all new facilities.

Reprinted from *AIBC Newsletter* (Fiss, 1994)

"Led by partner-in-charge Randle Iredale and Project Leader Jane Kinegal, Intern Architect, the team skillfully added a three-storey 660 m² addition [that] seamlessly blends in with the heritage original. A two-storey central glazed bay window is a welcome counterpoint to the traditional punched windows of the original brick facade. Behind these windows, flooded in daylight, is the reading area for the newly centralized school library. The open plan library resource centre combines with the welcoming, renovated administration/reception area and a spacious staff lounge/multi-purpose room to give the school a vital new heart. The secret to the success of this space, and for the project, is in doing double duty with each part. Rooms can be bigger when functions are combined. Structure can be both support and an expressive form. The requirements and budgets to make seismic upgrades and add access for the disabled can be used to improve the quality of all spaces affected."[1]

The lesson in this project is that we can learn from the old as well as the new. Daylight, adequate room size, and good materials will allow an institution to continue to be recycled and preserved. A continuity with our heritage buildings should be included in our curriculum for building the school district of the future.[1] ■

---

1 Eric Fiss, MAIBC, "Norquay Elementary School: The Three R's," *AIBC Newsletter*, Vol. 12, No. 6 (November / December 1994): 16.

Reception, Lounge, & Library below central stairway

The Library bay window forms a cozy reading alcove

Three-storey addition with two-storey bay window

Students at Norquay celebrate their 'new' school

In My Father's Footsteps

From an essay by, and an interview with, Richard Iredale.

When Rand and my mother, Kathryn, took me, my brother Talbot, and my sister Jennifer on a four-month trip to Europe in 1969, it made a lasting impression on all of us. Visits to ancient sites, art galleries, cathedrals, and museums had a powerful impact on my young mind, as did conversations with the architecture students at UBC's Studies Abroad program in Venice where we stayed for three months while Rand taught. I trace my passion for architecture and painting to this period.

After graduating from university, I worked with my dad during the 1990s, when he was in his sixties. I followed in his footsteps, completely, and shared his interest in integrating engineering into architecture. Rand believed that a building could and should originate in how it worked, structurally and mechanically. He also believed that science was good, that technology was good.

During that decade the practice's primary concerns continued to be the conservation of heritage buildings and townscapes. The firm actively advocated the gradual re-inhabitation of Vancouver's city core, which had been largely abandoned during the suburban exodus of previous decades. In designing such projects as Barclay Heritage Square in Vancouver and Maillardville Heritage Park in Coquitlam, we began to develop our ideas about how 'community places' can promote citizenship. We also explored alternative, ecologically sustainable construction methods.

Norquay School was a really interesting project for us. We had to figure out a way to economically reinforce a brick building. Not many of those had been done. So Dad and I put on our structural

Continued

Above:
Rand at Richard's graduation (M.Arch.) from the University of Washington (1990)

Opposite:
Rand, age 65, hiking the West Coast Trail (1994)

engineering thinking caps to figure that out. We worked well together; mostly, I did the structural engineering and Rand did the architecture. I learned a lot about his methods for managing and planning projects.

Rand strove to find a logical process for solving design problems. He hoped that his Project Manager's Manual would train almost any apprentice to become a good architect. He believed that if a problem could be properly understood and formulated, then the solution would be obvious; the main task for the designer, therefore, was to define the problem correctly through careful programming and site analysis. While there are many merits to this view, Rand's ideal of an orderly design process did not always fit the reality of working with the client which, as he well understood, could be more of a trial-and-error process than a tightly systematic one.

Forever Young

I remember hiking the West Coast Trail on Vancouver Island with my Dad when I was 35 and he was about 65. He was so keen to go. He loved to hike and he loved to be outside. It seemed like every time we organized a hiking trip it was cold and raining, but he was very willing to put up with the wind and the rain. Dad would happily put up with that deprivation.

On this particular trip Dad had started with our friend Ken King from Bamfield (at the northern end) and done a tough three-day leg—though the southern half of the Trail is the most difficult—and I was to meet them at Nitinat Lake. I got to the Narrows there, and got a ride in a speedboat from the Indians who run the little floating café at the north end of the lake. It was pouring rain, and I waited a couple of hours for Dad and Ken to show up.

Eventually I started hiking southward to try and find them. I got about four or five miles down the trail and there was Dad, soldiering along! He was too old to be doing the West Coast Trail, because it's like Marine Boot Camp. It's an incredibly difficult hike. He just looked at me in the rain and said, "Here, take this!" and gave me his backpack. That was the last trip he did on the West Coast Trail.

I hiked the southern part of the West Coast Trail in 2006 with my three daughters and their friends and we got rained on completely. It was really treacherous. And I thought, "This was not a good thing for a 65-year old guy to be doing in the pouring rain." I mean, Dad pushed himself really hard. He wasn't somebody who admitted to getting old. He wasn't somebody who said, "Maybe I shouldn't be doing this." He was forever young in his mind and he was a very stubborn, optimistic person.

Continued

Richard Iredale

Father, Architect, Teacher, Friend

I remember my Dad as a big family man who was very involved in everything we did together. When I was growing up, our family dinner table conversations were always lively, with lots of discussion about current social and political trends. The property on Mayne Island, initially only a weekend campsite, became his personal retreat and spiritual home. My own family's home is on Mayne Island, where we raised our three daughters and operated a small hobby farm.

Though architecture was truly the big adventure of Rand's life, he had a wide-ranging and curious mind. His keen interest in politics, economics, and sociology led him to become involved in civic affairs during the 1970s and 1980s. Rand contributed a lot to society in terms of promoting community projects. I think his genius was as a planner. He was probably one of only a few people there are to thank for the revitalization and livability of downtown Vancouver.

The other thing about Dad is that he was a good teacher. He was generous with his time and energy. Though he didn't suffer fools gladly, he was definitely willing to take the time to teach someone who really wanted to learn. He was very willing to communicate. I remember that you could always interrupt Dad; he never minded being interrupted. You could always go and bother him and he was always glad to talk.

And when Rand had good friends, they were very good friends. Most of the time, fortunately for him, he was able to find people he could enjoy working with, and that's all good—people like Bogue Babicki and Bob Hansen. Rand worked with Bob on Norquay, and the two of them got along like a house on fire.

Dad belonged to the generation of Canadian architects who grew up during the Depression and the ensuing war years and, as adults, entered into a period of unprecedented prosperity. He felt very optimistic about automobiles and jet planes and power dams and computers and all of the technologies that transformed life in the 20th century.

When I was about 19 Dad and I were on our way home from skiing up at Cypress Mountain. We got stuck in a huge traffic jam and Dad was frustrated at how long it was taking us, and he said we should be building a freeway. And I really disagreed with that. We had a huge argument about how freeways generate noise, cut up neighbourhoods, and only promote more traffic. I had taken a course on road design and learned that the more lanes you have, the more traffic you get. But Rand didn't buy it! He grew up in an earlier time when there was a love affair with the automobile.

Continued

Richard Iredale

A Vibrant Personality

The really best thing about my Dad ... well, there were several things that were really the best things about him. But the very best thing was his enthusiasm for life. He could make anything seem like fun. He could make building an outhouse seem like an exciting project.

I always remember, in the office, whatever project we did have, Dad would contrive to figure out a way of doing it in a unique and original manner and making it seem like a research project or something more than an everyday assignment.

Dad could do that. It was sort of like building castles in the air, but sometimes his dreams worked out and he really did come up with something interesting.

The dome project on Mayne Island is a good example. He fell in love with domes back in the 1970s. He was very stimulated by the hippie movement, even though he wasn't from that generation. Dad was always able to feed off youthful enthusiasm and naivety.

Dad decided that we would build this dome and we spent a Saturday cutting all of the pieces up in a plant over in North Van that Dad had with some partners for building pre-fabricated houses. And then we took all of the bits and pieces over to Mayne Island and actually assembled this thing in not very much time. And that was really fun.

Another example is when Rand would wake us up at four or five in the morning to go out on our speedboat on Mayne Island. We'd travel around to the other side of the island and go salmon fishing. Dad was convinced the fish would bite just as the rising sun struck the water. I remember watching the sun come up over Georgia Strait and putting the line out and catching a salmon and then bringing it back and cleaning it on the beach. It was really, really fun.

Dad liked to fish and he liked to be up early and he liked to be outside. He was essentially an outdoor person, and I think he was most himself in that kind of environment. We shared a lot around being outside. We shared fishing and hiking, and we shared being outside working, doing things, making things, building things.

Dad was a vibrant personality and he was writ large in Jennifer's and Tab's and my life. He was the one who always wanted to do things, who organized things. He was the one with the "let's go, let's do it" sort of approach. And so he got us out doing things.

And that's what I like to remember about him. ■

Excerpted from the "Development Plan: West Coast Railway Museum" (1993)

Project Team

Randle Iredale
Partner in Charge

Commonwealth Historic Resource Management

Historica Research Ltd.

Lord Cultural Resources Planning & Management

Project: Squamish Railway Museum

Working with the Prime Consultants, Commonwealth Historic Resource Management Limited, The Iredale Partnership provided the West Coast Rail Association with conceptual planning and capital cost estimates for the master plan of a new railway museum in Squamish BC.

The master plan provided museum operating and [artifact] collection policy and physical planning for the Squamish site. The planned facilities would provide space for the restoration and display of the largest collection of historic rail equipment in British Columbia.

The consulting team's market surveys showed that to assure the visitation required to sustain such a large operation, the museum must attract a wider range of visitors than only rail enthusiasts. In response, the wider implications of rail in British Columbia were incorporated in the master plan: a recreated historic railroad town complete with restaurants, shops, and a park. This wider vision of the historic importance of rail entailed facilities that could appeal to the whole family.

The Development Plan

Background

The West Coast Railway Association (WCRA) is in its fifth decade of collecting and restoring artifacts related to the railway history of British Columbia. The WCRA currently has more than 40 pieces of equipment in its roster, stored and exhibited at a number of locations in the Lower Mainland, and a supporting collection of smaller artifacts. It maintains a variety of activities and member services, including a highly successful series of rail excursions. The Association is a strong and well-established organization, with a broad base of membership and solid finances. The one component that it has lacked has been a permanent museum at which to exhibit and store its collection and from which to operate its activities.

After a long and careful search, the WCRA has secured a choice site for its museum: 12 acres (5 hectares) of land just north of Squamish, situated adjacent to the BC Rail yards and the Squamish River. It has also begun to acquire a collection of historic railway structures. The first and most important of these was the large PGE Car Shop, which was moved to the museum site from the nearby BC Rail Squamish Yards in 1992. At the time, it was the largest structure ever relocated in British Columbia.[1]

---

1 Text and images are excerpted from "Development Plan: West Coast Railway Museum" (1993), prepared by Commonwealth Historic Resource Management Limited in association with Lord Cultural Resources Planning & Management Inc. and The Iredale Partnership.

Excerpted from the "Development Plan: West Coast Railway Museum" (1993)

Mission Statement

The goal of the WCRA is to develop its museum into a lively attraction in keeping with its Mission Statement:

> The West Coast Railway Association, a registered non-profit society, collects, restores, preserves, operates and exhibits artifacts relating to the history of railways, particularly those of British Columbia.
>
> The role of the Association is of significance to the people of British Columbia and Canada in preserving a link to the past. It is important for all Canadians to understand the role of the railway in linking the country together and its impact on our general economic development.
>
> The West Coast Railway Museum develops entertaining and educational exhibits on the history of the railway that will appeal to the general public of all ages as well as the dedicated rail fan.
>
> The operation of the Museum will be of high professional standards attracting visitors to the Squamish / Howe Sound area, thereby having a positive economic value on the community and the province in general. Its programmes, operations, and exhibits will be seen both at the museum and by people in their own communities through the services of travelling displays and exhibitions of artifacts and rolling stock.
>
> The Association's tours program offers opportunities for the general public to travel on today's railways, generates revenues for the Association's projects, and supports the railway industry.
>
> Key strengths of the Association are a strong, committed membership, a broad base of financial support, and strong ties to the railway fraternity in Canada and the United States.

The Museum

The West Coast Railway Museum (WCRM) will present the public with an interesting, educational, and entertaining museum complex. It will combine the animation potential of open-air displays and activities with a variety of enclosed exhibits in a distinctive and high-quality museum building.

The visitor experience will begin in an attractive and distinctive visitor reception centre. An alluring multi-projector audio-visual display will orient people to the themes of the Museum, and amenities and sales outlets will serve people's needs and provide opportunities for revenues.

Visitors will then tour the museum building, where the most precious artifacts in the collection—from large locomotives, passenger cars, and freight equipment to uniforms, pocket watches, and documents—will be arranged in attractive and informative exhibits. Whether they are professional researchers or curious history-buffs, those who are interested may visit the library and archives.

Excerpted from the "Development Plan: West Coast Railway Museum" (1993)

People will then go outside and cross a watercourse on a railway bridge to arrive at the outdoor portion of the Museum. Here they will have the opportunity to explore a number of discrete zones, all integrated by a network of railway tracks on which equipment is displayed and operated. A crossing tower at the entry symbolizes the choices and offers a bird's-eye view of the entire complex. Old and new structures alike will give the flavour of both the community and working areas of a traditional railway community.

While some visitors may feel transported in time to an earlier era, they are touring a new Museum, not a historic site. The many exhibits and activities will be animated and fun, all framed by the spectacular backdrop of the snow-capped Coast Mountains and the Garibaldi Highlands, a setting of extreme natural beauty.

In the passenger and community zones, the themes will address the impact of railways on the society and economy of British Columbia. A reconstructed Pacific Great Eastern Railway station will offer interactive interpretive exhibits, a freight shed will feature an operating model railway display, restored passenger cars can be toured, and an excursion train will depart regularly on a scenic eight-mile excursion along the dyke adjacent to the Squamish River, to the head of Howe Sound. Food services will be available, from an elegant meal in a restored dining car to a quick take-out snack.

In the nearby yard zone, the emphasis will be on the history and technology of railway equipment. Locomotives and other equipment from the Museum's fine collection, representing a full range of types and ages of motive power and rolling stock used in British Columbia, will be presented for view—some of them in a stunning roundhouse, contemporary in design but clearly evocative of that traditional building type; some will be in the large and historic car shop that was built for the PGE in 1914; others will be displayed outdoors on the tracks.

Much equipment will have been fully restored. Children and adults can climb into the cab of a locomotive or take part in hand-car races. Those visitors who have purchased a premium 'Yardmaster' ticket can also have a tour behind the scenes, where they will see Museum staff and volunteers in the process of restoring other pieces of equipment. There will be some movements along the tracks, including steam locomotives taking on water, sand, and coal. Hungry visitors can partake of a 'Beanery Lunch' in one of the work cars.

Closer to the dyke and the river, the park zone offers recreational activities. Visitors can ride on a live-steam miniature railway, enjoy a picnic, take their children to a playground, or walk up a hill to the dyke to see the Squamish River and its bald eagles and other wildlife. A portion of the site will be devoted to railway logging activities, as they relate to Squamish history. Demonstrations will occur on a regular basis, and this area will be a centre of activity during the Squamish Days Logging Festival and other special events.

Excerpted from the "Development Plan: West Coast Railway Museum" (1993)

People will have learned about the Museum in a number of ways.

Some will have seen promotional brochures distributed by tour operators and other visitor attractions; others from hearsay. Many will have seen the displays in the Pacific Central Station in Vancouver, that city's rail and bus terminal. And a good number will be attracted by the catchy sign on Highway 99, as they drive from Vancouver to Whistler.

Some visitors will spend a day at the Museum, while others will have less time and save some of the activities for a second and third trip.

Noon hours during the summer will be particularly crowded with hurried visitors who have come to Squamish on the Royal Hudson and have only an hour before returning to Vancouver on the M.V. Britannia. They may only have time to visit the museum building and to take in the outdoor exhibits from the top of the crossing tower, but many will be back.

The Objectives

In the Fall of 1991, the WCRA commissioned a Development Plan for the West Coast Railway Museum (WCRM).

Funding assistance for the plan was provided by the Department of Communications, through its Museums Assistance Programme.

The Terms of Reference described the following objectives:

> The objective of the Development Plan Study is to examine in detail the physical, organizational, and financial requirements for the West Coast Railway Museum. This document will provide the framework within which the museum will be developed, operated, and funded. This document will serve as a Master Plan which will:
>
> - guide the long term planning process for the museum by elaborating on the Mission Statement and the aims and goals of the WCRA.
>
> - provide recommendations on the size of the museum and the phasing of development in relation to financial resources, population, community support, and other related factors.
>
> - provide a functional program for the museum which will become part of a design brief document to be presented to architects and engineering consultants.
>
> - provide a conceptual plan of the site showing phases of development and related cost estimates.
>
> - assist with and become part of a fundraising program targeting government, community, industry, general public, and railway enthusiast contributors. ∎

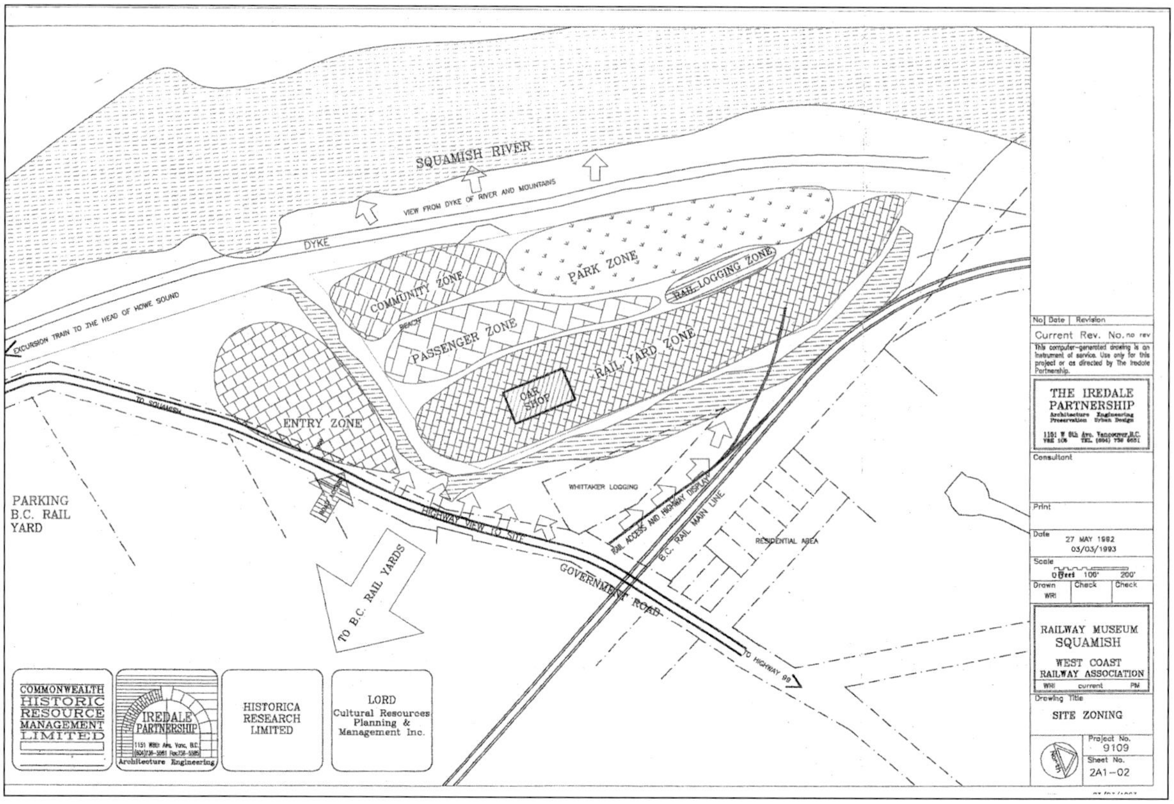

Excerpted from the "Development Plan: West Coast Railway Museum" (1993)

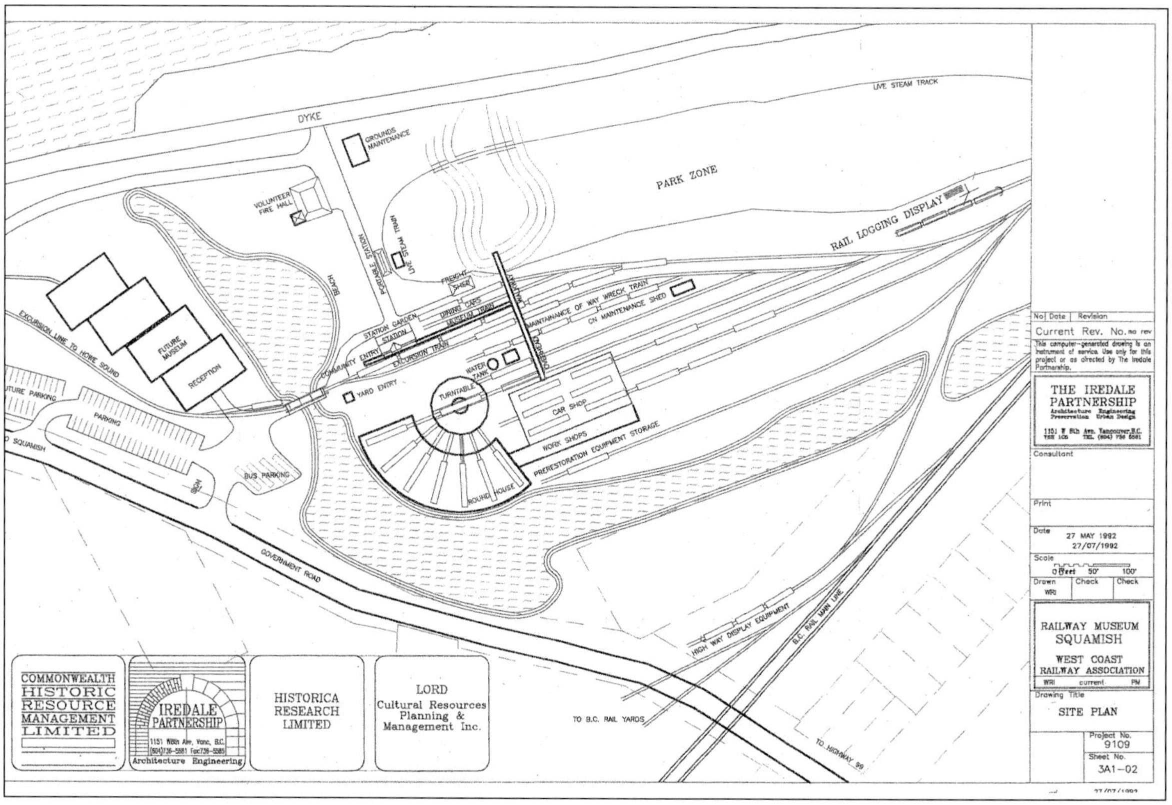

Excerpted from the "Development Plan: West Coast Railway Museum" (1993)

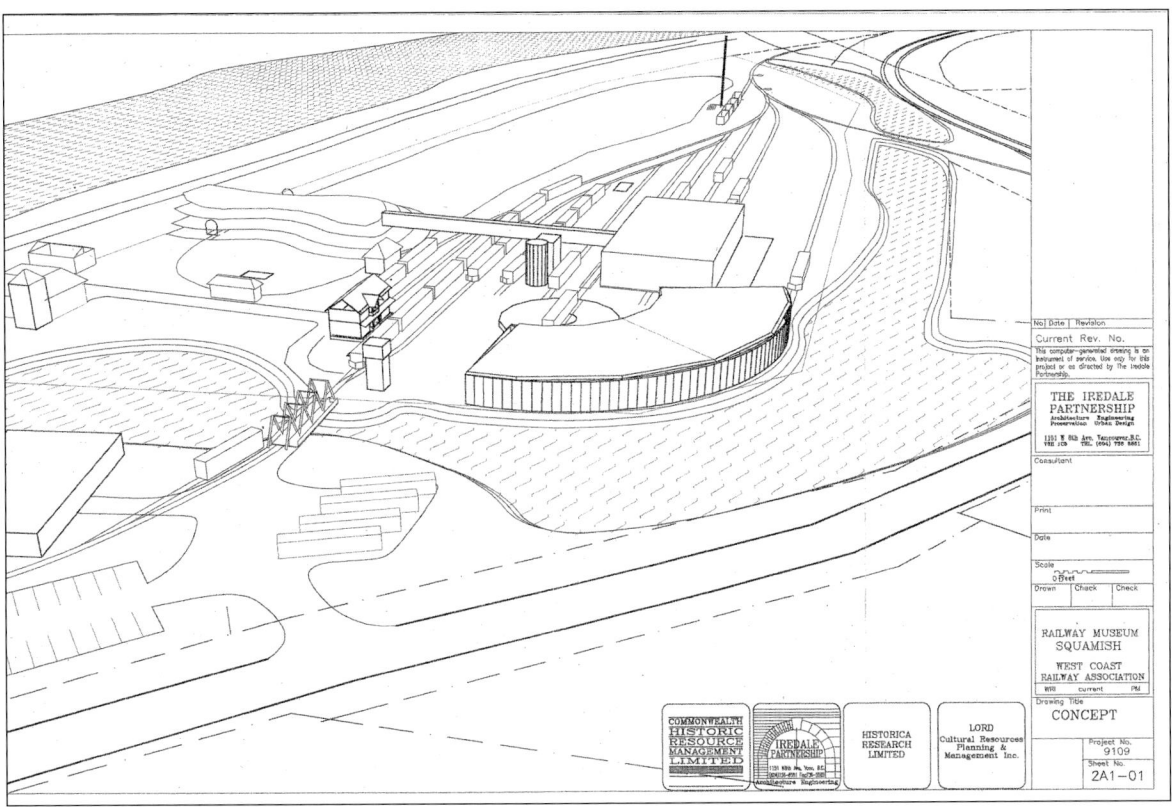

We Build a Shared Vision | 327

Excerpted from "Minnekhada Farm: Preliminary Feasibility Study" (1994)

Project: Minnekhada Heritage Park

Project Team

Randle Iredale
Partner in Charge

Richard Iredale
Project Architect

The Province of British Columbia purchased Minnekhada Farm [in Coquitlam] in 1975 to provide recreation opportunities for a planned community at the base of Burke Mountain. The non-agricultural portion—Minnekhada Lodge, the knolls and marsh adjacent to it—was dedicated as a GVRD Regional Park in 1983.

Obtaining Minnekhada Farm fits with every aspect of the GVRD Park's mandate, which includes "securing and caring for a legacy of diverse landscapes and natural and cultural features [that] express the character of the region."

Heritage Value

The property is adjacent to Minnekhada Regional Park and contains architecturally interesting barns, stables, outbuildings, and a farm house that date from the mid-1930s. The Minnekhada Farm and Minnekhada Regional Park were both originally part of the estates of Eric W. Hamber and Col. Clarence Wallace, former Lieutenant-Governors of BC.

The entire Minnekhada Farm was originally 416 hectares consisting of rocky knolls, forests, marshes, and farmland, and contained a historic lodge and numerous farm buildings. Minnekhada Farm is impressive because of both the number and character of the farm buildings. This cluster of historic farm buildings still exhibit style and grandeur. Minnekhada Farm is part of the region's heritage and provides valuable insight into a bygone era. The site has significant heritage value worth preserving.

Many of the buildings are structurally sound and have restoration potential. The stables and the main house are critical to the character, atmosphere, and visual aesthetic qualities of the site. They require immediate attention

Main Farm House

"This three-storey building has a gambrel roof that matches the stable barn, the milking barn, and the milk shed. Though the building has been extensively modified to accommodate tenants on each storey, it still contains considerable original material and is restorable."

328 | We Build a Shared Vision

Excerpted from "Minnekhada Farm: Preliminary Feasibility Study" (1994)

Photos & Sidebars

Opposite, adjacent, & overleaf:
Originally from Greater Vancouver Regional District Parks Department Draft Report, "Minnekhada Farm: An Assessment for Addition to Minnekhada Regional Park" (November 1993), and reproduced in referenced feasibility study (see footnote).

Smoke House

"This small, narrow building is 5' x 5' x 15' with a single-ridged shake roof and unpainted wall boards.

"The area for hanging the meat is separated by slats from the area where the smoke enters the building; there is a small back door for each area. There is a concrete containment area for the fire that is covered by corrugated tin."

Ice House

"The features of this small, square building suggest that it was constructed or modified in the 1950s. The thick, insulated walls are stainless steel on the lower portion and arborite on the upper portion.

"The building may have been machine-cooled and used for butchering and storing meat."

We Build a Shared Vision | 329

Excerpted from "Minnekhada Farm: Preliminary Feasibility Study" (1994)

to prevent further deterioration and are a high priority for restoration. Because of their historical significance, character, and current condition, the buildings should be stablilized, if not restored totally. ...

Heritage Attraction

Minnekhada Farm would be a regional attraction within one-half hour driving time from most municipalities in the Lower Mainland. It is a unique farm estate that combines recreational use with casual farming and reflects the stature and wealth of the previous owners. The BC Heritage Conservation Branch has examined Minnekhada Farm and confirmed the buildings and structures have heritage value. There are no other farm estates of this character in the Fraser Valley region and this contributes to its value as a heritage site.

None of the major heritage attractions are directly comparable to Minnekhada Farm, due to its unusual combination of farming and estate uses. There are no major heritage attractions in the north-east sector of the Lower Mainland. Minnekhada Farm would be a valuable addition to this region.

The vision for Minnekhada Farm restores the historic concept of a working farm estate. Minnekhada Farm would offer a broad range of uses, with four major themes: education, recreation, heritage value, and equestrian recreation.

Concept Plan

The concept plan developed provides a wide variety of uses and integrates the farm, the park, and the lodge. The single entrance into the park initially flows into the picnic area and provides significant parking with room for expansion. A short trail between the picnic area and the marsh effectively ties the marsh hiking trails with the farm. The short trail to the marsh also provides easy access up to Minnekhada Lodge from the picnic area.

A short pedestrian walk from the picnic area brings visitors down into the demonstration farm area and the central courtyard leading on to the entrance of the bed and breakfast and to the stables. The central garden courtyard provides a control point for the flow of visitors, with the ice house providing an overall park administration office.

The equestrian operation would include the stable areas, stable barn, and all fields on the eastern portion of the site. The allocation of the equestrian facilities to the lower eastern portion of the site effectively separates the equestrian activities from the public areas to the west. Public access would not be allowed into the equestrian area unless escorted by a tour guide.[1] ∎

---

1   Text, images, and sidebars excerpted from "Minnekhada Farm: Preliminary Feasibility Study for Consideration by GVRD Regional Parks" (1994), prepared for the Greater Vancouver Regional District Parks Department by West Bay Consultants Ltd. and The Iredale Partnership Architects / Engineers.

Excerpted from "Minnekhada Farm: Preliminary Feasibility Study" (1994)

Loafing Barn & Silo

"The primary purpose of the loafing barn was to provide animals with a refuge from the weather where they could feed, rest, and 'loaf.'"

"The second storey was used for hay storage and its large open space and wooden structure were impressive. The Silo is concrete, about 40' high, and 15' around."

Horse Track Garage & Mash Cooker

"The smaller, one-room building contains a cooker with a cover that can be raised and lowered over a cast iron cauldron. It was probably used to prepare mash for the horses."

"The cooker was located away from the stables and hay storage areas to avoid disturbing the horses."

Slaughter House

"This tall, narrow building has a single-ridged, shake roof and board and batten cladding. The main part of the building features a ceiling pulley system for hoisting animals."

"An extension on the back side contains a chimney and this portion of the building may have been used as a boiler room."

Excerpted from "Minnekhada Farm: Preliminary Feasibility Study" (1994)

Aerial View & Site Map

"Aerial view and map show the restored farm buildings of the historic Minnekhada Farm, incorporated as a demonstration farm into Minnekhada Regional Park.

"New parking, access roads, and visitor facilities would provide a welcoming entry to the park and connect the farm to the wildlife preserve beyond."

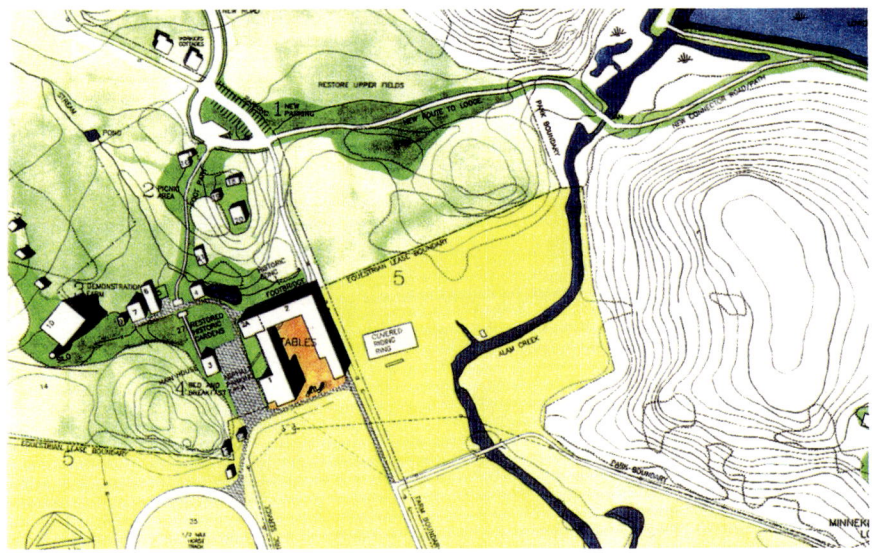

Images created by Rand Iredale and coloured by Richard Iredale

We presented these big boards to the Regional District Board ... at Minnekhada. I remember that as being a lot of fun. And I remember Dad looking very happy!

He was a Magician with a Spreadsheet

From an interview with Richard Iredale.

Minnekhada was an important project. It was a big planning exercise where we had to add 30 hectares to an existing Regional District Park of about 80 to 90 hectares. It involved working out all of the washrooms and parking and trails, and working out how people would visit the site and what they would see.

We had to look at why they would come to Minnekhada and where the revenue opportunities were. There were probably 15 small heritage buildings, and Dad went through it all in a day or so and worked out the cost to renovate all of these buildings. He was a magician with a spreadsheet.

We were involved in restoring these buildings over the last 10 years and a lot of Dad's numbers turned out to be quite accurate. He was numbers-oriented, among other things, and very good with estimating and planning and anticipating.

I remember Dad wearing his best suit and presenting his plan. He had an aerial photograph that he gleefully developed from a survey. Remember, it was the 1990s, when computers were just developing and half of the time stuff didn't work. But sometimes it did work, and when Dad could put this survey into 3D AutoCAD and actually rotate it and see the mountain have three-dimensional form, he was really excited.

So we had all of these 3-D boxes to represent the heritage farm buildings, and I got my water colours out and water-coloured them up, and we presented these big boards to the Regional District Board at their lodge at Minnekhada. I remember that as being a lot of fun. And I remember Dad looking very happy! ∎

There were probably 15 small heritage buildings, and Dad ... worked out the cost to renovate all of these buildings. He was a magician with a spreadsheet.

SHARED VALUES

Our Mission Statement is based on shared values and commitments to provide:

- professional services to create buildings and environments that fit our clients needs by designing structures that have the commodity, firmness, and delight that Vitruvius defined as architecture; and by managing the design to fit the highest aspirations of our clients and users within the realities of site, budget, and regulations;

- the highest standards of professional competence through integrity in all of our dealings, the use of common methodology to assure consistent quality of service, knowledge of the best technology available—from computers to building science—and peer review by design panel; and

- each member of the firm with a satisfying career in their chosen field through profit-sharing, continuing education, broadening experience, and recognition of the contribution of each member of the design team.

Rand Iredale, Project Manager's Manual (1997)

Marcus Vitruvius Pollio was a Roman writer, architect and engineer, active in the 1st century BC. Little is known about his life. He was the author of *De architectura*, known today as *The Ten Books of Architecture*, a treatise written in Latin and Greek on architecture, dedicated to the Emperor Augustus. It is the only surviving major book on architecture from classical antiquity.

Vitruvius is most famous for asserting in his book *De architectura* that a structure must exhibit the three qualities of *firmitas, utilitas, venustas*—that is, it must be strong or durable, useful, and beautiful. According to Vitruvius, architecture is an imitation of nature. As birds and bees built their nests, so humans constructed housing from natural materials. When perfecting this art of building, they invented the architectural orders: Doric, Ionic, and Corinthian.

Vitruvius is sometimes loosely referred to as the first architect, but it is more accurate to describe him as the first Roman architect to have written on his field. He was less an original thinker or creative intellect than a codifier of existing architectural practice. It should also be noted that Vitruvius had a much wider scope than modern architects. Roman architects practiced a wide variety of disciplines; in modern terms, they could be described as being engineers, architects, landscape architects, artists, and craftsmen combined.[1] ∎

---

1 Source: http://en.wikipedia.org/wiki/Vitruvius (2006).

A SHARED VISION

The firm considers design to be a joint search, by the client and the project team, for a fit of form to need. Design is an integral part of all work in an architectural office. For this reason, design is not assigned as a project task in the Iredale office. Whether a relationship diagram, the massing of a building, or an appropriate handrail is being designed, each must contribute to the building concept being developed. For this approach, we need more than coordination between members of the project team—*we need a shared vision.*

The procedures that have evolved over the years in the Iredale practice make this shared vision possible. By carefully developing the Program, which spells out the needs and aspirations to be fulfilled by the project, and the Site Analysis, which sets out the physical, legal, and budget constraints the design must fit, we build a shared vision of what is required, thereby making possible creative input from all members of the design team, including the consultants and the owner.

Rand Iredale, Project Manager's Manual (1997)

> By carefully developing the program and the site analysis, we build a shared vision of what is required, thereby making possible creative input from all members of the design team.

12 Place of Song and Dance

༃ One of Rand's last projects in the 1990s, and certainly one of the most challenging, was the five-year development of Maillardville Heritage Square in the City of Coquitlam. Rand was the Planning Partner, Charlotte Murray was the Heritage Partner, and Richard Iredale was the Structural Engineer. The project involved master planning and heritage restoration, as well as designing and expanding the existing Place des Arts to create a vibrant new arts and culture activity centre. Completing the project involved considerable civic controversy, as well as both conflict and collaboration among client and consultant team members. During this busy period in the practice Rand and I also did some travelling, as we slowly began to prepare for our retirement.

Travelling Together

One wonderful trip that Rand and I took together was to Hong Kong. It was a BCAA tour, and we went with my sister and brother-in-law, Daphne and Bill. Rand liked to explore on his own; he didn't much like tours, and he had been to Hong Kong previously. But we didn't know the language there, so I prevailed and we took the tour. The four of us flew to Hong Kong and had a wonderful time. Then we flew from Hong Kong to Bangkok and got caught in a terrible rainstorm. But it was a fascinating place, and we took a lot of little side trips.

We also went to Singapore, where one of Rand's clients was very hospitable. We were picked up in their big Mercedes and taken all around the city and then to their club. We had a great time with them. Singapore is an interesting place, a city-state that has a very good transportation system, as it costs a fortune to drive a car downtown. And then we took a trip up the Malaysian Peninsula, in a little van that carried eight people. We ended up in the beautiful Cameron Highlands, which was really good fun.

There was also a wonderful trip to Europe. We put 1,200 miles on our rental car travelling all over England. Rand had a lot of relatives! That trip was combined with a tour. We flew to the south of France and did some

travelling with Daph and Bill. We rented a boat to travel the lovely Canal du Midi in the south of France. The long canal boats don't go very fast because you have to go up a lot of locks; we meandered from near Avignon to Carcassonne. On one trip to Europe we visited Bogue Babicki and his wife, Marie, at their vineyard in Provence. Rand and Bogue had a great time preparing grapes for the crusher.

Keeping Up with Family

During these years our children were getting married, having children, and travelling, too. Rand and I were kept busy on Mayne Island—planning weddings and enjoying our new grandchildren—and, whenever our children travelled, we usually travelled, too, visiting them wherever they went.

Our son Richard was the first to wed. He and Lael were married in 1983 on Mayne Island. We spent the summer organizing the wedding and planning a sit-down meal for 150 people in the field. We had to build the tables and chairs! Lael's father came over from the Mainland to help. We had to run power down to the field from the Gingerbread House. And Lael's mother and I prepared a lot of salmon ahead of time and froze it so that we could feed everybody.

Richard and Tab were both working for Bogue at that time. That's when Richard did the computer drawings for the Science Centre in Vancouver. Eventually he and Lael wanted to travel and so they saved their pennies and then spent nine months seeing the world. Rand and I joined Richard and Lael in Europe for a while. Then when Tab and his wife, Paddy, decided they'd go off to Europe, we joined them, too. And we visited Jennifer when she was working up north and living in Wells BC.

Life did not slow down one bit! We started hiking and camping with our grandkids as they grew up, and Rand began his 'Camp School' on Mayne Island to teach them about the Great Outdoors.

Taking Our Last Trip

Rand and I also went to Cuba, just the two of us, in 2000. It was our last vacation together, the Spring before he died. It was another great trip. Again, I wanted to take a tour because of the lack of language—and also because when you arrive somewhere the place is open! But Rand liked to explore independently, so we compromised. I said, "Well, let's take a week with a tour and then we'll rent a car and we'll explore it on our own for a week."

We stayed in Old Havana and Rand used his camcorder to make a movie of the heritage buildings. We walked a lot and we had an excellent tour guide, Jorge, who spoke beautiful English. Jorge took a group of eight of us around the countryside in a small van. We visited a cave, a farm, a school; he really showed us life in Cuba.

Opposite:
Rand and Kathryn at the Mayne Island Fireman's Ball (June 1999)

When it came time to rent a car, Jorge helped us out. Cars are hard to rent in Cuba, and he told us how to get one. And he gave us some guidelines for travelling on our own. There's a lot of hitchhiking in Cuba. If you have a car you have to pick people up, because they don't have cars. That was fun.

We'd pick up hitchhikers and they would help us along the way, because none of the towns had any names on them, and the maps were hopeless! The towns were quite large, and you would arrive in a town and not even know where you were. Also, the hitchhikers wanted to learn English and we were trying to learn a little Spanish, though with not much luck!

Retiring Together

When Rand and I retired we just gradually withdrew from the practice and set up our offices at home. While I continued to run Kara Resources out of Tab's old bedroom, Rand and Richard set up an office in the basement of the Steamboat House and started a construction-online business.

Rand was a man of many talents. He loved camcording and programming, and he needed a place to work at home so that he could organize all of his films and files. He turned the stair landing into his office, and it's still there; I haven't changed it. That was his place to work, and our two computers were networked together. ■

Opposite:
Rand visited his old friend and colleague, Bogue Babicki, at Bogue's vineyard in Provence. Here they are preparing grapes for the crusher and adding wild asparagus to filter the wine.

Below:
Rand, 63, parachute-sailing from the beach in Puerto Vallarta, Mexico (1992).

Creating a Cohesive Design

From an essay written by Charlotte Murray.

In 1990 I received a phone call from a fellow I had met at a workshop on heritage park development that I had been invited to convene the year before in Mission. He was the City Clerk in Coquitlam, and he asked if we would be interested in submitting a proposal for the design of a heritage park in Maillardville. Of course this project was just perfect for us! Being a planning project, it was agreed that Rand would be in charge.

We all got busy assembling a hotshot proposal that included an eight-foot-long chart showing the work to be completed and the line of decision-making to be followed. Creating this chart was just Rand's cup of tea. We had a few practice runs so that each of us—Rand, Richard, and I—would have our part down pat before presenting our proposed approach to City Council. We must have wowed them, because soon after we had the job.

Focusing on the Big Picture

The site for the park had a long street frontage with a relatively short depth. The site was originally part of a lumber milling settlement, and most of the workers had come from Quebec. The only two houses left were the homes of the Manager and the Accountant for the mill and, as such, were high-class in their time. The Manager's house (Ryan House) was overcrowded by the then Arts Centre, and the Accountant's house (Mackin House) was being used for municipal offices.

The plan was to accommodate all of the present facility requirements—such as arts, music, and dance—by extending Ryan House and including a local museum in Mackin House. The heritage park as a whole was intended to celebrate the history of Maillardville and the lumber mill that had prompted its development.

When it came to planning, Rand was a visionary who focused on the big picture. His ideas were grand, and usually great, too! He was a firm believer in starting with an overall concept and keeping it open until all of the parts were identified and could come together as a whole. To start with a pretty picture was meaningless for him.

Rand believed that a valid concept generated a good design because all the parts came together logically to fit the concept and create a cohesive design. This approach is precisely how the Maillardville Heritage Square plan evolved.

Continued

Charlotte Murray

Three-Dimensional Reality

The client was really happy with the results of this commission, happy enough to give The Iredale Partnership the job of turning Mackin House into a museum and meeting place. As the Heritage Partner, I was to be the Partner in Charge and Richard would be the Structural Engineer. It was a nice little job and it went quite smoothly.

Following shortly after the heritage restoration and adaptive reuse of Mackin House was the job of extending the Arts Centre in Ryan House. Rand took on that project, even though it was a heritage house, because he had developed a rather great concept for extruding the addition out of the back of the house. As he explained, it was just like stretching the house in a long, narrow line until there was enough space to accommodate all activities of the Arts Centre. It was a great concept that fit the site and the client needs and that would look completely in proportion along the street.

The Director of the Arts Centre liked the idea and Rand went to work. The activities to be included in the extended centre grew considerably, however, as did the space needed and the budget required. The City Project Manager was not so happy—in fact, not happy at all—especially as Rand became increasingly frustrated by the City's interference with the design! It took a while but, finally, Rand was fired. It was a heavy blow. Richard, who had done the engineering, felt that we should have a meeting with the City Manager and the Chief Building Inspector to see if we could pick up the pieces.

The meeting was duly held between the three of us—Rand, Richard, and me—and three people from Coquitlam, including the Project Manager and the Arts Director. During the meeting Rand said very little; in fact, he seemed most contrite—a new side of Rand. Richard spoke eloquently about how he could complete the job to the client's satisfaction. In turn, the Arts Director was articulate about her need for the expanded facility and how the growing programs would provide increasing revenue to help cover the expanding costs. So it was that Richard took over the project and Rand worked quietly on the sidelines.

When the project was finished and all of the wonderful new space was filled with activities and displays—and after the grounds had been cleared for the grand new arena and the grass had grown back—the City, the Museum, and the Arts Director hosted a great opening event for Maillardville Heritage Square. The visitors were really impressed with all there was to see, the speeches were highly complimentary, and Rand was totally pleased to see and experience the three-dimensional reality of his concept. ∎

Excerpted from City of Coquitlam Brochure (circa 1990s)

History in the Making / Bâtir un passé

Maillardville Heritage Square is a celebration of 'community,' a tribute to Coquitlam's milltown past and a legacy to Coquitlam's evolving future. It is designed to preserve the city's heritage and enhance the region's arts services and programs in a time of accelerated change. Maillardville Heritage Square will provide the community with invaluable artistic and heritage educational opportunities.

Making History & Art More Accessible to More People
Rendre le passé et l'art plus accessibles à une plus grande population

Growth, change, urban development ... Today the boundaries of Coquitlam extend well beyond Maillardville, the turn-of-the-century Francophone community from which the city originated. Artistic and historical facilities are essential components of vibrant and dynamic communities. In a period of economic and demographic transition, it is necessary to ensure the concurrent development of such facilities with that of the community.

Reconciling a community's past with its future requires visionary thinking, leadership, and the efforts of individuals imbued with a strong sense of partnership. Such was the thinking of members of the Coquitlam community, the Coquitlam Maillardville Heritage Trust, and the City of Coquitlam when they initiated the innovative heritage preservation and arts centre expansion project: Maillardville Heritage Square.

The Harmony is Building

Two remaining landmarks of the mill's townsite, Mackin House and Place des Arts, will be renovated and restored through this project. Mackin House will be converted into a period house museum; Place des Arts will continue to function as the community's premiere arts teaching centre in an expanded facility designed to serve the artistic needs of Coquitlam's burgeoning population. The Maillardville CP Railroad Station will be relocated to the Square and remain the home of the Canadian Railroad Historical Association. A replica of the Fraser Mills Arch will be erected at the south end of the plaza that connects Mackin House and Place des Arts.

The Concept

A square or plaza is an architecturally defined space often indigenous to the origins of a community. A meeting place for citizens and visitors alike, it promotes the spirit of community. Maillardville Heritage Square will become that meeting place in Coquitlam for young and old, student and teacher, artist and artisan, visitor and resident. Conceptually unique, the Square not only links heritage and the arts structurally, it connects them dynamically in an evocative heritage ambiance that nurtures creative expression.

Excerpted from City of Coquitlam Brochure (circa 1990s)

"Place des Arts (Ryan House) and Mackin House are the two historic landmarks that remain of Maillardville's architectural heritage.

"The houses continue to serve as functional definitions of the community's forest industry origins and the pioneering spirit of the era—a spirit reflected in an industry that not only defined the course of the region's early history, but left an indelible imprint on the community's future development.

"The architecturally designed space will connect the heritage structures on site and reinforce the concept of community inherent in this project. Maillardville Heritage Square will provide a venue for community events, performances, and exhibits."[1]

---

1 The text on these two pages was excerpted from a brochure produced by the City of Coquitlam on behalf of the "Heritage Square Capital Campaign" (date unknown, circa 1990s).

It serves to illustrate the elaborate collaboration required between client, architect, and community to find the 'good fit' that Rand so ardently sought (and fought for) among need and aspiration, site and environment, cost and constraint.

It also illustrates, with foresight and hindsight, the great skill and success of Rand's Master Plan.

Phase 1: Mackin House / Project History

Restored under Phase 1 of Maillardville Heritage Square, Mackin House will be retrofit as a period house museum. It will serve as a centre for the documentation and interpretation of Coquitlam's regional history, a home for the Coquitlam Heritage Society and a public space for the exhibition of community artifacts and memorabilia. One of two main heritage structures anchoring the site, it figures significantly in the community's plans for the preservation of its heritage—a plan developed by the architectural group, The Iredale Partnership, after extensive consultation with numerous community groups.

Collaboration on the attainment of this objective resulted in the common vision of a heritage square that would preserve the cultural heritage of Maillardville and create a community landmark, anchored by an expanded arts centre, Place des Arts, and a period house museum, Mackin House. With the restoration of Mackin House in 1993, Phase 1 of the Master Plan was completed. Plans for the restoration and expansion of Place des Arts was initiated by the Place des Arts Board after recognition that the centre had reached its limit in growth. Phase 2 of the Architect's Master Plan is designed to accommodate the community's need for an expanded arts facility.

Phase 2: Heritage Square / Conversion of Concept to Reality

Education Annex

The expansion of Place des Arts will create state-of-the-art facilities, enhancing the programs and services presently being offered. With greatly improved programming and exhibition space, the arts centre can venture into new directions, reach new audiences, and serve a greater segment of the community.

Outdoor Theatre

An Outdoor Theatre will be constructed south of the Annex and Place des Arts. The site will be visually united through landscaping and site work. An extension of Place des Arts, the Theatre will offer additional space for outdoor performances and community events in a rich heritage environment.

Outdoor Museum

An Outdoor Museum will comprise the south boundary of the site. A sculptural wall with water cascading over it will reinforce the theme of the community's timber industry origins, as will exhibits of mill artifacts and timber displays on the site.

CP Railroad Station

The Station will celebrate the arrival of the town's settlers and reiterate the historical connection between the railroad and the mill. It will be relocated from Blue Mountain Park and strategically placed to anchor the east end of the Outdoor Museum.[1] ■

Excerpted and adapted from "An Urban Design" (Iredale, 1996)

Project: Maillardville Heritage Square

Project Team

Randle Iredale
Planning Partner in Charge
Site & Concept Plan
(Ryan House / Place des Arts)

Charlotte Murray
Heritage Partner in Charge
(Mackin House Restoration
& Adaptive Reuse)

Design Team
Randle Iredale
Richard Iredale
Warwick Ashley
Elizabeth Scremin
Hugh Bitz

Richard Iredale
Structural Engineer

Award
Urban Design Institute
Award for Community
Facilities (1999)

Maillardville Heritage Square is designed to be the eastern anchor of redevelopment of Coquitlam's Main Street. The community was founded at the turn of the century by French-Canadian mill workers who emigrated from Quebec in response to inducements of free transportation and housing to work at the Fraser River Mill. The theme of the Main Street redevelopment is based on this French-Canadian heritage.

Our scheme builds on this history of Coquitlam by adapting two heritage houses for cultural uses and by developing the 1.5-acre site to house museum, gallery, craft, and performance spaces as a focal point for community use.

Phase 1: Mackin House Heritage Museum

Mackin House was constructed in 1909 for Henry J. Mackin, General Sales Manager of Fraser Mills. The house was restored to its original state in 1994 by the City of Coquitlam and the Coquitlam Maillardville Heritage Trust. It previously provided office space for civic employees as well as exhibit and artifact storage for the Coquitlam Heritage Society.

Mackin House

Phase 2: Place des Arts

The multidisciplinary Place des Arts is 'the artistic heartbeat of Coquitlam': a learning centre, an art gallery, and a teaching facility; an arts and cultural centre and a meeting place for diverse community members and groups. A new 20,000 square foot building was designed to incorporate historic Ryan House, which was built in 1908 and, since 1972, has been the home of Place des Arts. The Great Hall provides a major art gallery venue as well as an open gathering space for members of the community. ∎

Excerpted and adapted from "An Urban Design" (Iredale, 1996)

An Urban Design / Heritage Preservation Submission

This urban planning design is based on a participatory planning process that responds to community needs, public support, and historical context. It also responds to such geophysical realities as noise, views, and slopes. The plan adapts the historic site and buildings to current needs and integrates community organizations, such as the *Société Maillardville-Uni*, which is an umbrella organization for some 20 local French-speaking organizations.[1]

Context

Village of Maillardville

The City of Coquitlam Planning Department's planning concept for this area proposes that Brunette Avenue from the intersection of Lougheed Highway to the City Hall be redeveloped as the "Main Street" of Maillardville. Design guidelines call for a "French-Canadian Character Area" based on its history as a French-Canadian mill town settlement.

This scheme picks up the planning theme to create an eastern terminus of this "Maillardville Main Street."

History

The site contains two of the few remaining heritage structures in the City of Coquitlam: Mackin House, built circa 1909, and Ryan House, built circa 1908, for managers of the mill.

Due to increased traffic, King Edward Avenue was rerouted in the 1960s to align with Marmont, leaving the road allowance that is now part of this site. As the original alignment of King Edward was the major access to the old mill, the axis is important and the historic buildings continue to face toward this area (which is no longer a street).

Geophysical

The site slopes south toward the Fraser River, providing views toward the river and sunny southern slopes for outdoor uses. The underlying soils are stable till affording good bearing. Brunette Avenue on the north boundary and the rerouted King Edward Avenue to the west are major traffic handlers creating a noise, pollution, and safety hazard. Neighbouring townhouses to the south of the site require a substantial buffer between the residential and public uses.

---

1   The text on this page and overleaf was excerpted and adapted from "An Urban Design / Heritage Preservation Submission" (1996), Rand Iredale's Planning Study for Maillardville Heritage Square in the City of Coquitlam. The above context categories were accompanied in the submission by a Site Analysis Plan.

Excerpted and adapted from "An Urban Design" (Iredale, 1996)

Planning Elements

Mackin House

This heritage building, the original Mill Manager's Home, was adapted to use as municipal offices with a longer-term plan to adapt to the Maillardville Museum. The building was restored as the first phase of this urban design project in 1994. The major adaptation required was to raise the building some four feet to restore its relation to the street level, which had been raised to accommodate the realignment of King Edward avenue for higher traffic.

Mackin House

Ryan House

Ryan House served as RCMP headquarters from the early 1950s until it was adapted in the 1980s to house Place des Arts. The homey character of the historic building was considered to be a major factor in the success of this community facility by the users. With completion of the Place des Arts expansion, this historic building is freed for restoration as part of the expanded facility.

Ryan House

Place des Arts Expansion

The second phase of this urban design project required expansion of four times the area of Ryan House while respecting the importance of the original building. The scale of the original house is maintained by breaking the addition into smaller-scale elements connected to a two-storey atrium. The atrium cuts into the historic building at the mid-bay of its tripartite form, providing an opportunity to deconstruct the historic structure and exposing and celebrating the original framing, as well as making clear that the new structure is generated by the original house.

Place des Arts Expansion

Amphitheatre

Expanding out from the Place des Arts entrance lobby, the amphitheatre provides outdoor performance space as well as a place for the public to gather and socialize in conjunction with other areas of the park.

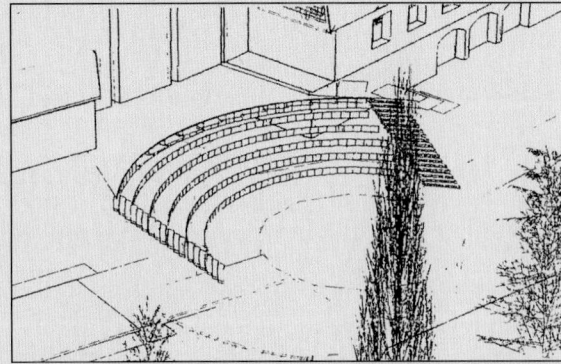

Amphitheatre

Excerpted and adapted from "An Urban Design" (Iredale, 1996)

Heritage Square

Computer massing view to south of Heritage Square

Computer massing model from King Edward

Computer massing model from eastern end

Heritage Square

The square at Maillardville Heritage Square is to be used for dances and other traditional street-related events in Maillardville such as *Le Gui Gnole* (caroling) and *Cabanea a Sucre*. It recreates a traditional street on the historic alignment of King Edward Avenue, the original main road to the mill, and restores the traditional siting required by the two historic houses.

The traditional view to the south is evoked by the reconstruction of the mill gate of 1905, beyond which is the residential buffer wall symbolizing the old mill and the Fraser River, part of the Forestry Museum.

The grade of the street is raised to align with the raised grade of Brunette Avenue and to create the 'trench' for the Forestry Museum and symbolic Fraser River.

Outdoor Forestry Museum

The Outdoor Forestry Museum commemorates the role of the forest industry and the mill in the life of Maillardville. This element is supported by the forest industry through contributions of money and historic equipment. It will be used for orientation and teaching about the role and importance of the forest industry in the community.

The museum buffers the residential neighbours from the public square with a sculptural wall covered with planting on the residential side and forming the backdrop theme on the forestry museum side.

This museum wall recalls the form of a traditional mill in a two dimensional wood form and symbolizes the Fraser River, as it flows from Boston Bar to the Maillardville Mill, with a concrete wall fountain flowing from the eastern viewpoint to the symbolic mill.[1] ∎

---

1   *Ibid.*, "An Urban Design / Heritage Preservation Submission."

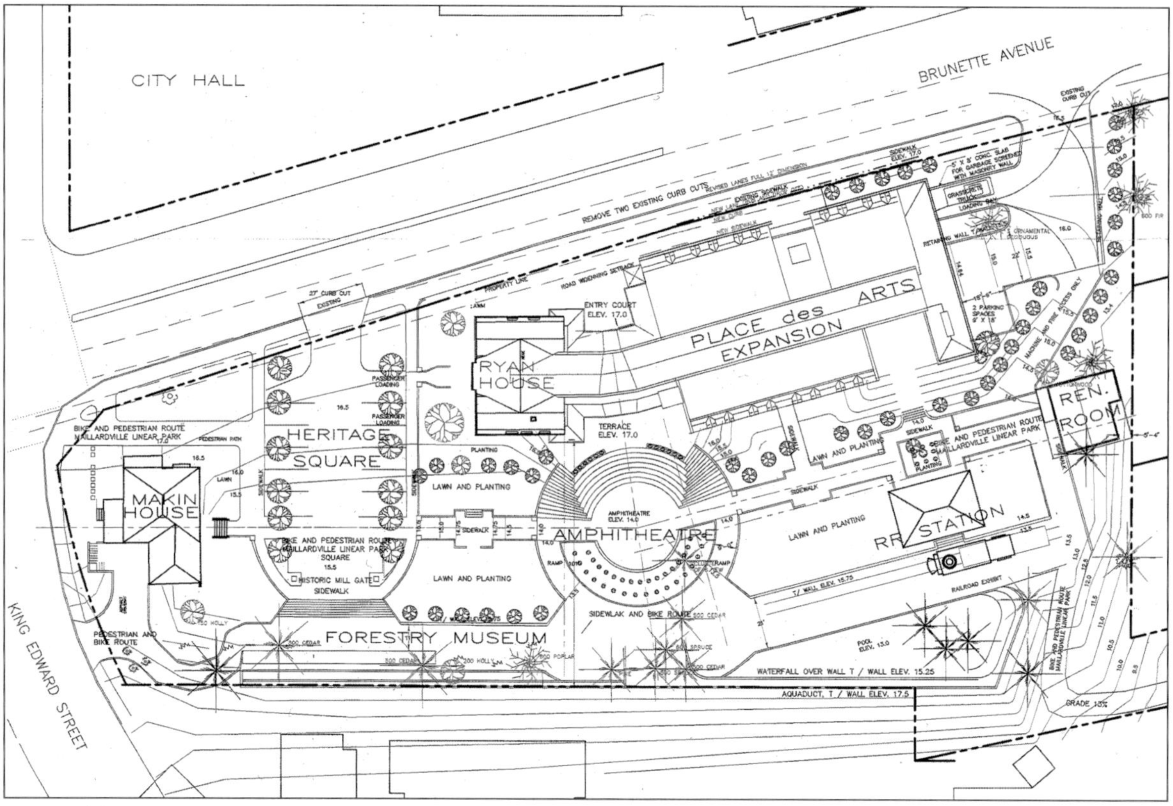

Excerpted and adapted from "An Urban Design" (Iredale, 1996)

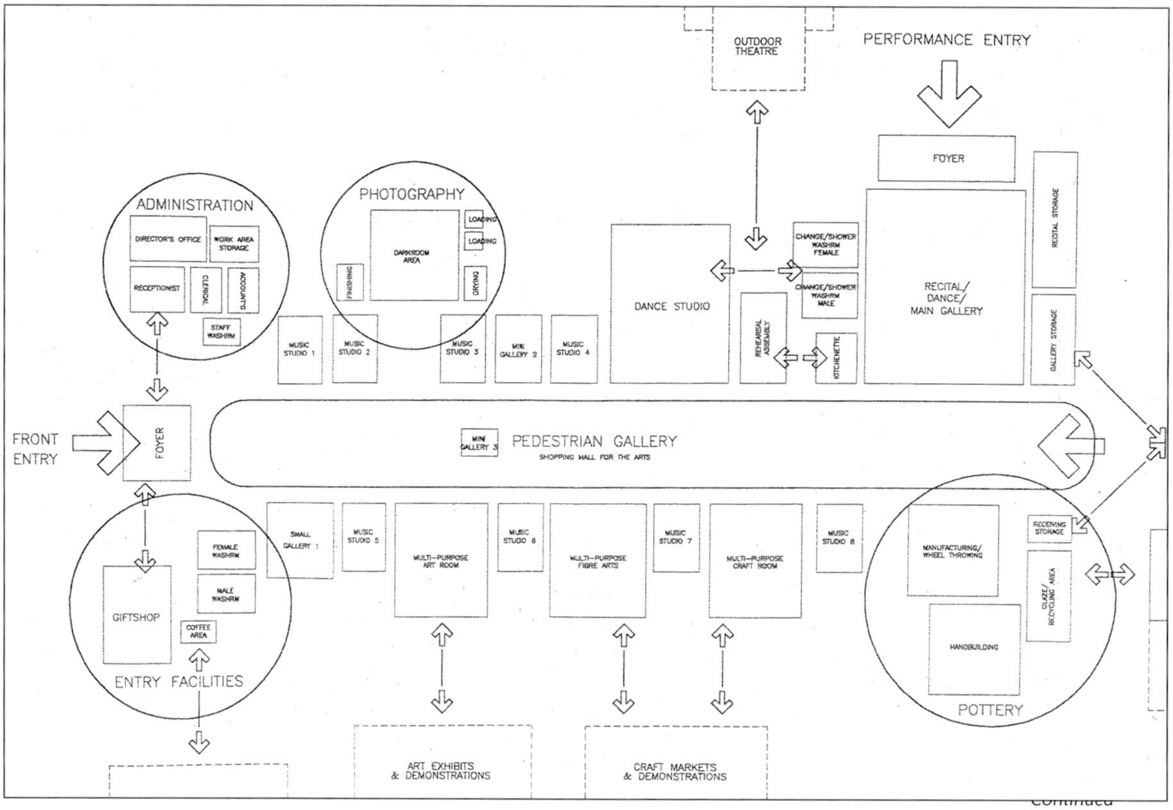

Brutally Tight Budgets

From an interview with Richard Iredale.

The Maillardville project was challenging. It was painful for me, and for Dad, and for Charlotte. It was painful for all of us. The client wanted $10 million worth of good stuff, and they didn't really have any money. Coquitlam was not a wealthy community; it was very much a blue-collar municipality, which didn't have liberal ideas about public works and building the common good. The civic leaders did, but they didn't get support from the electorate. They couldn't pass the bond issue. They depended entirely on corporate donations, which were hard to come by.

The whole project was done on a shoestring with brutally tight budgets. I think we did it over four or five phases and in almost every phase we had to bid twice to get the cost down and go through a difficult process of cost-saving with the local contractor. The contractors felt hard done by. So I got my friend Ken King his first contracting job building Phase 3 of Maillardville Heritage Square, which he did, but the job lost money.

Dad did a big site plan for the project, which was slowly built out. It worked really well. The first phase was restoring Mackin House, the second phase was building the wing addition (Place des Arts), and the third phase was restoring the old Ryan House and building the link between Ryan House and the addition.

The project also involved moving an old CPR rest station, which had been located nearby, up onto the site. Dad planned decking around a square, which would be a people place. Place des Arts was a 10,000 sq. ft. addition to create an arts and culture centre. Dad and I designed it together, but he did the bulk of the design detail with Liz Scremin.

At some point during this process, Dad was fired from the project. I think it all came down to a personality conflict with the client's representative, who was a City employee with the job of seeing the project through to completion. And I think he was under a lot of stress because he didn't have the money to do this project. But he had to do it. They had any number of volunteers coming to the meetings and saying that it had to be done. But nobody had enough money to actually do it! The classic community project—lots of people, and no money!

But Dad was getting older and he would not suffer fools gladly. That more or less summarizes it. There were contractual problems, but they couldn't get anyone else to take the job over. I think the real reason why they fired us was that Dad was asking for more fees and they didn't want to give us more fees. I think it was

Continued

352 | Place of Song and Dance

Richard Iredale

about money. So Dad suggested to the client, "Well, if you're tired of working with me, why don't you work with Richard or with Charlotte?" And we decided among ourselves that I would officially take the lead on the job [without raising the fees].

The new building, Place des Arts, was more or less Phase 2 and Dad took care of that. It's rather complicated—you have to look at it on the floor plan—but, basically, Phases 2 and 3 both involved building Place des Arts. The first half of it got done, but the municipality didn't have enough money for the second half. There were huge hassles, and that was when Dad was supposedly fired. But we kept doing it, including Dad; it's just that I was the one who went to the meetings instead of him. Place des Arts was designed and it was just a question of getting it built. It took about six years to complete the overall project. ∎

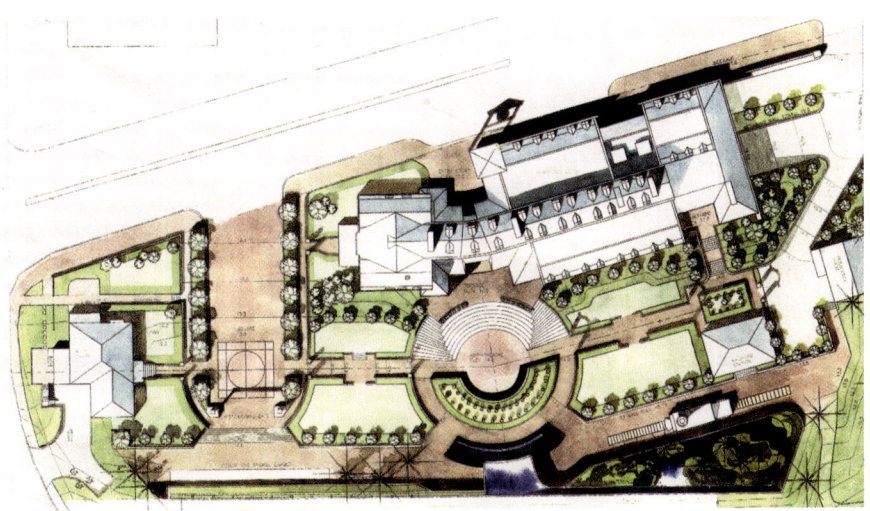

Above:
Site Plan showing the overall Heritage Square concept, with historic Ryan House restored and connected via an Atrium to the new Place des Arts.

Adjacent:
View showing the entry to Place des Arts. The completed complex includes an outdoor Amphitheatre and traditional garden.

Place des Arts

Place des Arts was conceived as a cluster of heritage style studio buildings arranged around a central glass atrium gallery.

The smaller studio buildings match the scale and style of existing heritage buildings on the site.

Historic Ryan House, before (above) and after (adjacent) restoration, renovation, and addition of The Great Hall to Place des Arts

Adjacent:
Entry to the Great Hall of Place des Arts; partial view of seating for the outdoor amphitheatre

Background:
The Great Hall, or 'pedestrian gallery,' linking arts, crafts, and performance studios

An Environment of Collaboration

From an essay written by Charlotte Murray.

Richard Iredale became a registered architect sometime after the completion of Maillardville Heritage Square. He proved to be an excellent marketer, and had soon promoted more new work than anyone else in the office. Rand became more and more involved with upgrading and maintaining our computers. Eventually he more or less handed the practice over to Richard and began developing an idea that had been growing in his mind.

The concept was to create a computer software program that would allow all of the complex and time-consuming bidding procedures on a project to be handled through computer communications. He pursued this concept with typical enthusiasm, taking over the lower-floor office space and persuading one or two others to join him. But I think that project got washed out one weekend when the water from our washroom overflowed and flooded the office below, drowning all of the papers and incapacitating the computers.

After his retirement, Rand still came to the office from time to time with his dog, Bing, and Bing made the rounds to say hello to everyone while Rand carried on discussions with staff. After Richard joined the firm we wanted to bring in more partners in preparation for our impending retirements, though I wasn't going to retire until the heritage restoration of Christ Church Cathedral was finished (which came in 2004, nine years after it began!).

I feel very fortunate that circumstances, such as the trip to Venice in 1969, brought me together with Rand. Our partnership extended to feeling very close to his whole family and being included in the Mayne Island scene. My partnership with Rand led to close relationships with Kathryn, Richard, and Jennifer. And Tab and I often found ourselves turning the spit together at the summer lamb bakes.

I have a strong and continuing admiration for Rand. He was a good friend and an architect with special gifts for planning and organization. He excelled in terms of organizing the work and also in terms of creating working relationships among the people in the office. Architectural offices can be very competitive, and Rand created an environment of collaboration.

I suppose that true lasting friendships are often tested with reversals or differences—but they never amount to anything, they are soon overcome, and the friendships deepen. When Kathryn asked me to say a few words at Rand's funeral, I was very, very touched to be given that honour. ■

CONTEXT ANALYSIS

Cultural Factors

It is important to be aware of the complexity and richness of the natural and built environment in which you are about to build. Man is an unusual creature; other living things are figures in the landscape but man is a shaper of the landscape. Recognize that your new building is an intervention in a complex social and ecological system. We cannot forget the responsibility that comes with our ability to shape our environment. What we build will either disrupt or enhance the existing condition:

"We shape our buildings; thereafter they shape us" (Sir Winston Churchill).

The Chicago housing project that had to be demolished some ten years after it was built is a cautionary tale for those of us who presume to replace slums with new buildings. Too often we know not what we do: when we demolish the buildings we unknowingly lose social organization built into the urban fabric.

Implied Values

Be aware of the value systems that underlie the stated aims of your project. Architecture has been used to enhance power since the dawn of civilization. The Egyptian Pyramids still evoke the absolute power of an omnipotent king and we are uplifted to the power of monotheism expressed in the great medieval cathedrals, while small American towns with their clapboard churches and townhalls 'bespeak of free men and democrats.'

Today, the smooth slab of an office tower is an obelisk dedicated to the power of the great corporation, while the campus layout of such head offices as Microsoft or Weyerhaeuser evolved to reflect a more horizontal, democratic organization.

Another implied value that we as architects must be aware of is architecture as a sub-culture. From the schools of architecture, the glossy architectural magazines, and the awards system, we have developed an inward-looking value system that is not shared by the rest of our society.

When Venturi wrote *Learning from Las Vegas* there was a glimmer of hope that the avant-garde intellectualism that had isolated the architectural establishment from mainstream culture would be replaced with a search for form that would resonate with our times. The mainstream of post-modernism, however, has not fulfilled this promise. Gold-plated television antennas to signify a seniors' home or

---

"In 1972 Robert Venturi, Denise Scott Brown, and the late Steven Izenour wrote *Learning from Las Vegas*,[1] a revolutionary case study that opened the world's eyes to vernacular architecture and iconography—the 'ugly and ordinary' structures and signage born to satisfy the needs of regular people, not architects.

"Today, the Las Vegas they wrote about no longer exists, but the ideas brought to the fore by the pioneering architects, who once famously declared that 'less is a bore,' now inform the urban planning and construction of areas intended for mass use."[2]

---

[1] Robert Venturi, Denise Scott Brown, and Steven Izenour, *Learning from Las Vegas: The Forgotten Symbol of Architectural Form*, Rev. ed. (Cambridge, MA: MIT Press, 1994, 1977, 1972).

[2] Source: Internet (2006).

Roman Pediments to express Imperial America leave architecture a sub-culture. I suggest we be wary of the glossy magazine architectural sub-culture. Architecture, as I believe is the case with all art, is not achieved by a direct approach. It should be an aspiration, not a goal. If we can be competent builders, architecture may follow—as verse may become poetry—if it is well-crafted and has that resonance with time and place that conveys a significant insight.

Historical Context

A grasp of what has shaped the context in which we build provides insight and inspiration. History was critical, for instance, with the Maillardville Place des Arts Project.

In this case, rather than merely locating the two heritage structures to be preserved on the site analysis, we devoted one complete map to the historic structures and views on the site, the original street alignment, the historic view to the mill, and other historic structures such as the gate to the mill.

It was from this analysis that the concept of restoring the axial view toward the mill with a reconstructed gate and a wall that evoked the distant view of the mill on the Fraser River emerged as an organizing principle for the redevelopment of the site.

Rand Iredale, Project Manager's Manual (1997)

> Architecture, as I believe is the case with all art, is not achieved by a direct approach. It should be an aspiration, not a goal. If we can be competent builders, architecture may follow—as verse may become poetry—if it is well-crafted and has that resonance with time and place that conveys a significant insight.

A Natural Curiosity for Life

From an essay written by Richard Iredale.

One of my first vivid childhood recollections was of my dad popping the cork on a champagne bottle. The year was 1962. Rand and his partner, Bill Rhone, had just won second prize in the competition to design Simon Fraser University. Their design for a series of academic villages stepping down the forested hillside was bold and innovative. Instead of a central, imposing edifice for the university, Bill and Rand intended to create a series of smaller colleges similar to those at UC Berkeley, each sensitively nestled into the landscape. Though Arthur Erickson's grander design won the competition, the vision of Rhone & Iredale foreshadowed the movement toward more informal, village-like college campuses.

Bill Rhone and Rand Iredale each contributed unique and valuable skills to their shared design practice. From his training at Berkeley, Bill brought a Californian's sensitivity to landscape and natural building materials; Rand had a highly inventive and analytical mind, and a brilliance for site planning and innovative uses of building materials and mechanical and electrical systems.

Photos of their buildings still hang on our office walls, and I often marvel at their sculptural elegance and clarity of concept.

Rand's partnership with Bill Rhone came to an end in 1980 and it was a difficult time for him. He had turned 50, and the optimism of his younger years began to give way to the uncertainty and doubt that, for many people, accompanies the latter half of life. He soldiered on with his own architectural practice, aided by my mother, Kathryn, who joined him as the bookkeeper and office manager. Hard economic times hit in 1982. Rand had borrowed money to finance his development project on Mayne Island, and soaring interest rates threatened to bankrupt him. My mother vividly remembers the fear and uncertainty of this period.

Meanwhile, Rand formed a new partnership with an old friend, Charlotte Murray. One of the first women to graduate from UBC's School of Architecture—in 1969; followed by an M.Arch. from UBC in 1980—Charlotte brought a tremendous interest in heritage preservation to the practice. Their pioneering heritage work in the 1980s was a precursor to the new urbanism that would dominate the 1990s. Together with colleague Robert Lemon, Rand and Charlotte developed the pre-eminent heritage conservation practice in British Columbia. Heritage projects were small-scale, pedestrian-oriented, highly-textured, decorative, and whimsical projects. The rediscovery of heritage, in a way, led to new ideas about how to design buildings and cities that work.

Continued

Richard Iredale

A Most Engaging Companion

Rand had a natural curiosity for life that made him a most engaging companion. During my ten years working with him in the 1990s, we had many wonderful conversations over lunch about politics, history, and architecture.

Toward the end of Dad's life he would sometimes come into the office and sit by the coffee machine all morning, ready to chat with anyone who happened by. A short design discussion would often expand into a seminar on the secrets of community-building, the ethics of conservation, or the future of cities.

Rand's curiosity made him an excellent teacher, for which many younger architects remember him. This same curiosity led to the innovative flair that characterized his best work.

Ever an Optimist

Every life is an intellectual and spiritual journey through the landscape of a particular place and time. Rand's life encompassed the greater part of the 20th century. The setting for his childhood was the Canadian Prairie during the hard-luck times of the 1930s dustbowl. His adolescence was shaped by World War II, when the very existence of Western Canada seemed to hang in the balance. The prosperous second half of the 20th century formed the backdrop for his adult life in British Columbia, and during these years he helped to build a great city.

Continued

Rand at work in the Steamboat House on the Fairview Slopes, with a cloudy view of downtown Vancouver and the North Shore mountains in the background (1995)

Richard Iredale

Rand belonged to an optimistic and enthusiastic generation. Like his peers, he embraced the values of modernism; he believed in progress and was proud of the technological advances mankind had made during his lifetime. His generation was in love with the automobile and the seemingly infinite power of machinery, and that love affair shaped their concept of the 'good life.' Looking back on that time from an era when our dependence on fossil fuel threatens the survival of our planet's climate and ecosystems, I can't help but wish they'd had more foresight. Even my father, in his later years, began to question the fast-paced, consumer lifestyle of modern society, and to quite naturally yearn for the older, simpler, and more sustainable lifestyles of traditional societies.

I'm sorry that Dad didn't live for another 10 years, because he had so much curiosity. Were he alive today, he would apply his enthusiasm, exuberance, and keen intelligence to working on the environmental problems that now confront us. Ever an optimist, he would tell us not to give up hope. He loved brainstorming and problem-solving, and he would urge us to put on our thinking caps and work together to find solutions. I know he would have embraced the challenge of designing a more sustainable future. ∎

Place of Song and Dance

Rand believed strongly that communities needed town squares as a focus of community life. All of his municipal and community planning work featured town centres, markets, plazas, or squares. His work with architectural students on Mayne Island in the 1970s proposed a town square on a then privately-owned piece of land across from the small store that made up the village at Miners Bay.

When Rand passed away in 2000, our family wanted a memorial that would make a positive difference in the world, as Rand had made a difference during his life. There was a community project on Mayne Island at this time to preserve a piece of land in the village centre as a park. The family decided the band stand proposed for this park would be a suitable memorial, as it would create an outdoor gathering place in the village for music, performances, and community celebrations.

Our family's contribution, along with those of other donors, made it possible for the community to purchase the property for Miners Bay Park. Our family also provided the funds for the band stand. Richard donated his time to design and manage construction of the new band stand, as well as the new library, both located in Miners Bay Park. Many other community members donated their time, skill, and money to finish this work.

Library & Band Stand at Miners Bay Park

Architect
Richard H. Iredale, MAIBC, MRAIC, P.Eng., LEED AP, Partner, Iredale Group

Photos: Andrew Doran
(www.andrewdoran.com)

Rand celebrating his 70th birthday on Mayne Island, and admiring the Log House made with Tootsie Rolls and slabs of chocolate by Talbot and his three boys (1999)

Left to right:
Richard, Kathryn, Jennifer, and Talbot, commemorating the Miners Bay Band Stand in Rand's memory (2005)

The Band Stand at A'lele̱n

A gift from the family and friends of
William Randle Iredale
1929 – 2000
Pioneer Architect Mentor

"A'lele̱n" was the Coast Salish name for Miners Bay, and means "Dance House" in the Seńćoten language

362 | Place of Song and Dance

In recognition of the First Peoples of Mayne Island, the family chose to call the memorial the "Band Stand at A'lelen." The name *A'lelen* is a *Senćoten* word that means 'winter dance house.' It specifically refers to Miners Bay, where once the *W'Sáneć* (Saanich) people lived for periods of the year. John Elliott, First Voices Language Administrator, agreed to this naming.

It seems the naming is appropriate, as Miners Bay Park, or *A'lelen,* is the place where the community gathers to celebrate on Christmas Eve. The huge cedar tree in the park is decked with Christmas lights, and we gather around a large bonfire to drink hot chocolate and sing Christmas carols—and sometimes to dance. Musical groups lead the singing from the band stand.

The band stand was first opened in August of 2005 at a community music festival featuring the many fine musicians on the Island. There were performances by Rand's daughter-in-law Lael, with her band Jaiya, and two of his teenaged grandchildren, Adam and Marlies, with their band Belljar.

In May 2006 the community erected a may pole in the park and celebrated the first May Day Dance there. Elaborately costumed locals and visitors came to dance around the may pole and crown the May Day Queen. The park, the library, and the band stand are taking their place as a focal point for community gatherings and festivities.

Rand would love it. We found a good fit. ∎

Overleaf:
The Band Stand at Sunset (2006)

Photo: Andrew Doran
(www.andrewdoran.com)

INDEX

Index

1095 West 7th Avenue, 10, 265
1100 West 7th Avenue, 10, 11, 23, 179, 216, 227–229
1151 West 8th Avenue, 11
    SEE ALSO Steamboat House

A

Abbeyfield Heritage House, 314
Abbeyfield Houses, 305
Active Pass Growers' Association (Mayne Island), 38
Adler, Dankmar, xviii
Alexander House, 314
Amphitheatre at Maillardville Heritage Square, 348
Andrews, John, 7, 267, 268, 269
Anthem Properties, 127
architects, career advice to in 1949, 20–21
architecture
    cultural and emotional function of, 97, 356–357
    heritage, 234, 279, 295–296; Heritage Studio, 11, 263; preservation philosophy in, 5, 263
    Modern Movement in, 97
    practice of in Iredale firms, 334–335; budgets and budgeting, 36–37, 315, 351–353; computerization, 5, 7, 237, 284–289, 355; management style, 187–189, 304–305, 306–307; quality control, 301; site analysis, 118; team approach to, 131, 166, 168, 175, 179, 185
    SEE ALSO design philosophy and process
Autonomous House, The (by Brenda and Robert Vale), 213

B

Babicki, Bogue, 71, 127, 130, 134, 320
    memories: of Rand, 88–89;
        of Rand and Bill, 131
    on structural systems, 115, 131
band stand at Miners Bay Park, 361–365
Barclay Heritage Square, 237, 254, 255–262, 318
    SEE ALSO Vancouver Park Site 19
Barclay Manor (Barclay Heritage Square), 257
Barnard, Frank, 27
Bartlett, John, 61
Bawlf, Sam, 198, 200, 206
BC Electric, 27
BC Ferry Corporation, 40
BC Place, 5, 211
    SEE ALSO Downtown Stadium
BC Power Commission, 27
Beckman, Paul, 227
Bell, Douglas, 50
Bell Bay Strata development (Mayne Island), 41, 56–57, 231
Bennett, Bill
    & Expo '86, 207
Bennett, Fred, Sr, 41
Bennett, W.A.C., 26, 40, 71, 96
Bennett Road townhouses, 291
Bernardo (sawmill owner), 61–62
Berton, Pierre, 174
Bingham, Janet, 255, 260
Binnie, G.M., 96
Blomfield Company (art glass firm), 239
Boddy, Trevor
    Tribute to Rand, xviii–xix
Bogue Babicki and Associates Inc.
    SEE Babicki, Bogue
Bridger, Paul, 214
Brinkman & Associates (tree planters), 61
Brinkman, Dirk, 61
British Columbia Hydro and Power Authority, 27, 73
    SEE ALSO Portage Mountain Hydro-Electric Development
British Columbia Institute of Technology, campus expansion, 190–191
Brown, Frank, 42
Bullpitt, Errol, 130
Burnaby Lake Sports Complex, 212
Burnaby Village Museum, 274
Burrard Medical Building, 179, 182–183
Busby, Peter, xviii
    memories of Rand, 212–214
Busby Bridger Architects, 214

C

Campbell, Bob, 17
Campbell, Gordon (BC Premier), 195
    remarks by, 196–197
Canadian Cellulose Company, 212
Canadian Environmental Sciences (CES), 3, 166, 195
CanCel, offices of, 212
Cardew, Peter, xviii, 123, 166, 212, 227
Carlson, Eric, 127
Chang, Tao, 130
Channel 8 Television Studios project, 30–33
Chilkoot Trail, 174, 176–177
Choklit Park, 10
    townhouses at, 265
Christ Church Cathedral, 270
church architecture, 270
Cividin, Glen, 109
Clark, Joe, 207
computers in architectural practice.
    SEE UNDER architecture, practice of
conservation ideology, 263
Cotton, Peter, 260
Cowie, Art, 3, 123, 166, 214
    remarks by, 294
creativity, nature of, 192–193
Crooks and Money (firm), 56
Crown Life Building, 212
Cruise, Martin, 236, 294
culture of design in Iredale practices, 166–171, 179

D

Dalibard, Jacques
    on Park Site 19, 258–262
Daon Development Corporation, 215
de Bono, Edward, 192–193
Deacon, Wilbur, 43
Demming, W. Edwards, 301

design panels. *SEE UNDER* design philosophy and process
design philosophy and process, 141, 159, 167–168, 253
   creativity, nature of, 192–193
   design panels in, xix, 168, 221, 294, 306–307, 334
   interactive, 129
   iterative, 220–221
   SEE ALSO culture of design in Iredale practices
desire lines in architecture, 148
Diamond, Larry, 257
Dodd, John and Jeannine, 61
Donny (American conscientious objector), 48–49, 54–55
Downs, Barry, 260
Downtown Stadium, 195, 197, 206, 211
   SEE ALSO BC Place
Duke Energy, 127
Durante, Jane, 257

E
EIKOS, 3
Elder, Henry, 46, 100, 108, 171, 266, 268
elemental estimating, 36–37
Emery, James, 11, 29
Empire Stadium, 206
Erickson, Arthur, xviii, 166, 171, 358
Erickson and Massey (architects), 104, 109, 116, 214
Erskine, Ralph, 169
Expo '86, 5, 195, 196, 265
   Roundhouse complex at, 237

F
Fabco Ltd., 3
Fabtec Structures Ltd., 3
Fairview Cottage. *SEE* Gingerbread House
Fairview Slopes townhouses, 216–217
False Creek, 5, 23, 199
   redevelopment of, 195, 196, 206, 215
False Creek Housing (The Lagoons), 212, 215
Fassler, Rainer, xviii, 123, 130
   memories of Rand, 166–171, 174–175, 179, 272

Feilden, Richard, 42
Festival of Architecture Awards Program, 266
Fitzpatrick, Ross, 130
Flavelle, Charles, 10
Fleming, Rhonna, 260
Forest Industrial Relations, 9
Forestry Museum (Maillardville Heritage Square), 349
Forster, Kurt, 7, 267, 268
Freschi, Bruno, 46, 171

G
Gaitanakis, John, 45, 188
Gaitanakis, John and Jania, 44
Gehry, Frank, xviii
geodesic dome (Mayne Island), 48–49, 51–53, 169–171
George W. Pearkes Elementary School, 80–81
Georgia Gateway (Vancouver), 199
Gingerbread House, 58–59, 238, 240–243
Gordon M. Shrum Generating Station, 71
Governor General's Medals for Architecture Awards Program, 266–269
Green, Aaron, 100
Greenwood Village (townhouses), 290
Grouse Mountain Chalet project, 34–35
Gruft, Andrew, xviii

H
Haebler Construction, 58
Hansen, Bob, 320
Harris, Gordon, 18
Harrison, Bob, 109
Hart, John, 40
Henriquez, Richard, xviii, xix, 123, 166, 175, 214
Henriquez and Partners Architects, 232
heritage architecture. *SEE* architecture, heritage
Heritage Studio, 11, 263
Hodson Manor, 238, 239
Hopping Kovach Grinnell (design consultants), 109
Horne-Payne, Robert, 27
Howarth, Thomas, 100
Hudson's Hope Housing, 79
Hull, Bob, 175
Hume, Jim, 200

Index | 371

I

International Power and Engineering Consultants of Vancouver, 73
Iredale, Betty (Isabel), xviii–xix, 8, 12, 23, 40, 42
    memories of Rand's childhood, 14–15
Iredale, Jennifer, 10, 234, 236, 239
    & Barclay Heritage Square, 237–238
    & Gingerbread House, 58, 240, 247
    & heritage architecture, 162, 163
    memories of Rand, 244–248
Iredale, Kathryn, xx–xxi, 9–10, 222, 230
Iredale, Rand, 167
    biography, 3–7, 8–10, 12–13, 17–19
    SEE ALSO Project Manager's Manual (by Rand Iredale)
Iredale, Richard, 10, 305, 316
    career of, 11, 29, 89, 218
    memories of Rand, 318–321, 333, 351–352, 358–360
    wedding of, 59
Iredale, Talbot, 10, 39, 89
    memories of Rand, 284–287
Iredale, William E., 8, 14, 40
Iredale, William Randle. *SEE* Iredale, Rand
Iredale family life, 9–10, 12–13, 39, 244–247, 337–341
    in Venice, 161–165, 245
    SEE ALSO Iredale Place (Mayne Island)
Iredale Group Architecture, 11, 232–233
Iredale Partnership, The, 3, 7, 11, 29, 265, 314
Iredale Place (Mayne Island), 39–67
Iredale Report (1985), 7, 266–269

J

Jefferson, Randy, xviii
Jessiman, Kendall B., 11, 29, 232
John Norquay Elementary School, 310–317, 318–319
Jones, Art, 22

K

Kadonaga, Gontaro, 38
Kadonaga, Victor, 38
Kamloops Indian Centre, 293
Kara Resources Ltd., 230, 240, 241, 251
Karlsen, Eric, 166, 174
Keenleyside, Hugh, 77
Kennedy, Warnett, 100, 108
Kinegal, Jane, 317
King, Ken, 319, 351
Kiss, Zoltan, 109
Klondike Gold Rush International Historic Park, 176–177
Knoppe, Bill, 22
Kovach, Rudy, 109

L

Ladysmith Heritage Harbour, 265, 292
Lagoons, The. *SEE* False Creek Housing (The Lagoons)
Langley, Arthur, 255, 260
Lanskail, Don, 9
Lasserre, Frederick, 9
Lemon, Robert, xviii, 127, 254, 358
Log House (Mayne Island), 54–55, 60
Loh, C.Y., xviii, 166

M

MacFarlane, Hugh, 46
Mackin House (Maillardville Heritage Square), 342–349, 346
Maillardville CP Railroad Station, 344–345
Maillardville Heritage Square, 318, 337, 342–355, 357
Maki, Fumihiko, 7, 267, 268
Manning, Paul, 207–208
Manning Park Housing Study, 184
Massey Medals Award Program, 266, 269
Mathers, Alvan S., 20
Mathers and Haldenby (Toronto architects), 20
Mayne Island, 38–67, 169–171, 231, 240–243, 321, 361–363
McCann, Leonard, 260
McCarter Nairne and Partners (architects), 3, 108, 214
McGarva, Graham, 260
McHarg, Ian, 118
McIlraith, David, 50
McKee and Gray, Architects and Engineers, 3
McKinley, David, 100
McMahon, Frank, 130

McMicking, Robert, 27
McNab, Duncan, 109
Miller, Dave, 175
Miller and Hull (architects), xviii, 175
Miners Bay Park (A'lelen), 361–363
Minnekhada Heritage Park, 328–333
Montgomery, Roger, 137
Morris, William, 97
Morton, Bob, 212, 227
Mummery, Jack, 42
Murray, Charlotte, xviii, xix, 11, 29, 234, 305
    & Architecture School workshops, 44–47
    & heritage preservation, 263, 270, 358
    & Studies Abroad Program in Venice, 162
    career of, 230, 236
    memories of Rand, 186–189, 236–238, 254, 294, 304–305, 342–343, 355
Murray, Gordon, 44, 162
Museum of Science and Technology, 198

N
Nagata, John, 38
Nagata, Kumazo, 38
Nagata, Lynn, 38
Nanson & Dyer (graphic designers), 229
Nelson Park, 259
Nichol, Walter C., 251
Nickel Bros. (house movers), 58, 241
Norquay Elementary School. SEE John Norquay Elementary School

O
Old Territorial Administration Building (Dawson City), 265, 294–299
Oswald, Patrick and Patricia, 44

P
Paulus, Stanley, 316
peg board (project management tool), 304–305
Phillips, Art (Mayor), 197
Pickstone, Harry, 10
Piconi (Bell Bay developer), 58
Pierce, Robin and Freda, 59
Pither, Ron, 49

Place des Arts (Maillardville Heritage Square), 344–346, 348, 350, 352–354, 357
Pollio, Marcus Vetruvius, 334
Portage Mountain Hydro-Electric Development, 5, 26, 71–97
    Central Control Building, 84–87, 94
    George W. Pearkes Elementary School, 80–81
    Hudson's Hope Housing, 79
    intake structure, 83
    power scheme perspective, 82
    Powerhouse, 90–91
    Tourist Development master plan, 92–93
    Tourist Lookout Building, 75–76, 93
Power Corporation, 27
Project Manager's Manual (by Rand Iredale), xv, xvii, 167, 192, 319

Q
Qube (condominium complex), 123

R
Randle Iredale Architect, 3, 29
Randle Iredale Architects, 236–237
Rattenbury, Francis, 259
Read Jones Christoffersen (engineers), 36, 88
Redpath, Laurie, 109
Reid, Sir John Watt, 250–251
relationship diagrams in architecture, 150, 335
Rhone, Bill, xix, 10, 29, 214, 234, 358
    memories of Rand: collaborative work relationship, 22–23, 114–115, 189; Peace River Dam housing project, 77–78; Sedgewick Undergraduate Library, 146; SFU design competition, 108–109, 114–115; Westcoast Transmission Building, 130–131
Rhone & Iredale Architects, xix, 3, 10, 29
    dissolution of partnership, 227
    growth and development of, 123
    offices of, 23–25
Rhone, Louise, 10, 22
Ri-Rite (computer software), 5, 237, 284
Roedde House (Barclay Heritage Square), 255, 257, 259, 260

Rogatnick, Abraham, 161, 174
Rombout, Luke, 207
Roundhouse complex at Expo '86, 237
Royal Architectural Institute of Canada
    awards program, 266–269
Ryan House/Place des Arts (Maillardville
    Heritage Square), 342–348

S

Safdie, Moshe, 7, 267, 268
Saint Catherine's Anglican Church, 270
Saint Cuthbert's Anglican Church Hall, 270
Saint Francis of Assisi Rectory, 270
Saint Helen's Anglican Church, 271–273
Saint John's Anglican Church, 265
Scott, Alan, 166
Scremin, Liz, 305, 351
    memories of Rand, 306–309
Sedgewick, Garnet Gladwin, 154
Sedgewick Undergraduate Library (UBC),
    5, 123, 142–158
Segger, Martin, 260
Seymour Medical Clinic, 179, 180–181
Shadbolt, Douglas, 281
Shadbolt, Jack, 174
Sharp & Thompson (architects), 108, 281
Sholi shelter (Mayne Island), 42
Shrum, Gordon, Jr, 77–78
Shrum, Gordon M., 9, 26, 71, 99, 100, 108
    on Simon Fraser University Design
        Competition, 101
Simon Fraser University, 117
    design competition for, 99–109
    Science Complex, 5, 110–113, 116;
        Babicki structural system for, 115
Sinclair Centre. *SEE* Vancouver City Block 15
Sinclair Centre Clock Tower, 232–233
site analysis, 118
SkyTrain, 196, 197
Smith, Charles, 30
Smith, Gwen, 314
Smith, Neville, 278
Smith Bros. & Wilson, 36
Sommerville, Ken, 56, 61
Sommerville, Ken and Karen, 59
Spence-Sales, Mary and Harold, 10

Squamish Railway Museum, 322–327
Steamboat Heritage House, 11, 216,
    218–219, 222, 250–253
Stewart, Robert, 228
Still Creek Park, 265, 275–277
Strangway, David, 282
Sullivan, Louis, xviii, 300–301
Swaisland, George and Margaret, xxi
Swan Wooster Engineering, 40
Swangard, Erwin, 200, 209
Swanson, Cecil, xx
synectics (problem-solving tool), 7, 193

T

Taylor, Matt, 63
tecton cottage (prefabricated modular
    building systems), 34
Tecton Structures Ltd, 3, 42
Thom, Bing, 171
Thompson Berwick & Pratt (architects),
    108, 206, 214
Toby Russell Buckwell Partners (architects),
    146, 232
Tonio (horse-logger), 61, 62
Tonn, Jim, 209
Trade & Convention Centre, 196
Transpo (World's Fair). *SEE* Expo '86

U

University of British Columbia
    School of Architecture, 9; Studies Abroad
        Programs, 161–165
    SEE ALSO Sedgewick Undergraduate
        Library (UBC); Walter C. Koerner
        Library (UBC)

V

Vale, Brenda and Robert, 213
Van der Rohe, Mies, 253
Vancouver Art Gallery, 207
Vancouver Centenary 1886–1986 Study,
    195, 198–210
Vancouver City Block 15, 232–233
Vancouver Heritage Awards, 311, 314
Vancouver Park Site 19, 254, 258–262

VanTel Broadcasting (Channel 8), 22–23, 30–33
Venice, Italy, 161, 162, 165
Venice Island of Studies group, 165
Vernon, Phil (American conscientious objector), 48–49, 54–55
Vetruvius, 334
Victoria Electric Illuminating Company, 27
Volrich, Jack, 207–208

W
W.A.C. Bennett Dam, 5, 71
Walter C. Koerner Library (UBC), 123, 154
Watt, Robb, 239, 260
Waugh, Captain, 41
Waugh, Captain and Mrs, 43
Weaver, Martin, 254, 260
Weeks House (Barclay Heritage Square), 257
Weinstaup, Kevin, 60, 61
Weldwood Canada, office building at, 130
West Coast Railway Association Museum, 322–325
Westcoast Transmission Building, 5, 123–141
Whitehead, Lael, 39, 59, 363
Wilkes, Barry, 54
Williams, Stewart, 100
Williams, Terry, xviii, 130, 166, 214
Wood, Bud, 46
Wood, Jack, 40